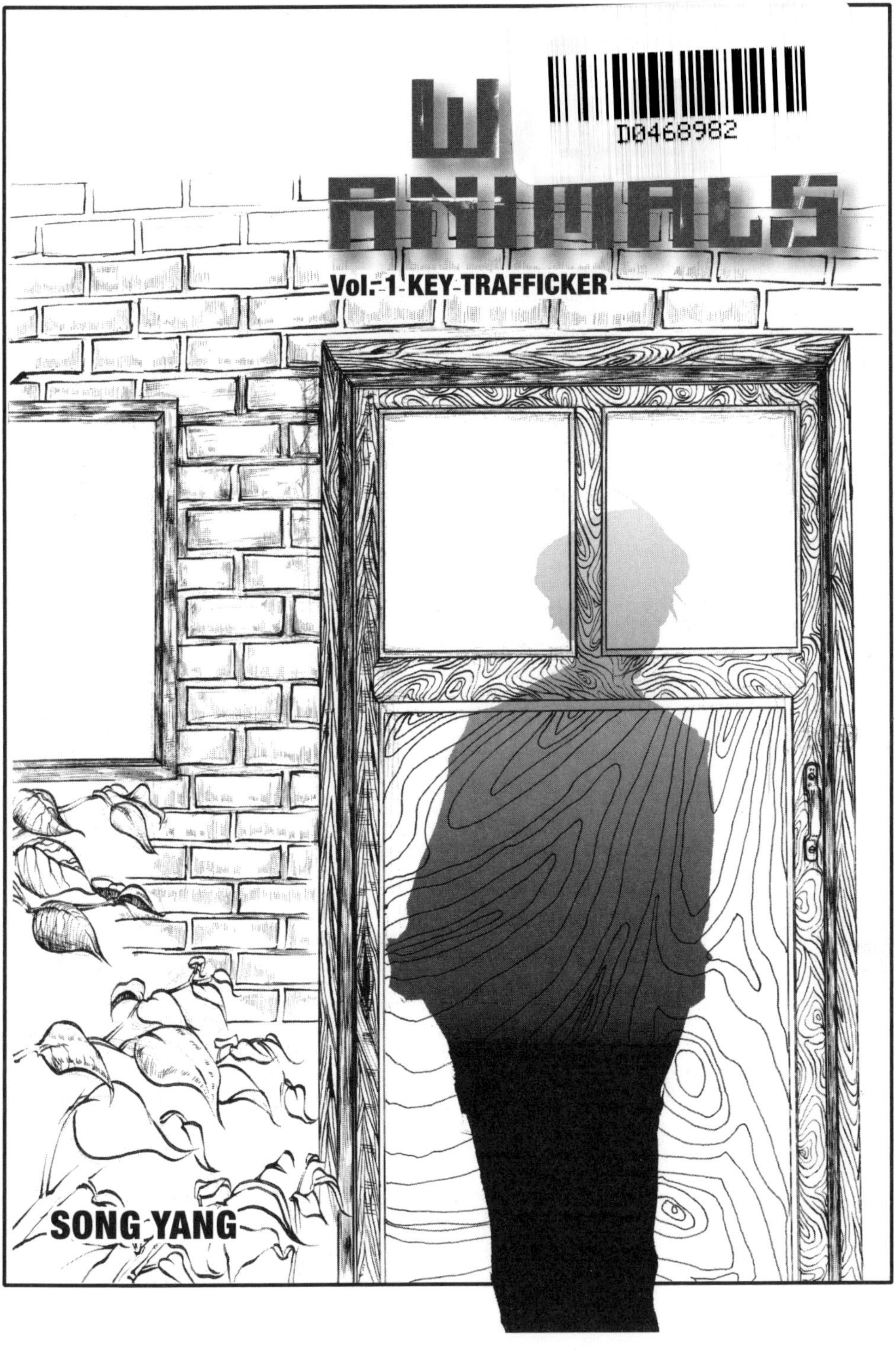
W
ANIMALS
Vol. 1 KEY TRAFFICKER
SONG YANG

ARTIST'S PREFACE

Summer, 2003. Since I'd begun the adaptation of **WILD ANIMALS** in my workshop in Tianjin, sleep had become an inaccessible illusion.

The novel (*Days of Dazzling Sunshine*) and its film adaptation (*In the Heat of the Sun*) are my favorite works.

The story takes place in an era which is at once mysterious and familiar to all of us. One of the problems we had during the creative process was adequately capturing this era, so we completely immersed ourselves in documents from the time: "The Magazine of the Liberation Army," "The Little Red Book," the "Live" and "Red Era" films, some picked up at the flea market, others kindly loaned by the father of the husband of the sister of the mother of a friend. In other words, we were able to finish this work, but we did so only through the important prep work with various documents and numerous discussions and exchanges with the editors (especially with Mr. HE Yue).

The work intuitively reflects the character of an individual within a group. The original Chinese graphic novel should also reflect the spirit that is unique and particular to Chinese culture. This special spirit is totally linked to culture, local style, and historic heritage. For many years now, we have been hoping for original Chinese comics, but, even now, most of these works just copy the Japanese style. Still, for a work to be artistic, it has to be more than just the manifestation of a new and original thought, both on the technical and narrative level. It also needs to completely understand and integrate elements of Chinese culture. The term "Chinese culture" here doesn't mean the creation of Chinese comics using pencils and ink made in China, but a precise analysis of the constructions, the language, the clothing, and the decorations which are unique to China. That is the only way to get results and make new discoveries. In a certain way, the process coincides with the principles of contemporary design.

Because of my unlimited adoration of this story, I used the totally anti-commercial "aligned cases" in the creative process. For the color sketches, I paid extra attention to the play of shadows and light; the colors I chose are essentially warm colors (the color of the time) that imitate natural light, and the décor has a to-the-millimeter precision in order to reflect the sincere and simple character of the era. For standard constructions, I left sketching, and finished with ink drawings where every brick was individually drawn!

I basically used only flat planes to reflect the placid and reserved but also impetuous character of the youth of the era. For the story, I not only used flashbacks, insertions, and subjective planes, but also in the last chapter included different drawing styles to demonstrate a single story could have several more or less subversive endings, and also to stay close to the general impression given by the film. Mr. Wang Shuo himself has said that drawings were "very cinematic."

Creating the comic was a drawn-out task accomplished by a team of a dozen people that worked from dawn to midnight for about ten months. During this time, we had to switch up team members three times, mostly because some left us for a cooler job. Nevertheless, I kept drawing with a smile on my lips and happiness in my heart.

Comics: a loveable life, but an imperfect one.

SONG YANG
2/24/2004
Tianjin

I - Memories, Memories

WHEN I WAS VERY YOUNG,
I LEFT MY PLACE OF BIRTH TO COME TO
THIS LARGE CITY, AND I'VE NEVER LEFT. NOW
IT IS MY BIRTHPLACE. EVERYTHING HERE CHANGES AT
AN INSANE CLIP—THE HOUSES, THE STREETS,
THE CLOTHING, AND THE TOPICS OF
CONVERSATION AMONG
ITS INHABITANTS.

TODAY, EVERYTHING IS DIFFERENT.
IT'S A NEW CITY,
A MODERN CITY,
A "TRENDY" CITY.

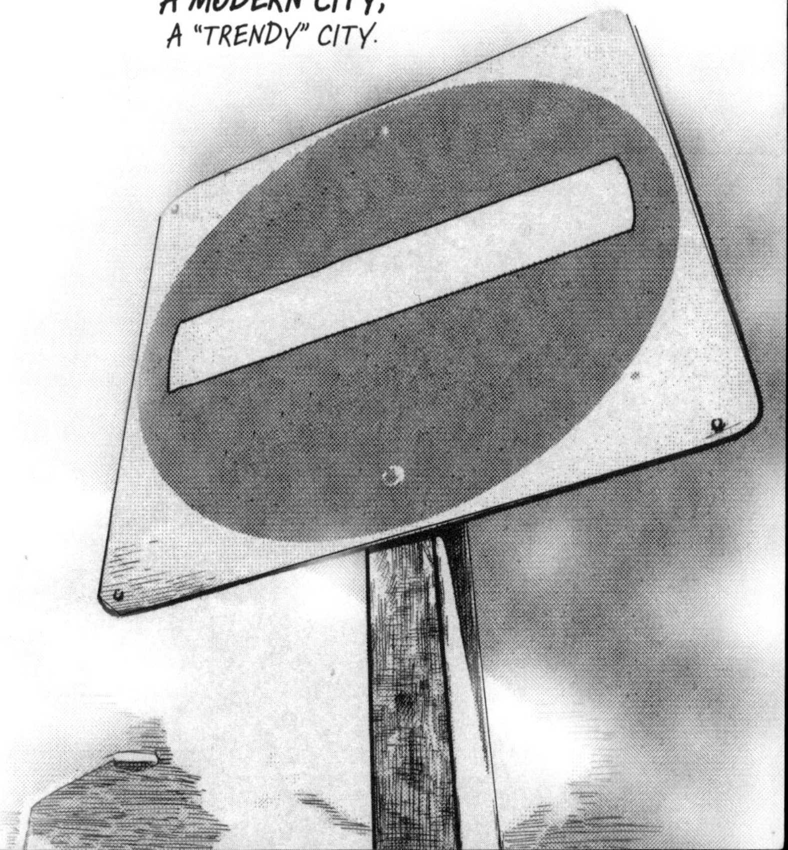

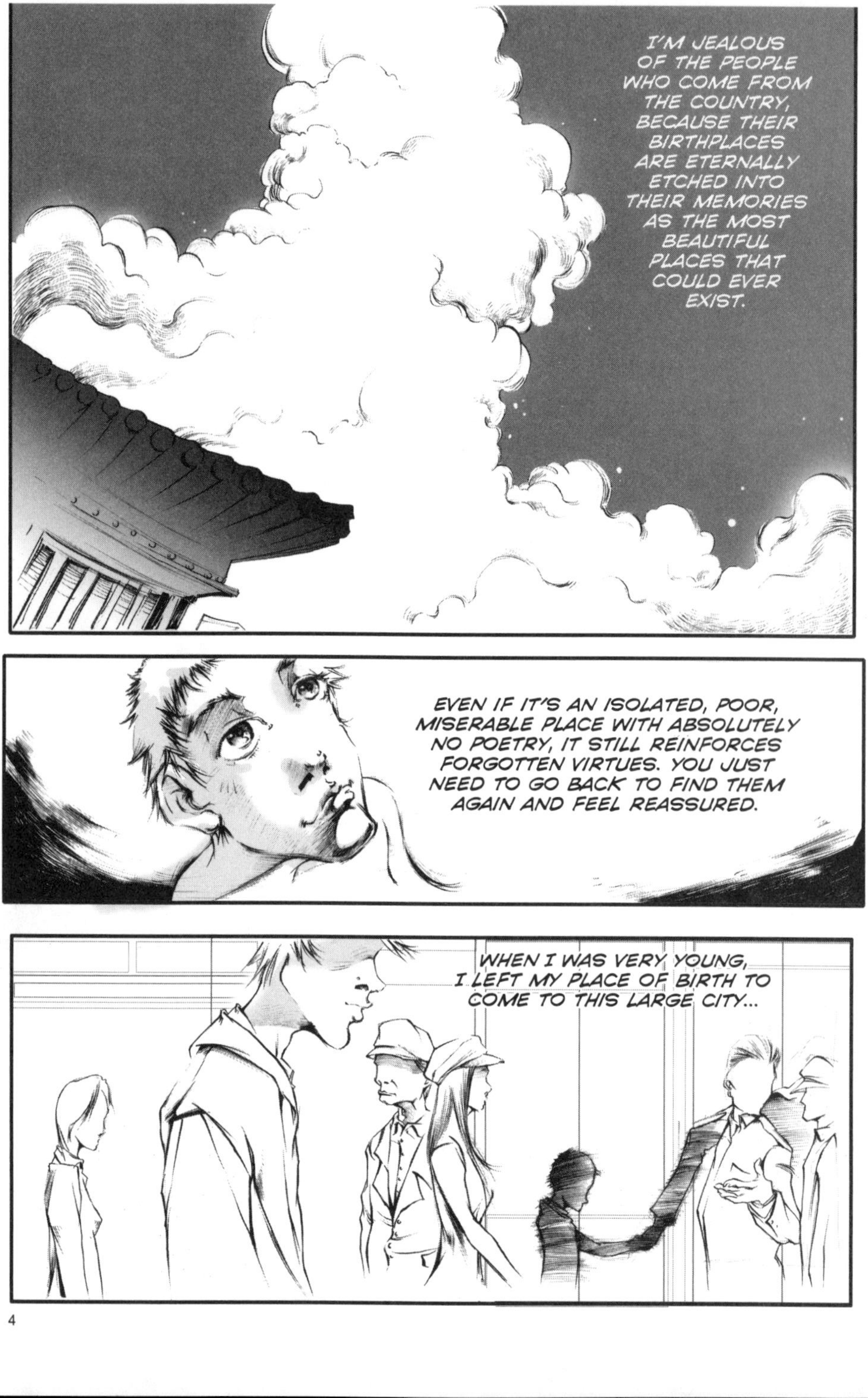
I'M JEALOUS OF THE PEOPLE WHO COME FROM THE COUNTRY, BECAUSE THEIR BIRTHPLACES ARE ETERNALLY ETCHED INTO THEIR MEMORIES AS THE MOST BEAUTIFUL PLACES THAT COULD EVER EXIST.
EVEN IF IT'S AN ISOLATED, POOR, MISERABLE PLACE WITH ABSOLUTELY NO POETRY, IT STILL REINFORCES FORGOTTEN VIRTUES. YOU JUST NEED TO GO BACK TO FIND THEM AGAIN AND FEEL REASSURED.
WHEN I WAS VERY YOUNG, I LEFT MY PLACE OF BIRTH TO COME TO THIS LARGE CITY...

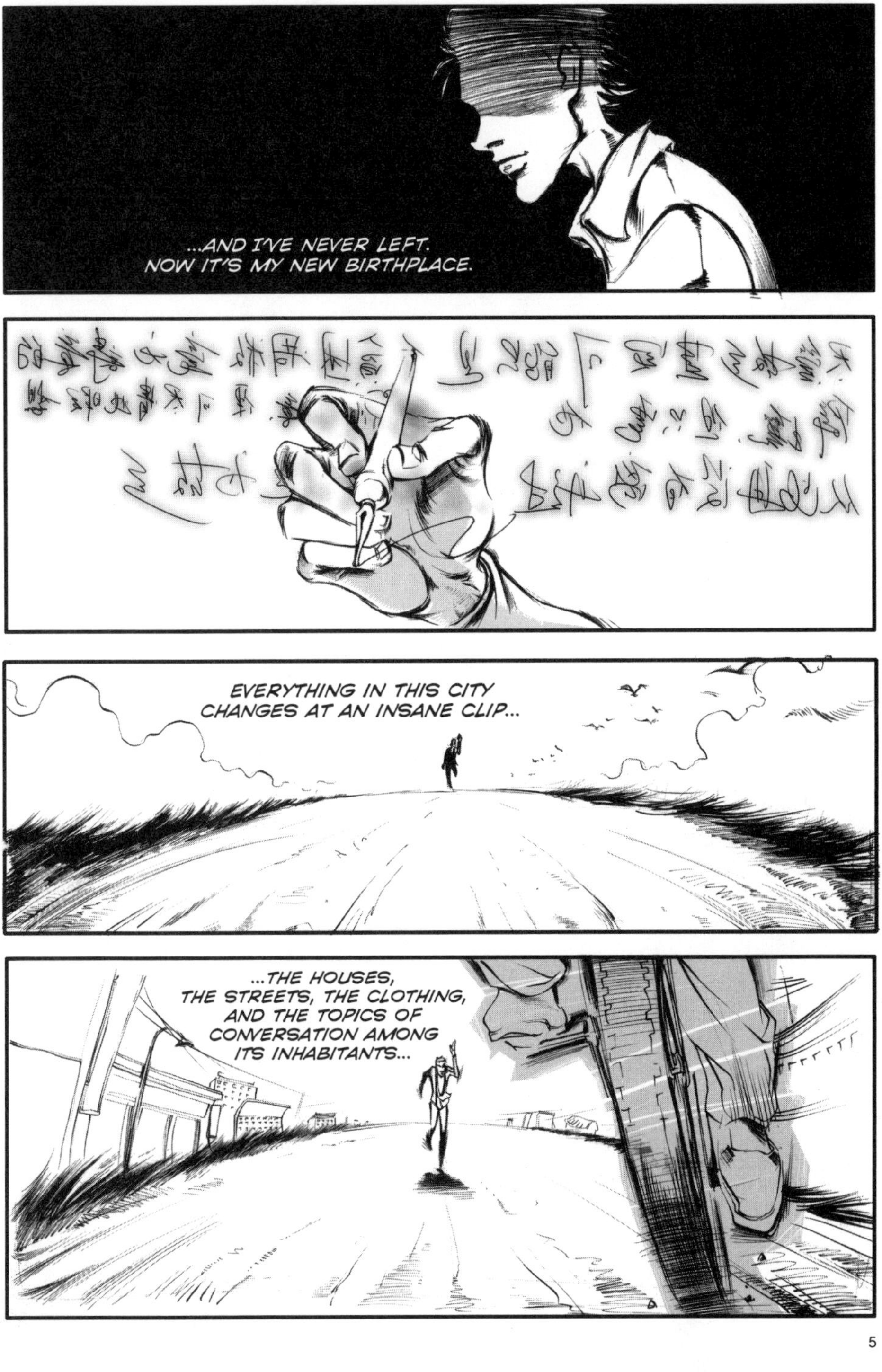
...AND I'VE NEVER LEFT. NOW IT'S MY NEW BIRTHPLACE.
EVERYTHING IN THIS CITY CHANGES AT AN INSANE CLIP...
...THE HOUSES, THE STREETS, THE CLOTHING, AND THE TOPICS OF CONVERSATION AMONG ITS INHABITANTS...

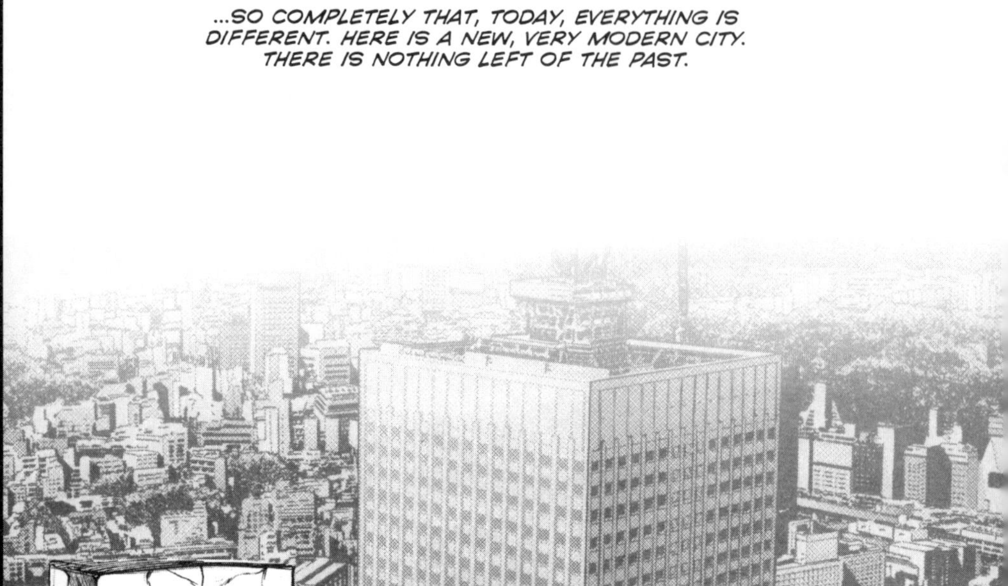
...SO COMPLETELY THAT, TODAY, EVERYTHING IS DIFFERENT. HERE IS A NEW, VERY MODERN CITY. THERE IS NOTHING LEFT OF THE PAST.
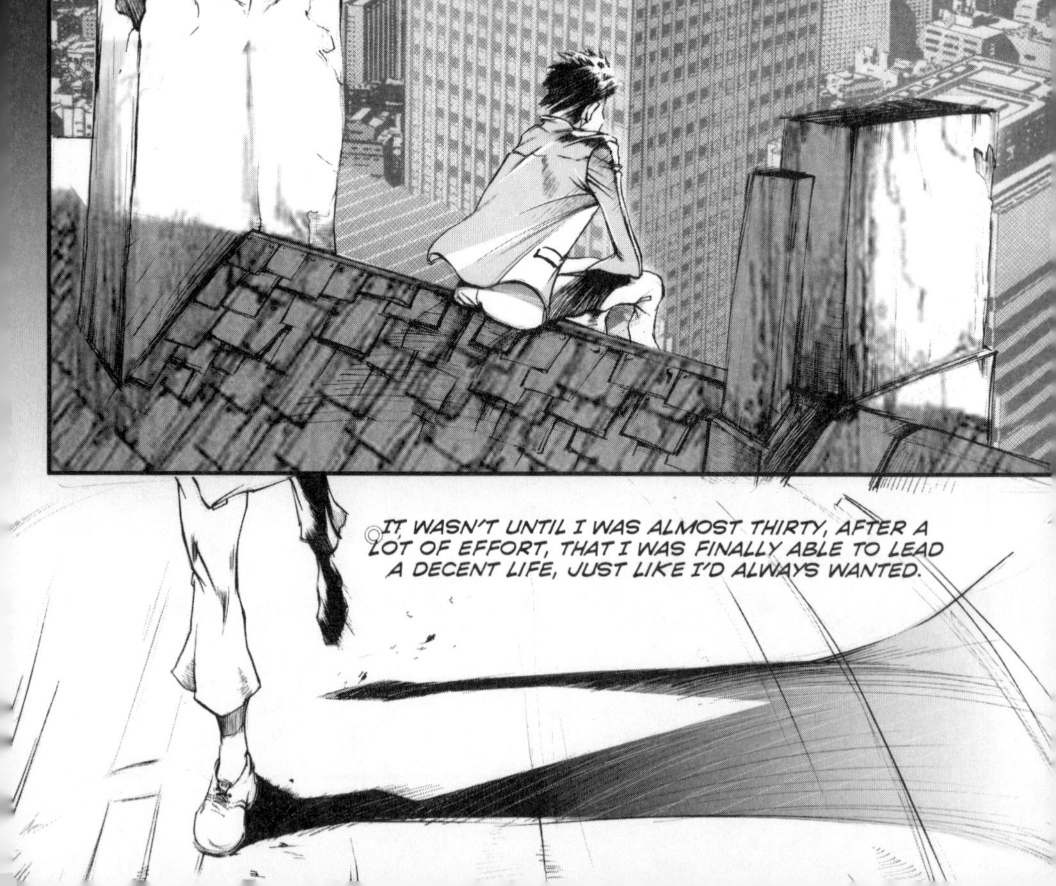
IT WASN'T UNTIL I WAS ALMOST THIRTY, AFTER A LOT OF EFFORT, THAT I WAS FINALLY ABLE TO LEAD A DECENT LIFE, JUST LIKE I'D ALWAYS WANTED.

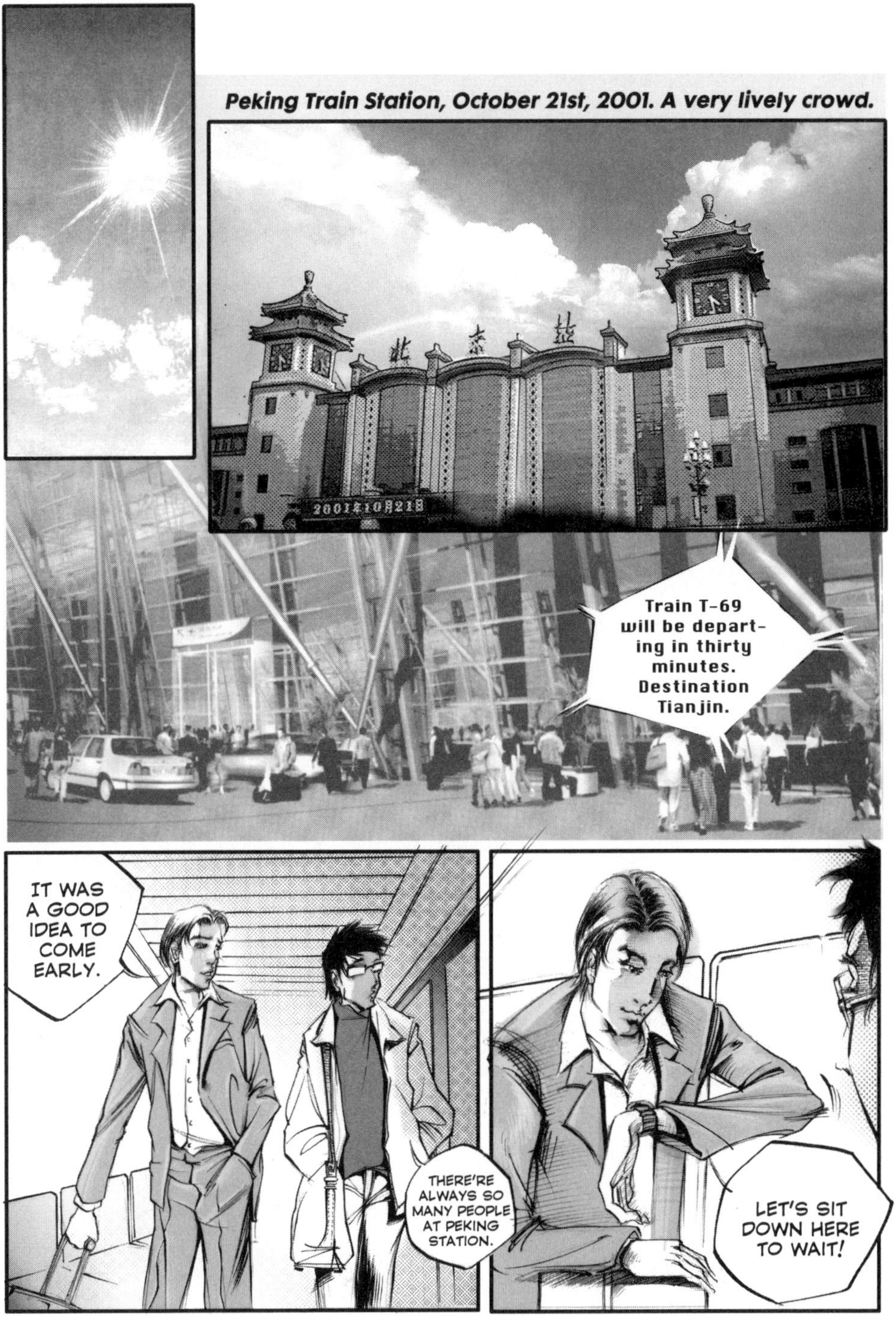
Peking Train Station, October 21st, 2001. A very lively crowd.
Train T-69 will be departing in thirty minutes. Destination Tianjin.
IT WAS A GOOD IDEA TO COME EARLY.
THERE'RE ALWAYS SO MANY PEOPLE AT PEKING STATION.
LET'S SIT DOWN HERE TO WAIT!

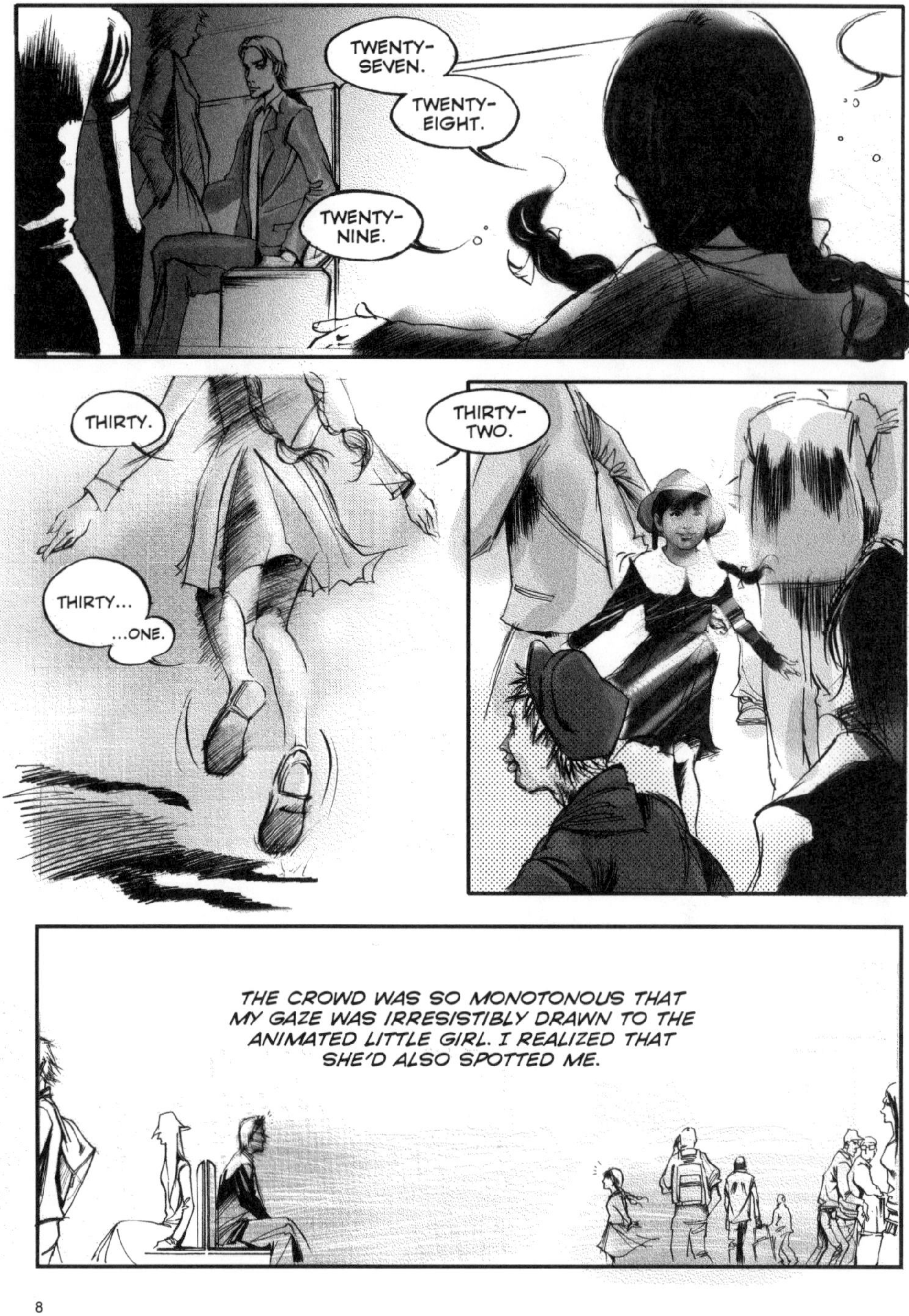
TWENTY-SEVEN.
TWENTY-EIGHT.
TWENTY-NINE.
THIRTY.
THIRTY...
...ONE.
THIRTY-TWO.
THE CROWD WAS SO MONOTONOUS THAT MY GAZE WAS IRRESISTIBLY DRAWN TO THE ANIMATED LITTLE GIRL. I REALIZED THAT SHE'D ALSO SPOTTED ME.

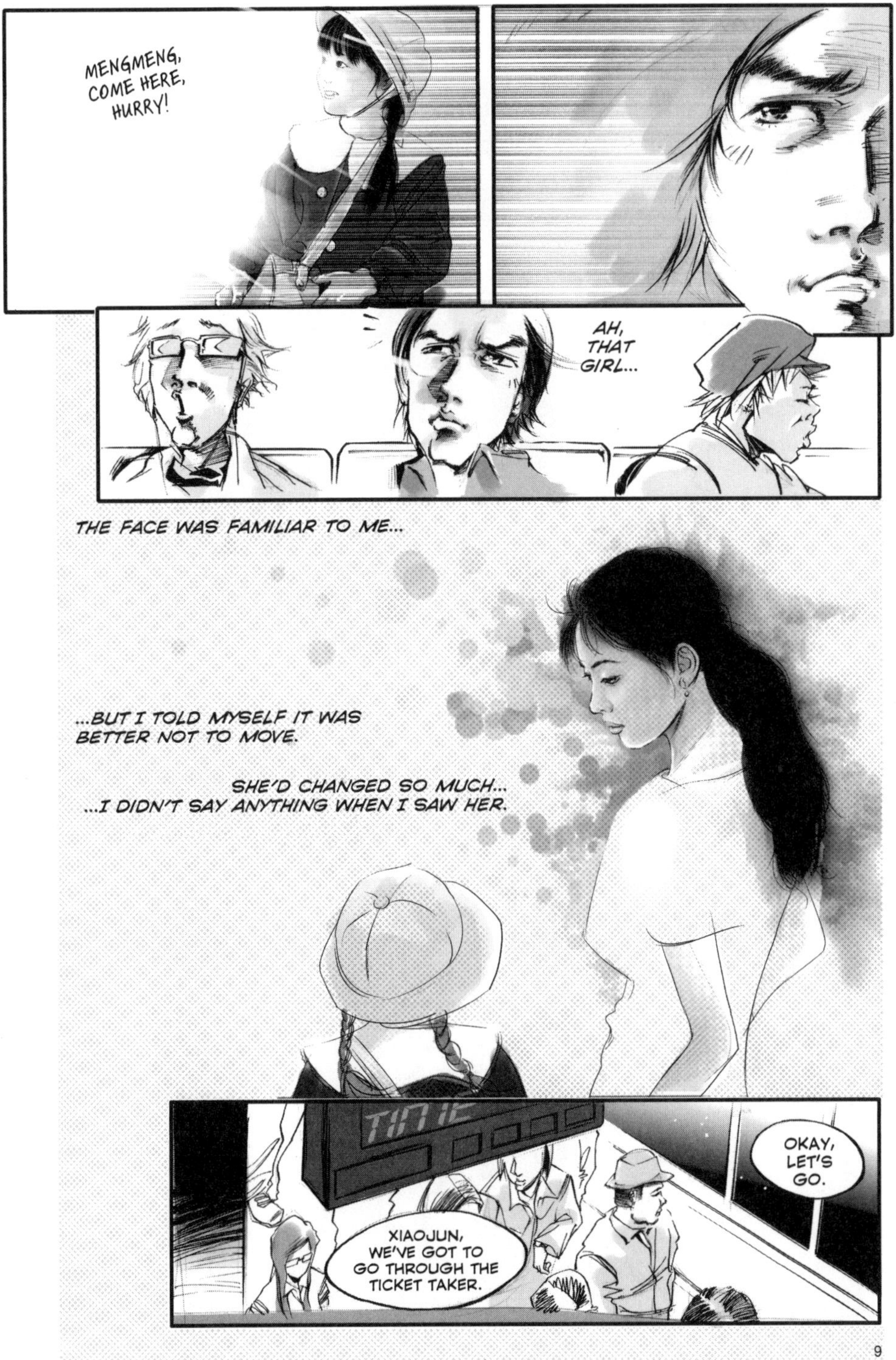
MENGMENG, COME HERE, HURRY!
AH, THAT GIRL...
THE FACE WAS FAMILIAR TO ME...
...BUT I TOLD MYSELF IT WAS BETTER NOT TO MOVE.
SHE'D CHANGED SO MUCH...
...I DIDN'T SAY ANYTHING WHEN I SAW HER.
XIAOJUN, WE'VE GOT TO GO THROUGH THE TICKET TAKER.
OKAY, LET'S GO.

Seafood Restaurant Chutian

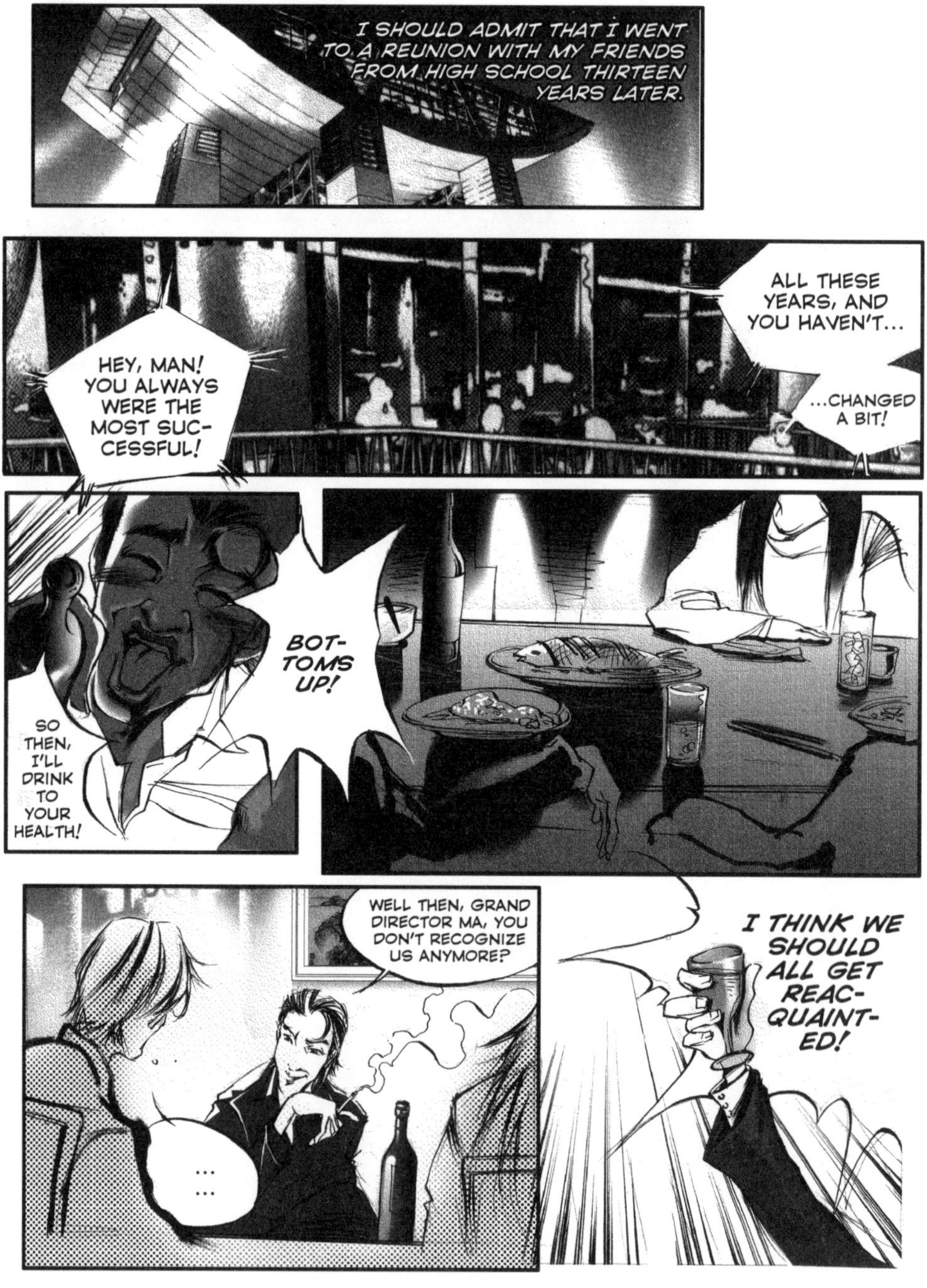

I SHOULD ADMIT THAT I WENT TO A REUNION WITH MY FRIENDS FROM HIGH SCHOOL THIRTEEN YEARS LATER.
HEY, MAN! YOU ALWAYS WERE THE MOST SUC-CESSFUL!
ALL THESE YEARS, AND YOU HAVEN'T...
...CHANGED A BIT!
SO THEN, I'LL DRINK TO YOUR HEALTH!
BOT-TOMS UP!
WELL THEN, GRAND DIRECTOR MA, YOU DON'T RECOGNIZE US ANYMORE?
... ...
I THINK WE SHOULD ALL GET REAC-QUAINT-ED!

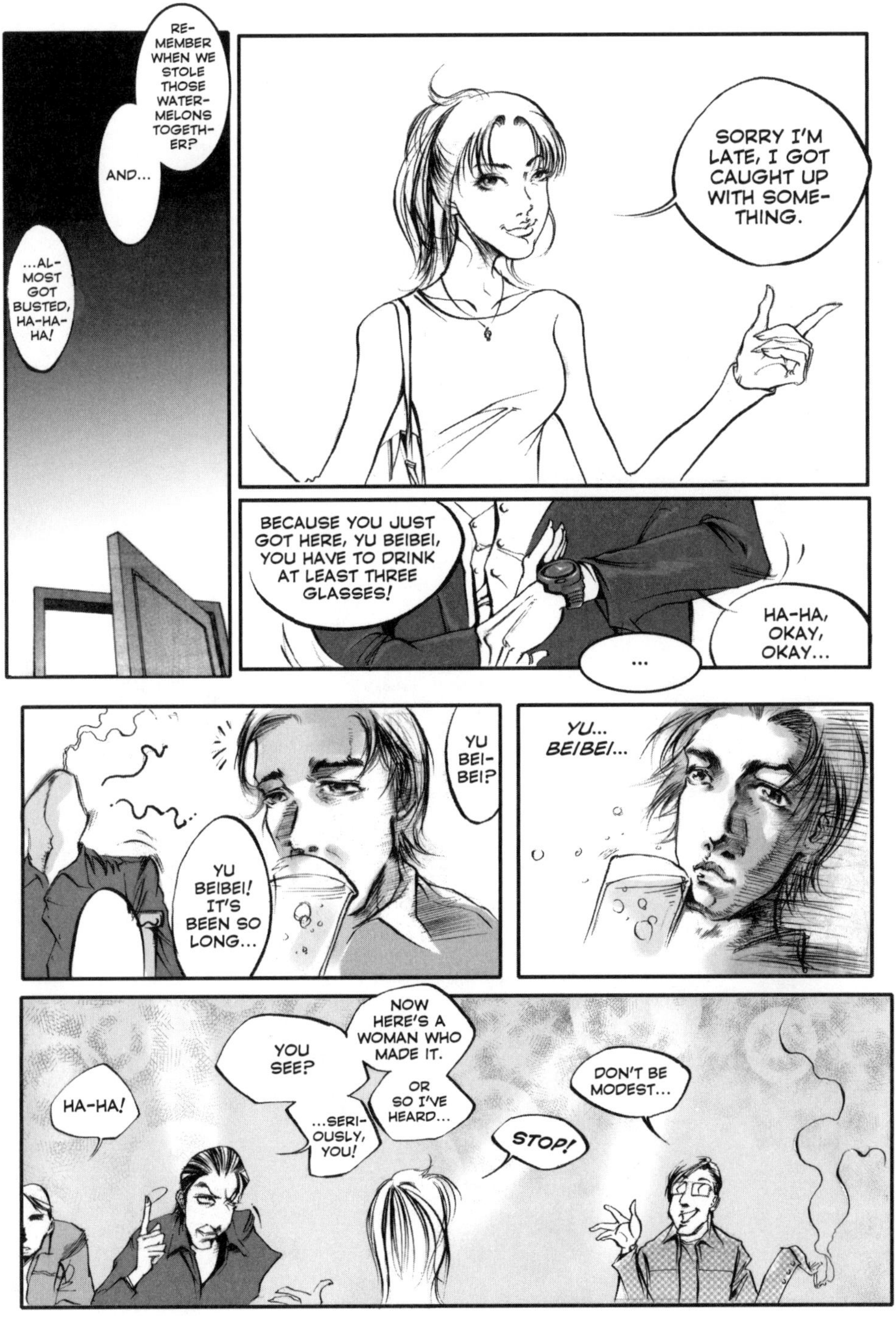
REMEMBER WHEN WE STOLE THOSE WATERMELONS TOGETHER?
AND...
...ALMOST GOT BUSTED, HA-HA-HA!
SORRY I'M LATE, I GOT CAUGHT UP WITH SOMETHING.
BECAUSE YOU JUST GOT HERE, YU BEIBEI, YOU HAVE TO DRINK AT LEAST THREE GLASSES!
HA-HA, OKAY, OKAY...
...
YU BEIBEI?
YU BEIBEI! IT'S BEEN SO LONG...
YU... BEIBEI...
HA-HA!
YOU SEE?
NOW HERE'S A WOMAN WHO MADE IT.
...SERIOUSLY, YOU!
OR SO I'VE HEARD...
STOP!
DON'T BE MODEST...

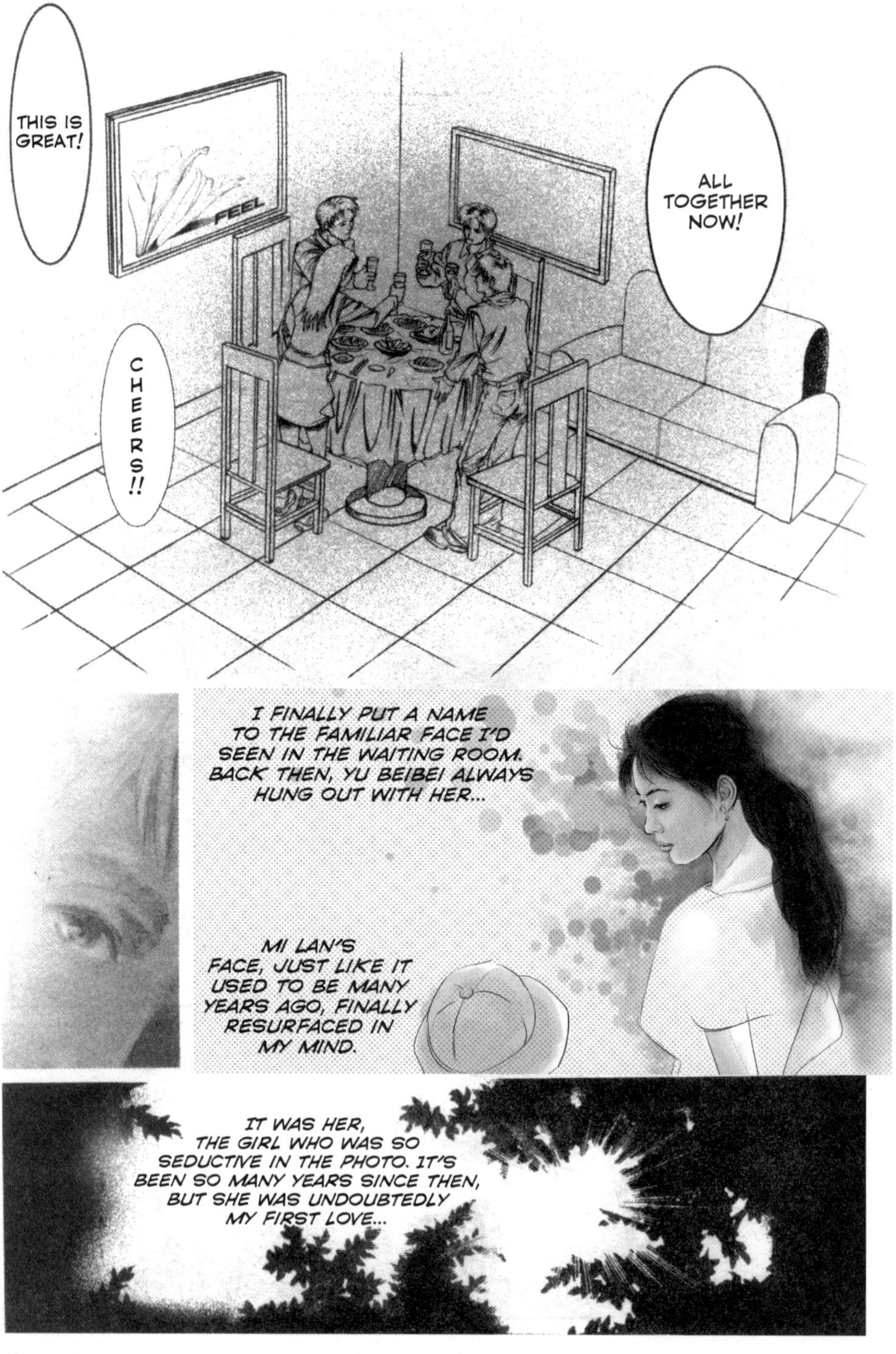
THIS IS GREAT!
CHEERS!!
ALL TOGETHER NOW!
I FINALLY PUT A NAME TO THE FAMILIAR FACE I'D SEEN IN THE WAITING ROOM. BACK THEN, YU BEIBEI ALWAYS HUNG OUT WITH HER...
MI LAN'S FACE, JUST LIKE IT USED TO BE MANY YEARS AGO, FINALLY RESURFACED IN MY MIND.
IT WAS HER, THE GIRL WHO WAS SO SEDUCTIVE IN THE PHOTO. IT'S BEEN SO MANY YEARS SINCE THEN, BUT SHE WAS UNDOUBTEDLY MY FIRST LOVE...

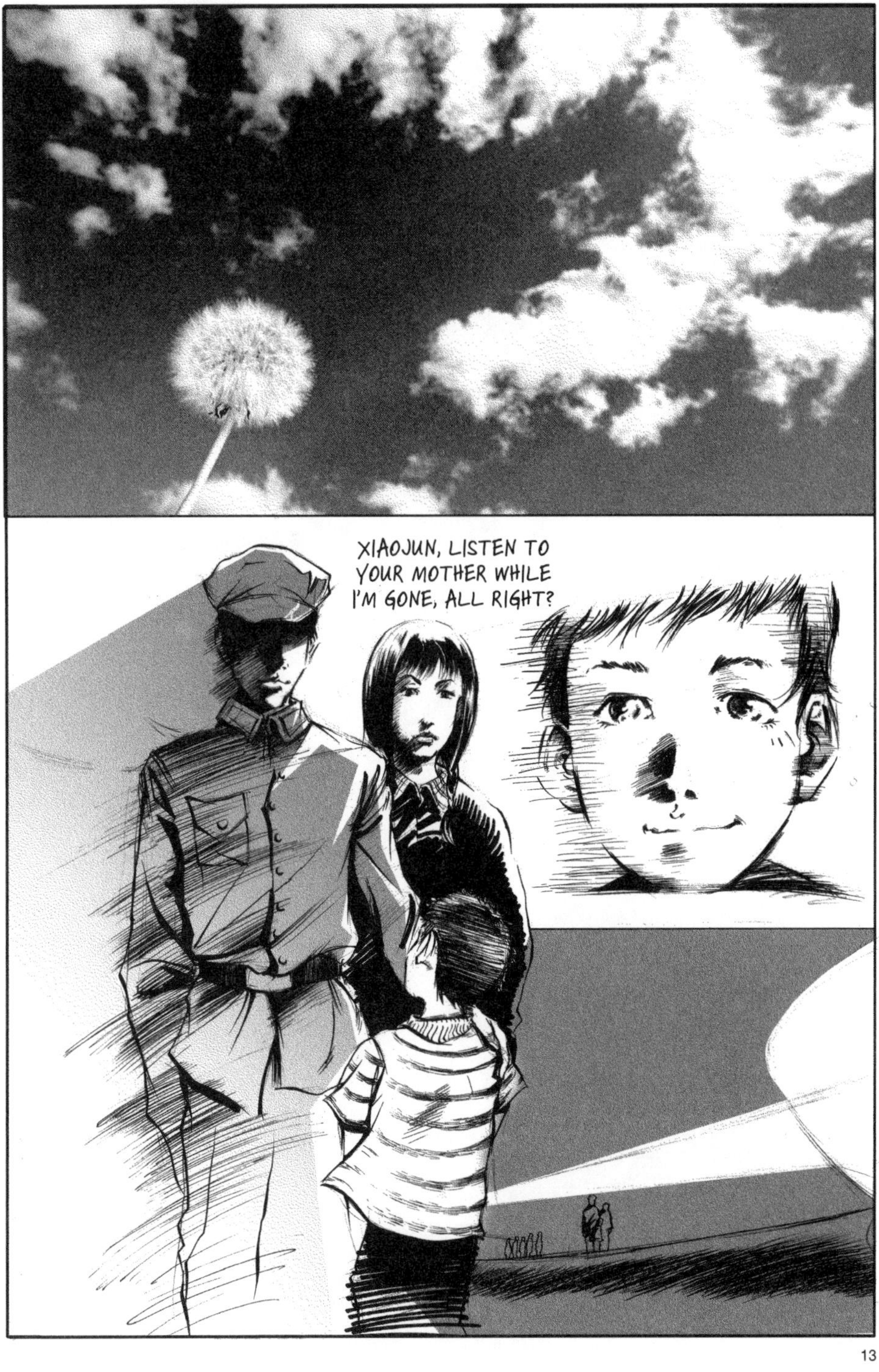
XIAOJUN, LISTEN TO YOUR MOTHER WHILE I'M GONE, ALL RIGHT?

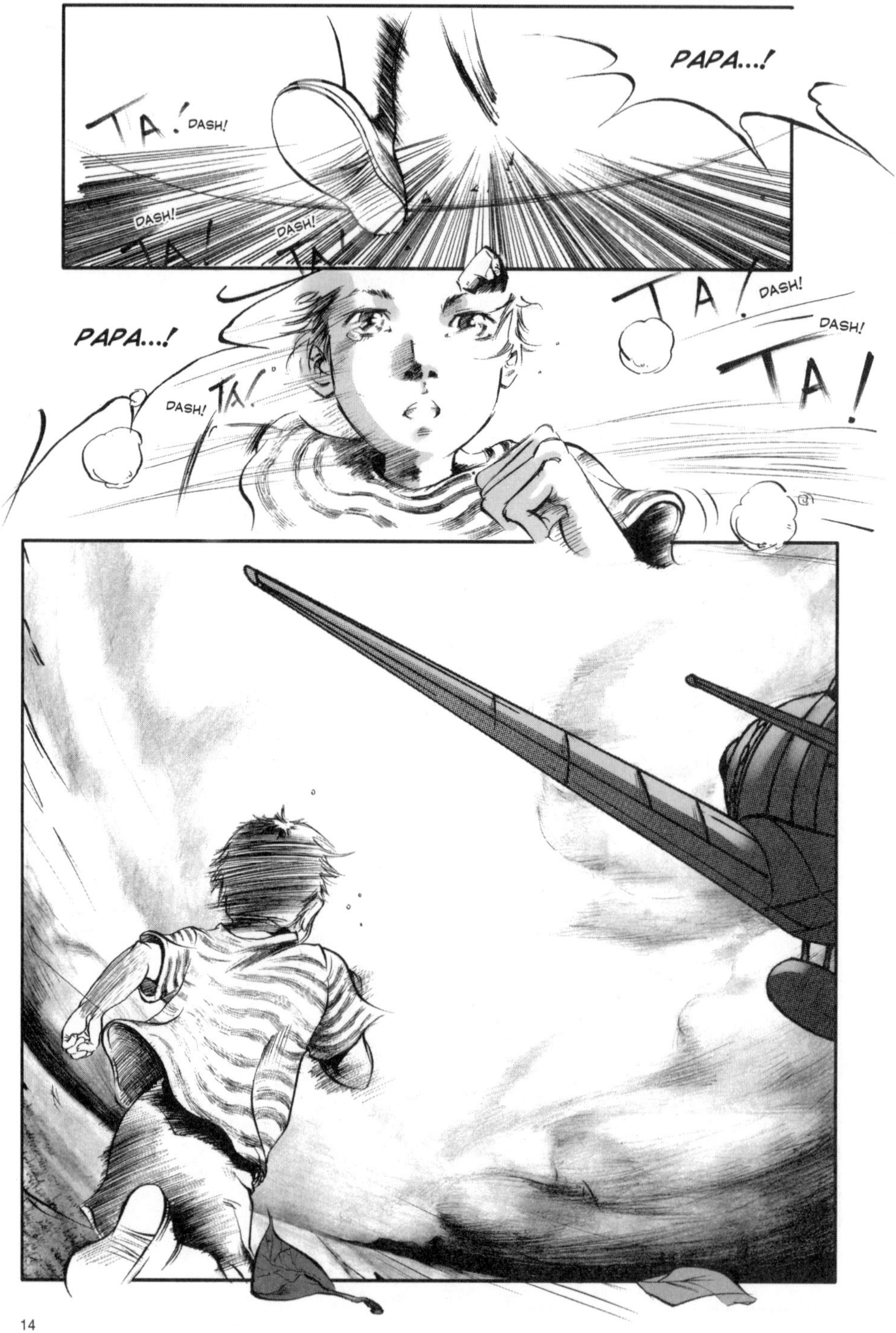
PAPA...!
TA! DASH!
DASH! TA!
DASH! TA!
TA! DASH!
PAPA...!
DASH! TA!
DASH! TA!

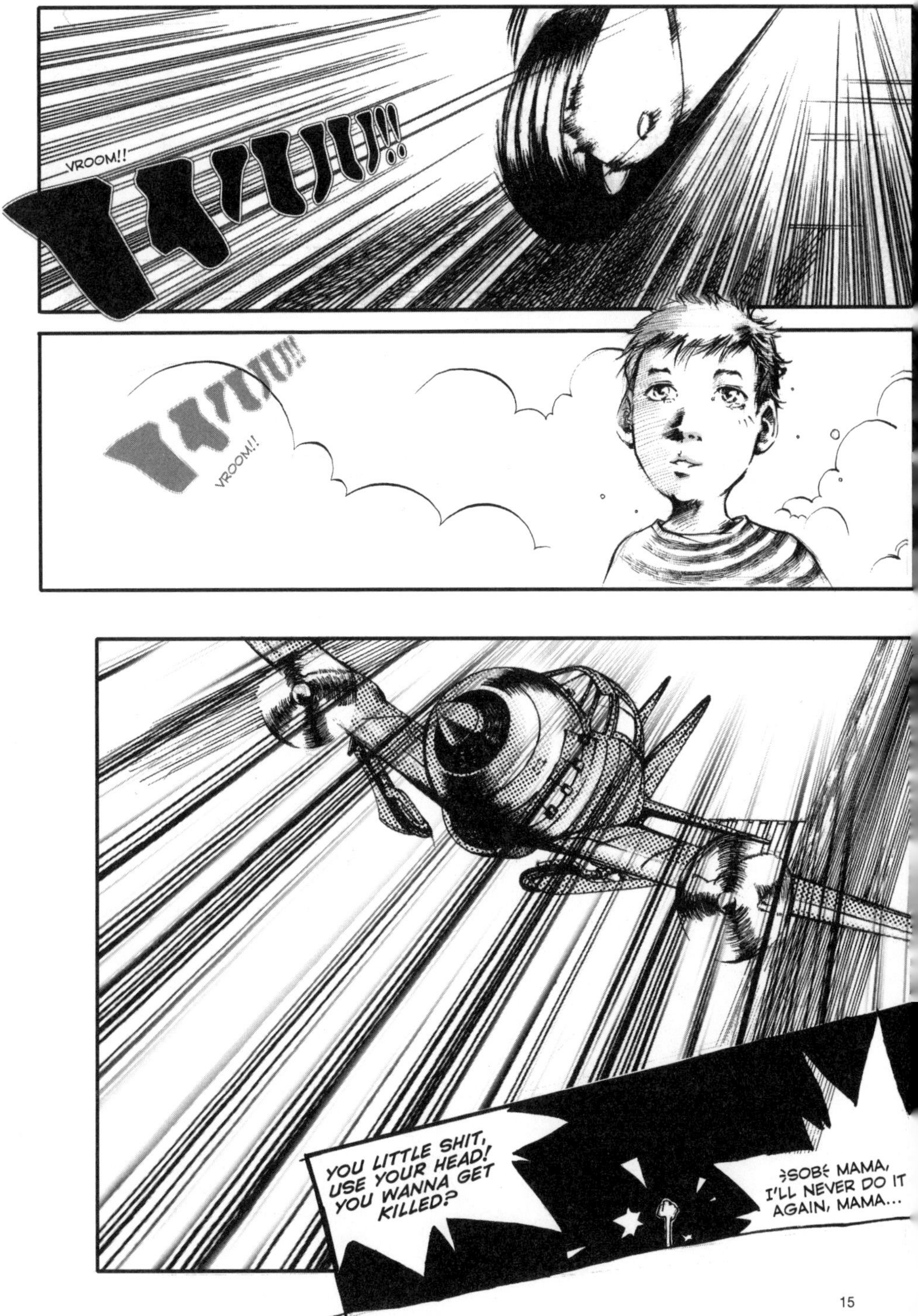
VROOM!!
VROOM!!
YOU LITTLE SHIT, USE YOUR HEAD! YOU WANNA GET KILLED?
≯SOB≼ MAMA, I'LL NEVER DO IT AGAIN, MAMA...

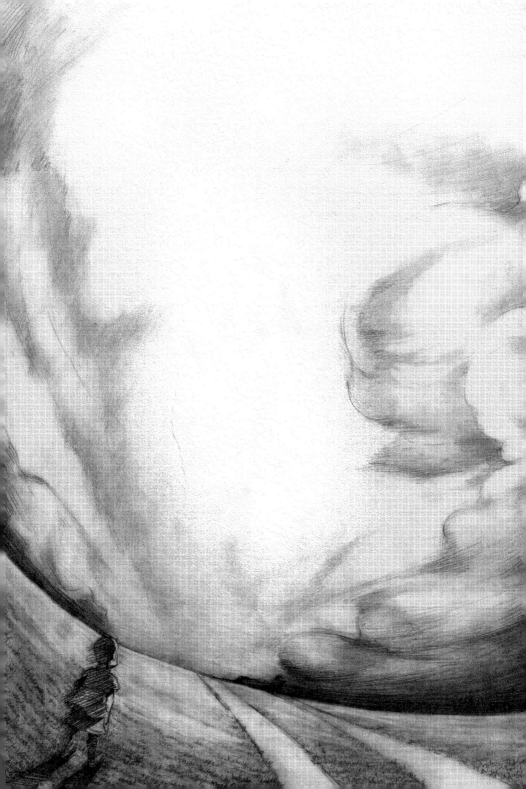

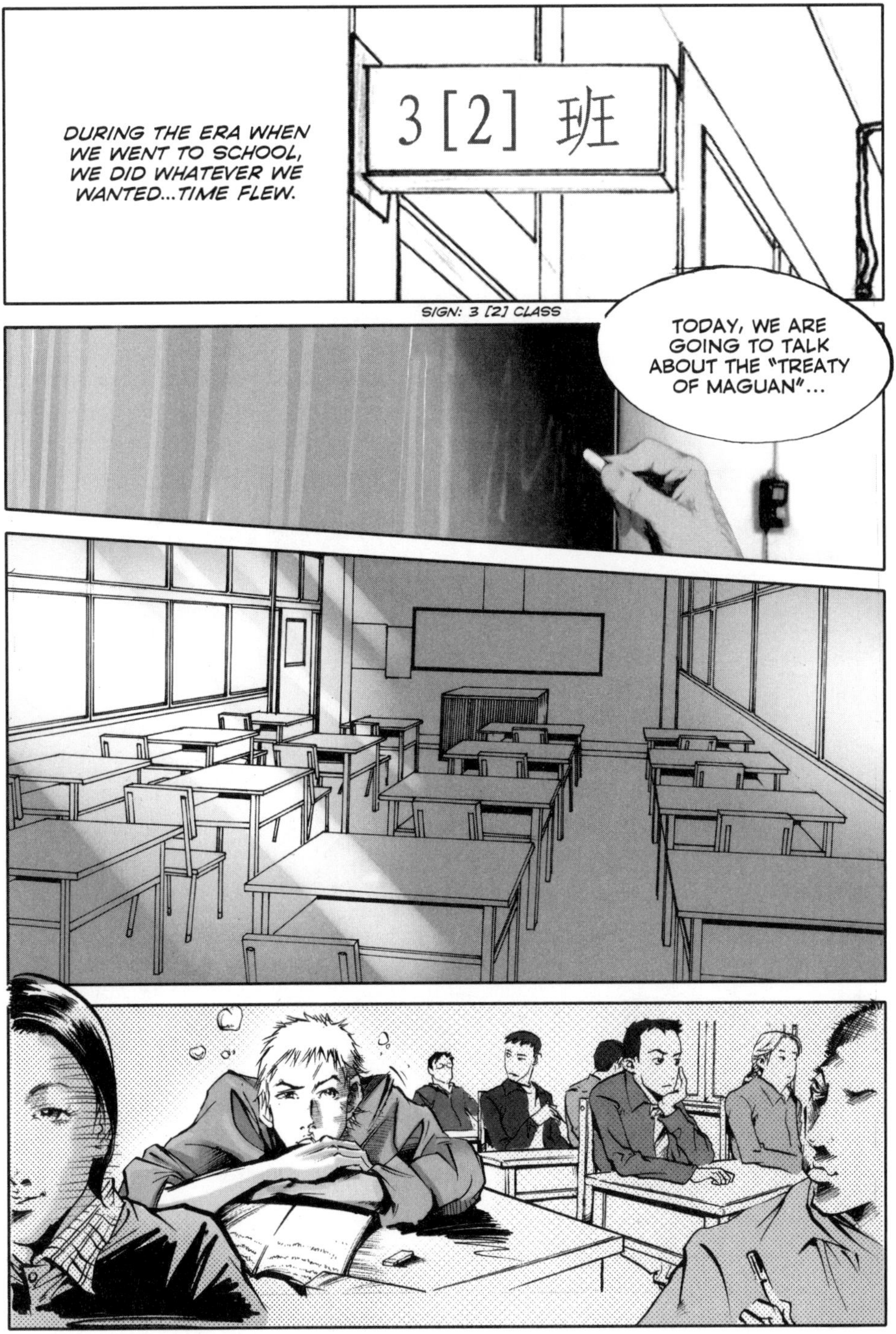
DURING THE ERA WHEN WE WENT TO SCHOOL, WE DID WHATEVER WE WANTED...TIME FLEW.
3 [2] 班
SIGN: 3 [2] CLASS
TODAY, WE ARE GOING TO TALK ABOUT THE "TREATY OF MAGUAN"...

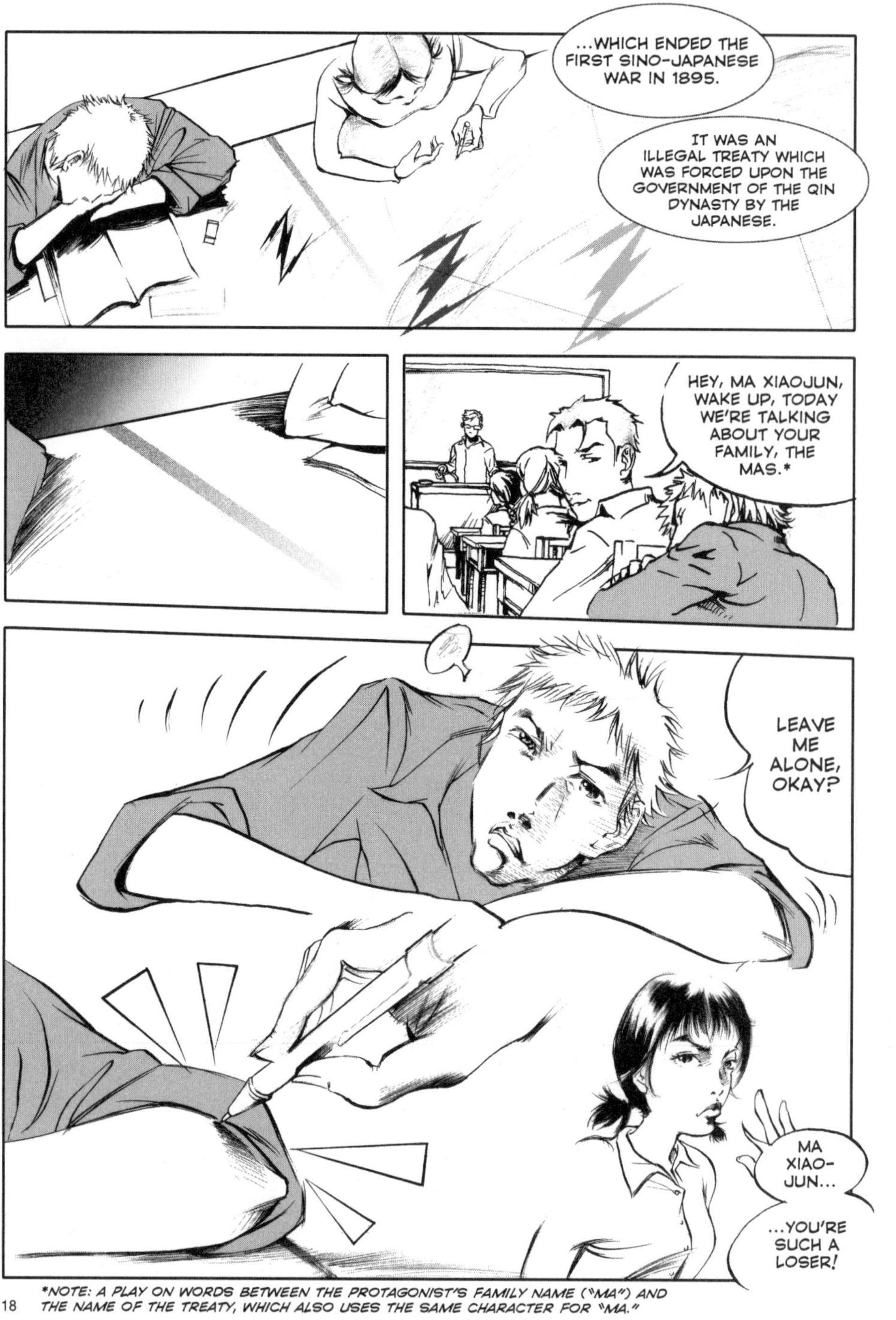
...WHICH ENDED THE FIRST SINO-JAPANESE WAR IN 1895.
IT WAS AN ILLEGAL TREATY WHICH WAS FORCED UPON THE GOVERNMENT OF THE QIN DYNASTY BY THE JAPANESE.
HEY, MA XIAOJUN, WAKE UP, TODAY WE'RE TALKING ABOUT YOUR FAMILY, THE MAS.*
LEAVE ME ALONE, OKAY?
MA XIAO-JUN...
...YOU'RE SUCH A LOSER!

**NOTE: A PLAY ON WORDS BETWEEN THE PROTAGONIST'S FAMILY NAME ("MA") AND THE NAME OF THE TREATY, WHICH ALSO USES THE SAME CHARACTER FOR "MA."*

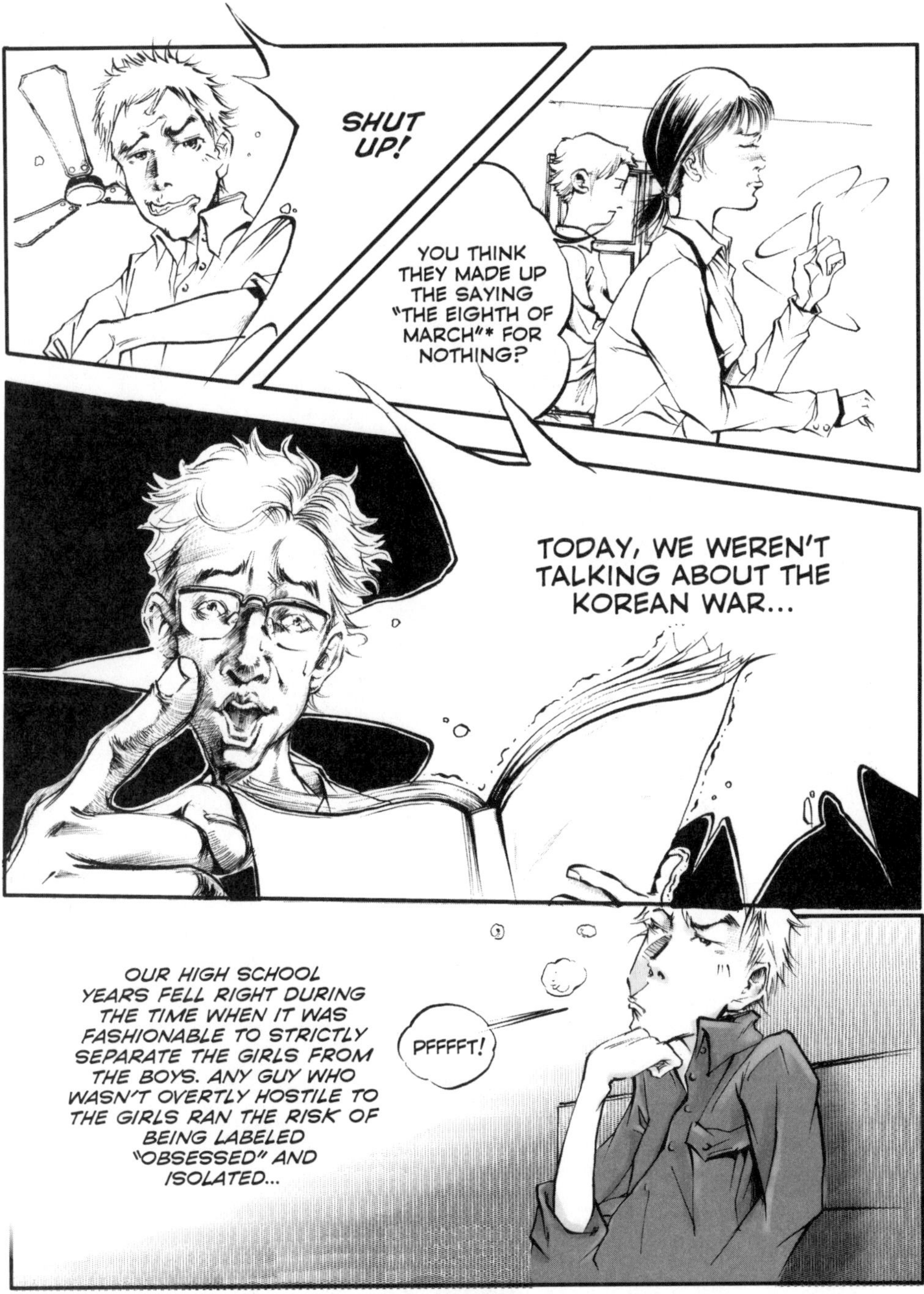
SHUT UP!
YOU THINK THEY MADE UP THE SAYING "THE EIGHTH OF MARCH"* FOR NOTHING?
TODAY, WE WEREN'T TALKING ABOUT THE KOREAN WAR...
OUR HIGH SCHOOL YEARS FELL RIGHT DURING THE TIME WHEN IT WAS FASHIONABLE TO STRICTLY SEPARATE THE GIRLS FROM THE BOYS. ANY GUY WHO WASN'T OVERTLY HOSTILE TO THE GIRLS RAN THE RISK OF BEING LABELED "OBSESSED" AND ISOLATED...
PFFFFT!

*NOTE: IN CHINA, THE 3RD OF MARCH IS THE DAY OF WOMEN.

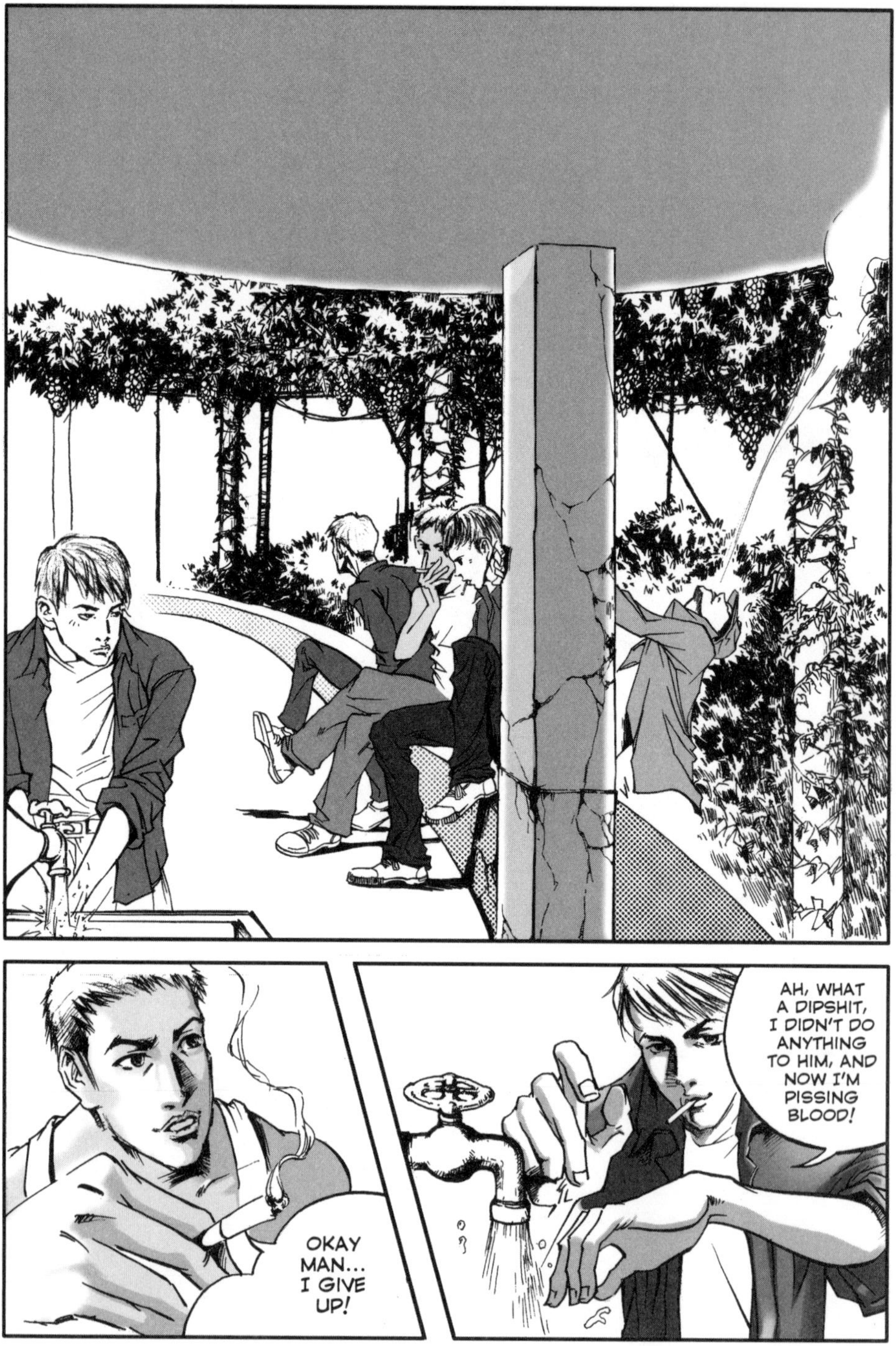
OKAY MAN... I GIVE UP!
AH, WHAT A DIPSHIT, I DIDN'T DO ANYTHING TO HIM, AND NOW I'M PISSING BLOOD!

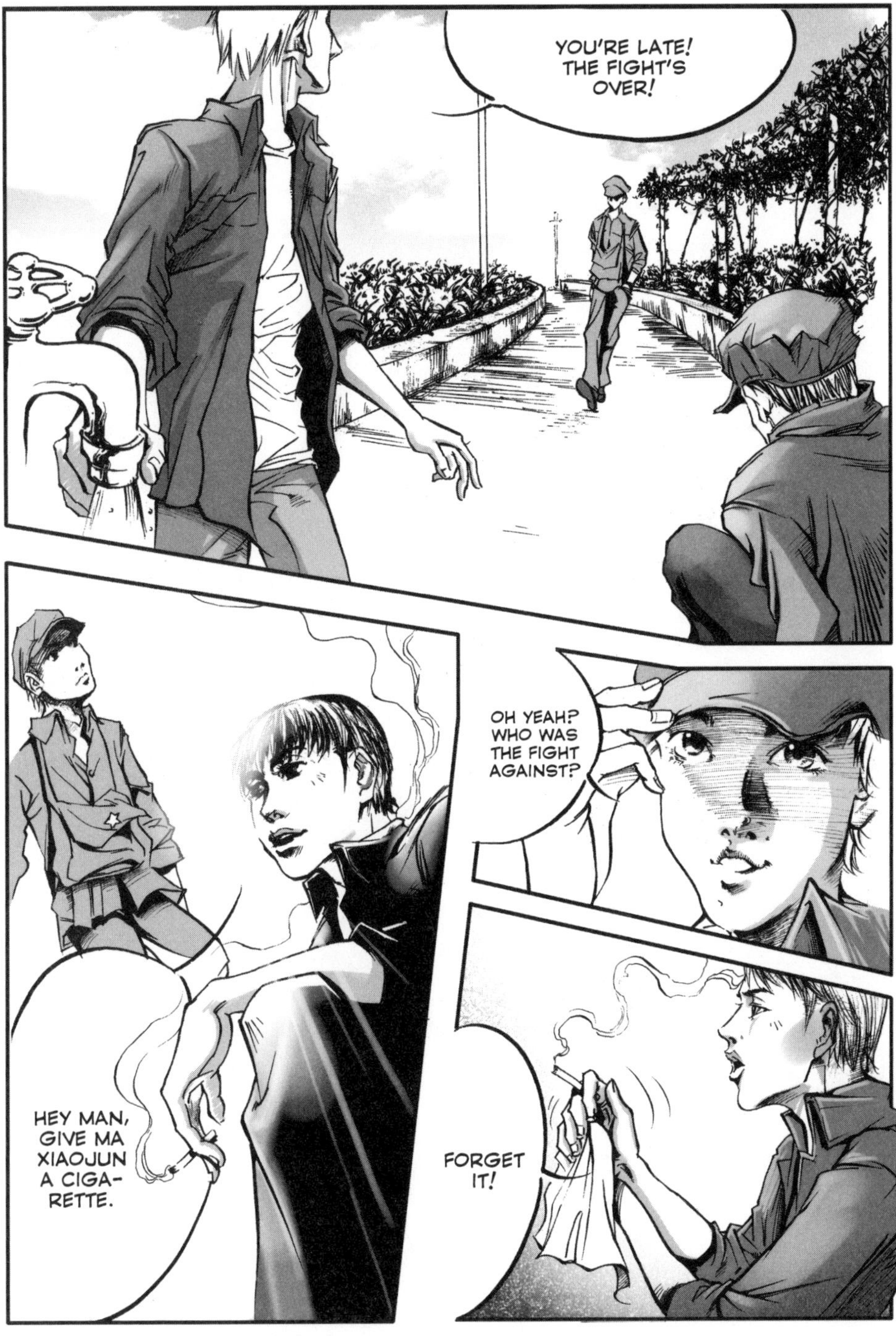
YOU'RE LATE! THE FIGHT'S OVER!
HEY MAN, GIVE MA XIAOJUN A CIGA-RETTE.
OH YEAH? WHO WAS THE FIGHT AGAINST?
FORGET IT!

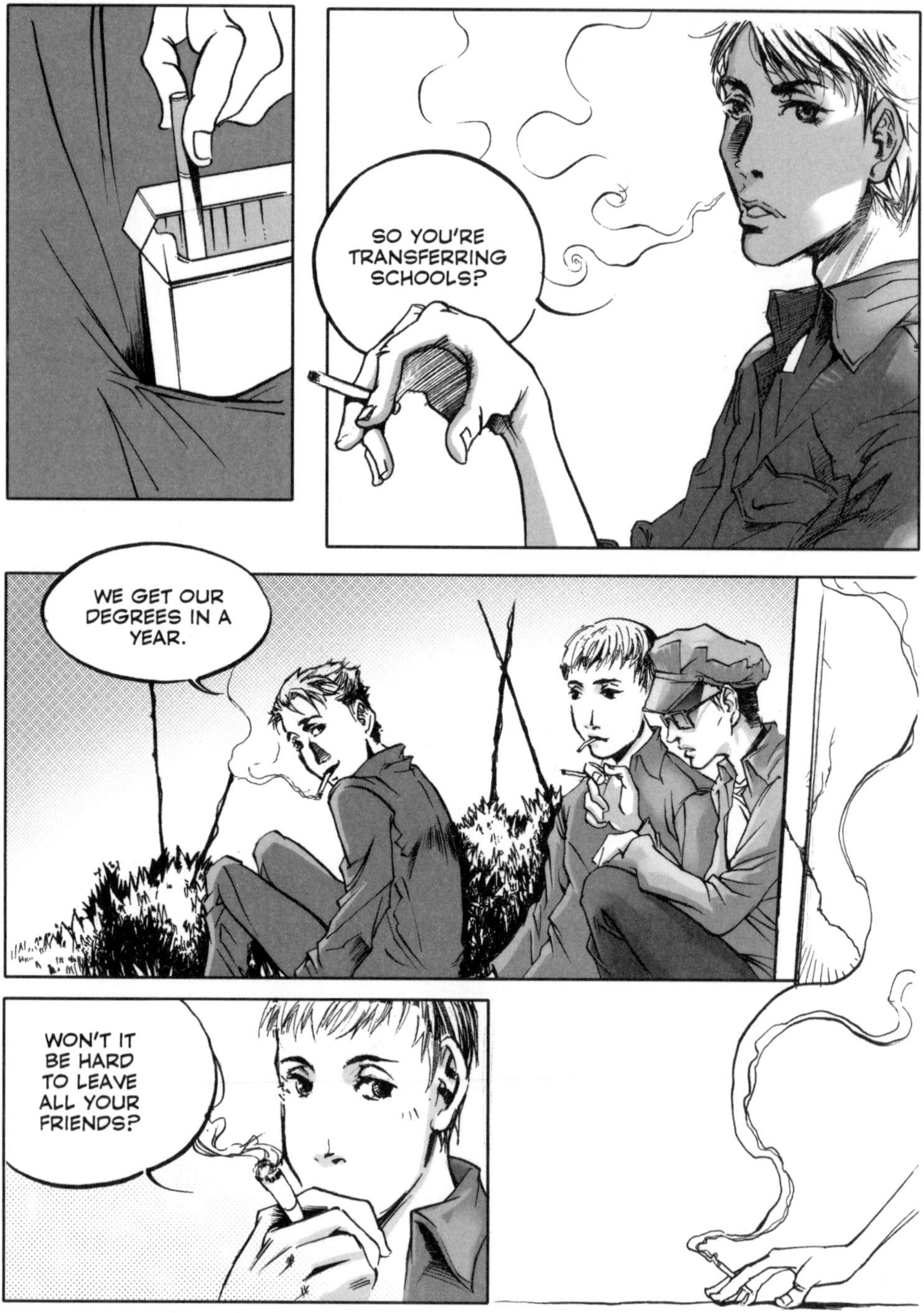
SO YOU'RE TRANSFERRING SCHOOLS?
WE GET OUR DEGREES IN A YEAR.
WON'T IT BE HARD TO LEAVE ALL YOUR FRIENDS?

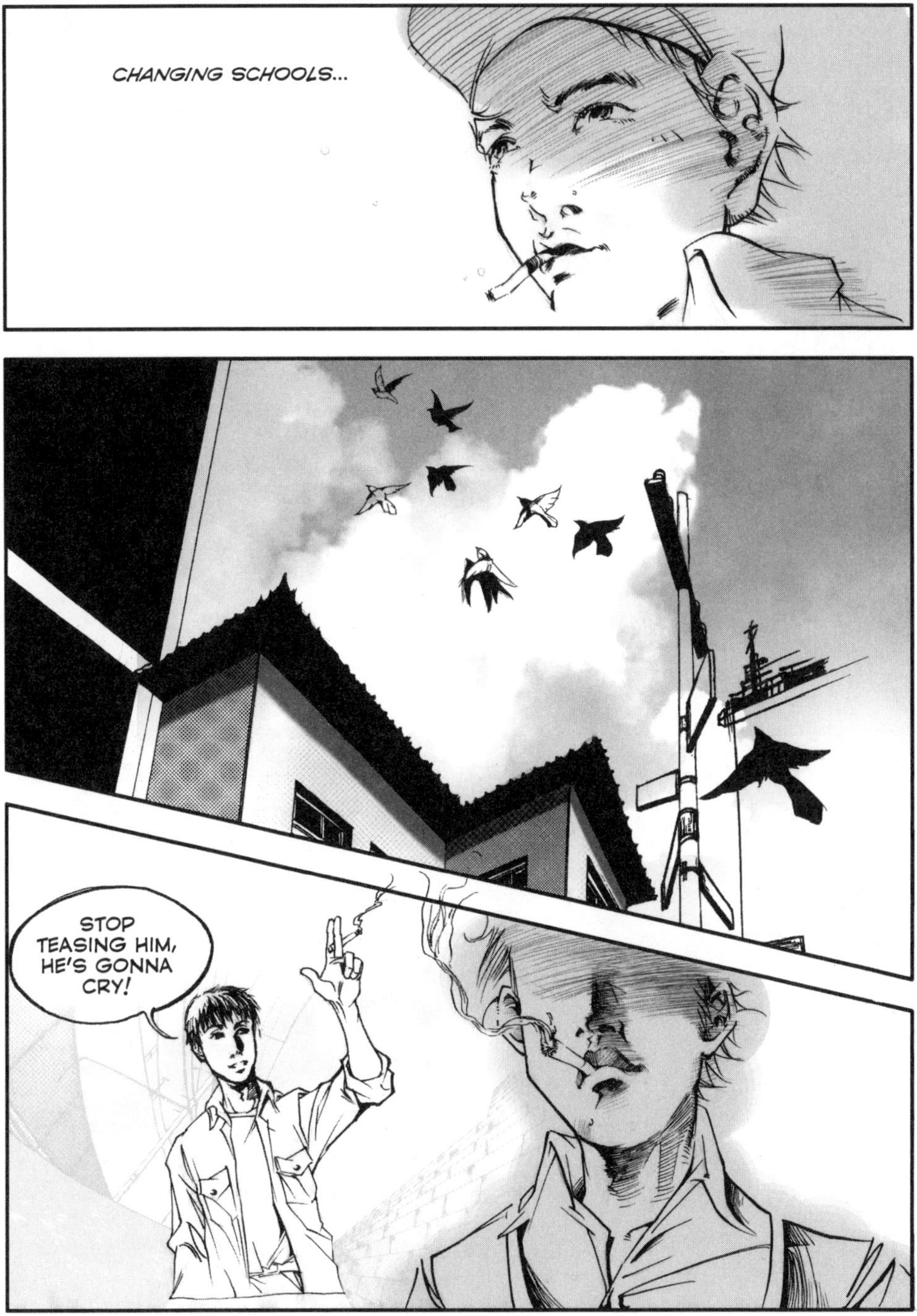
CHANGING SCHOOLS...
STOP TEASING HIM, HE'S GONNA CRY!

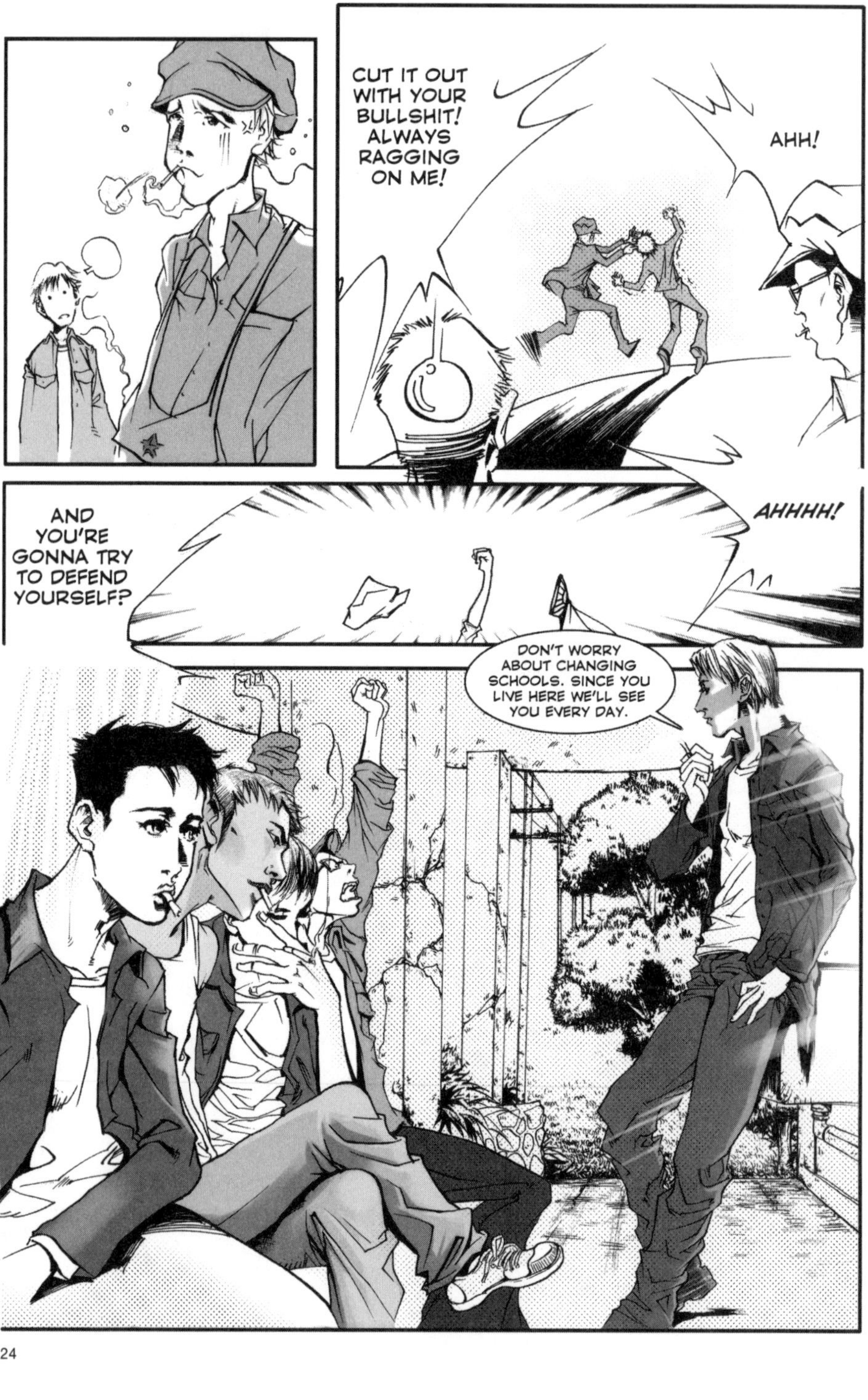
CUT IT OUT WITH YOUR BULLSHIT! ALWAYS RAGGING ON ME!
AHH!
AND YOU'RE GONNA TRY TO DEFEND YOURSELF?
AHHHH!
DON'T WORRY ABOUT CHANGING SCHOOLS. SINCE YOU LIVE HERE WE'LL SEE YOU EVERY DAY.

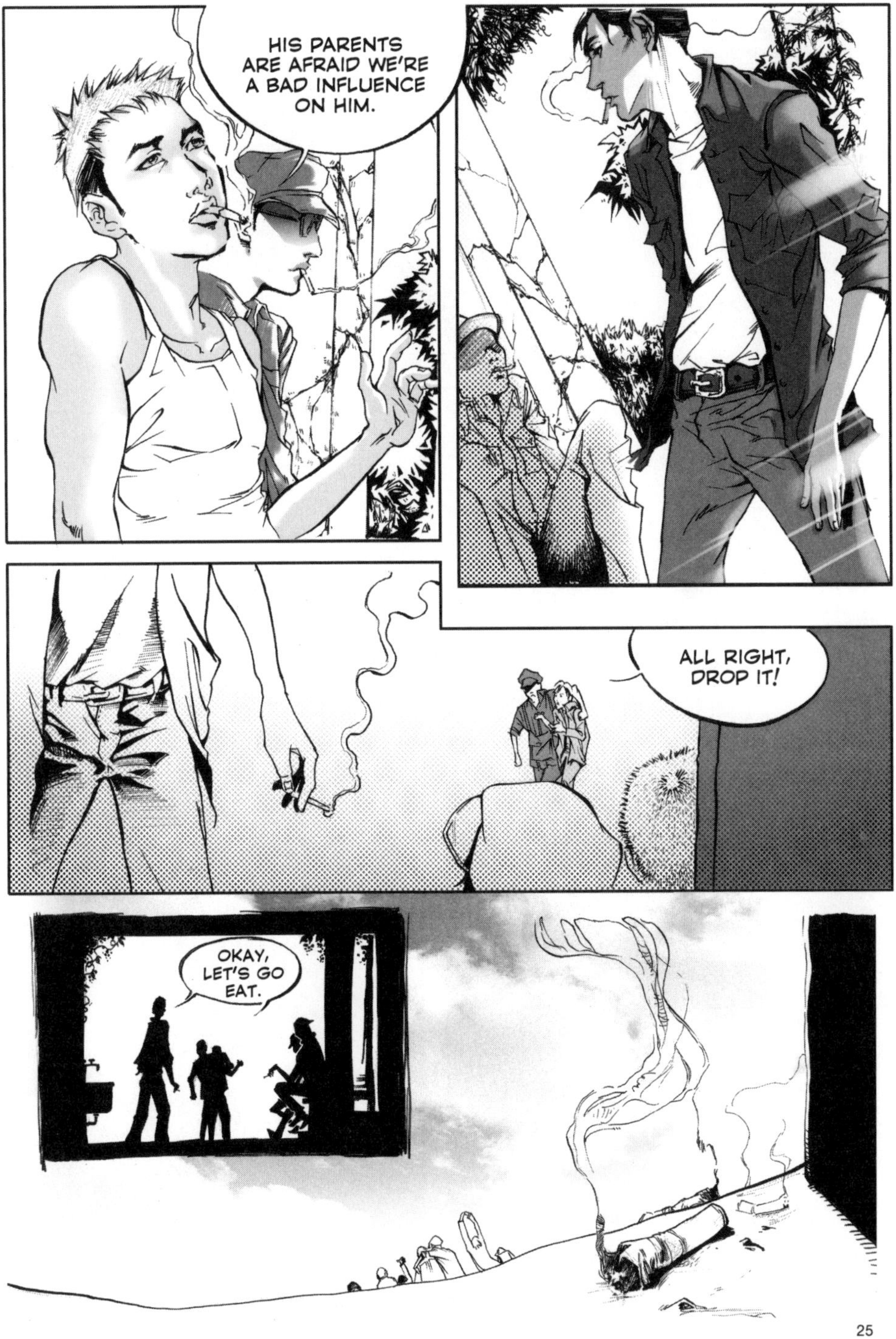
HIS PARENTS ARE AFRAID WE'RE A BAD INFLUENCE ON HIM.
ALL RIGHT, DROP IT!
OKAY, LET'S GO EAT.

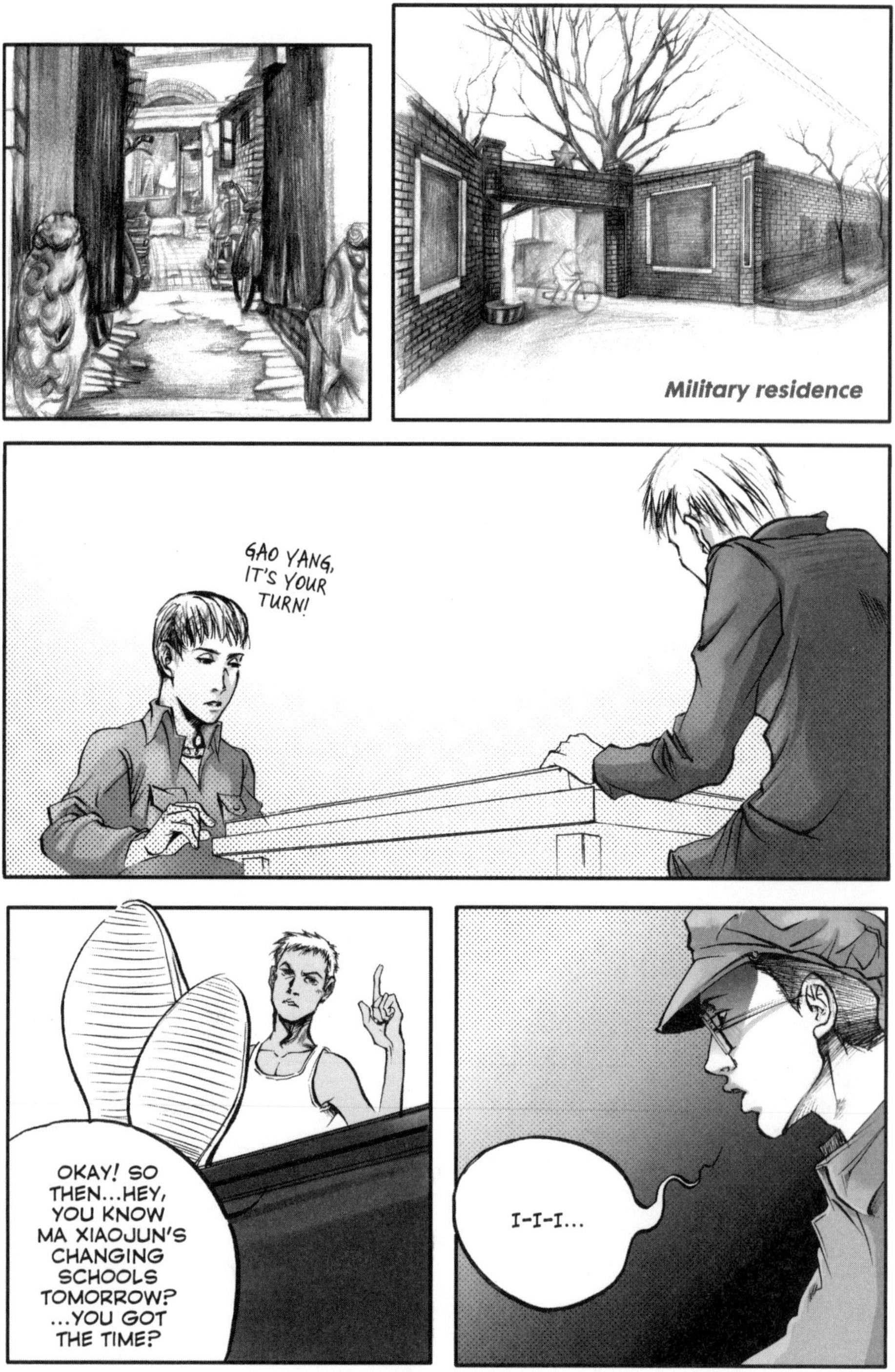
Military residence
GAO YANG, IT'S YOUR TURN!
OKAY! SO THEN...HEY, YOU KNOW MA XIAOJUN'S CHANGING SCHOOLS TOMORROW? ...YOU GOT THE TIME?
I-I-I...

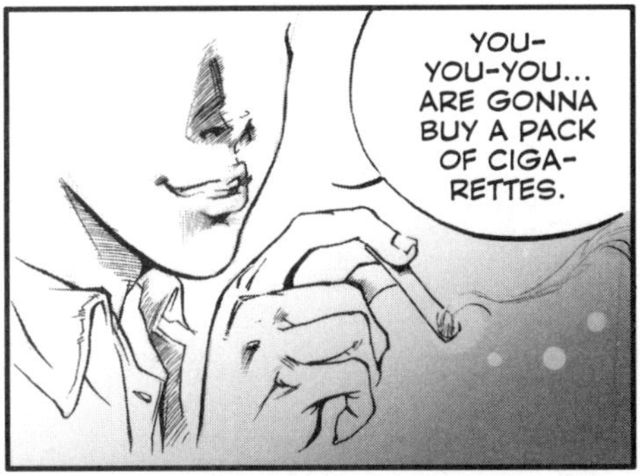
YOU-YOU-YOU... ARE GONNA BUY A PACK OF CIGA-RETTES.

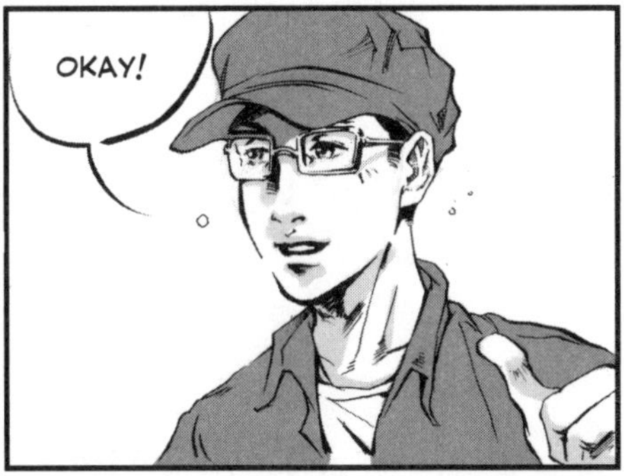
OKAY!

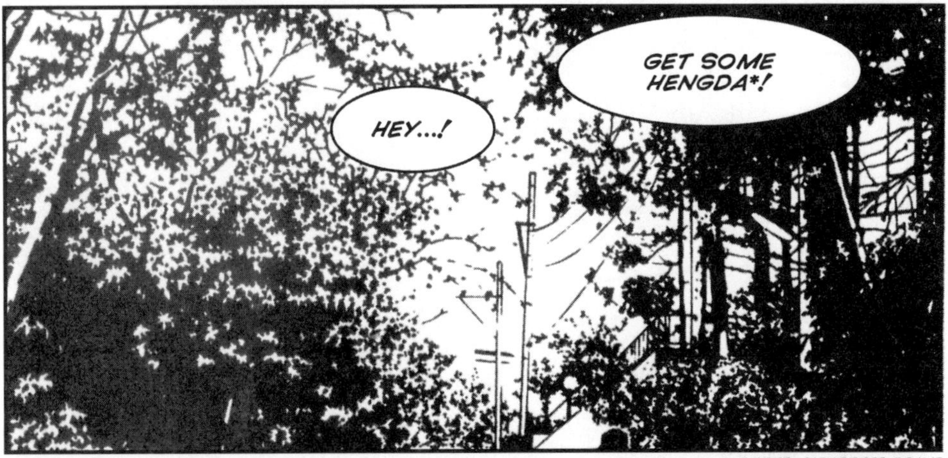
HEY...!
GET SOME HENGDA*!

*NOTE: CIGARETTE BRAND

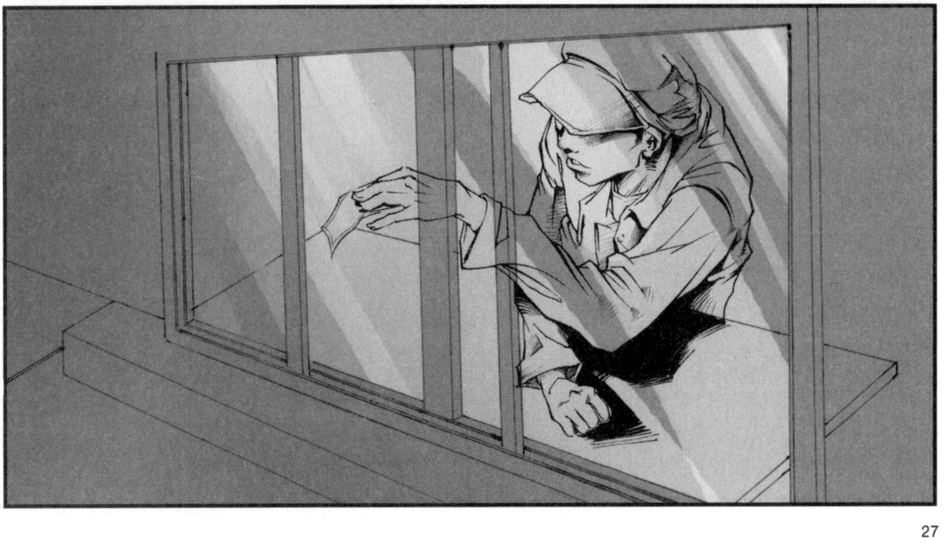

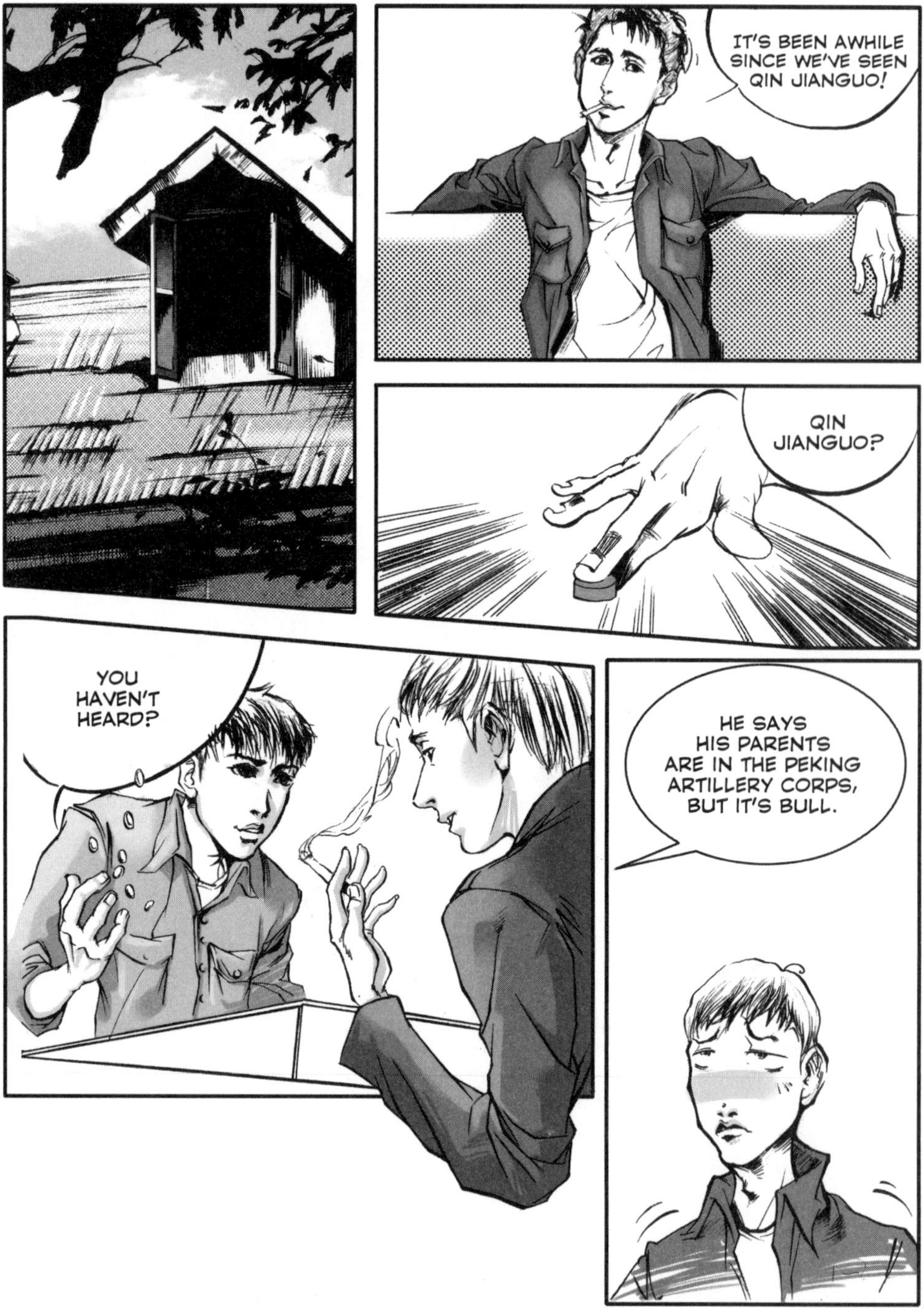
IT'S BEEN AWHILE SINCE WE'VE SEEN QIN JIANGUO!
QIN JIANGUO?
YOU HAVEN'T HEARD?
HE SAYS HIS PARENTS ARE IN THE PEKING ARTILLERY CORPS, BUT IT'S BULL.

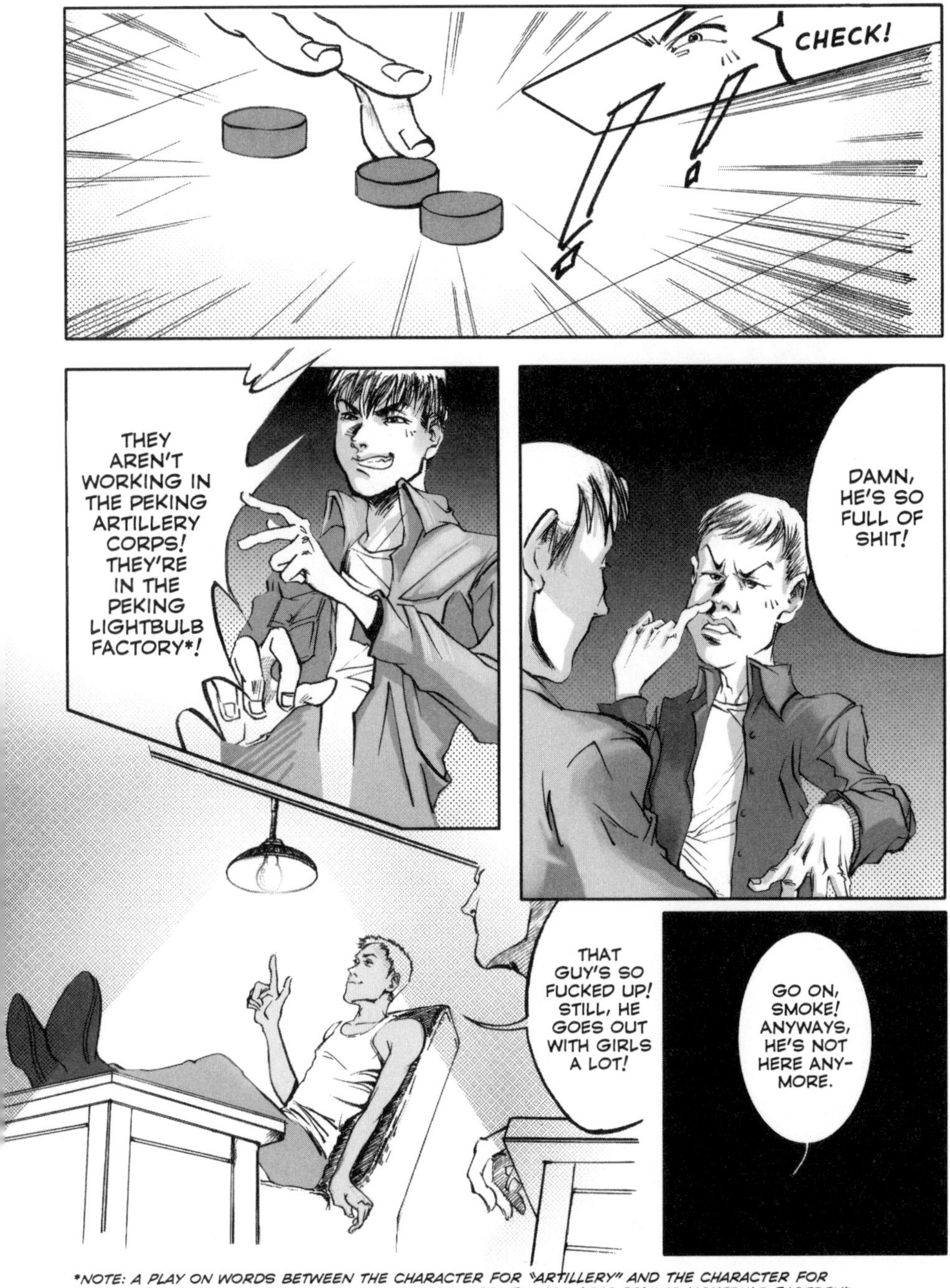
CHECK!
THEY AREN'T WORKING IN THE PEKING ARTILLERY CORPS! THEY'RE IN THE PEKING LIGHTBULB FACTORY*!
DAMN, HE'S SO FULL OF SHIT!
THAT GUY'S SO FUCKED UP! STILL, HE GOES OUT WITH GIRLS A LOT!
GO ON, SMOKE! ANYWAYS, HE'S NOT HERE ANYMORE.

*NOTE: A PLAY ON WORDS BETWEEN THE CHARACTER FOR "ARTILLERY" AND THE CHARACTER FOR "LIGHTBULB," WHICH ARE HOMONYMS IN CHINESE. SPECIFICALLY, "THE PEKING LIGHTBULB FACTORY" AND "THE PEKING ARTILLERY CORPS" HAVE THE SAME PRONUNCIATION.

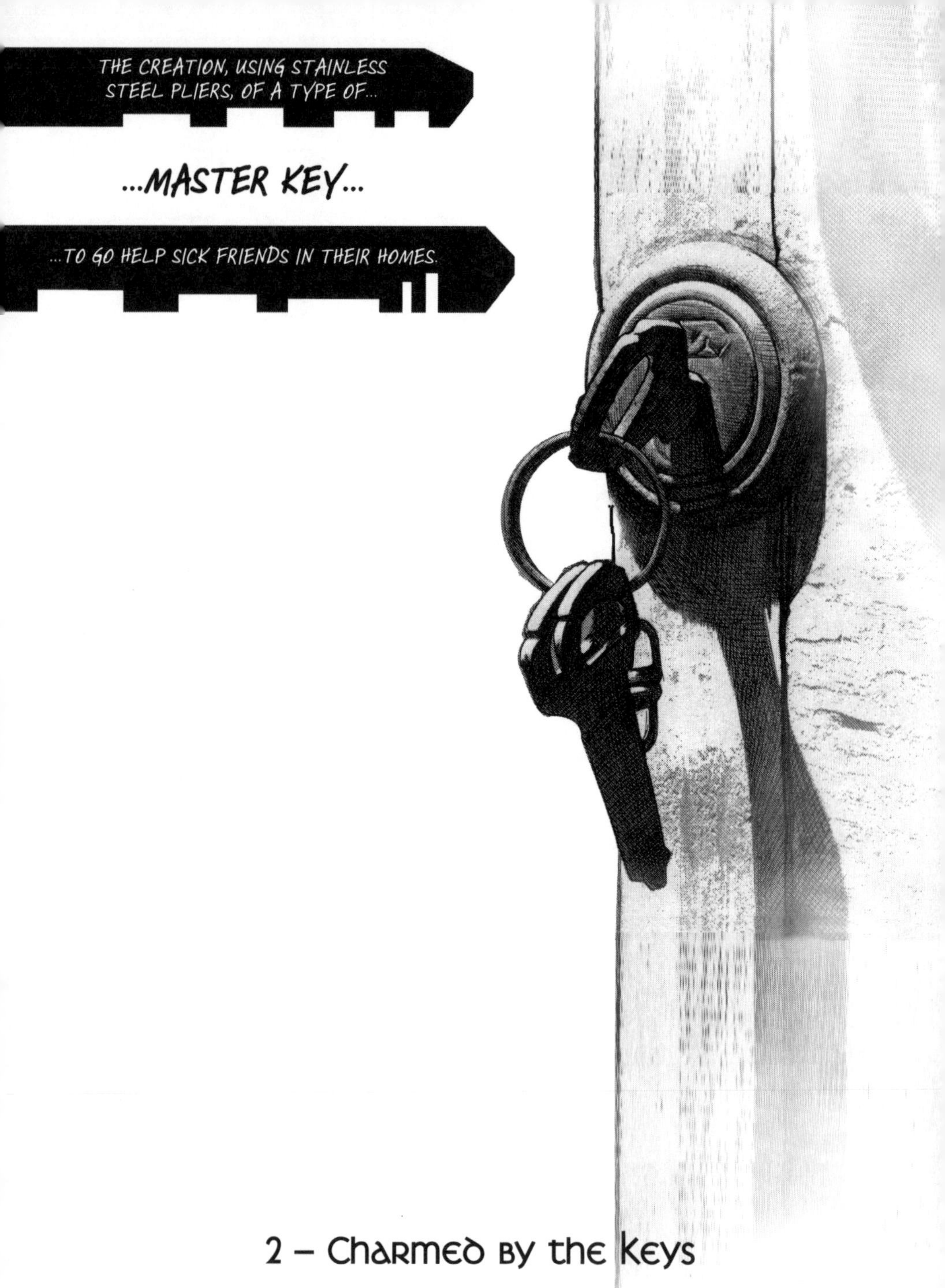
THE CREATION, USING STAINLESS STEEL PLIERS, OF A TYPE OF...
...MASTER KEY...
...TO GO HELP SICK FRIENDS IN THEIR HOMES.

2 – Charmed by the Keys

IT WAS A REALLY STRICT SCHOOL. EVEN THE BRAVEST STUDENTS WERE TERRIFIED BY THE TEACHERS.

IT WAS IMPOSSIBLE TO FIND EVEN ONE BROTHER-IN-ARMS.

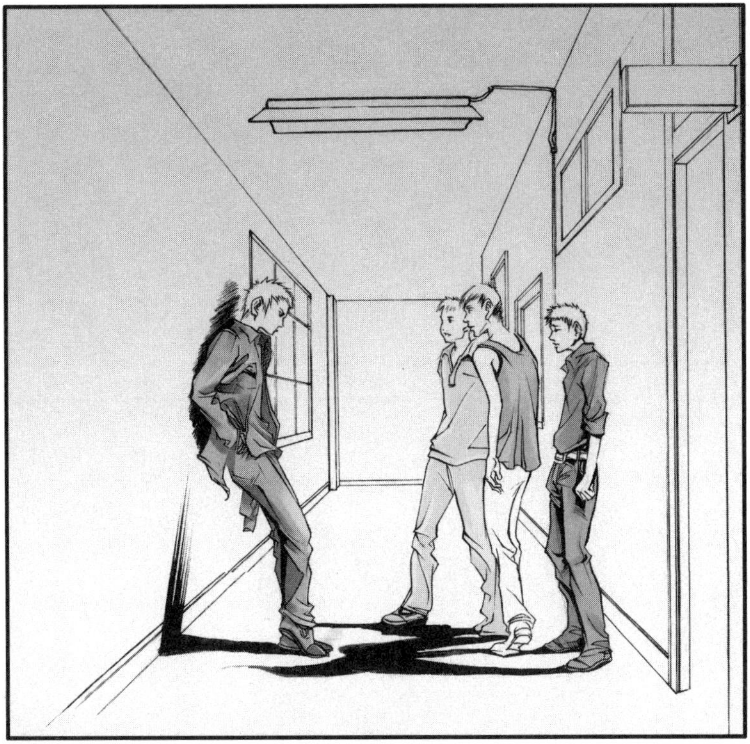

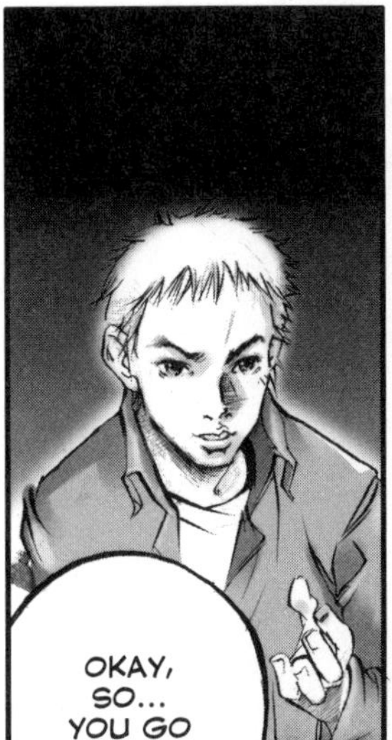
OKAY, SO... YOU GO LIKE THIS, AND...

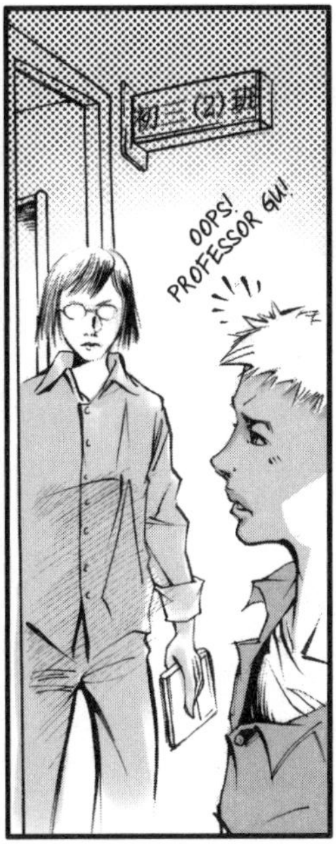
初三(2)班
OOPS! PROFESSOR GU!

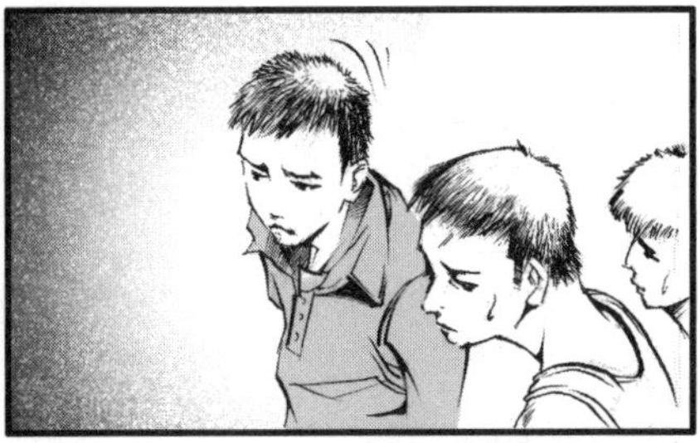

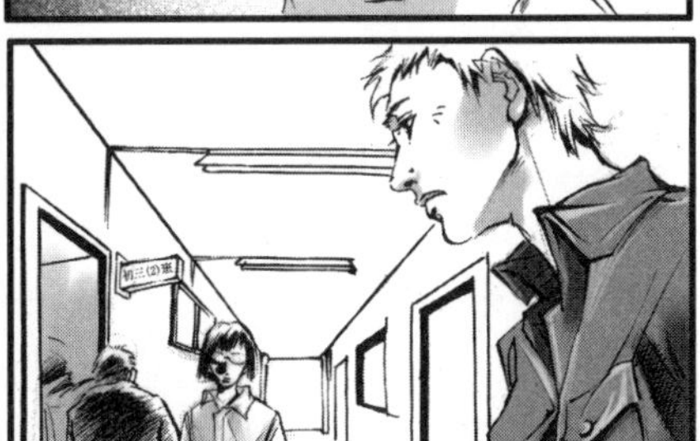

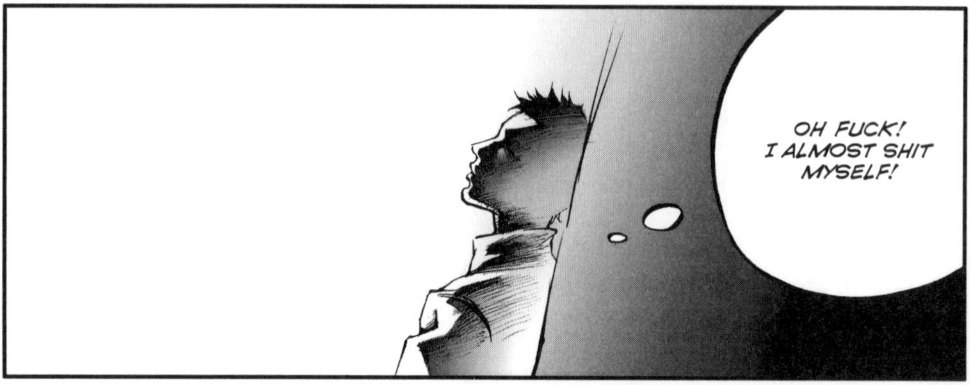
OH FUCK!
I ALMOST SHIT MYSELF!

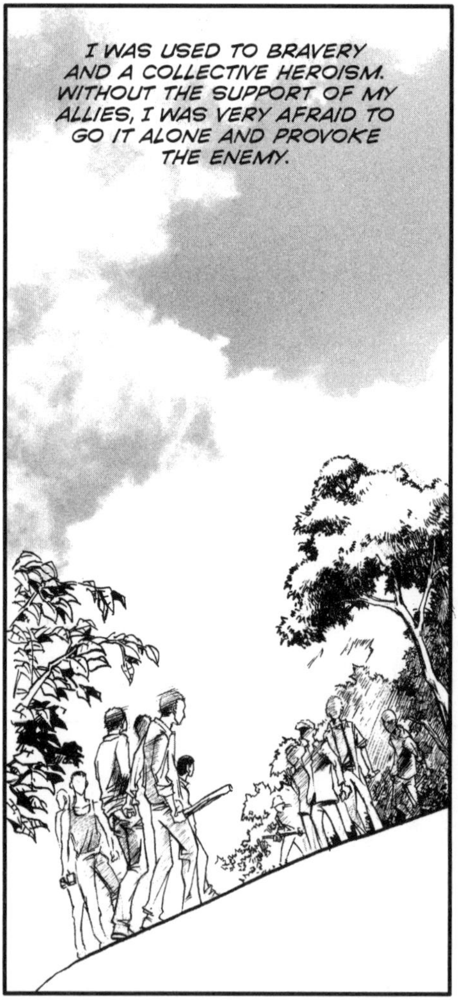
I WAS USED TO BRAVERY AND A COLLECTIVE HEROISM. WITHOUT THE SUPPORT OF MY ALLIES, I WAS VERY AFRAID TO GO IT ALONE AND PROVOKE THE ENEMY.

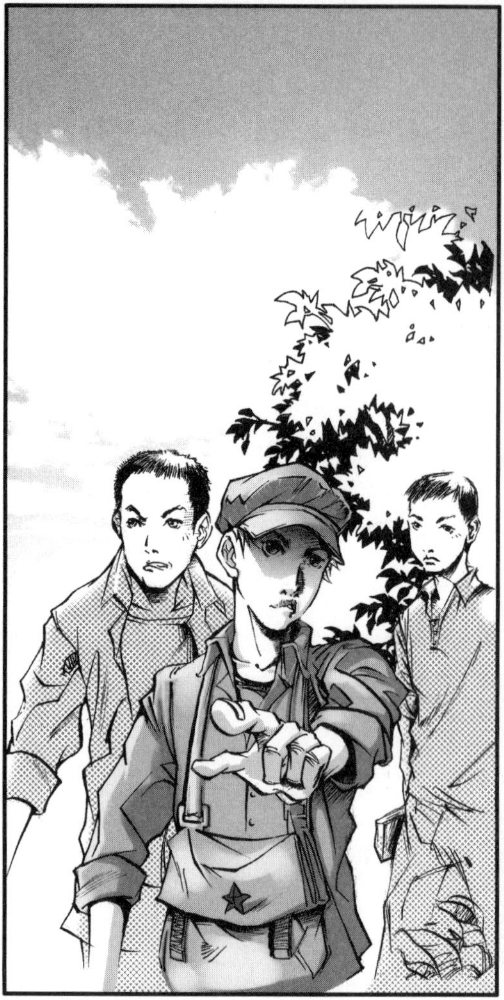

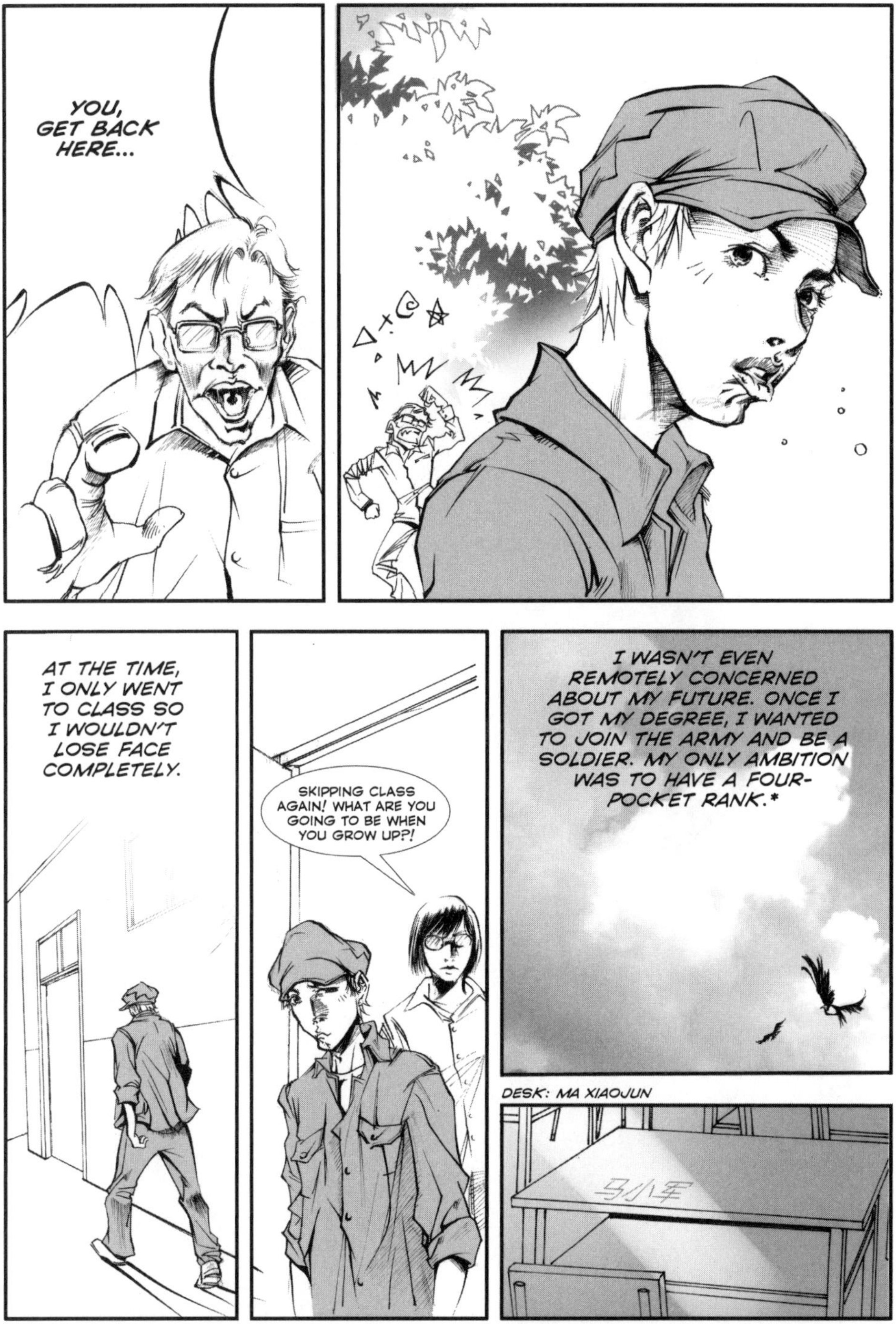
YOU, GET BACK HERE...
AT THE TIME, I ONLY WENT TO CLASS SO I WOULDN'T LOSE FACE COMPLETELY.
SKIPPING CLASS AGAIN! WHAT ARE YOU GOING TO BE WHEN YOU GROW UP?!
I WASN'T EVEN REMOTELY CONCERNED ABOUT MY FUTURE. ONCE I GOT MY DEGREE, I WANTED TO JOIN THE ARMY AND BE A SOLDIER. MY ONLY AMBITION WAS TO HAVE A FOUR-POCKET RANK.*
DESK: MA XIAOJUN
马小军

*NOTE: THE HIGHER A SOLIDER IS IN RANK, THE MORE POCKETS HE HAS ON HIS UNIFORM.

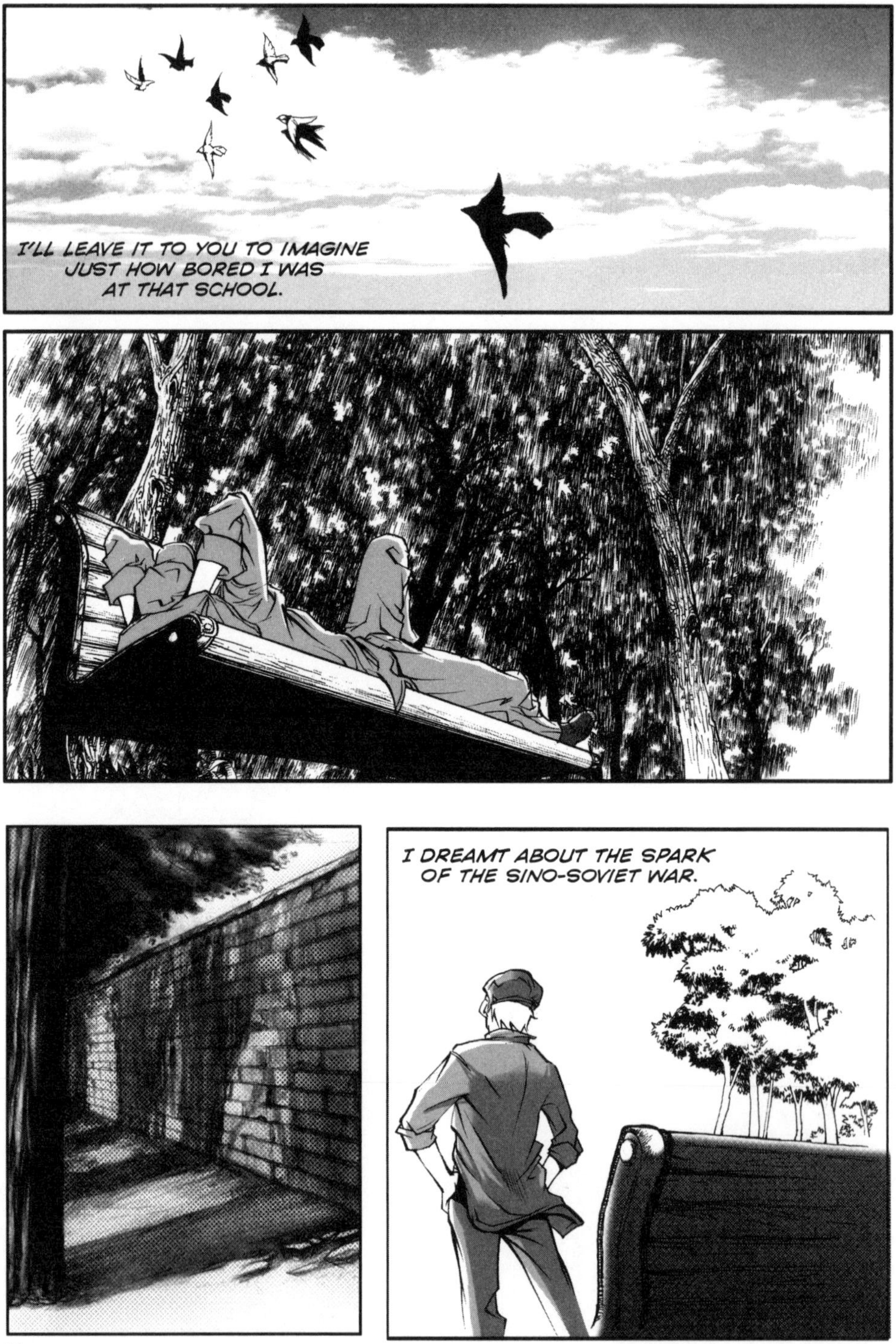
I'LL LEAVE IT TO YOU TO IMAGINE JUST HOW BORED I WAS AT THAT SCHOOL.
I DREAMT ABOUT THE SPARK OF THE SINO-SOVIET WAR.

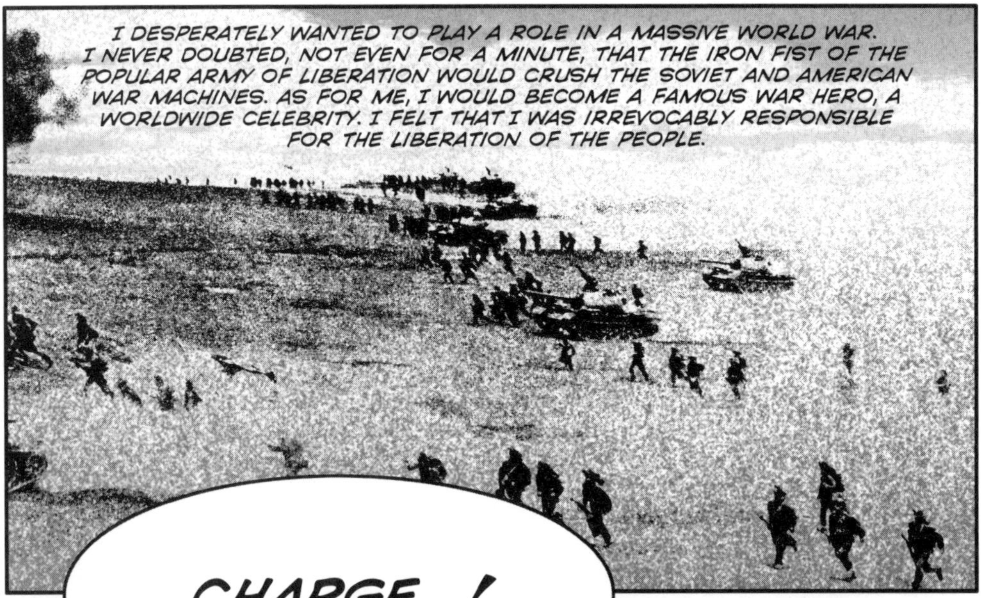
I DESPERATELY WANTED TO PLAY A ROLE IN A MASSIVE WORLD WAR. I NEVER DOUBTED, NOT EVEN FOR A MINUTE, THAT THE IRON FIST OF THE POPULAR ARMY OF LIBERATION WOULD CRUSH THE SOVIET AND AMERICAN WAR MACHINES. AS FOR ME, I WOULD BECOME A FAMOUS WAR HERO, A WORLDWIDE CELEBRITY. I FELT THAT I WAS IRREVOCABLY RESPONSIBLE FOR THE LIBERATION OF THE PEOPLE.

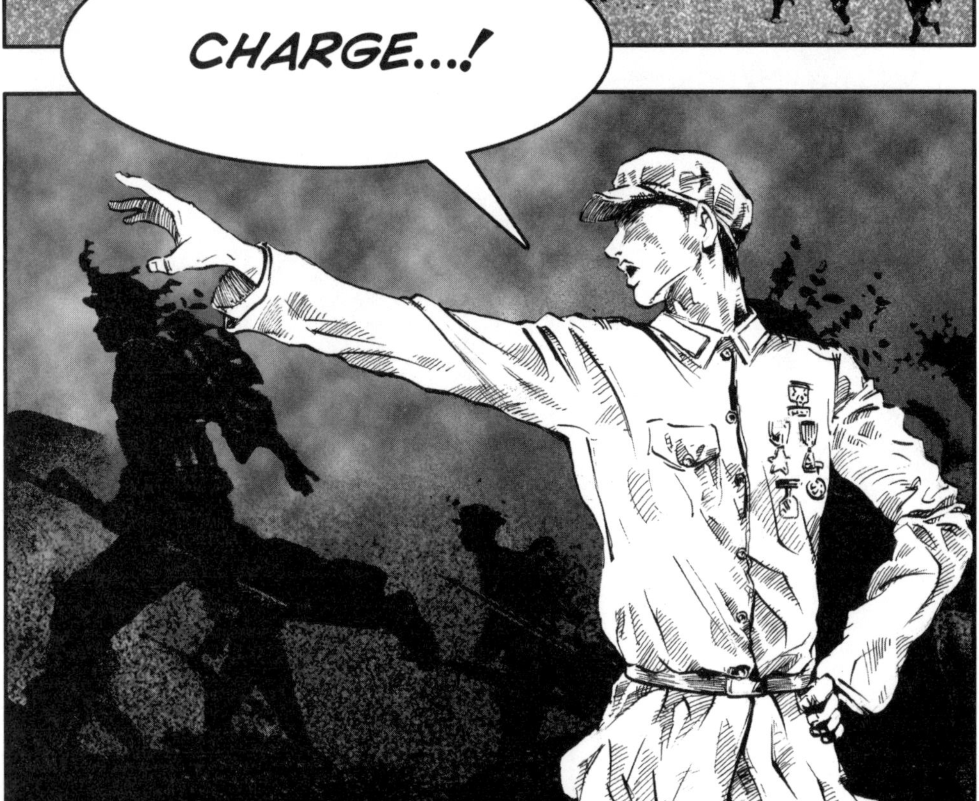
CHARGE...!

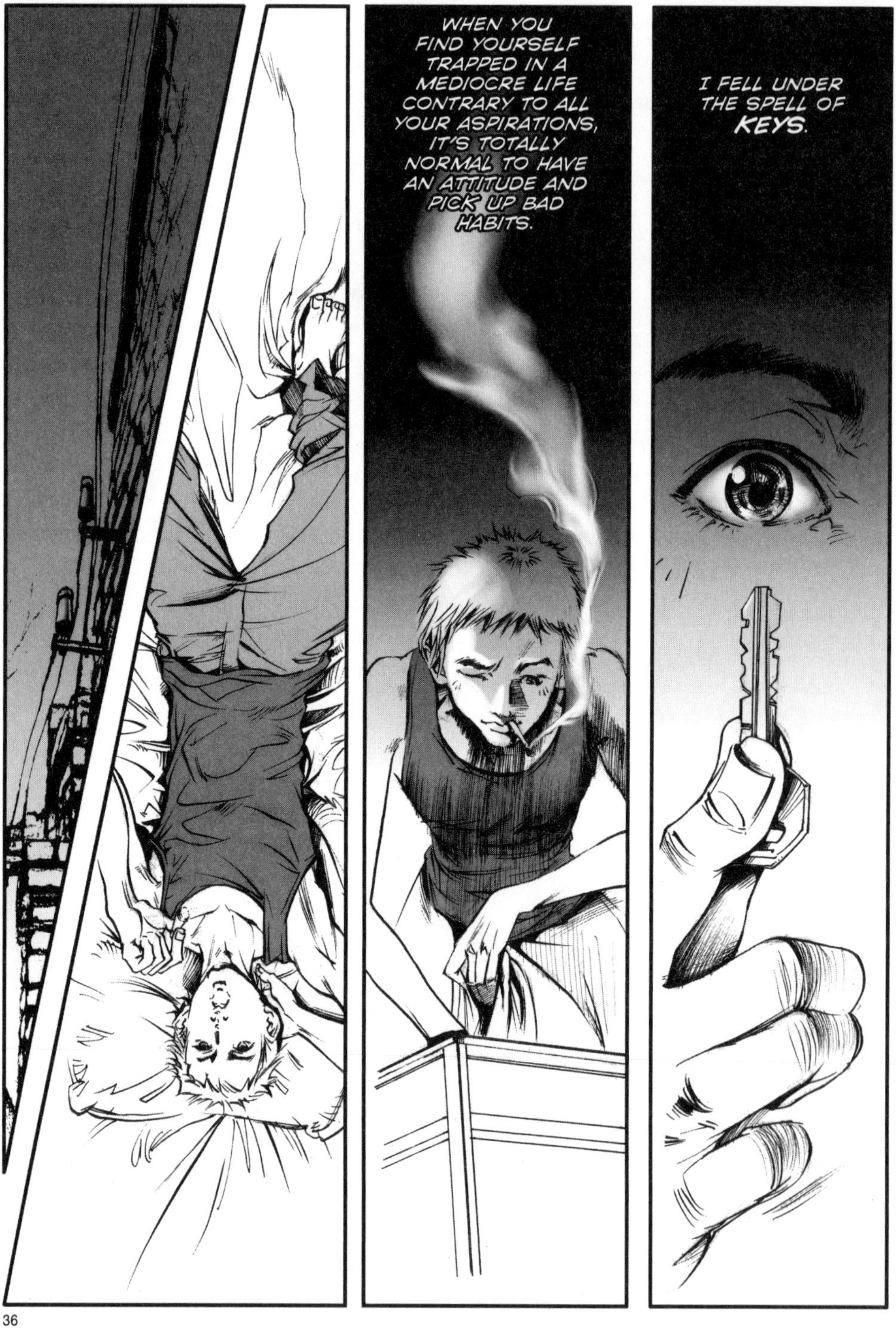
WHEN YOU FIND YOURSELF TRAPPED IN A MEDIOCRE LIFE CONTRARY TO ALL YOUR ASPIRATIONS, IT'S TOTALLY NORMAL TO HAVE AN ATTITUDE AND PICK UP BAD HABITS.
I FELL UNDER THE SPELL OF KEYS.

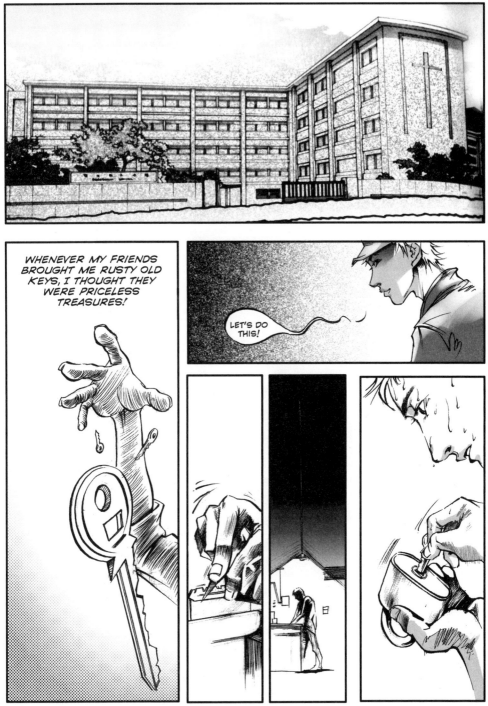

WHENEVER MY FRIENDS BROUGHT ME RUSTY OLD KEYS, I THOUGHT THEY WERE PRICELESS TREASURES!

LET'S DO THIS!

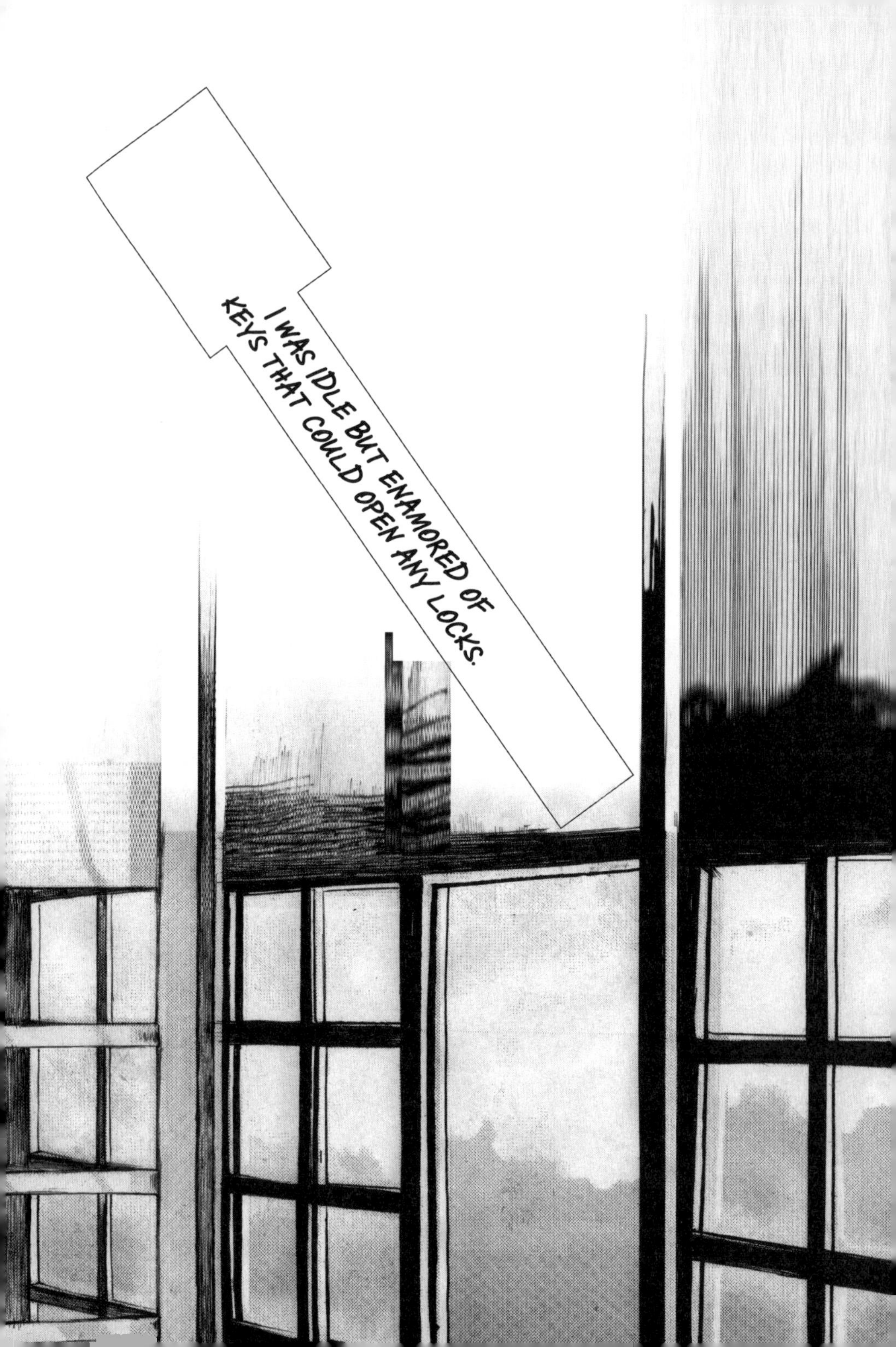
I WAS IDLE BUT ENAMORED OF KEYS THAT COULD OPEN ANY LOCKS.

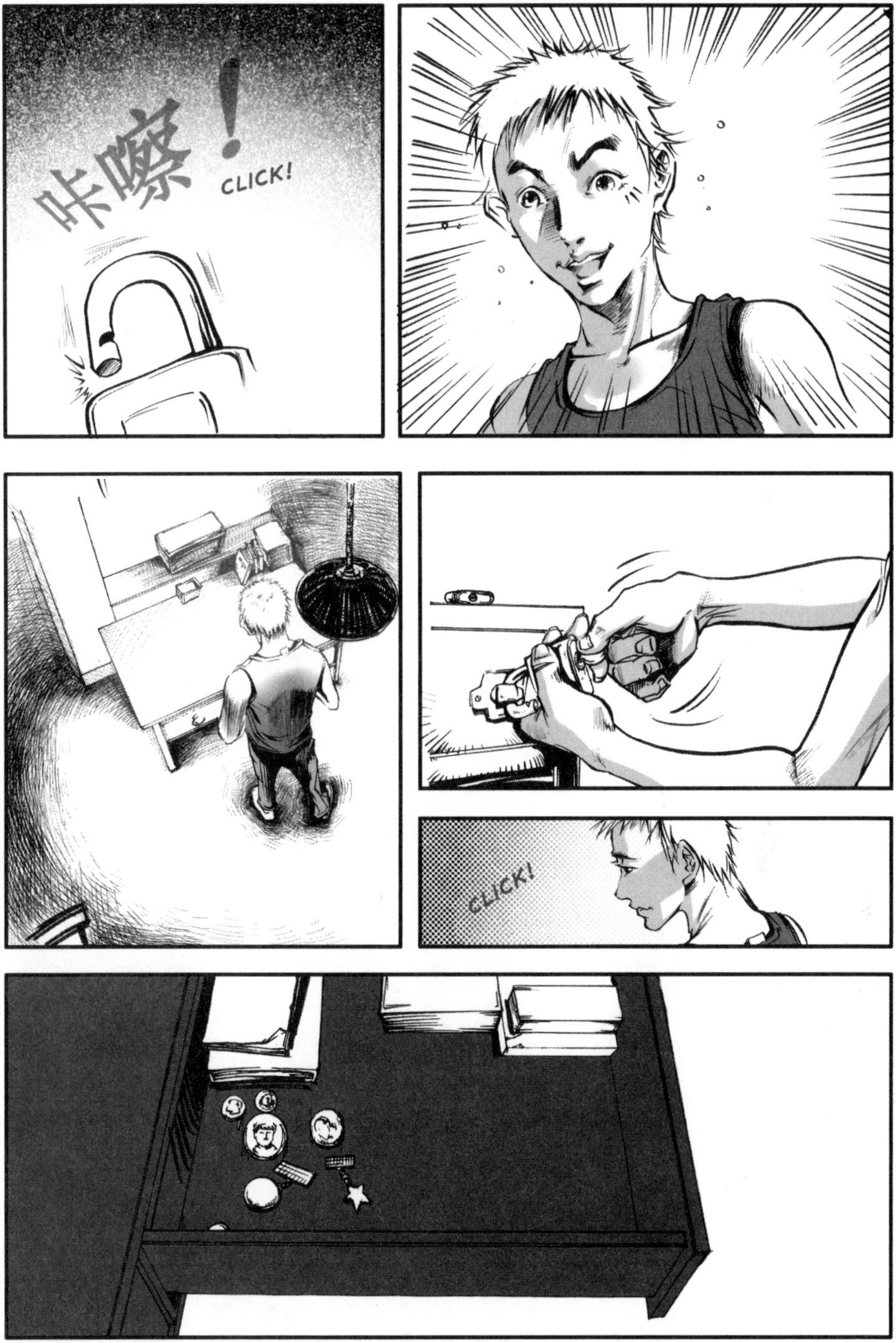
咔嚓!
CLICK!
CLICK!

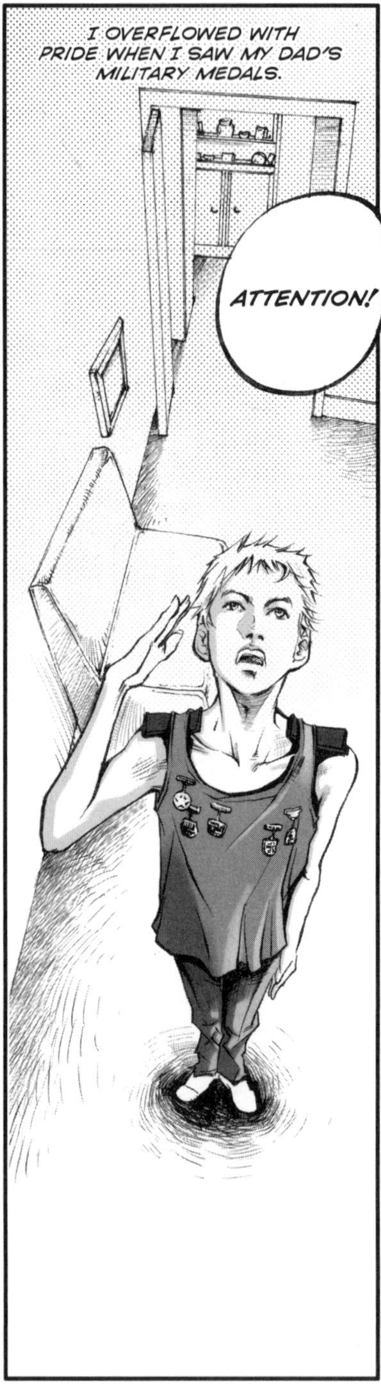
I OVERFLOWED WITH PRIDE WHEN I SAW MY DAD'S MILITARY MEDALS.
ATTENTION!

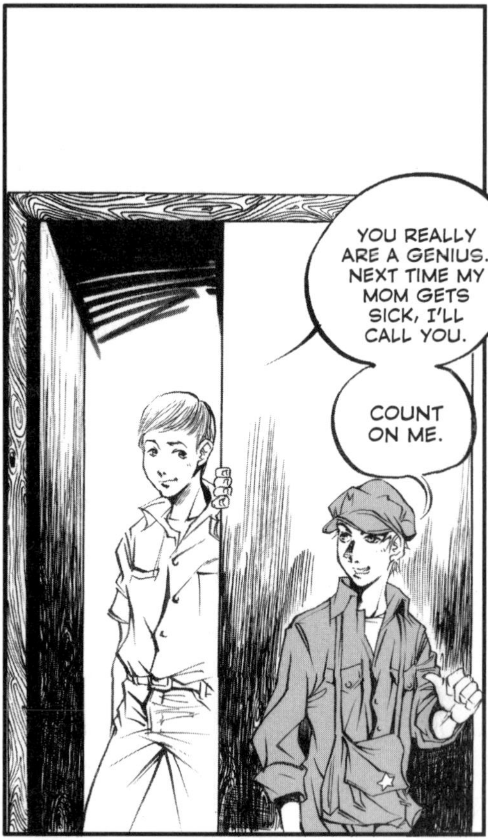
YOU REALLY ARE A GENIUS. NEXT TIME MY MOM GETS SICK, I'LL CALL YOU.
COUNT ON ME.

SFX: ≶WHOOO WHOOO≶

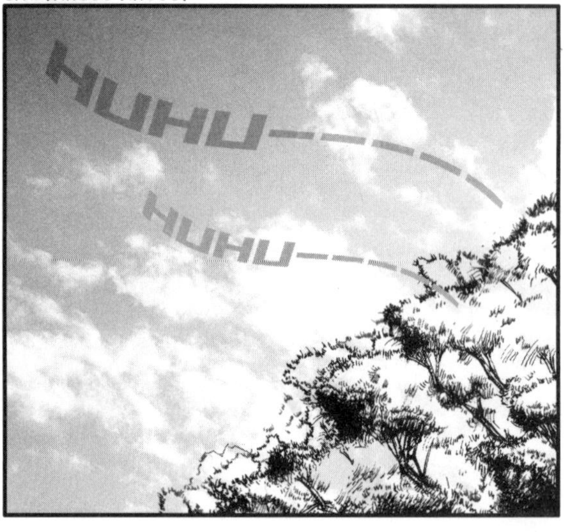
HUHU------
HUHU----

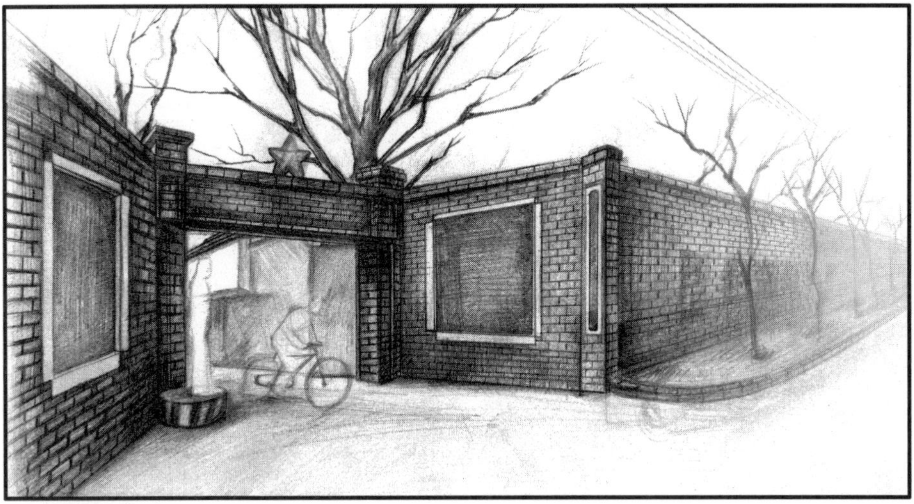

SIGN: LONG LIVE THE PARTY

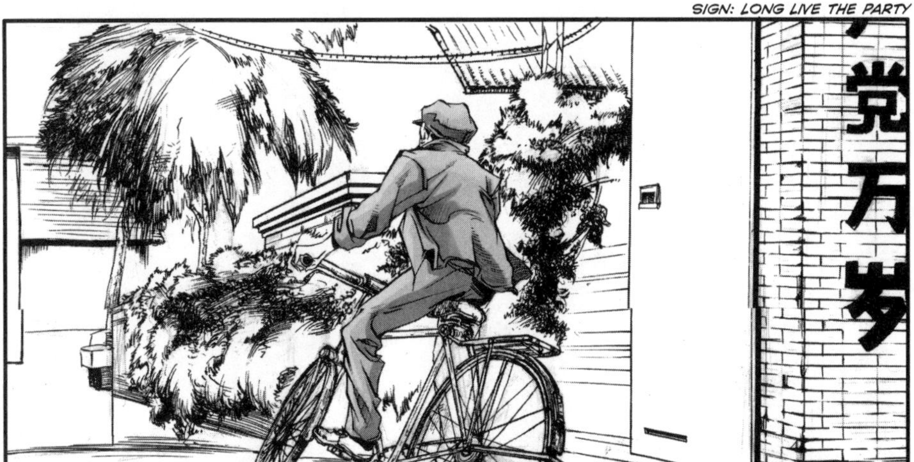
党万岁

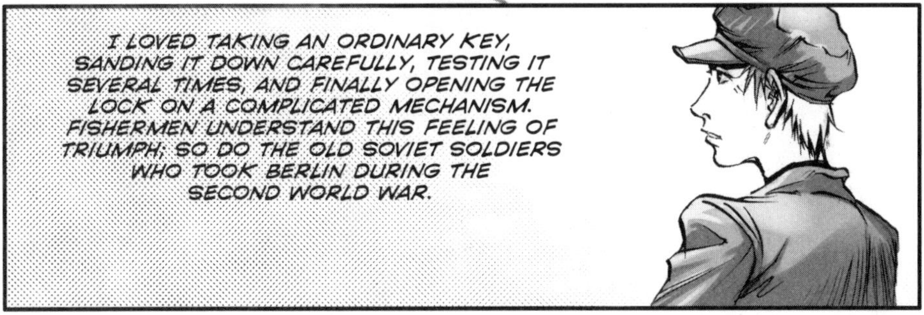
I LOVED TAKING AN ORDINARY KEY, SANDING IT DOWN CAREFULLY, TESTING IT SEVERAL TIMES, AND FINALLY OPENING THE LOCK ON A COMPLICATED MECHANISM. FISHERMEN UNDERSTAND THIS FEELING OF TRIUMPH; SO DO THE OLD SOVIET SOLDIERS WHO TOOK BERLIN DURING THE SECOND WORLD WAR.

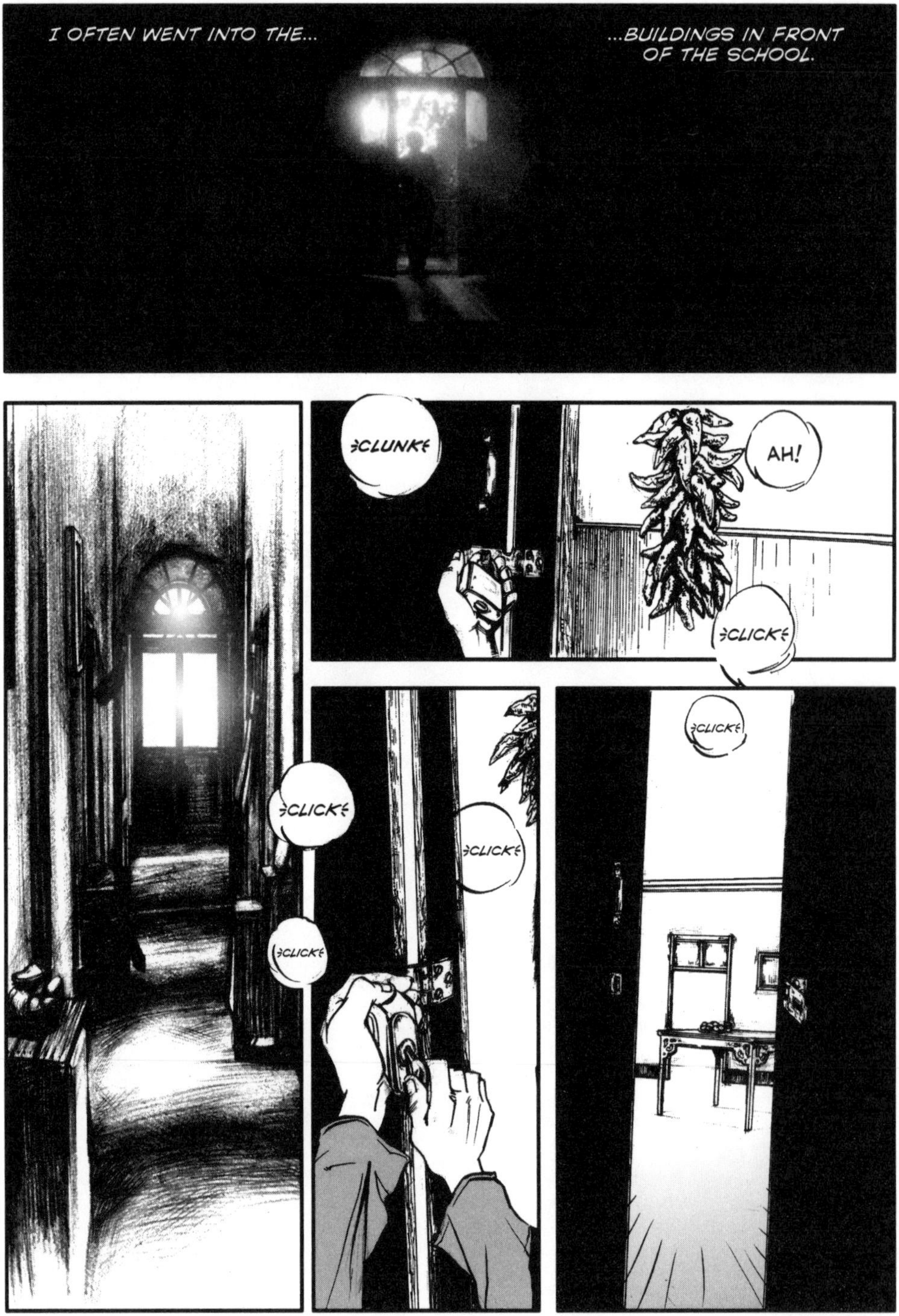
I OFTEN WENT INTO THE...
...BUILDINGS IN FRONT OF THE SCHOOL.
CLUNK
AH!
CLICK
CLICK
CLICK
CLICK
CLICK

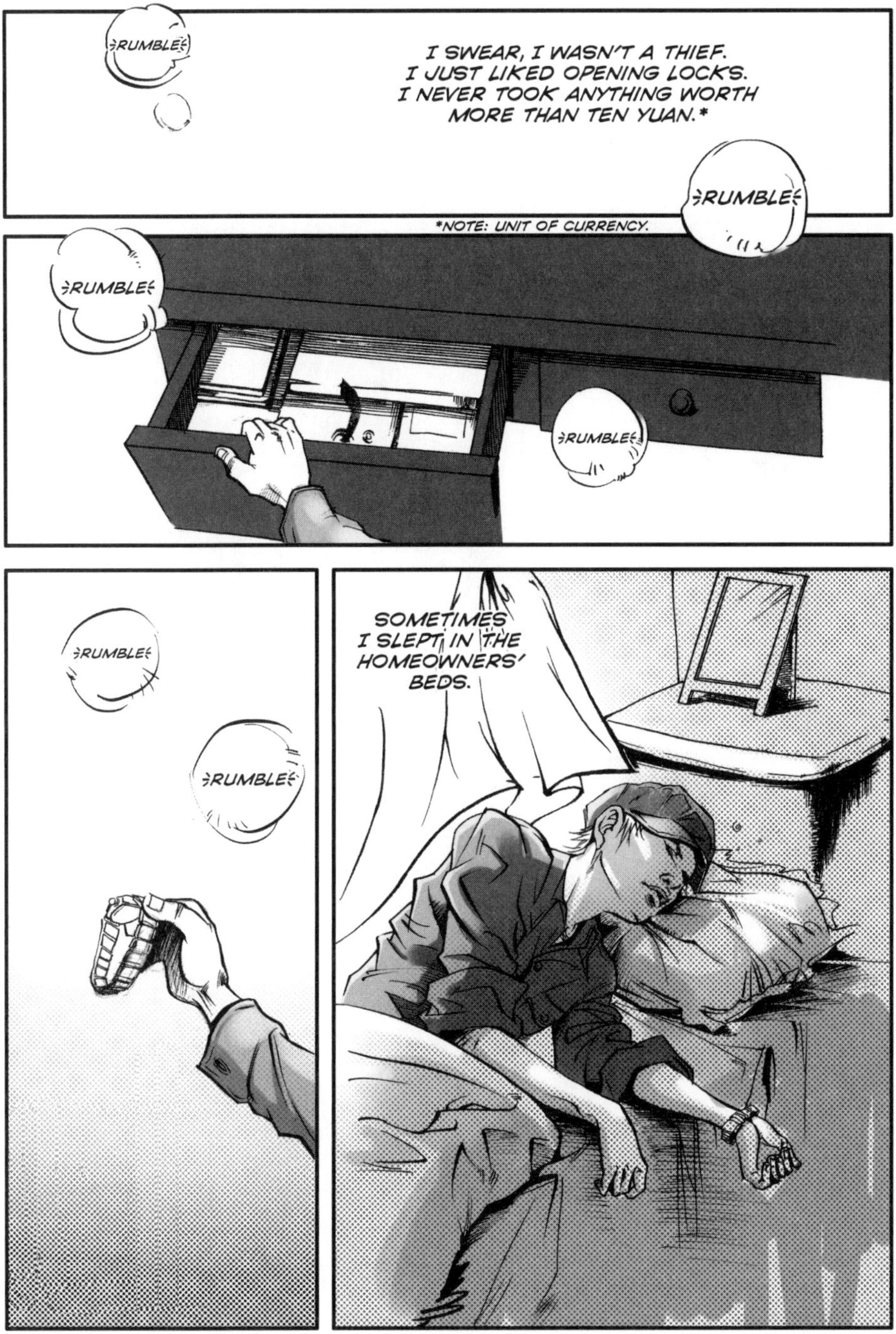
RUMBLE
I SWEAR, I WASN'T A THIEF. I JUST LIKED OPENING LOCKS. I NEVER TOOK ANYTHING WORTH MORE THAN TEN YUAN.*
RUMBLE
*NOTE: UNIT OF CURRENCY.
RUMBLE
RUMBLE
RUMBLE
RUMBLE
SOMETIMES I SLEPT IN THE HOMEOWNERS' BEDS.

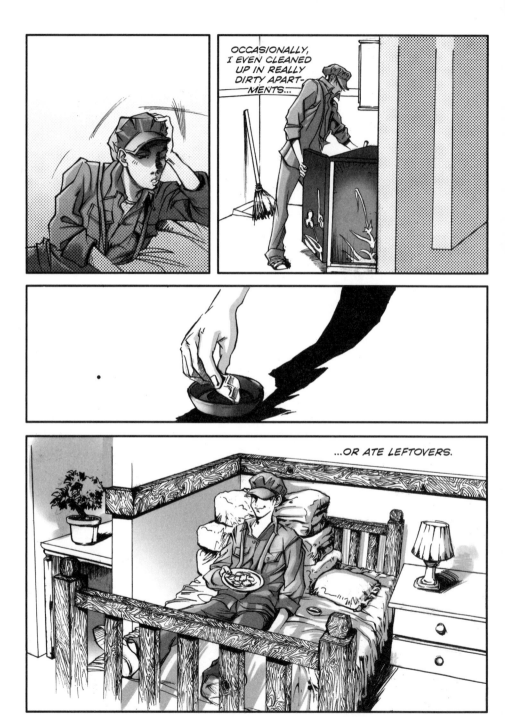

OCCASIONALLY, I EVEN CLEANED UP IN REALLY DIRTY APART-MENTS...

...OR ATE LEFTOVERS.

44

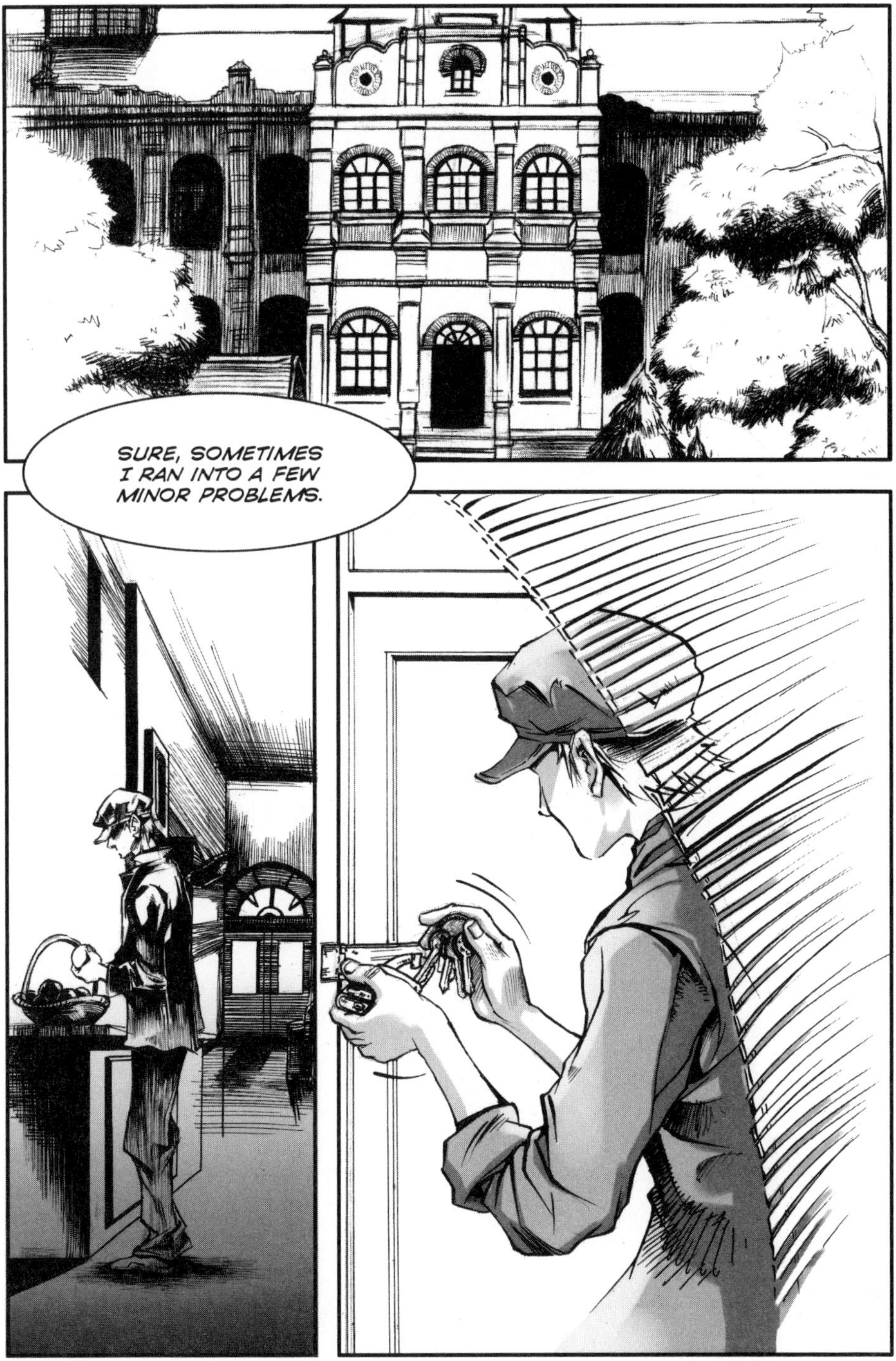
SURE, SOMETIMES I RAN INTO A FEW MINOR PROBLEMS.

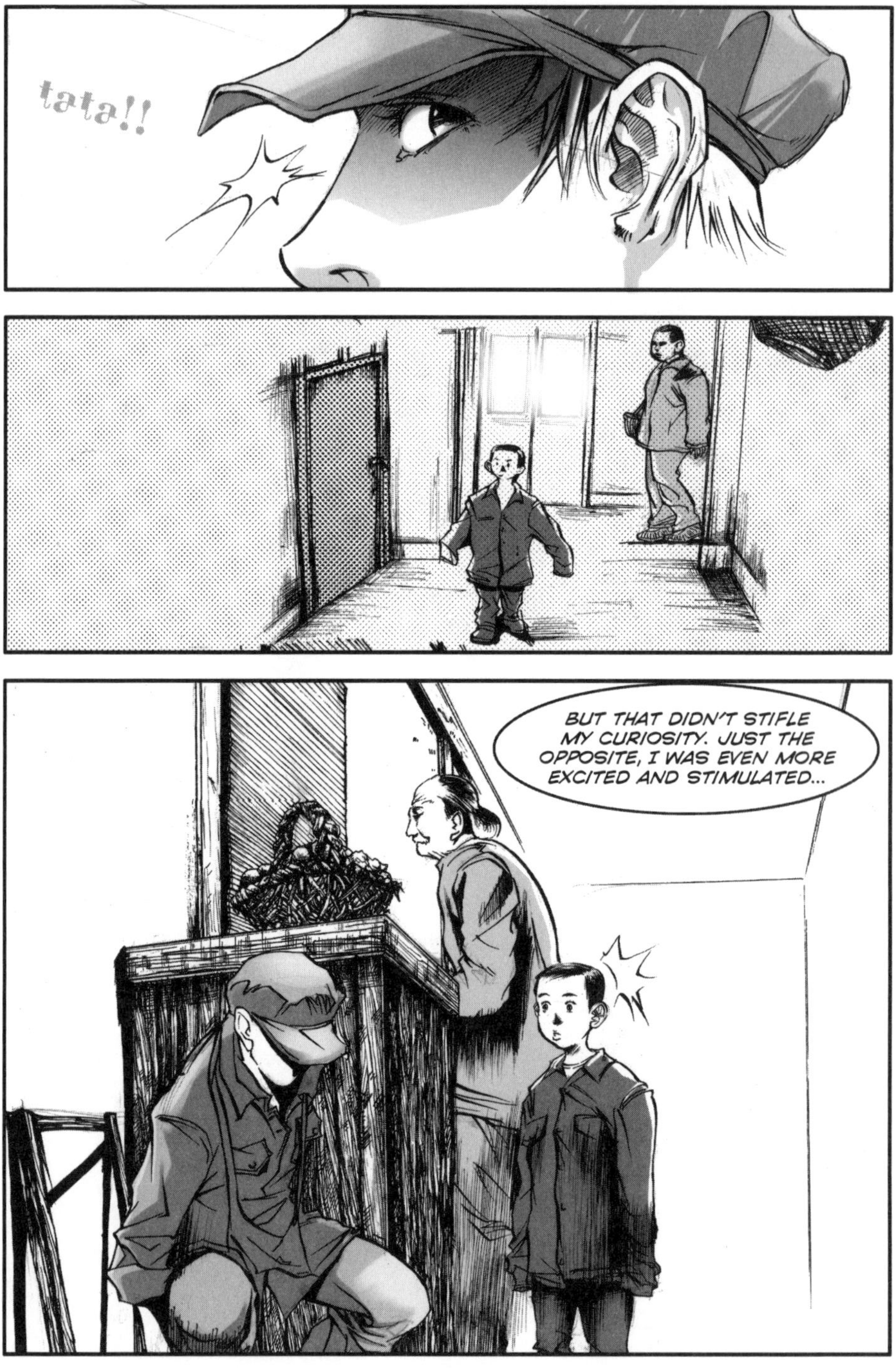

tata!!
BUT THAT DIDN'T STIFLE MY CURIOSITY. JUST THE OPPOSITE, I WAS EVEN MORE EXCITED AND STIMULATED...

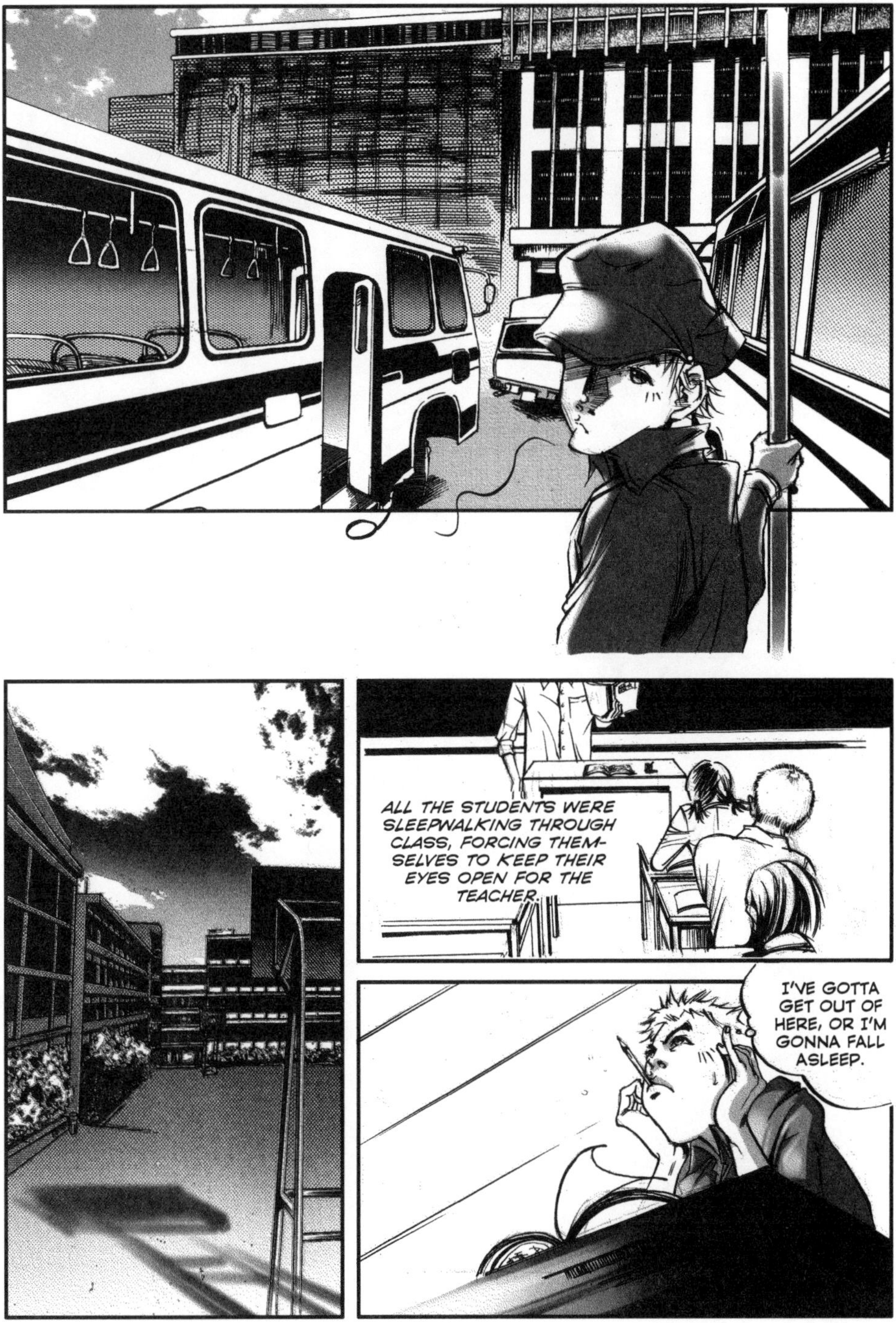
ALL THE STUDENTS WERE SLEEPWALKING THROUGH CLASS, FORCING THEMSELVES TO KEEP THEIR EYES OPEN FOR THE TEACHER.
I'VE GOTTA GET OUT OF HERE, OR I'M GONNA FALL ASLEEP.

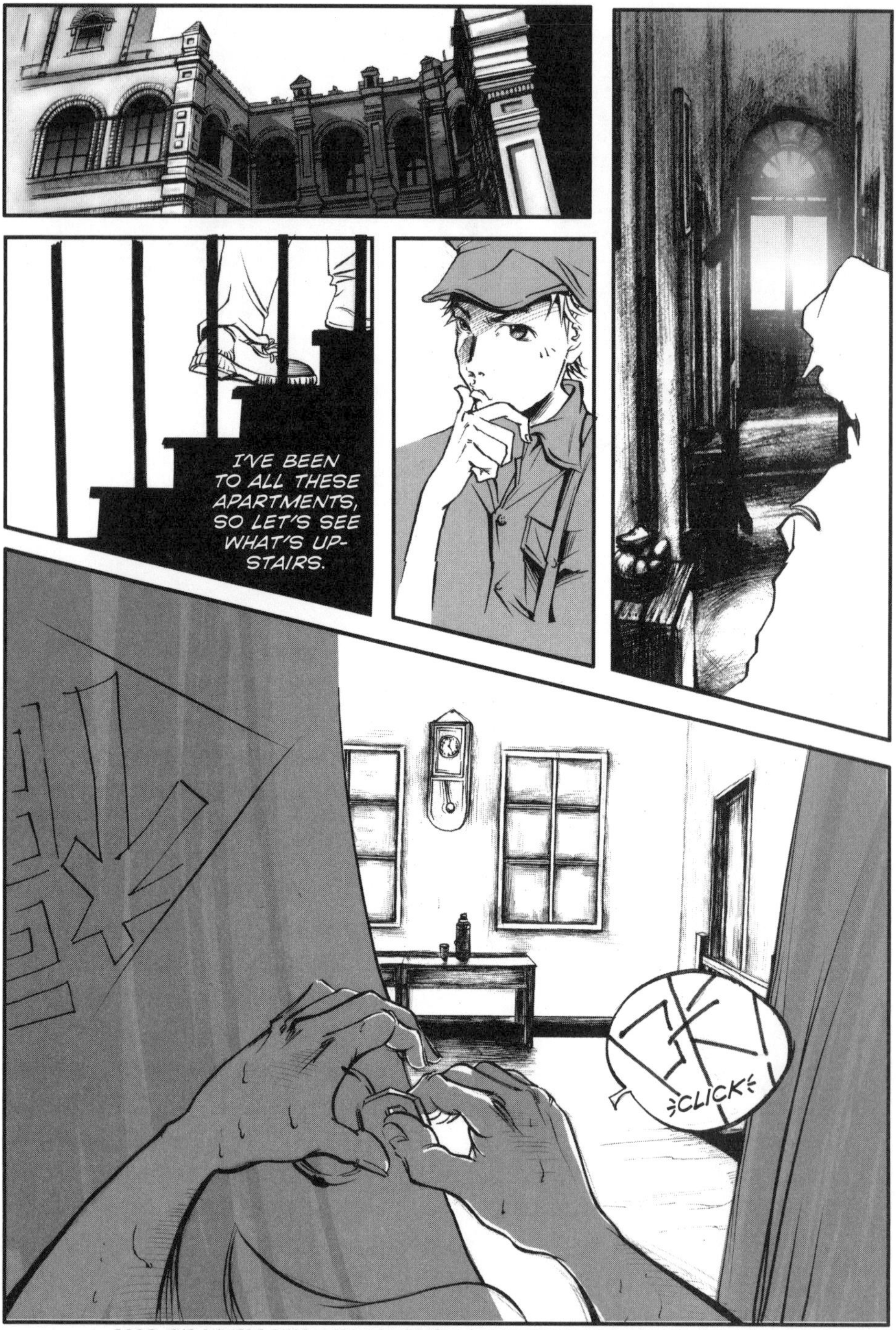
I'VE BEEN TO ALL THESE APARTMENTS, SO LET'S SEE WHAT'S UP-STAIRS.
CLICK

DOOR: THE CHINESE CHARACTER STANDS FOR "GOOD FORTUNE" OR "HAPPINESS." TURNING IT UPSIDE DOWN MEANS "GOOD FORTUNE/HAPPINESS ARRIVES (OR WILL ARRIVE)."

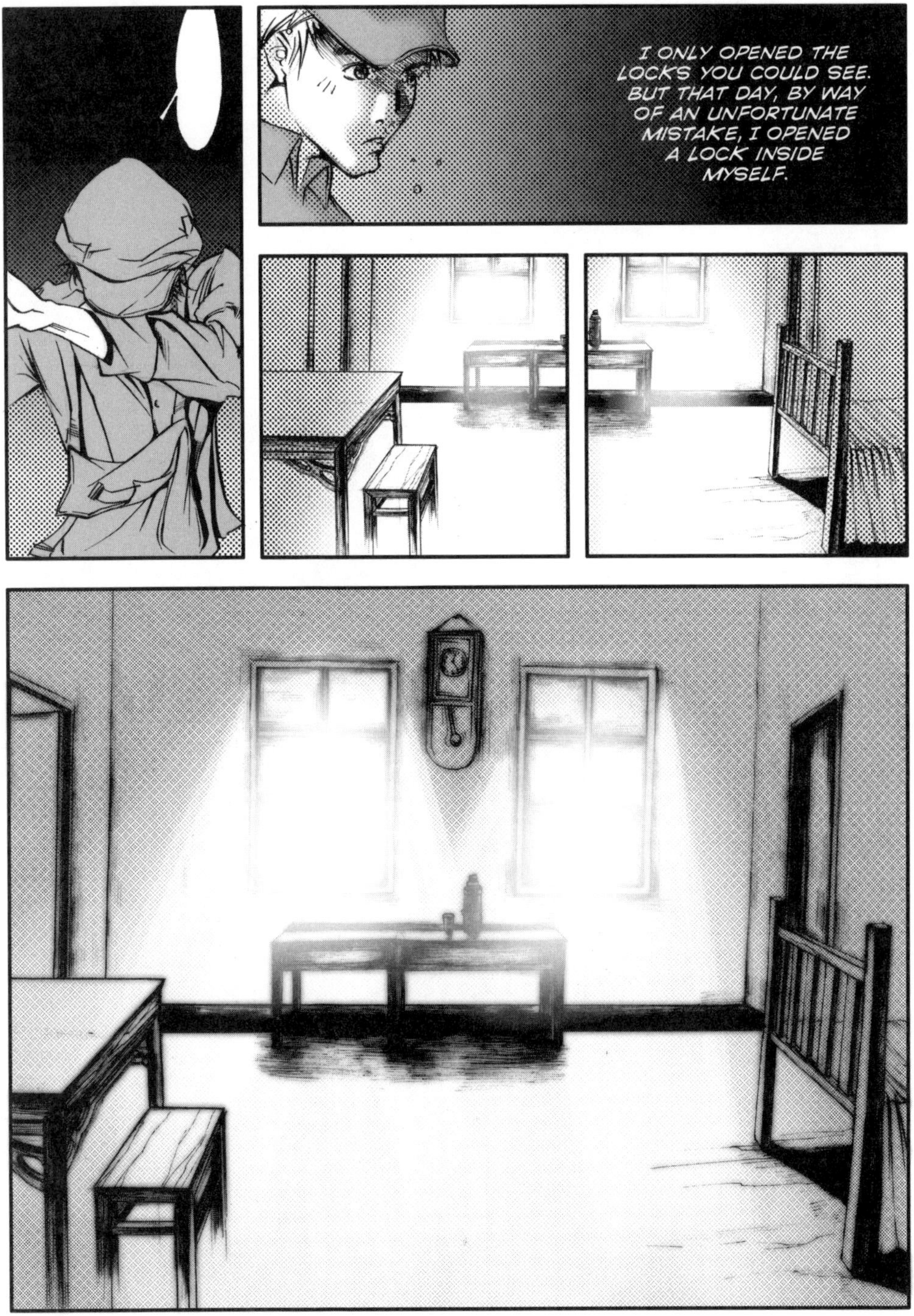
I ONLY OPENED THE LOCKS YOU COULD SEE. BUT THAT DAY, BY WAY OF AN UNFORTUNATE MISTAKE, I OPENED A LOCK INSIDE MYSELF.

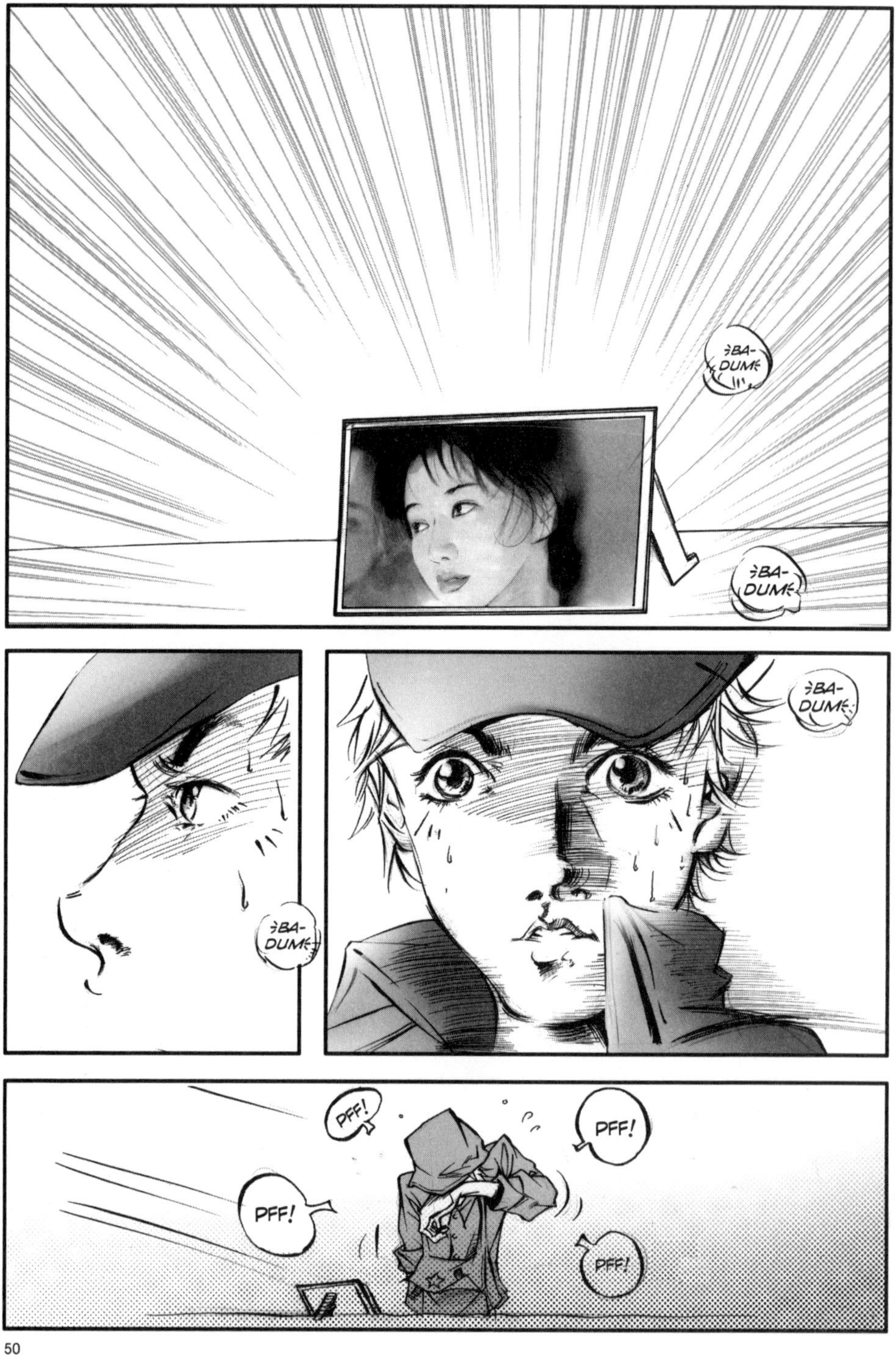
BA-DUM
BA-DUM
BA-DUM
BA-DUM
PFF!
PFF!
PFF!
PFF!

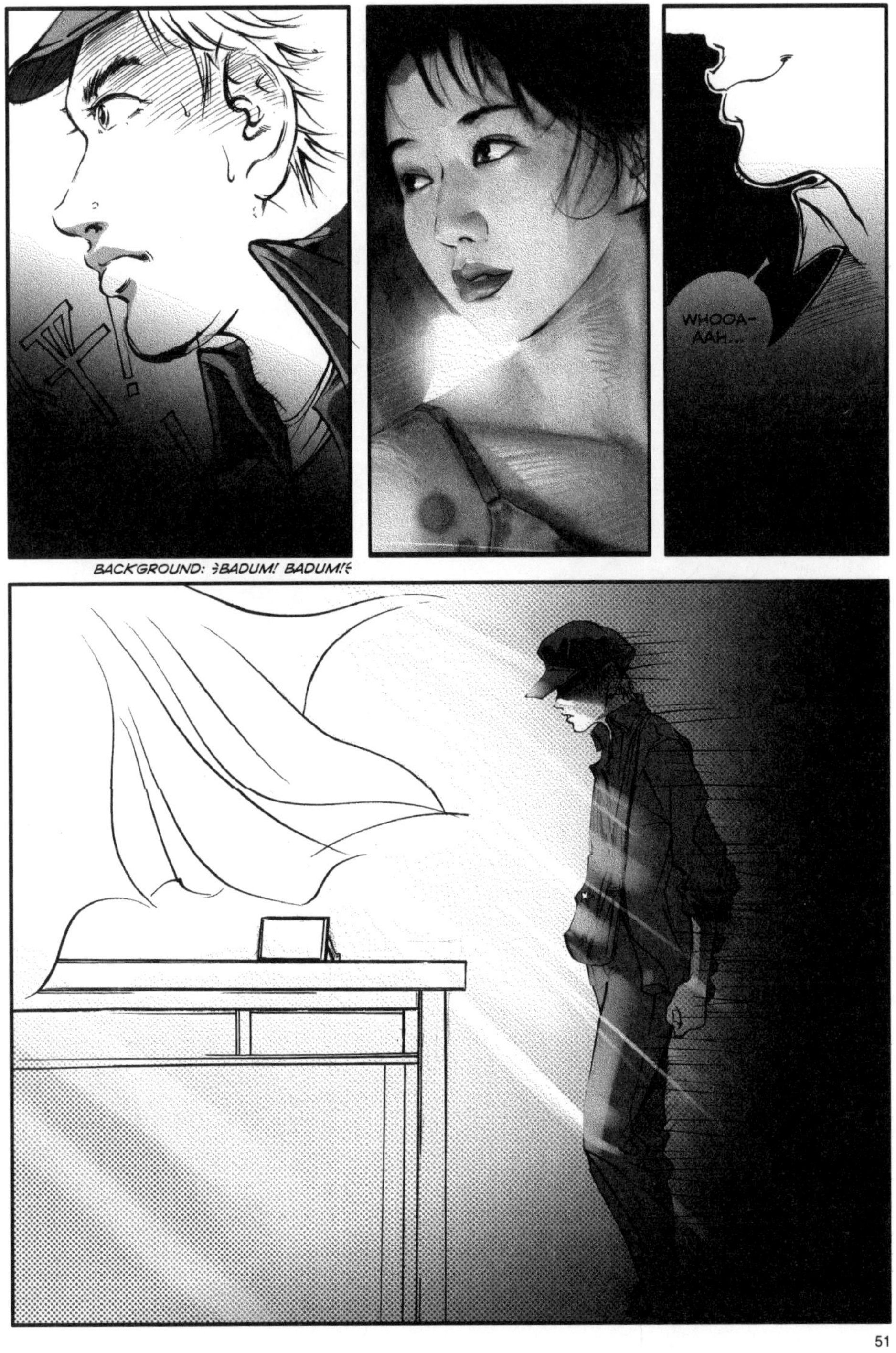
WHOOA-AAH...
BACKGROUND: BADUM! BADUM!

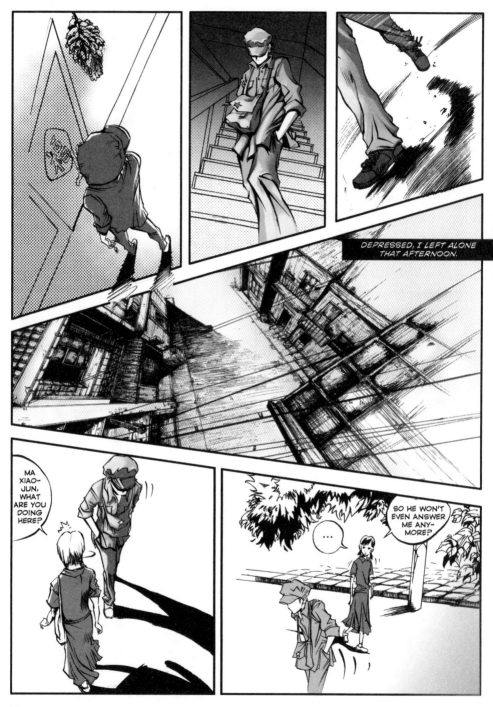

DEPRESSED, I LEFT ALONE THAT AFTERNOON.

MA XIAO-JUN, WHAT ARE YOU DOING HERE?

...

SO HE WON'T EVEN ANSWER ME ANY-MORE?

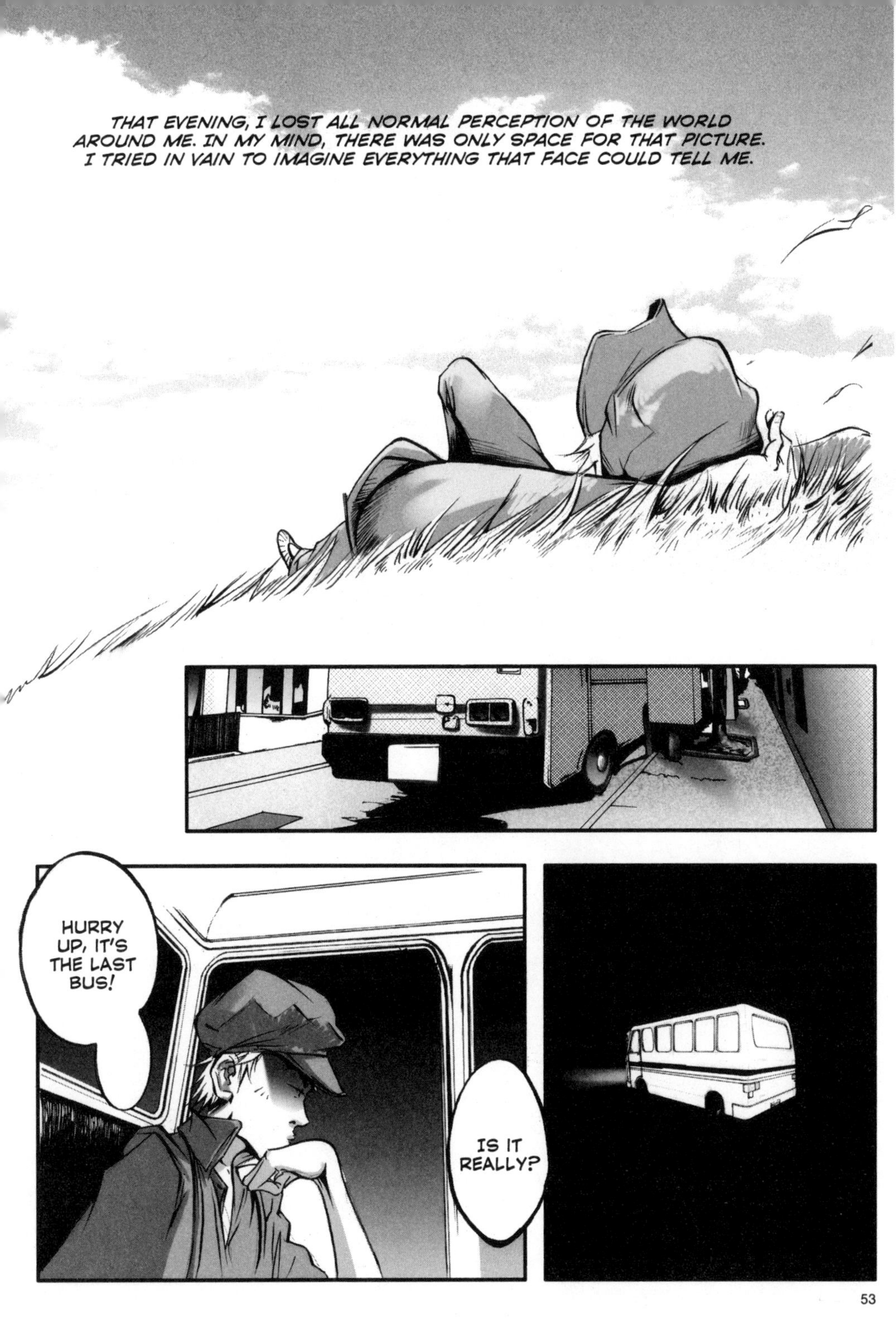
THAT EVENING, I LOST ALL NORMAL PERCEPTION OF THE WORLD AROUND ME. IN MY MIND, THERE WAS ONLY SPACE FOR THAT PICTURE. I TRIED IN VAIN TO IMAGINE EVERYTHING THAT FACE COULD TELL ME.
HURRY UP, IT'S THE LAST BUS!
IS IT REALLY?

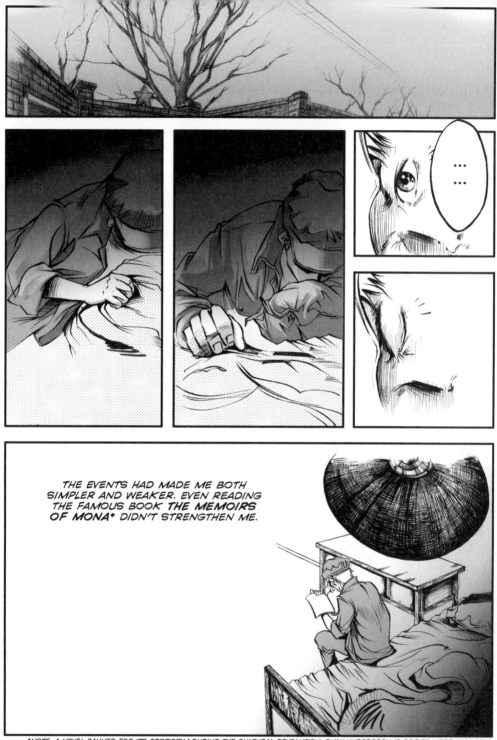

THE EVENTS HAD MADE ME BOTH SIMPLER AND WEAKER. EVEN READING THE FAMOUS BOOK *THE MEMOIRS OF MONA** DIDN'T STRENGTHEN ME.

*NOTE: A NOVEL BANNED FOR ITS EROTICISM DURING THE CULTURAL REVOLUTION. ONLY UNDERGROUND COPIES WERE AVAILABLE.

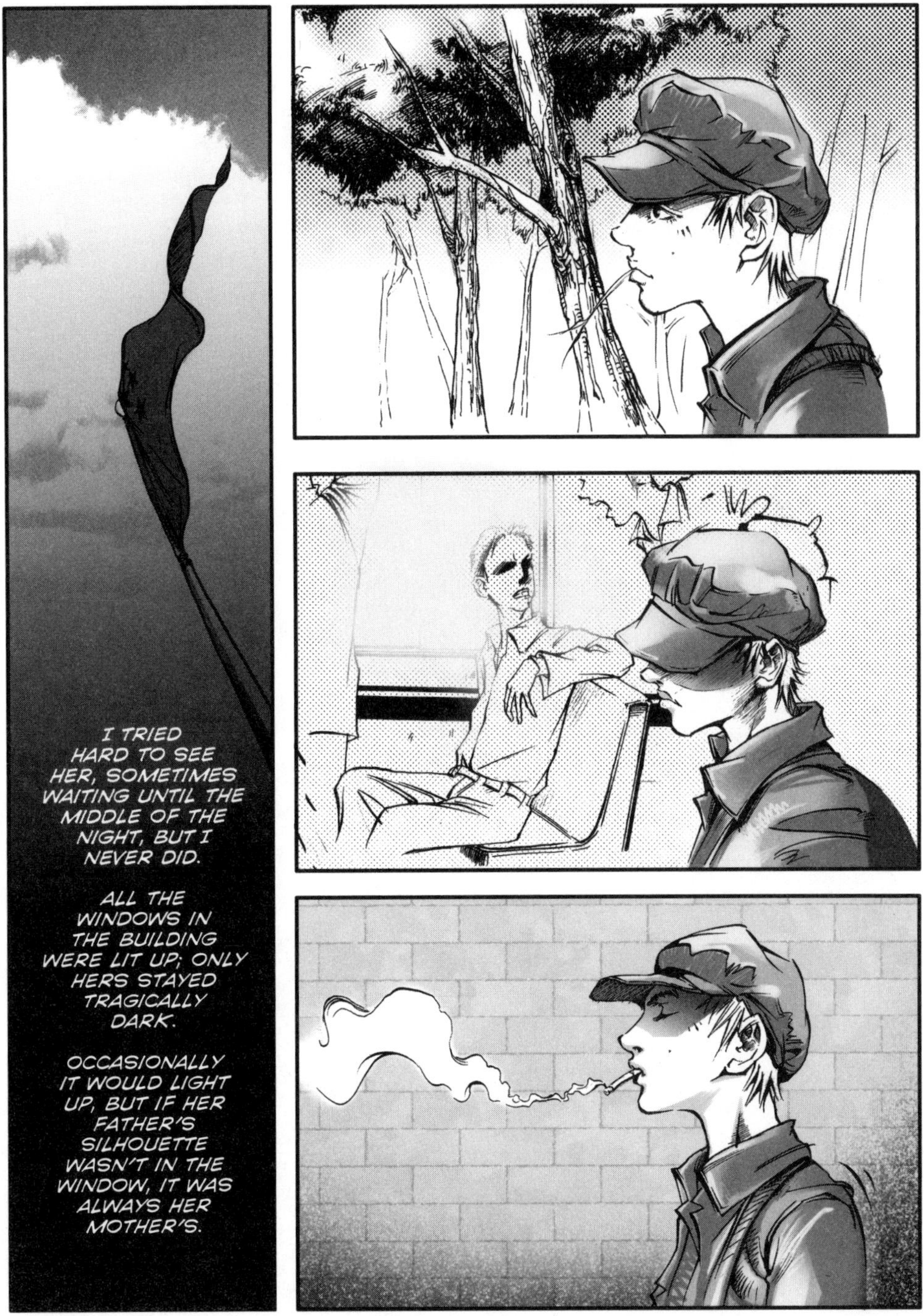
I TRIED HARD TO SEE HER, SOMETIMES WAITING UNTIL THE MIDDLE OF THE NIGHT, BUT I NEVER DID.
ALL THE WINDOWS IN THE BUILDING WERE LIT UP; ONLY HERS STAYED TRAGICALLY DARK.
OCCASIONALLY IT WOULD LIGHT UP, BUT IF HER FATHER'S SILHOUETTE WASN'T IN THE WINDOW, IT WAS ALWAYS HER MOTHER'S.

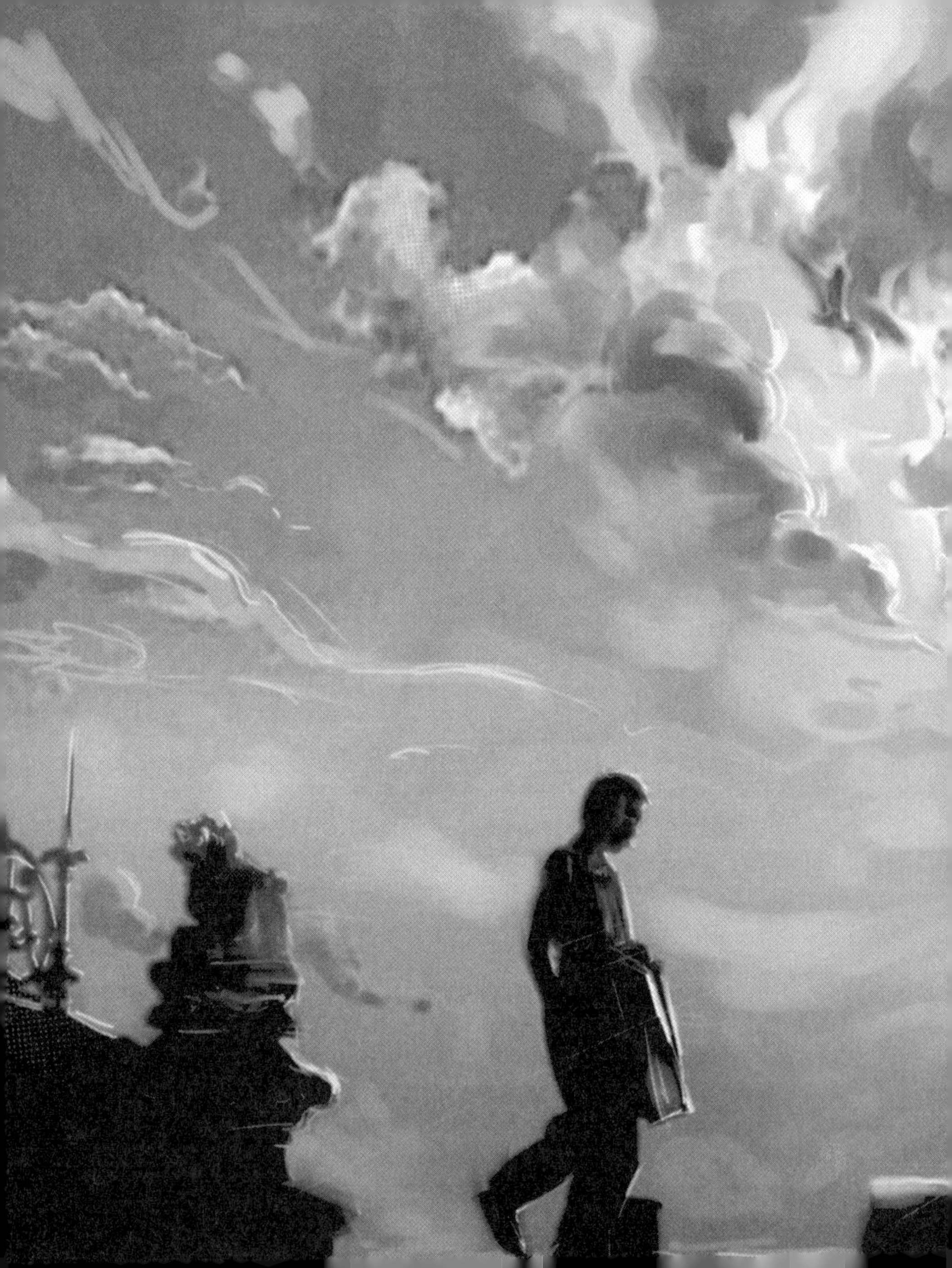

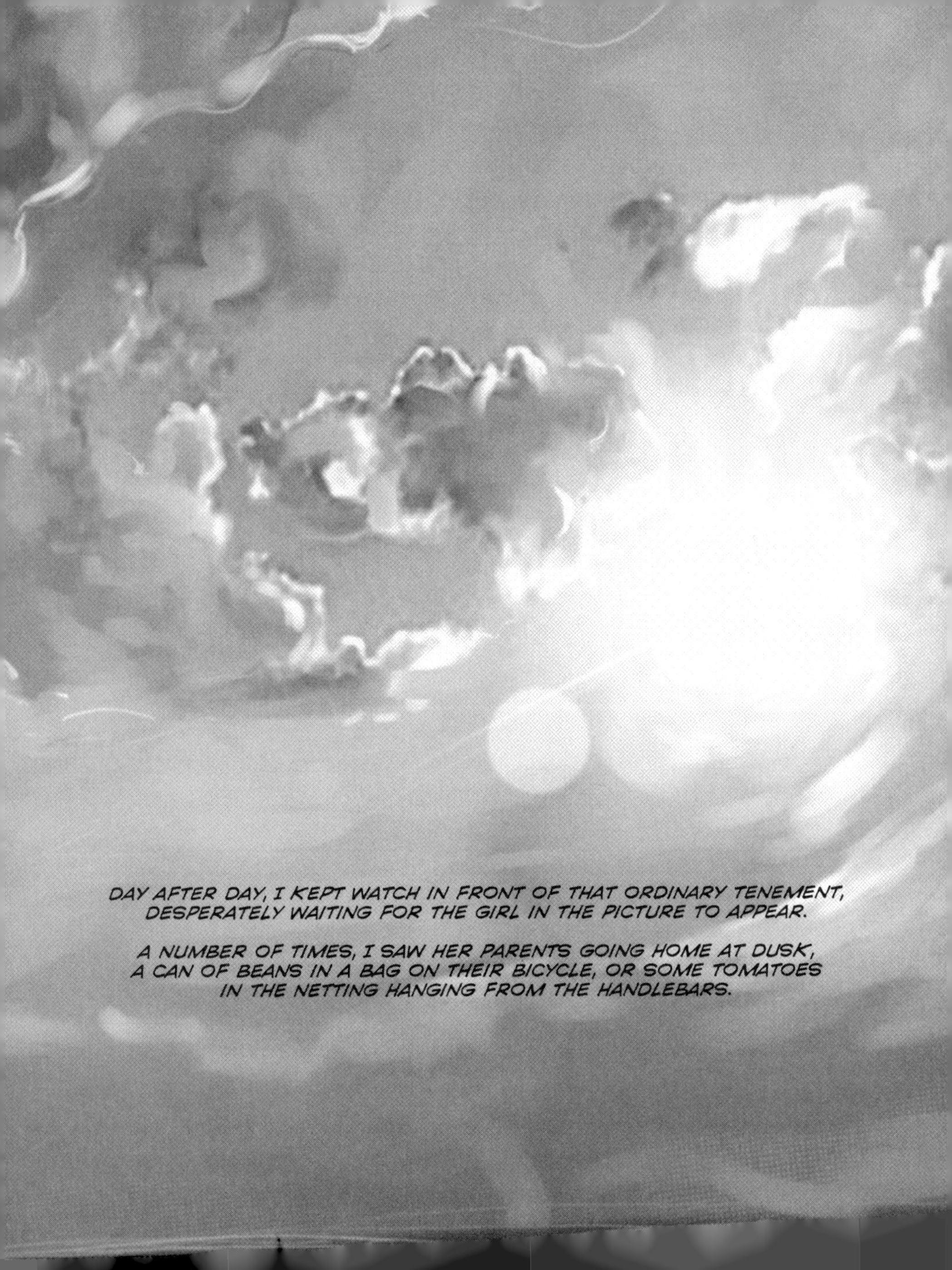
DAY AFTER DAY, I KEPT WATCH IN FRONT OF THAT ORDINARY TENEMENT, DESPERATELY WAITING FOR THE GIRL IN THE PICTURE TO APPEAR.
A NUMBER OF TIMES, I SAW HER PARENTS GOING HOME AT DUSK, A CAN OF BEANS IN A BAG ON THEIR BICYCLE, OR SOME TOMATOES IN THE NETTING HANGING FROM THE HANDLEBARS.

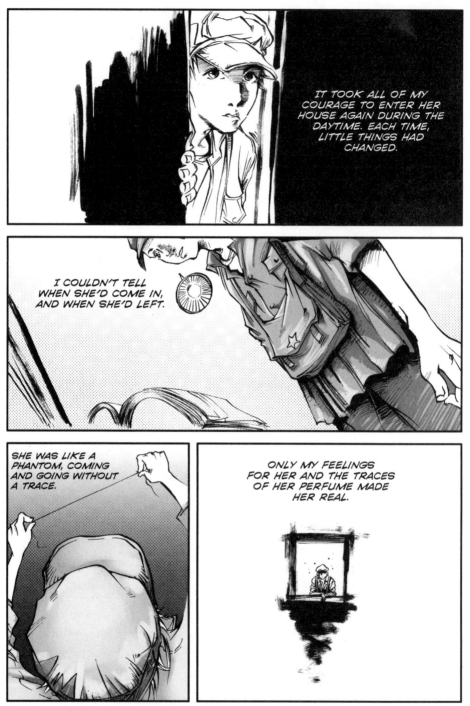

IT TOOK ALL OF MY COURAGE TO ENTER HER HOUSE AGAIN DURING THE DAYTIME. EACH TIME, LITTLE THINGS HAD CHANGED.

I COULDN'T TELL WHEN SHE'D COME IN, AND WHEN SHE'D LEFT.

SHE WAS LIKE A PHANTOM, COMING AND GOING WITHOUT A TRACE.

ONLY MY FEELINGS FOR HER AND THE TRACES OF HER PERFUME MADE HER REAL.

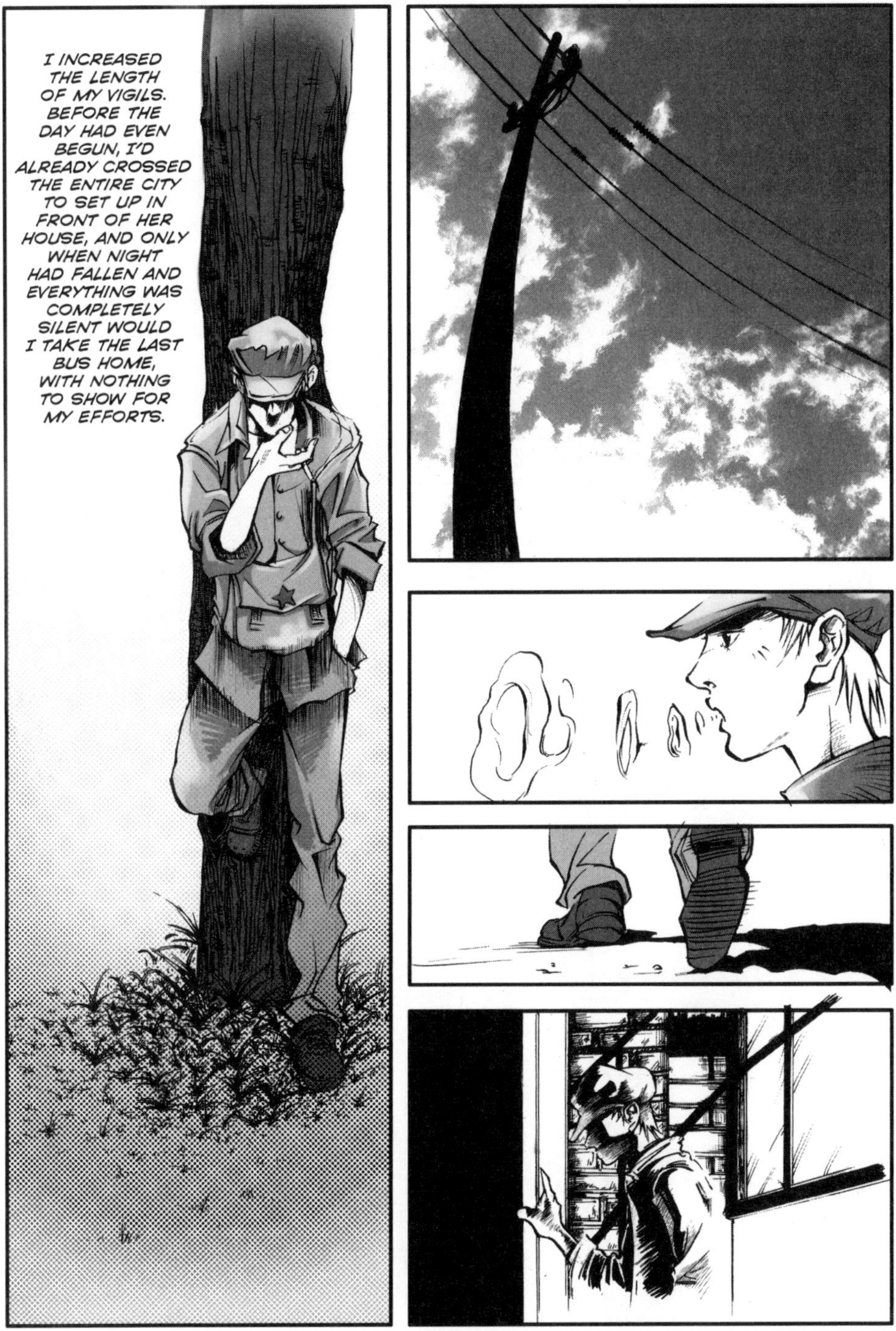
I INCREASED THE LENGTH OF MY VIGILS. BEFORE THE DAY HAD EVEN BEGUN, I'D ALREADY CROSSED THE ENTIRE CITY TO SET UP IN FRONT OF HER HOUSE, AND ONLY WHEN NIGHT HAD FALLEN AND EVERYTHING WAS COMPLETELY SILENT WOULD I TAKE THE LAST BUS HOME, WITH NOTHING TO SHOW FOR MY EFFORTS.

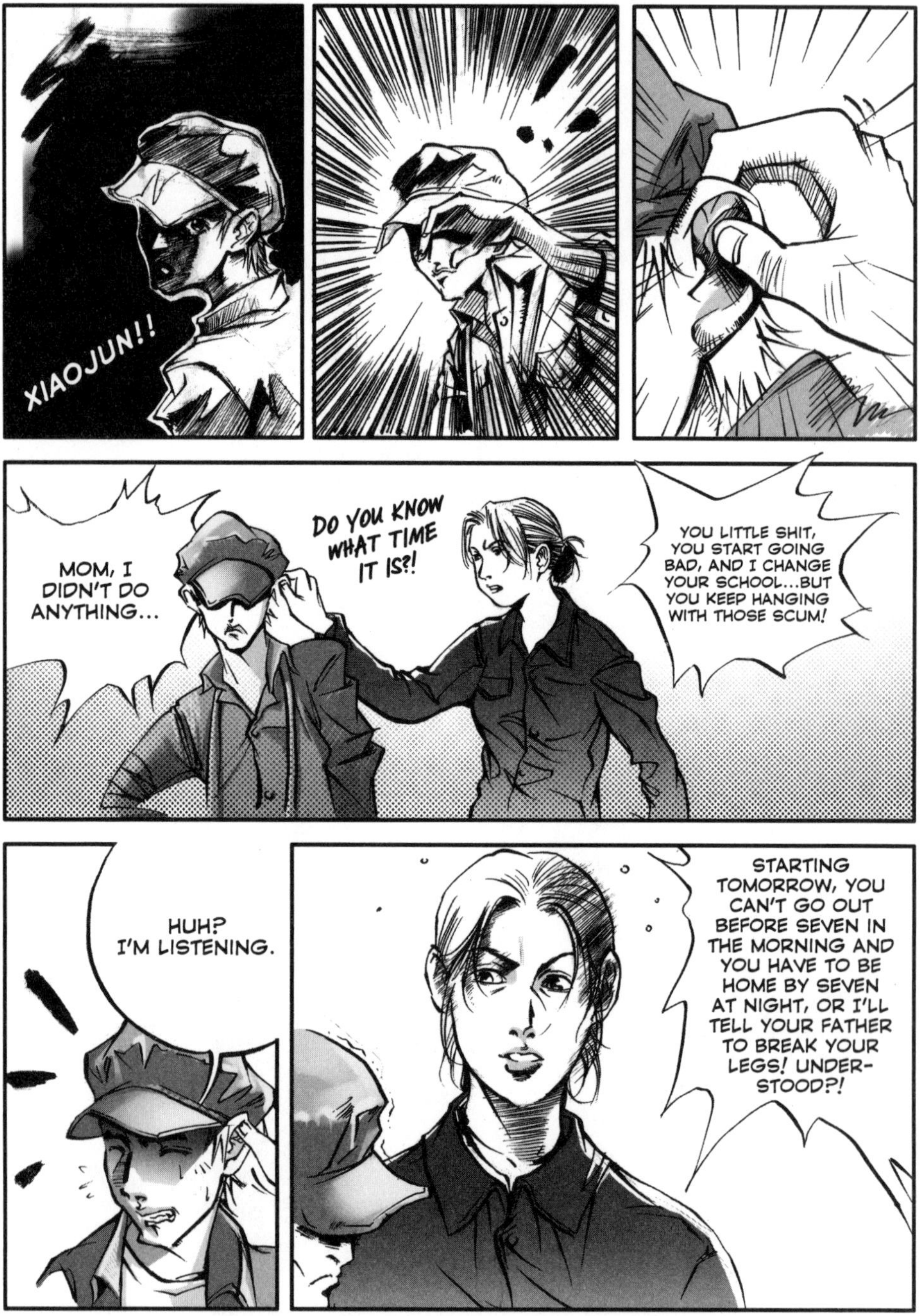
XIAOJUN!!
MOM, I DIDN'T DO ANYTHING...
DO YOU KNOW WHAT TIME IT IS?!
YOU LITTLE SHIT, YOU START GOING BAD, AND I CHANGE YOUR SCHOOL...BUT YOU KEEP HANGING WITH THOSE SCUM!
HUH? I'M LISTENING.
STARTING TOMORROW, YOU CAN'T GO OUT BEFORE SEVEN IN THE MORNING AND YOU HAVE TO BE HOME BY SEVEN AT NIGHT, OR I'LL TELL YOUR FATHER TO BREAK YOUR LEGS! UNDER-STOOD?!

3 - The Day I Met Yu Beibei

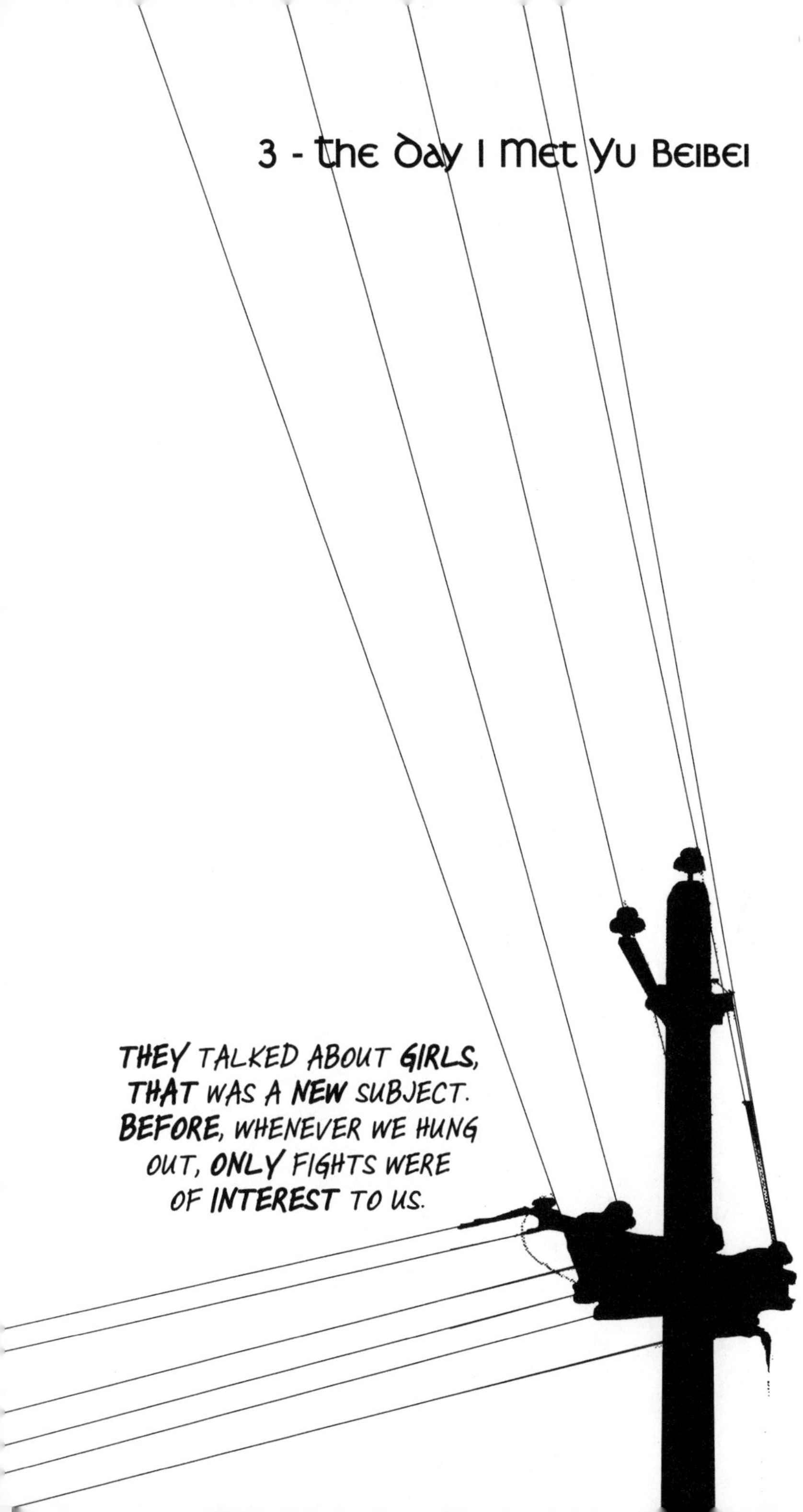
THEY TALKED ABOUT GIRLS, THAT WAS A NEW SUBJECT. BEFORE, WHENEVER WE HUNG OUT, ONLY FIGHTS WERE OF INTEREST TO US.

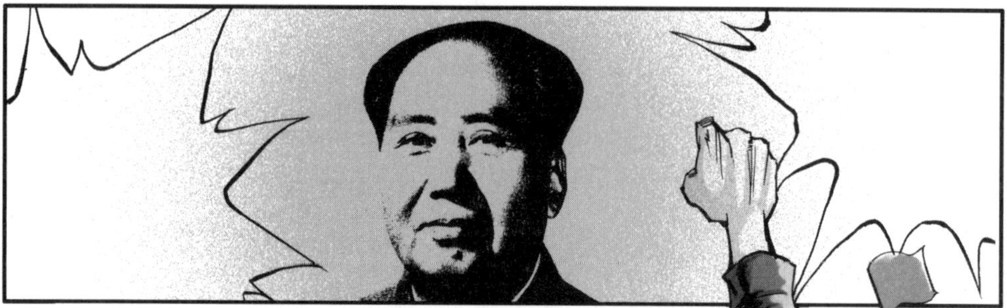

I'VE FORGOTTEN WHAT DAY IT WAS. I DON'T THINK IT WAS A HOLIDAY, MORE LIKE A PROTEST. I FOLLOWED IT ALL DAY LONG, THROUGHOUT THE WHOLE CITY, LED BY DRUMMERS. I WAS WAVING A PAPER FLAG AND CHANTING SLOGANS WITH THE TEACHERS.

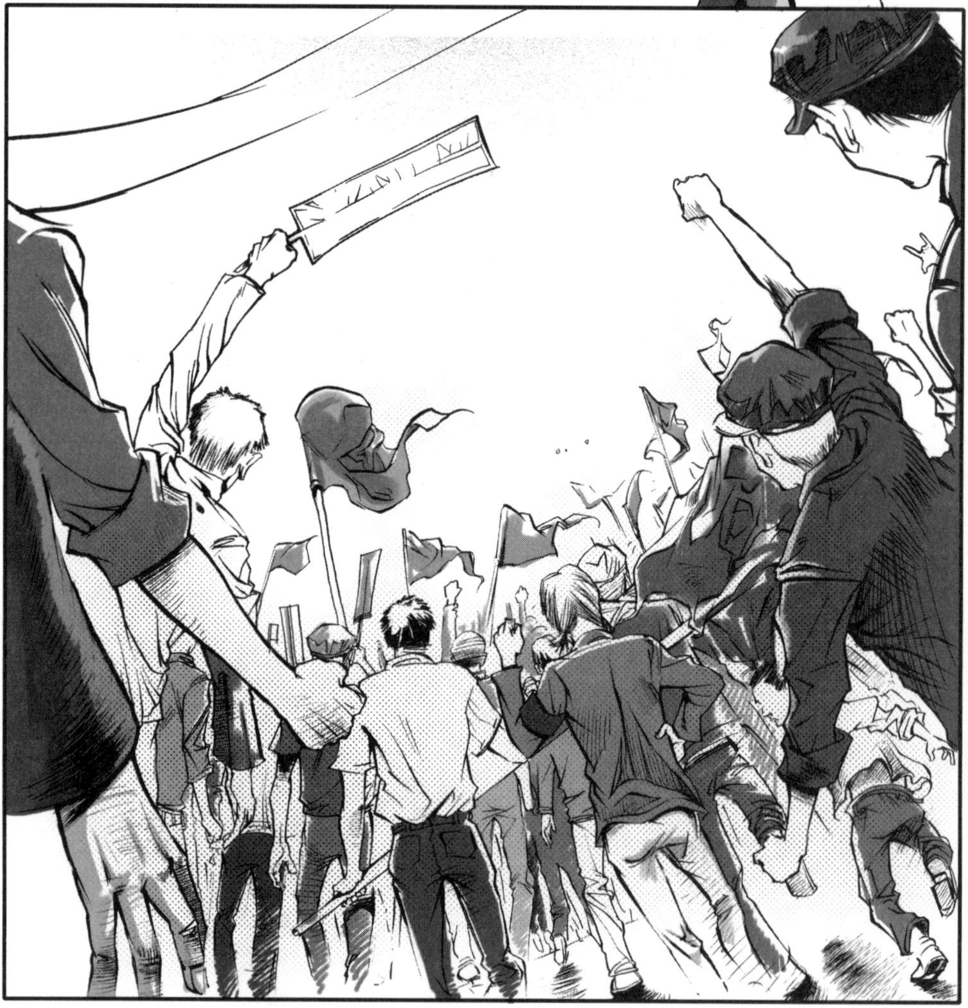

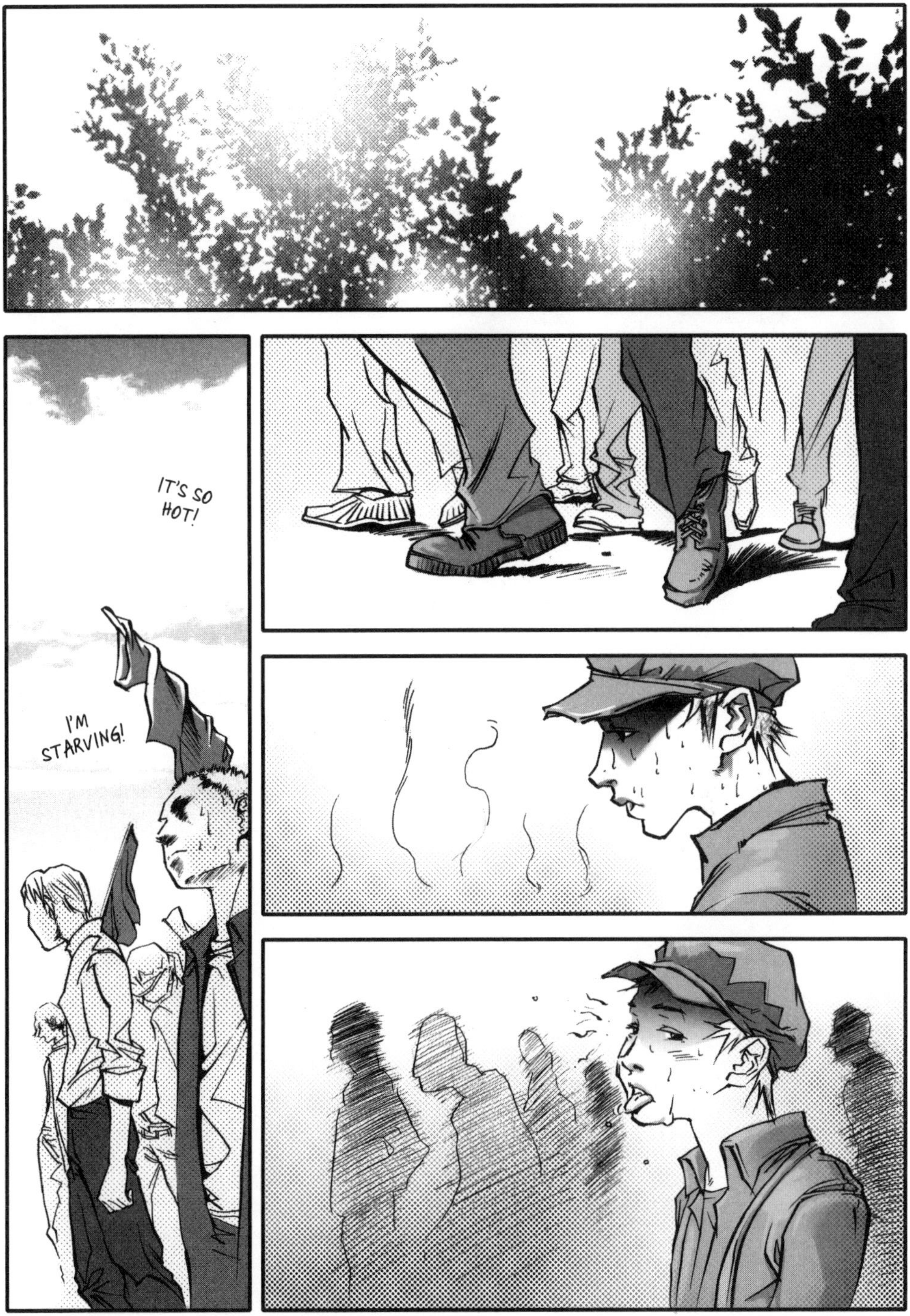
IT'S SO HOT!
I'M STARVING!

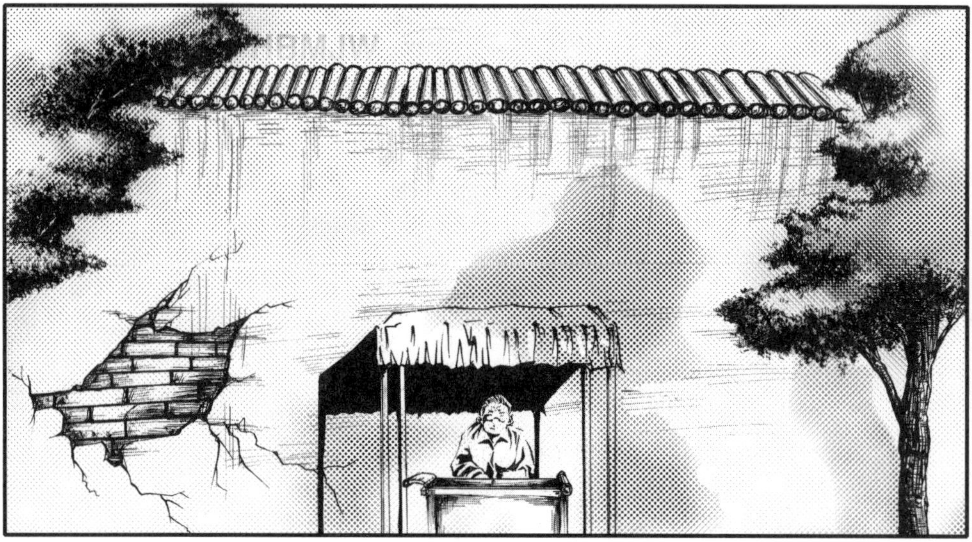
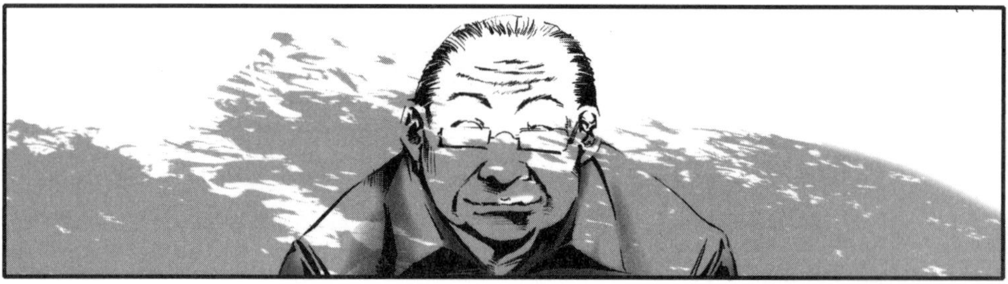
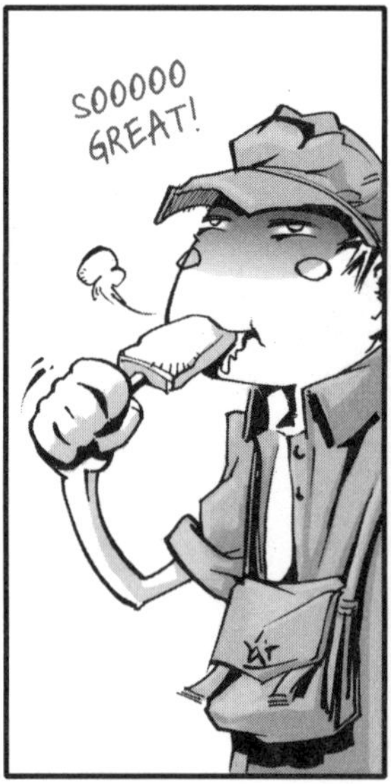
SOOOOO GREAT!
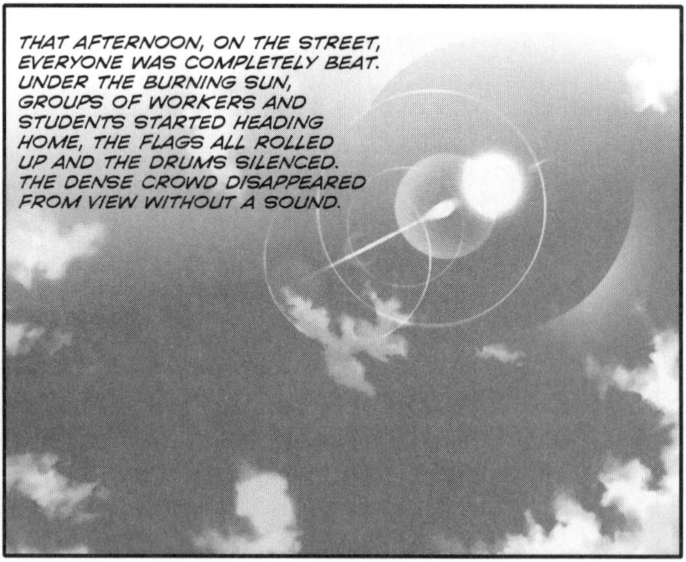
THAT AFTERNOON, ON THE STREET, EVERYONE WAS COMPLETELY BEAT. UNDER THE BURNING SUN, GROUPS OF WORKERS AND STUDENTS STARTED HEADING HOME, THE FLAGS ALL ROLLED UP AND THE DRUMS SILENCED. THE DENSE CROWD DISAPPEARED FROM VIEW WITHOUT A SOUND.

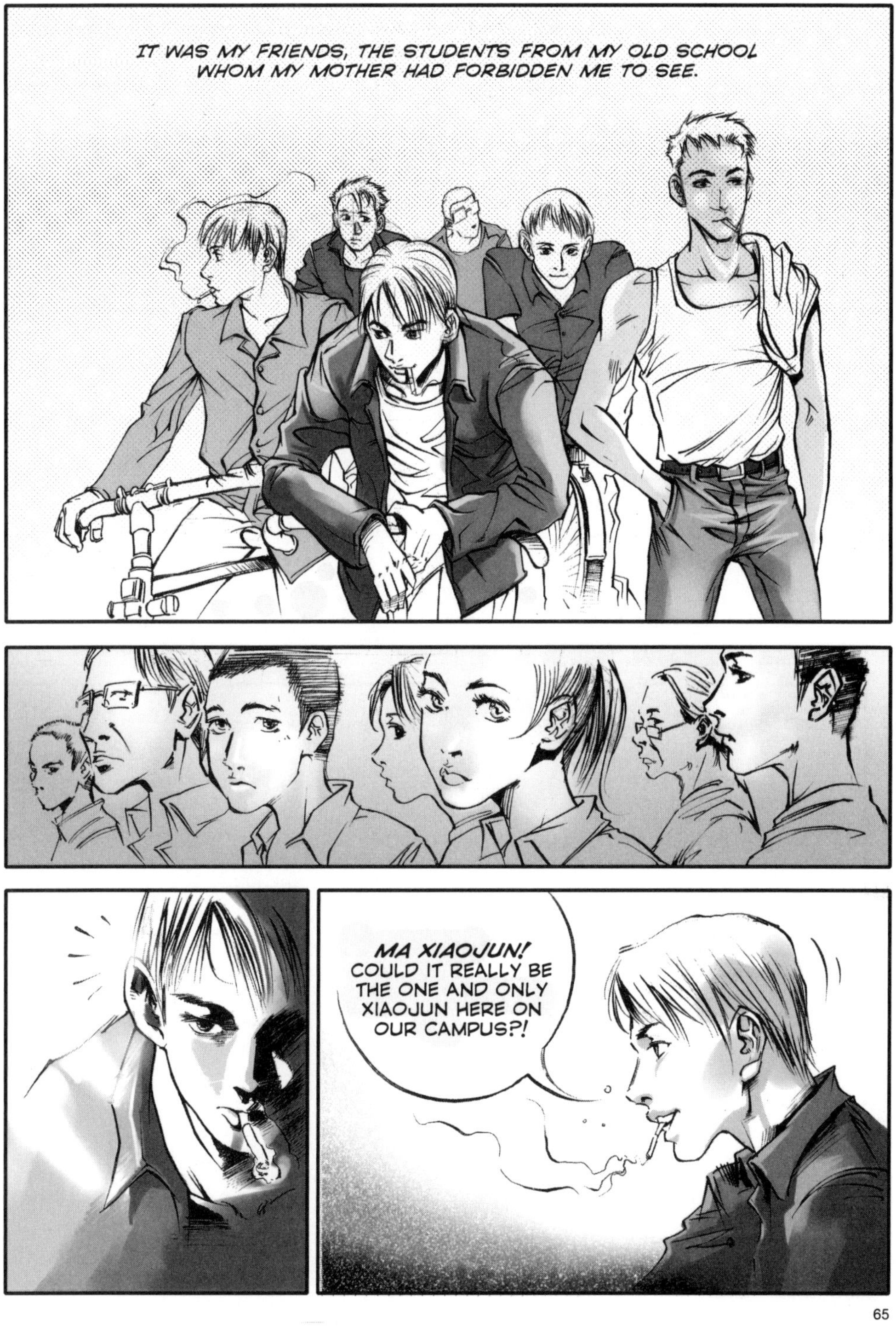
IT WAS MY FRIENDS, THE STUDENTS FROM MY OLD SCHOOL WHOM MY MOTHER HAD FORBIDDEN ME TO SEE.
MA XIAOJUN! COULD IT REALLY BE THE ONE AND ONLY XIAOJUN HERE ON OUR CAMPUS?!

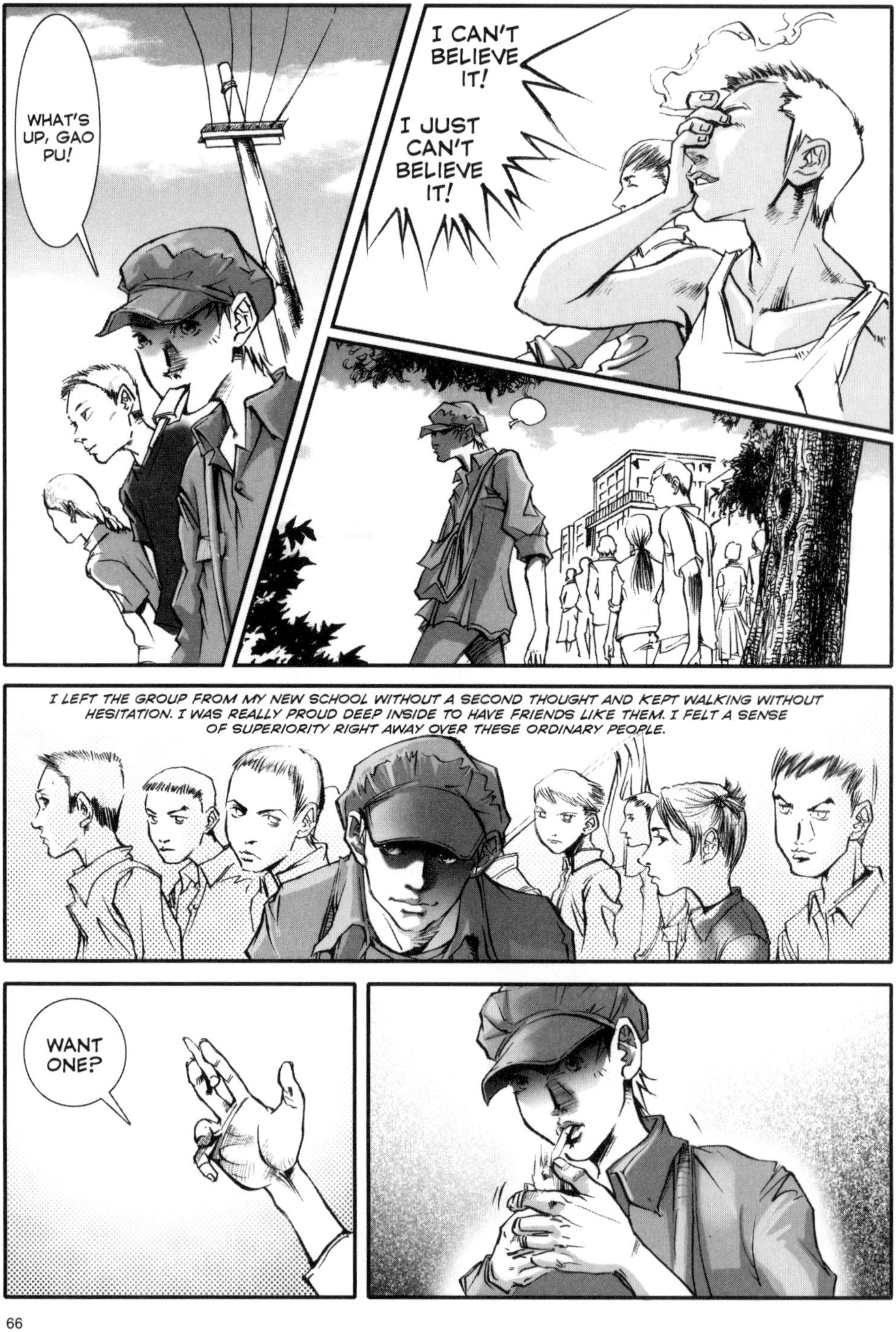
WHAT'S UP, GAO PU!
I CAN'T BELIEVE IT!
I JUST CAN'T BELIEVE IT!
I LEFT THE GROUP FROM MY NEW SCHOOL WITHOUT A SECOND THOUGHT AND KEPT WALKING WITHOUT HESITATION. I WAS REALLY PROUD DEEP INSIDE TO HAVE FRIENDS LIKE THEM. I FELT A SENSE OF SUPERIORITY RIGHT AWAY OVER THESE ORDINARY PEOPLE.
WANT ONE?

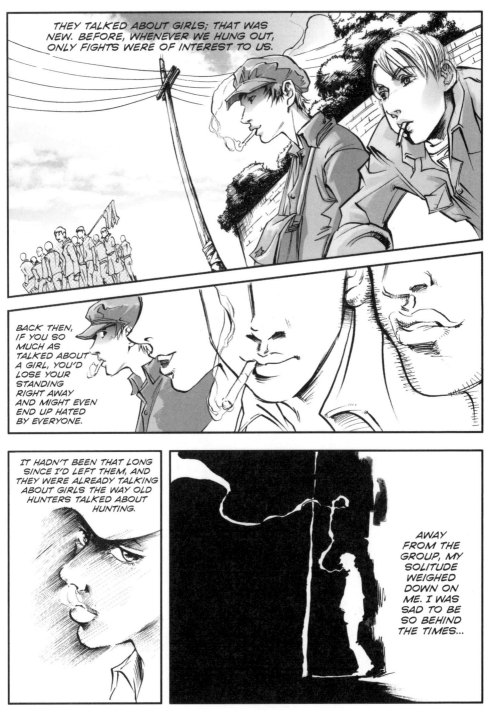

THEY TALKED ABOUT GIRLS; THAT WAS NEW. BEFORE, WHENEVER WE HUNG OUT, ONLY FIGHTS WERE OF INTEREST TO US.

BACK THEN, IF YOU SO MUCH AS TALKED ABOUT A GIRL, YOU'D LOSE YOUR STANDING RIGHT AWAY AND MIGHT EVEN END UP HATED BY EVERYONE.

IT HADN'T BEEN THAT LONG SINCE I'D LEFT THEM, AND THEY WERE ALREADY TALKING ABOUT GIRLS THE WAY OLD HUNTERS TALKED ABOUT HUNTING.

AWAY FROM THE GROUP, MY SOLITUDE WEIGHED DOWN ON ME. I WAS SAD TO BE SO BEHIND THE TIMES...

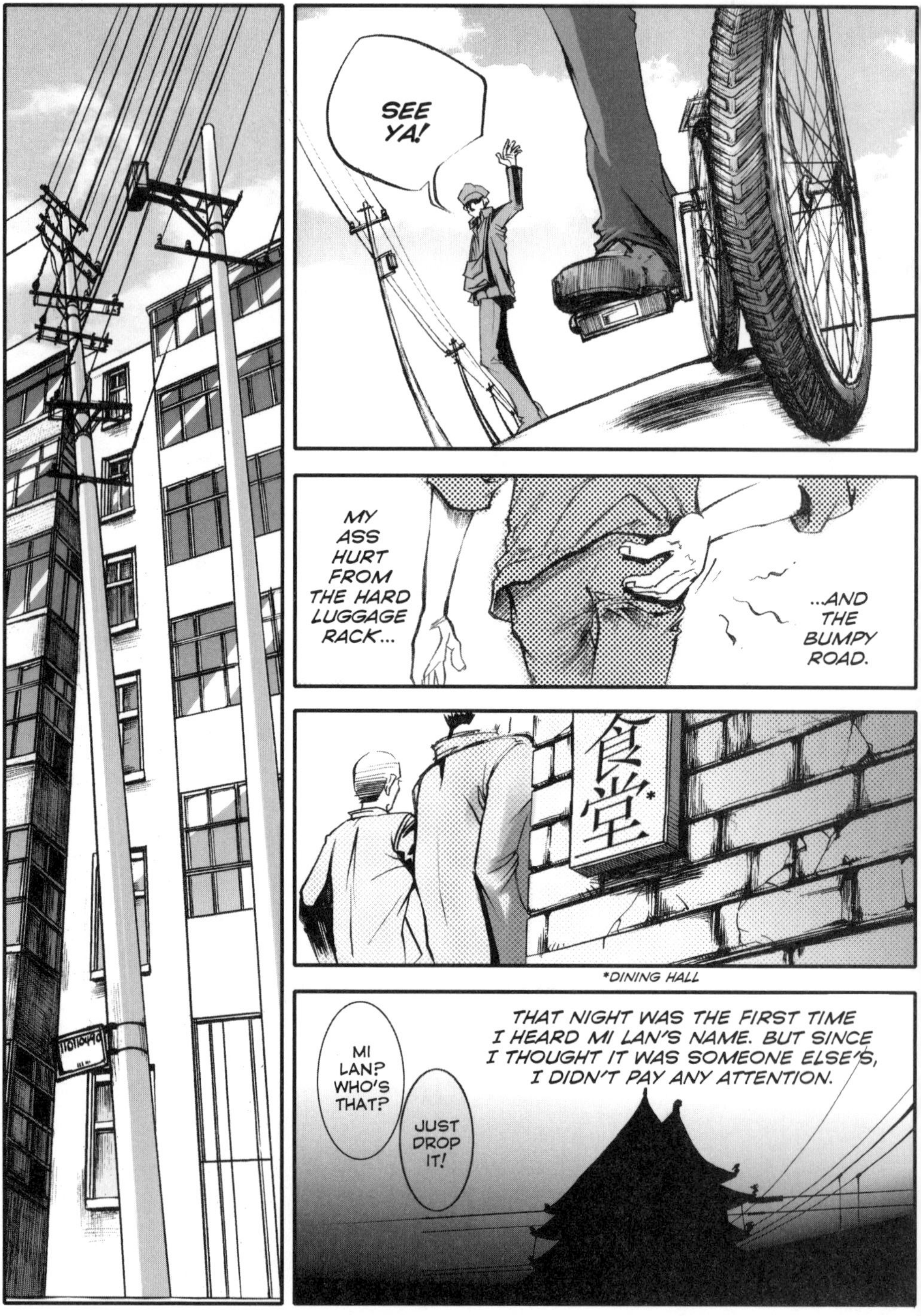
SEE YA!
MY ASS HURT FROM THE HARD LUGGAGE RACK...
...AND THE BUMPY ROAD.
食堂*
*DINING HALL
THAT NIGHT WAS THE FIRST TIME I HEARD MI LAN'S NAME. BUT SINCE I THOUGHT IT WAS SOMEONE ELSE'S, I DIDN'T PAY ANY ATTENTION.
MI LAN? WHO'S THAT?
JUST DROP IT!

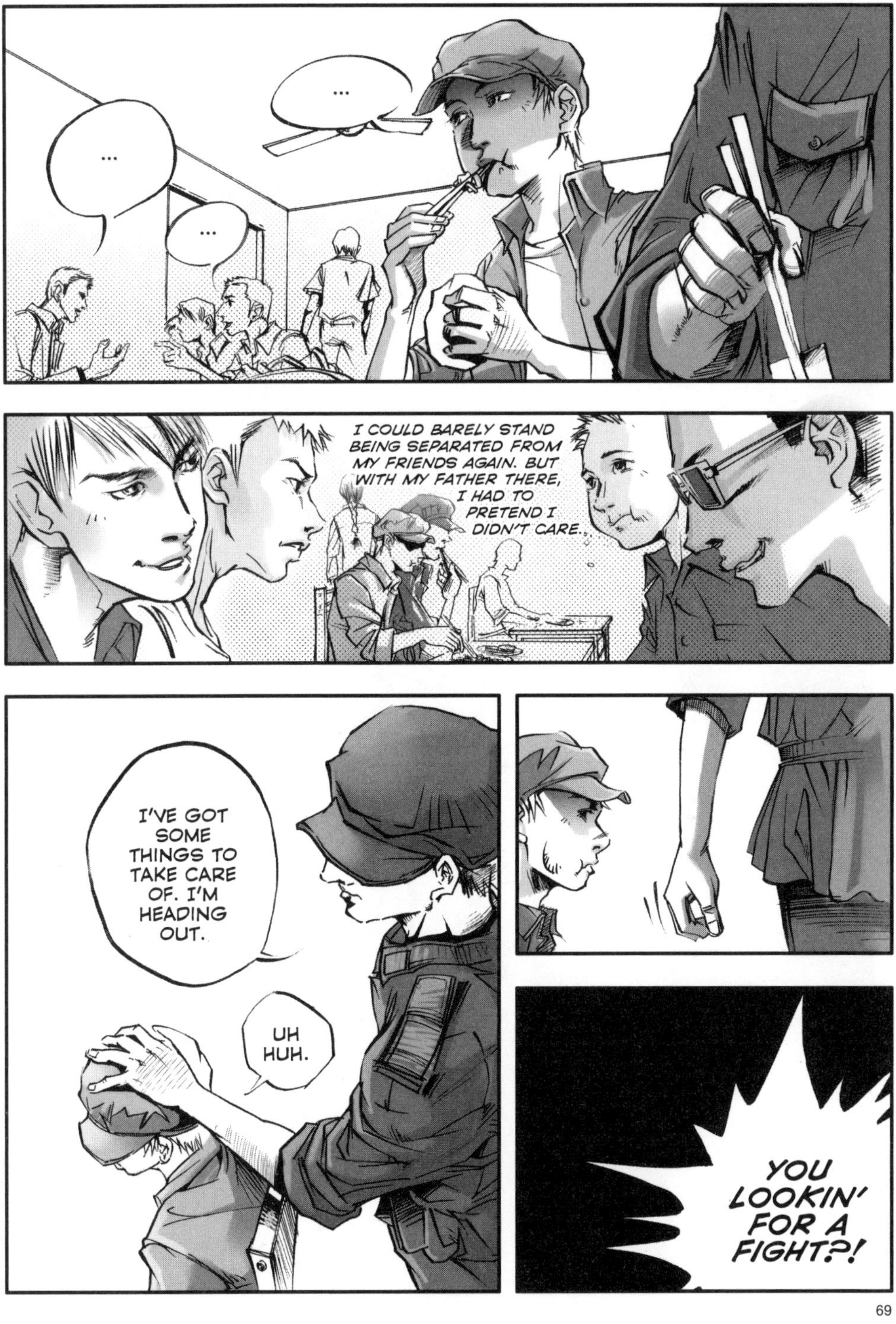
...
...
...
I COULD BARELY STAND BEING SEPARATED FROM MY FRIENDS AGAIN. BUT WITH MY FATHER THERE, I HAD TO PRETEND I DIDN'T CARE..
I'VE GOT SOME THINGS TO TAKE CARE OF. I'M HEADING OUT.
UH HUH.
YOU LOOKIN' FOR A FIGHT?!

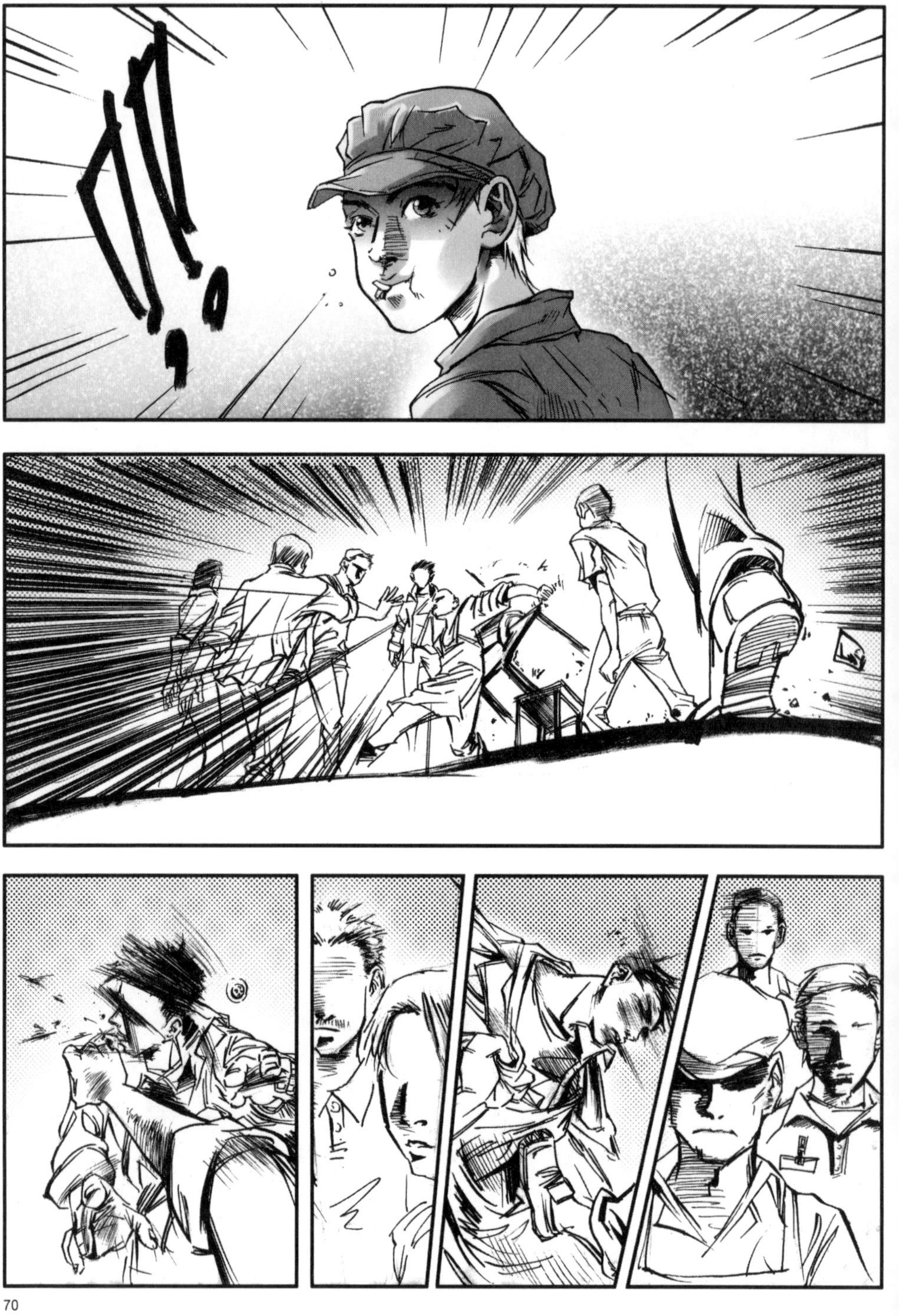

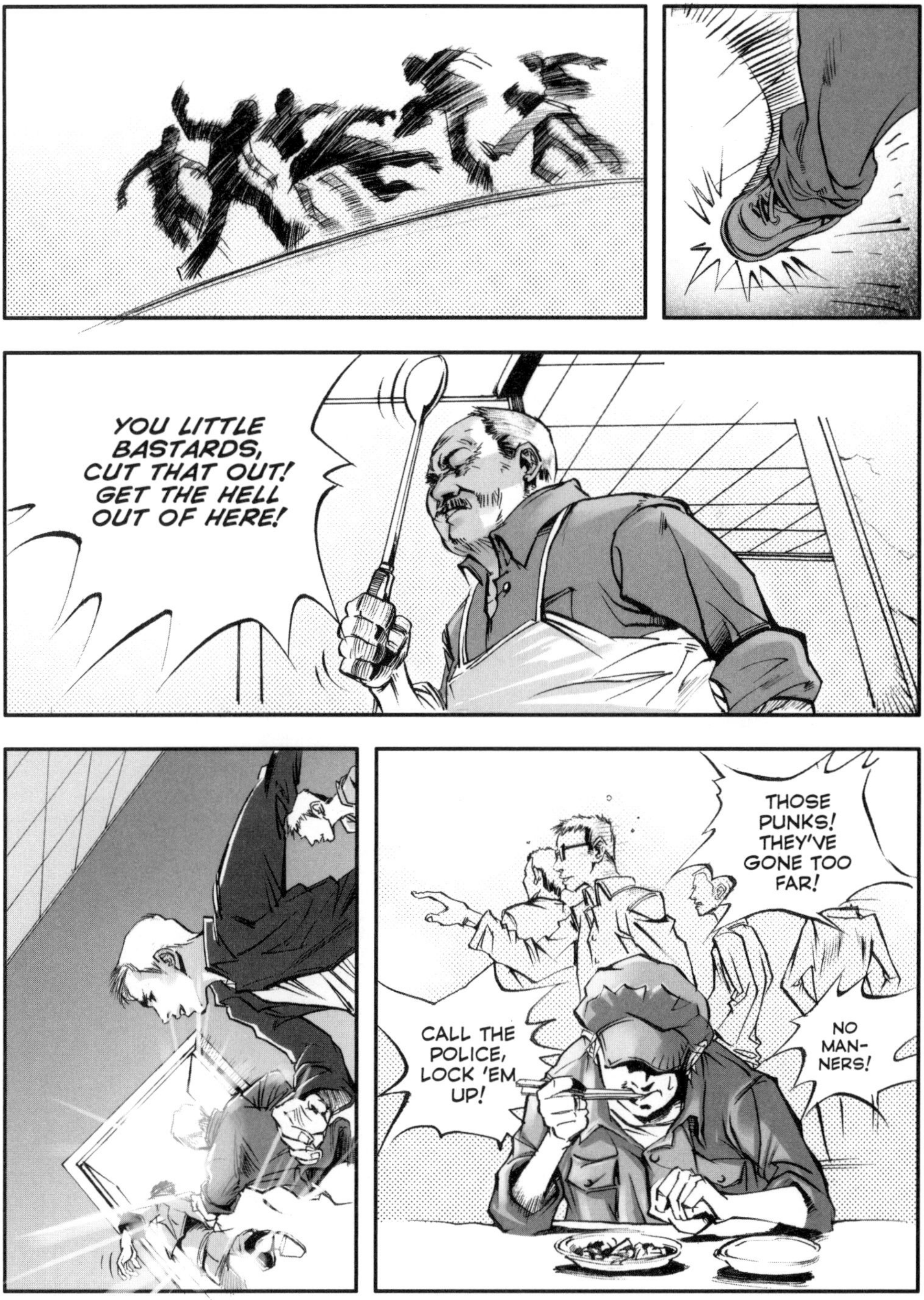
YOU LITTLE BASTARDS, CUT THAT OUT! GET THE HELL OUT OF HERE!
THOSE PUNKS! THEY'VE GONE TOO FAR!
CALL THE POLICE, LOCK 'EM UP!
NO MAN-NERS!

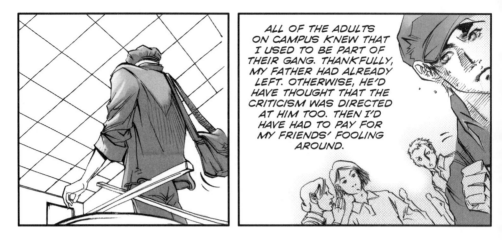

ALL OF THE ADULTS ON CAMPUS KNEW THAT I USED TO BE PART OF THEIR GANG. THANKFULLY, MY FATHER HAD ALREADY LEFT. OTHERWISE, HE'D HAVE THOUGHT THAT THE CRITICISM WAS DIRECTED AT HIM TOO. THEN I'D HAVE HAD TO PAY FOR MY FRIENDS' FOOLING AROUND.

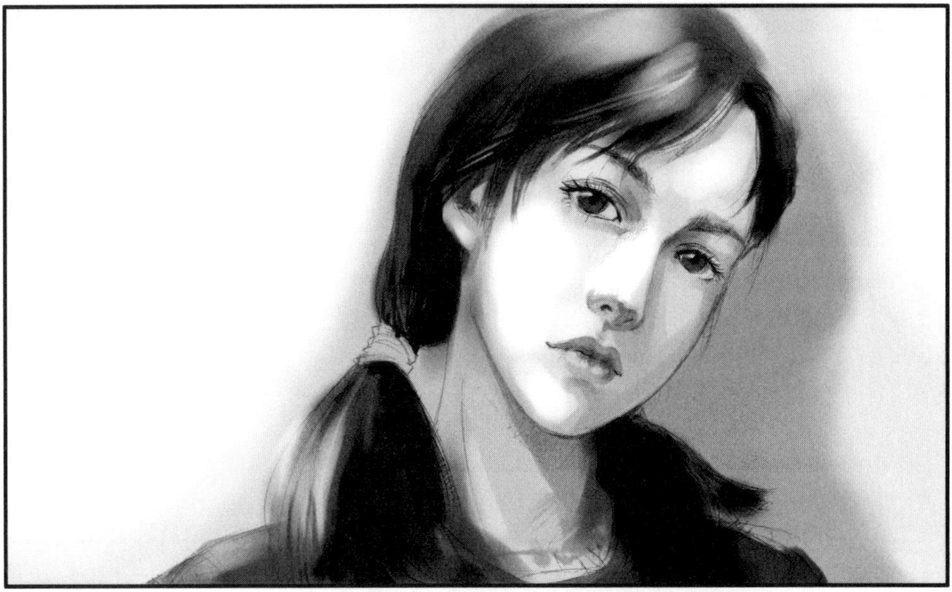
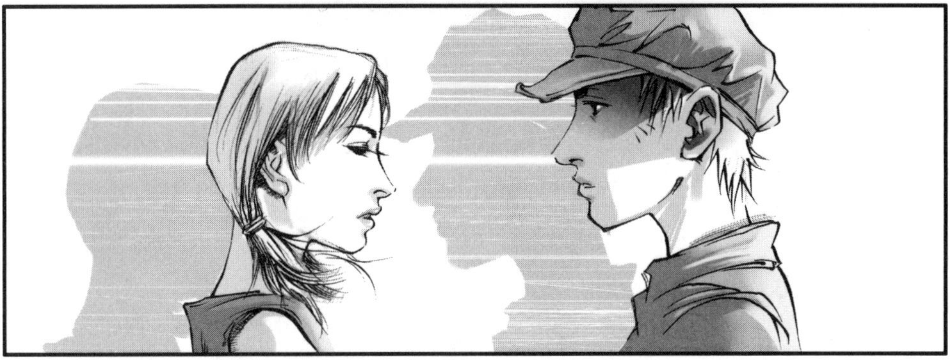
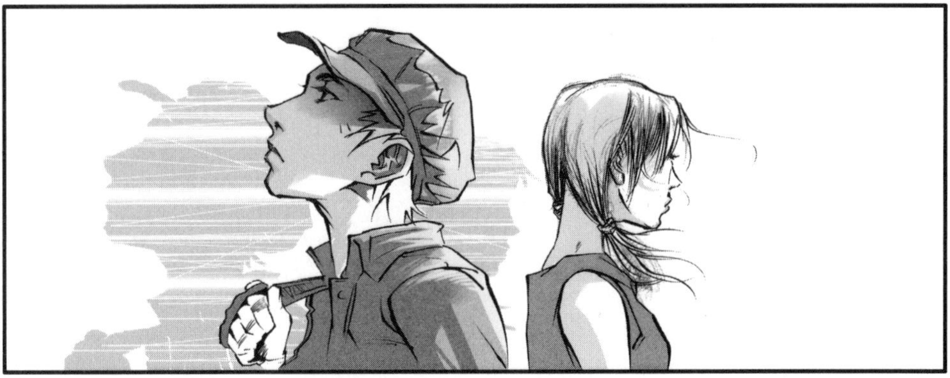

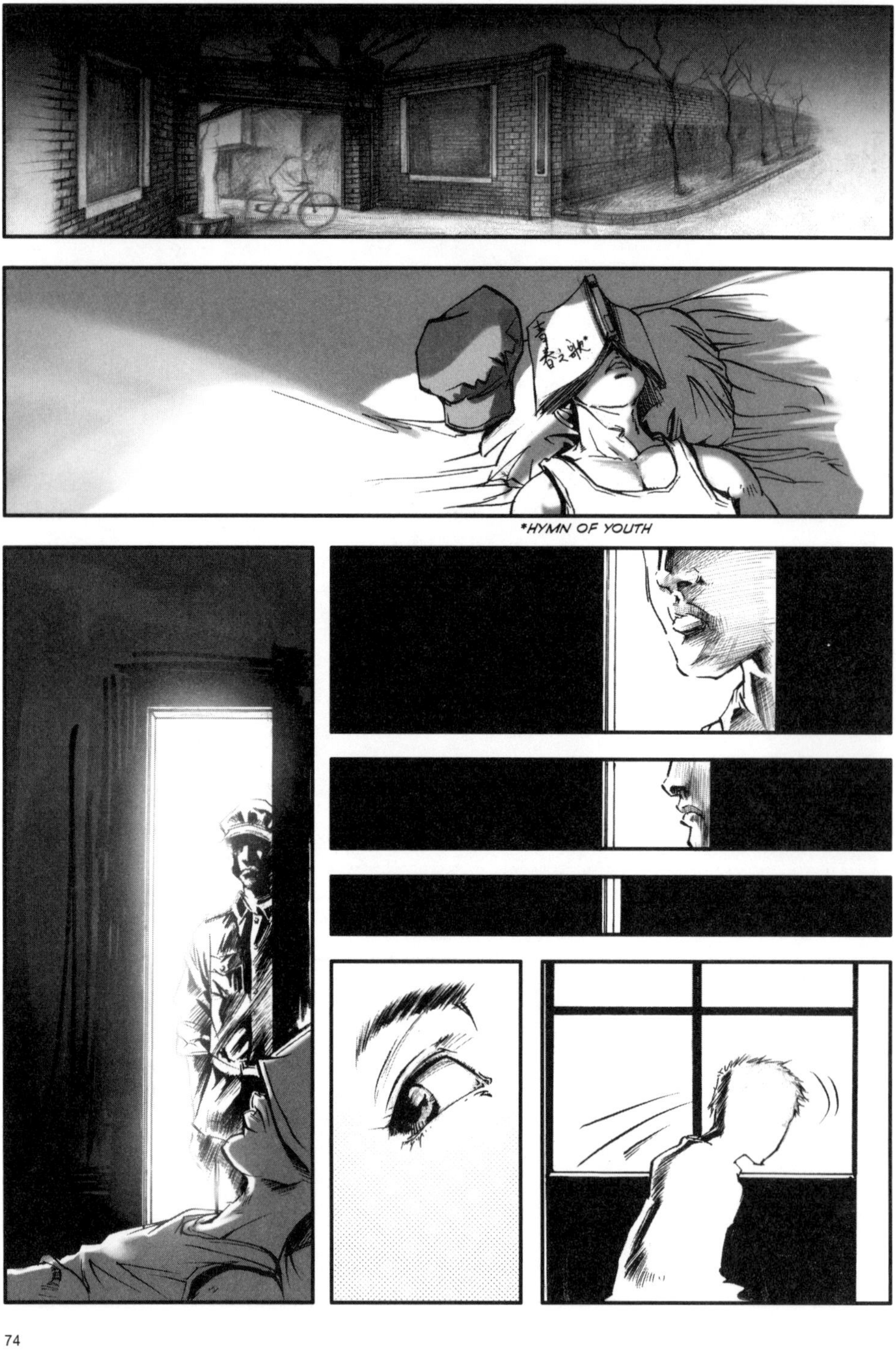
青春之歌*

*HYMN OF YOUTH

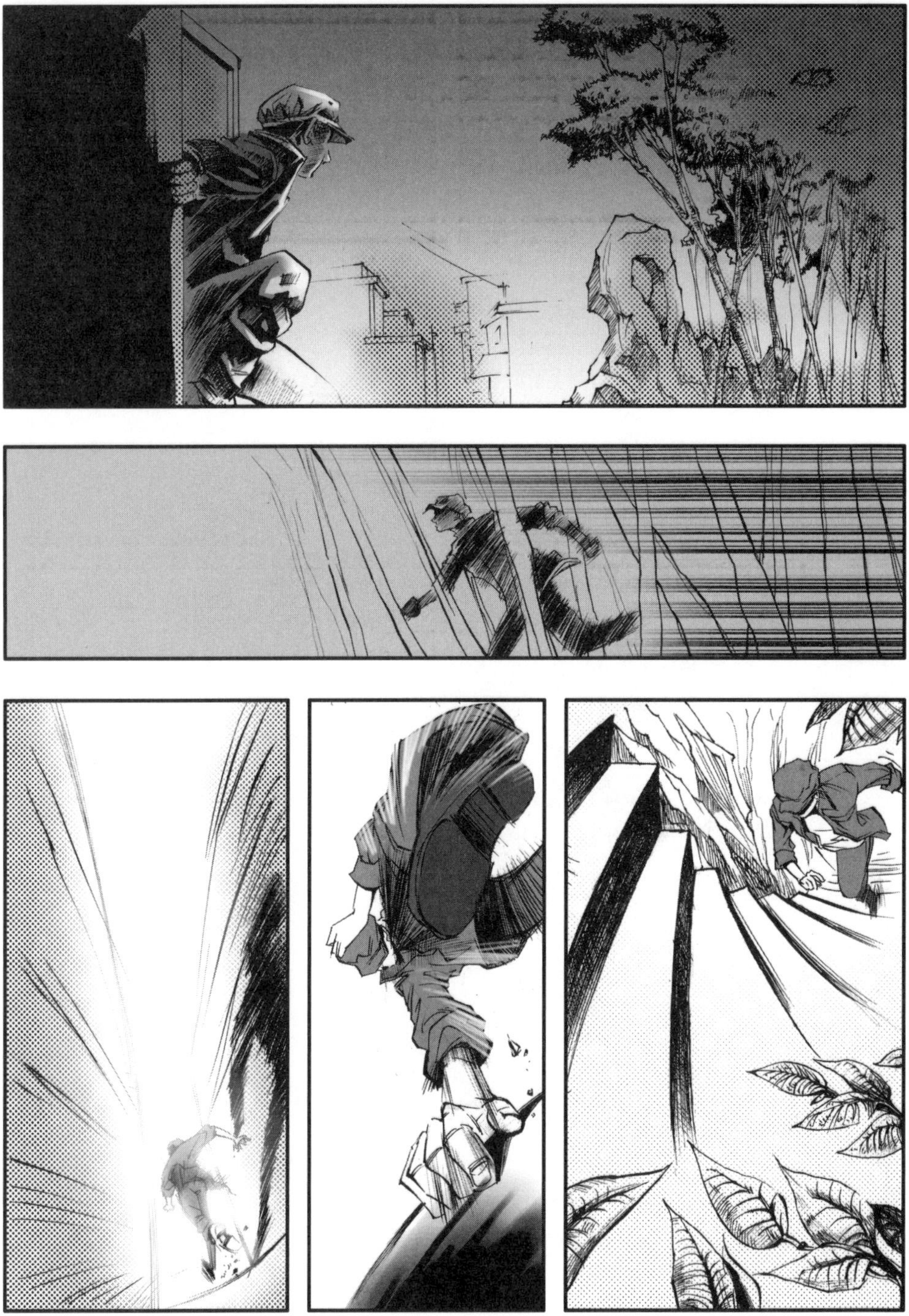

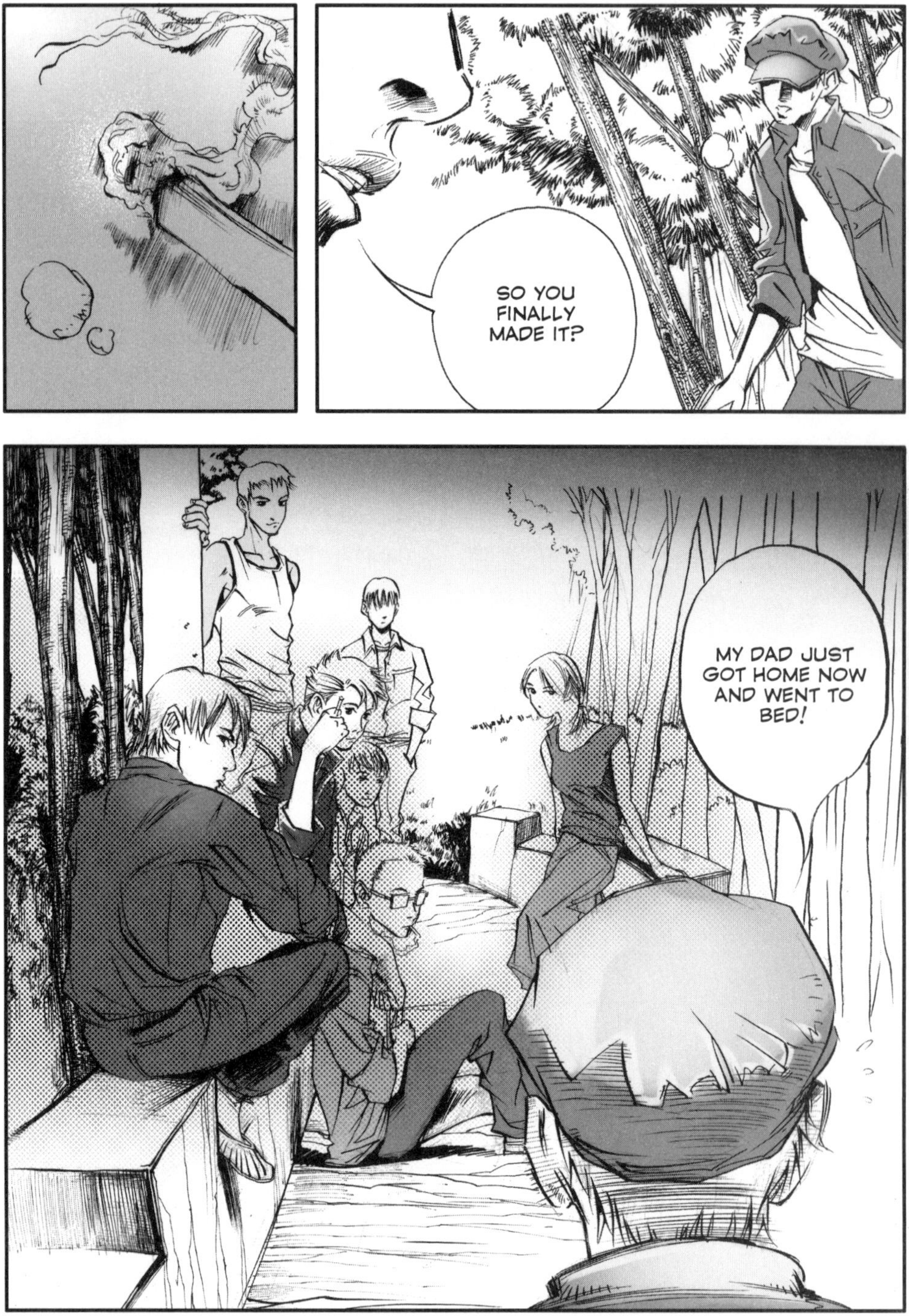
SO YOU FINALLY MADE IT?
MY DAD JUST GOT HOME NOW AND WENT TO BED!

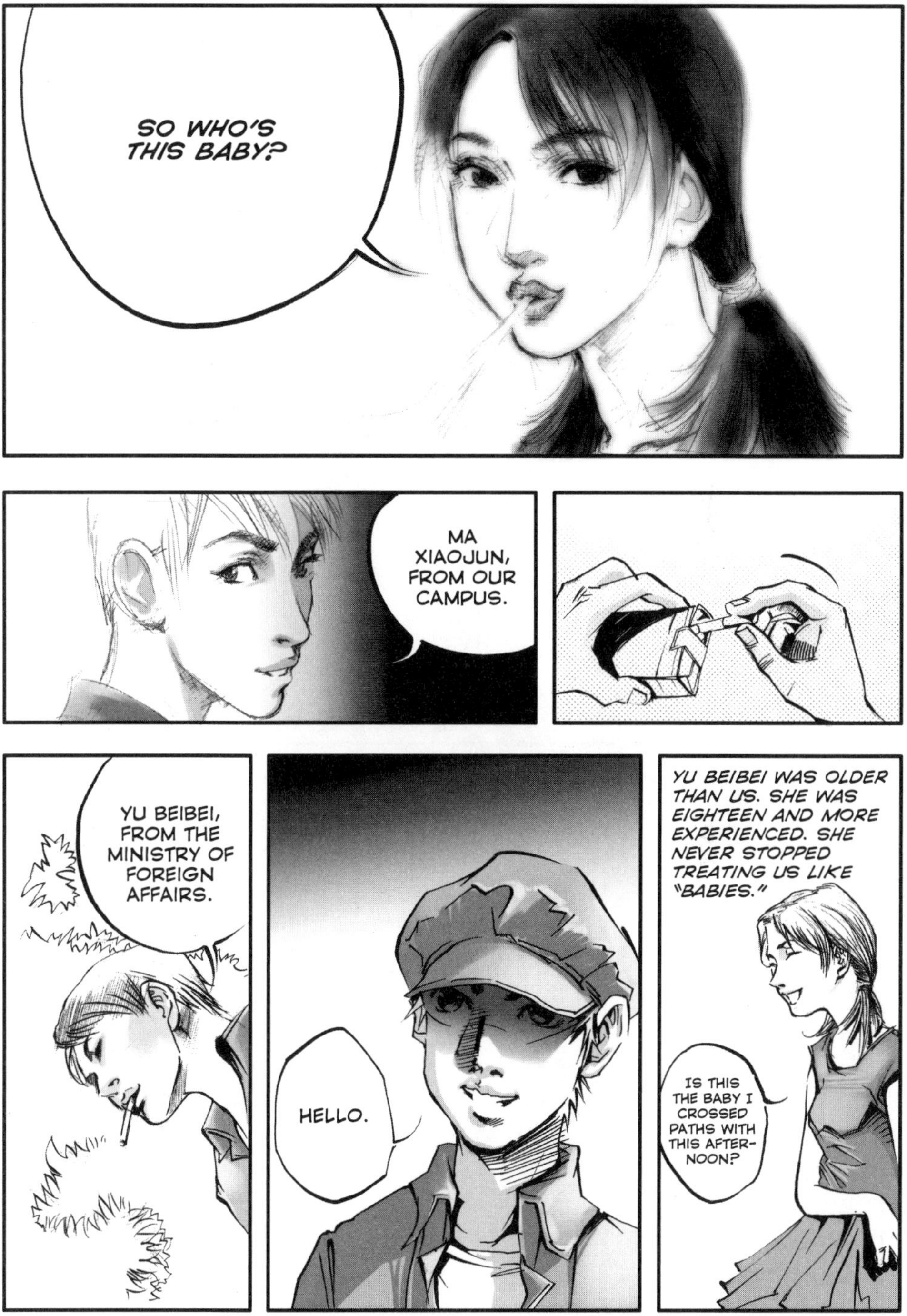
SO WHO'S THIS BABY?
MA XIAOJUN, FROM OUR CAMPUS.
YU BEIBEI, FROM THE MINISTRY OF FOREIGN AFFAIRS.
HELLO.
YU BEIBEI WAS OLDER THAN US. SHE WAS EIGHTEEN AND MORE EXPERIENCED. SHE NEVER STOPPED TREATING US LIKE "BABIES."
IS THIS THE BABY I CROSSED PATHS WITH THIS AFTER-NOON?

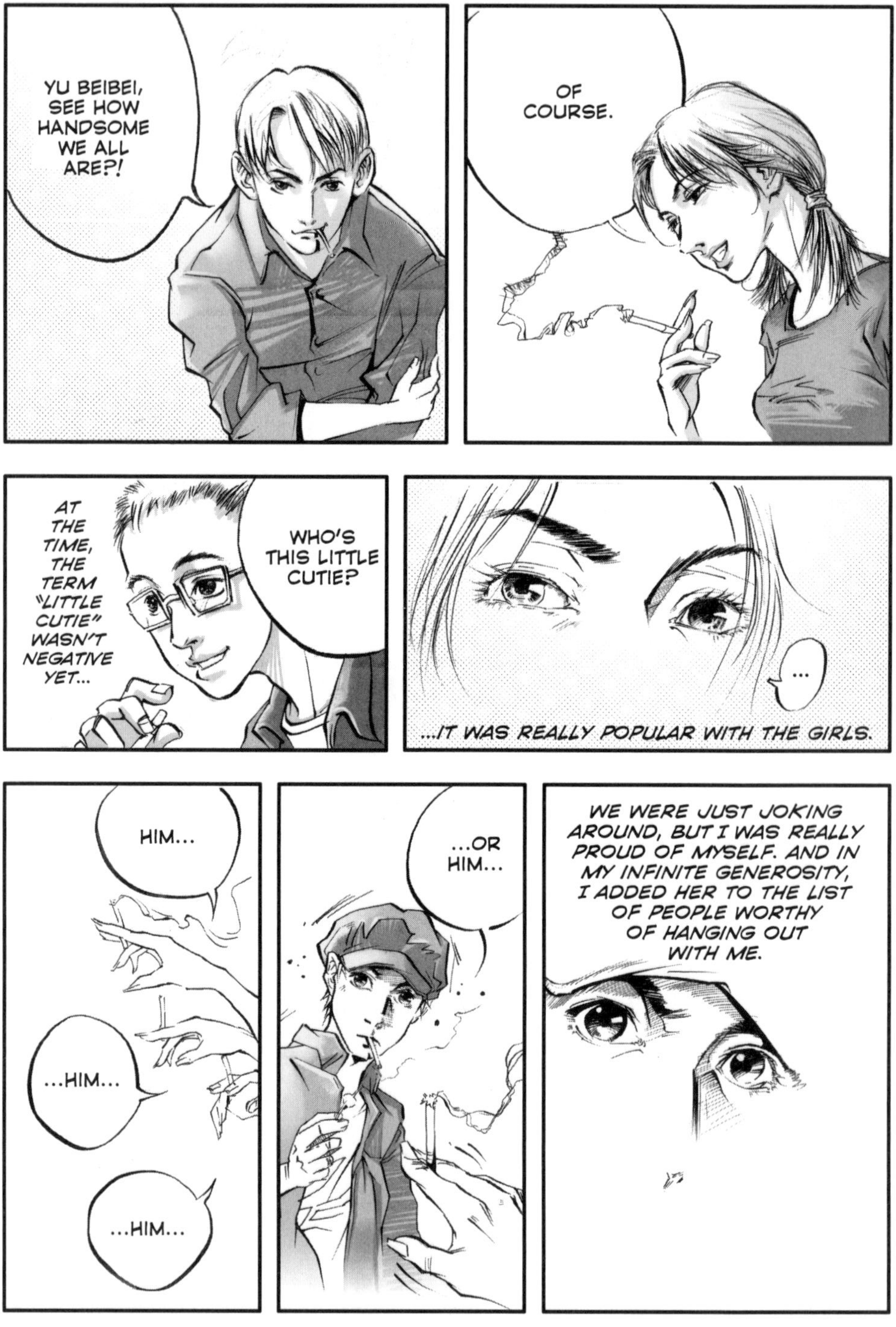
YU BEIBEI, SEE HOW HANDSOME WE ALL ARE?!
OF COURSE.
AT THE TIME, THE TERM "LITTLE CUTIE" WASN'T NEGATIVE YET...
WHO'S THIS LITTLE CUTIE?
...
...IT WAS REALLY POPULAR WITH THE GIRLS.
HIM...
...HIM...
...HIM...
...OR HIM...
WE WERE JUST JOKING AROUND, BUT I WAS REALLY PROUD OF MYSELF. AND IN MY INFINITE GENEROSITY, I ADDED HER TO THE LIST OF PEOPLE WORTHY OF HANGING OUT WITH ME.

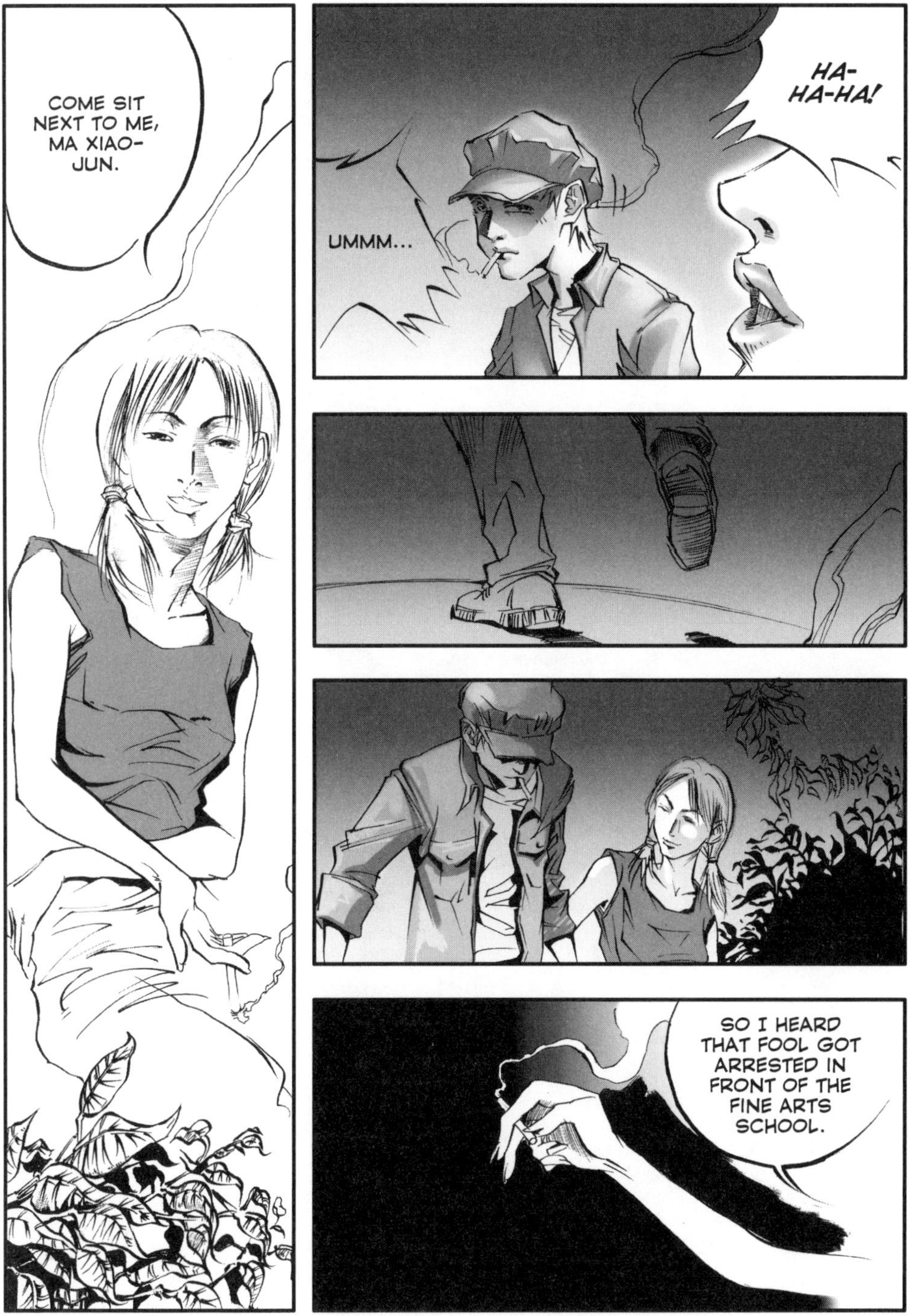
COME SIT NEXT TO ME, MA XIAO-JUN.
HA-HA-HA!
UMMM...
SO I HEARD THAT FOOL GOT ARRESTED IN FRONT OF THE FINE ARTS SCHOOL.

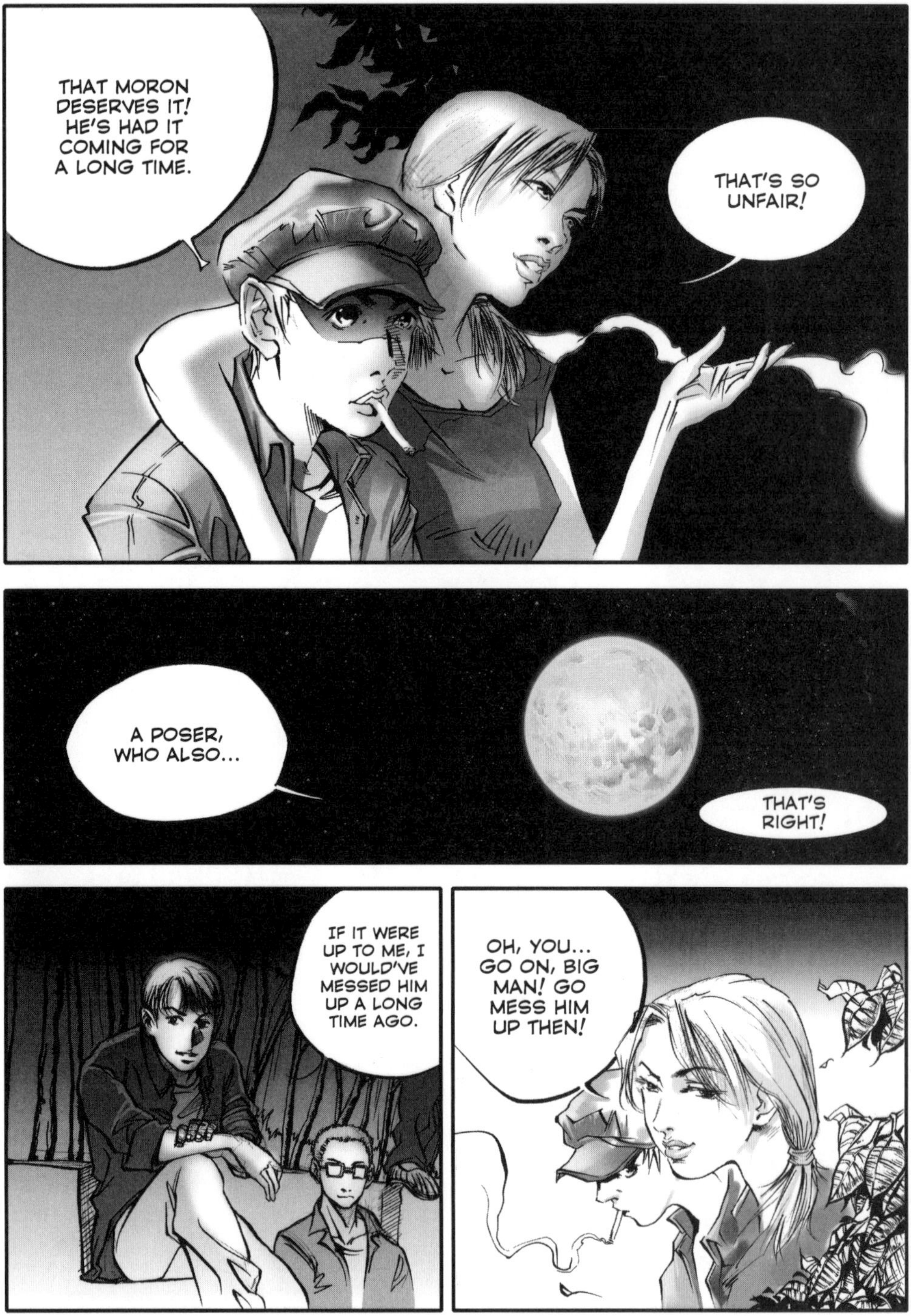
THAT MORON DESERVES IT! HE'S HAD IT COMING FOR A LONG TIME.
THAT'S SO UNFAIR!
A POSER, WHO ALSO...
THAT'S RIGHT!
IF IT WERE UP TO ME, I WOULD'VE MESSED HIM UP A LONG TIME AGO.
OH, YOU... GO ON, BIG MAN! GO MESS HIM UP THEN!

HER ARM WAS DRAPED OVER MY SHOULDER, CIGARETTE IN HAND. FROM TIME TO TIME, SHE TURNED HER NECK TO TAKE A DRAG AND, IN DOING SO, PULLED ME CLOSER, HER FACE AGAINST MINE.

I COULD ALMOST FEEL THE BATTING OF HER LASHES AGAINST MY CHIN, LIKE THE DOWNY CARESS OF A WEEPING WILLOW.

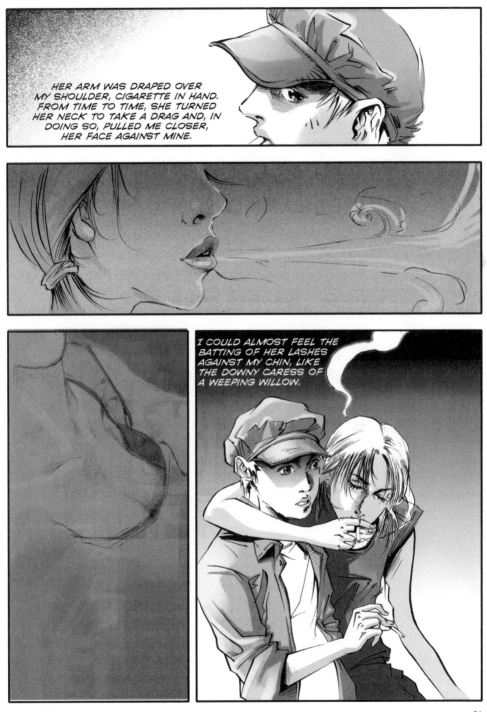

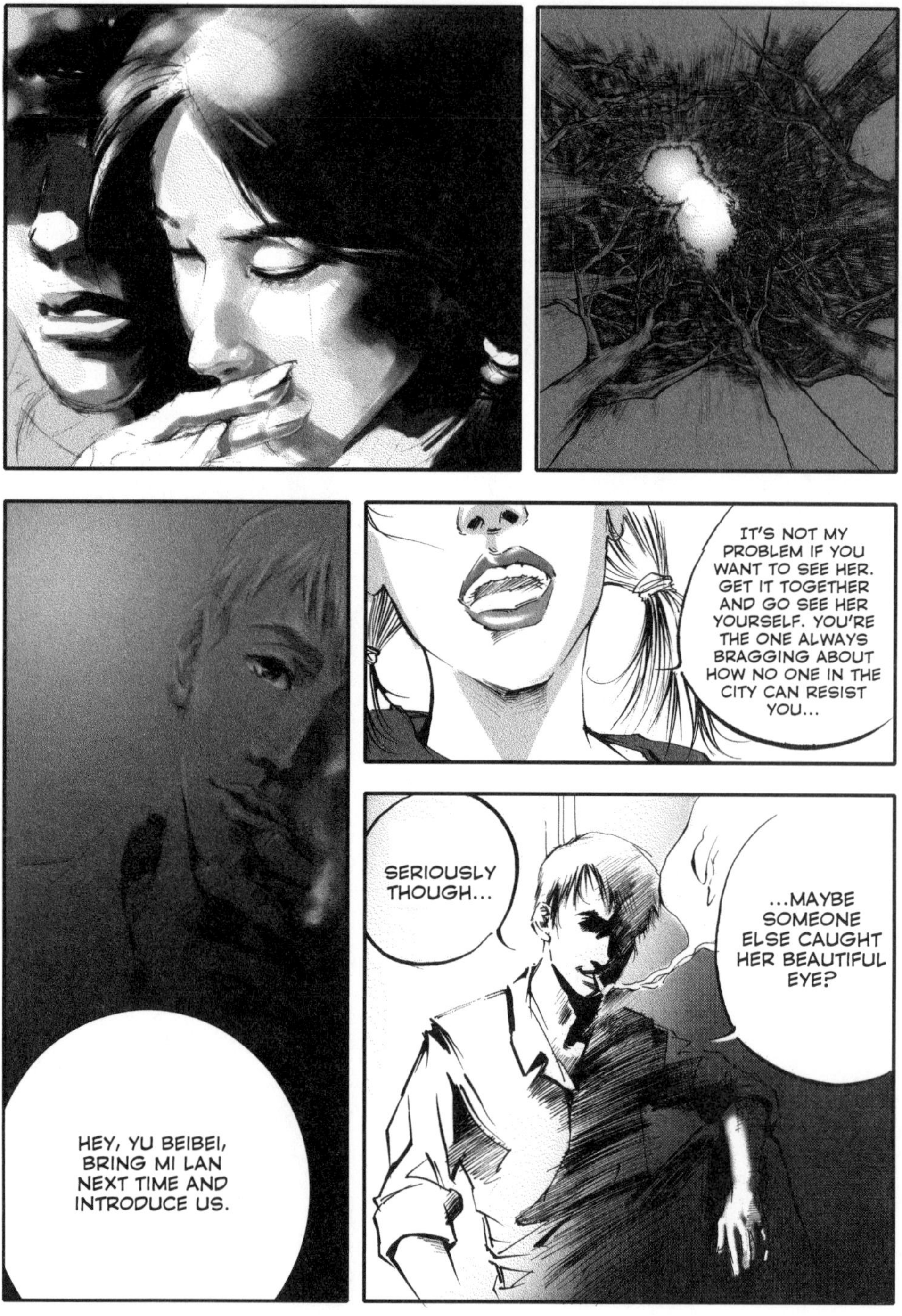
HEY, YU BEIBEI, BRING MI LAN NEXT TIME AND INTRODUCE US.
IT'S NOT MY PROBLEM IF YOU WANT TO SEE HER. GET IT TOGETHER AND GO SEE HER YOURSELF. YOU'RE THE ONE ALWAYS BRAGGING ABOUT HOW NO ONE IN THE CITY CAN RESIST YOU...
SERIOUSLY THOUGH...
...MAYBE SOMEONE ELSE CAUGHT HER BEAUTIFUL EYE?

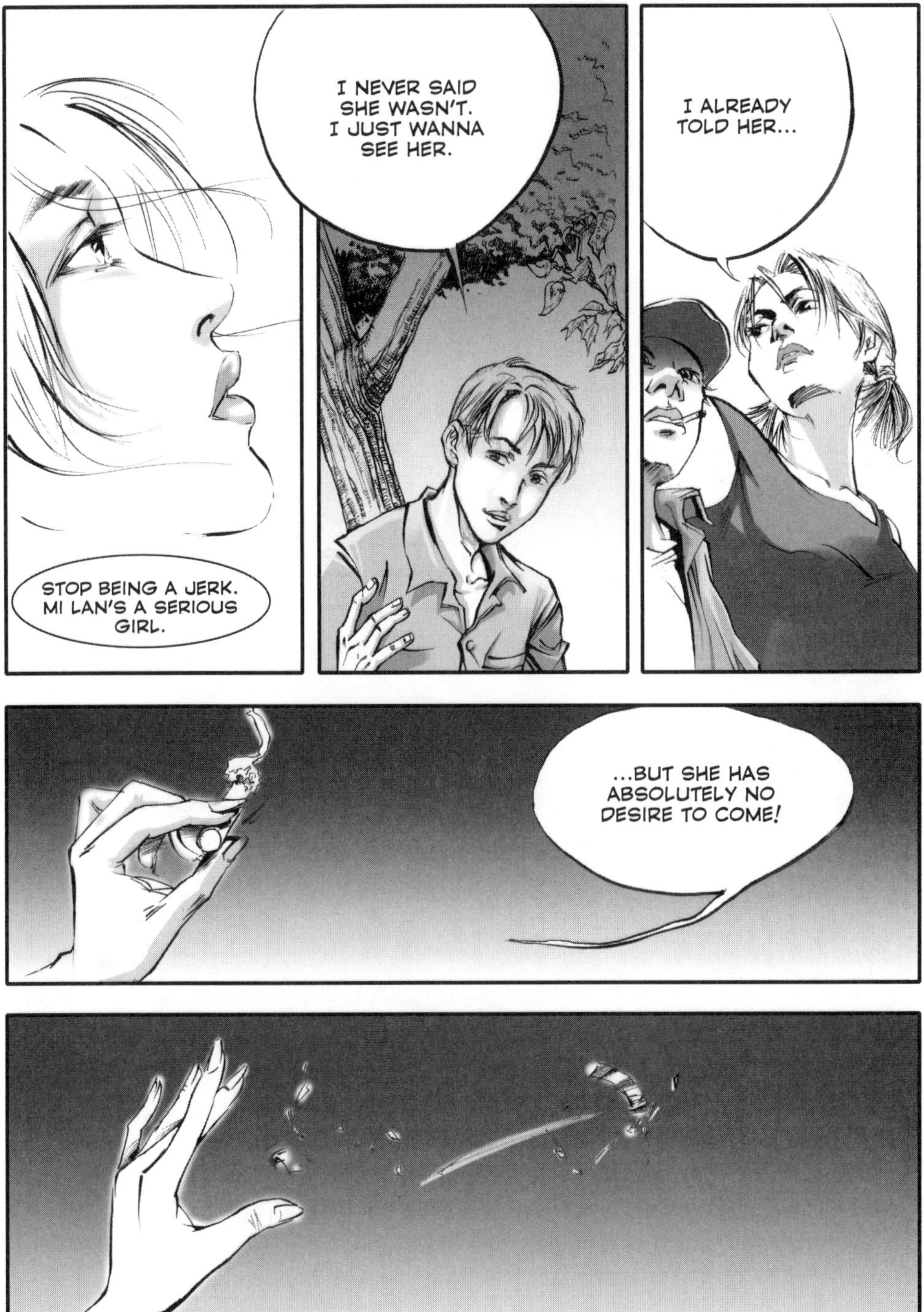
STOP BEING A JERK. MI LAN'S A SERIOUS GIRL.
I NEVER SAID SHE WASN'T. I JUST WANNA SEE HER.
I ALREADY TOLD HER...
...BUT SHE HAS ABSOLUTELY NO DESIRE TO COME!

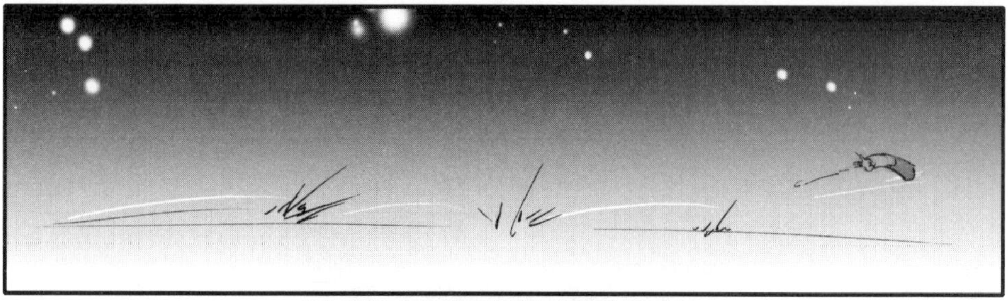

ALL THE CIGARETTES WERE GONE...

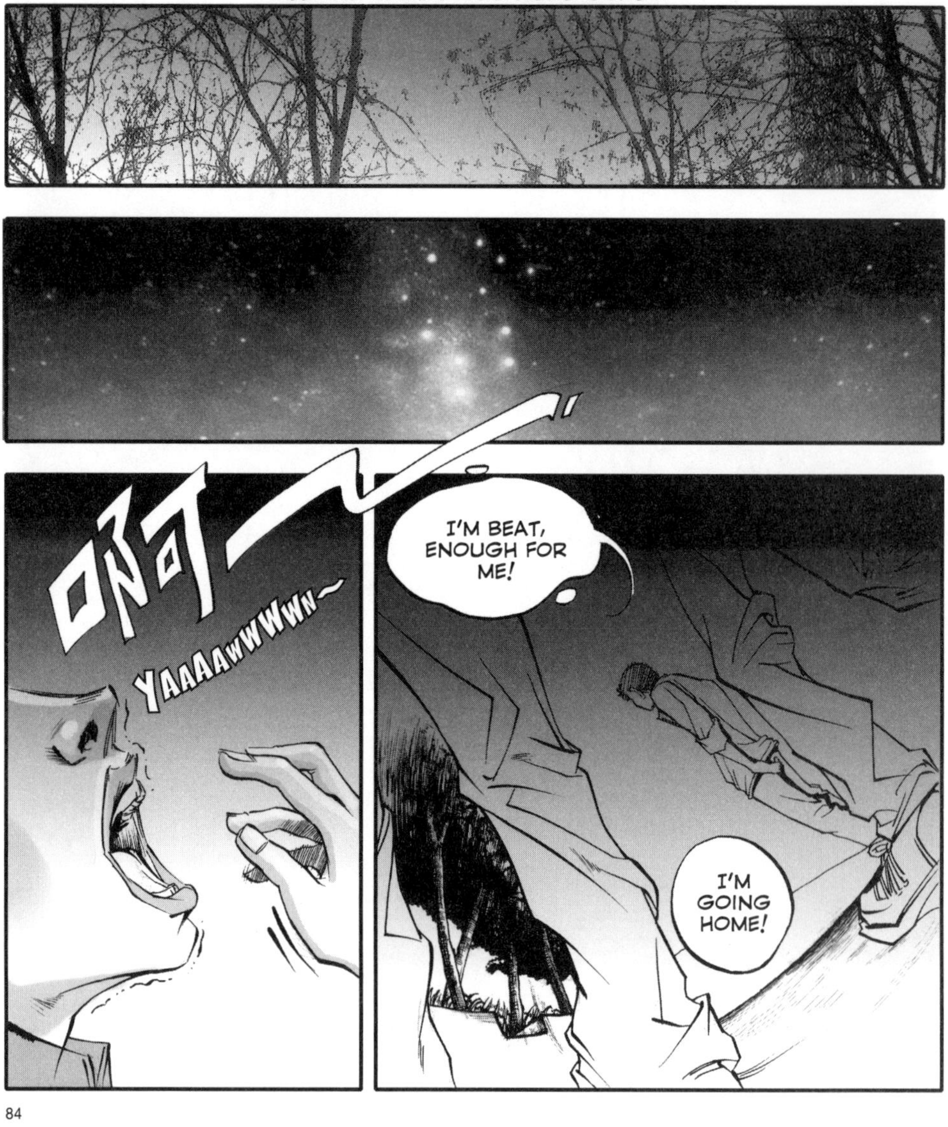
YAAAAWWWN~
I'M BEAT, ENOUGH FOR ME!
I'M GOING HOME!

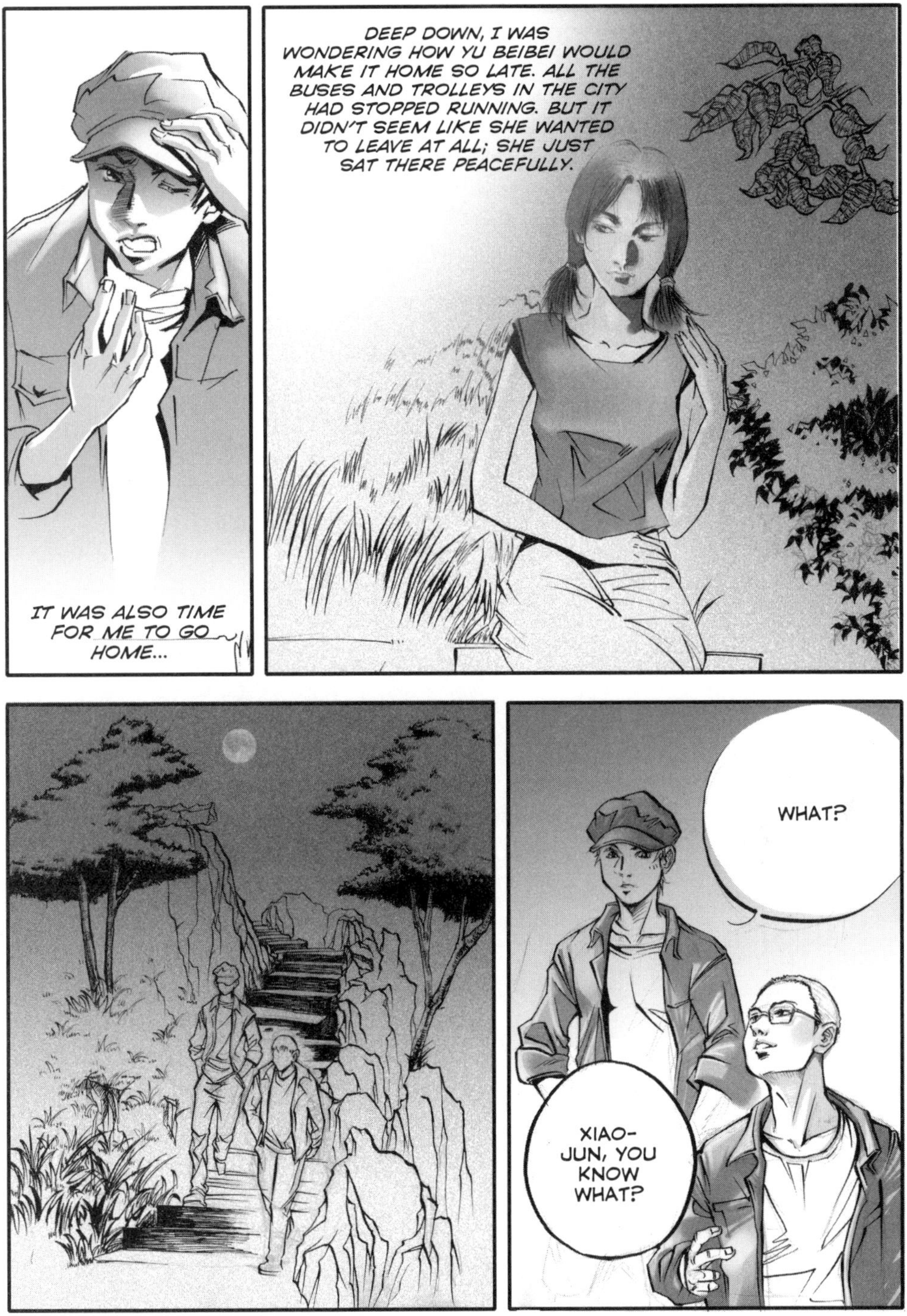
IT WAS ALSO TIME FOR ME TO GO HOME...
DEEP DOWN, I WAS WONDERING HOW YU BEIBEI WOULD MAKE IT HOME SO LATE. ALL THE BUSES AND TROLLEYS IN THE CITY HAD STOPPED RUNNING. BUT IT DIDN'T SEEM LIKE SHE WANTED TO LEAVE AT ALL; SHE JUST SAT THERE PEACEFULLY.
WHAT?
XIAO-JUN, YOU KNOW WHAT?

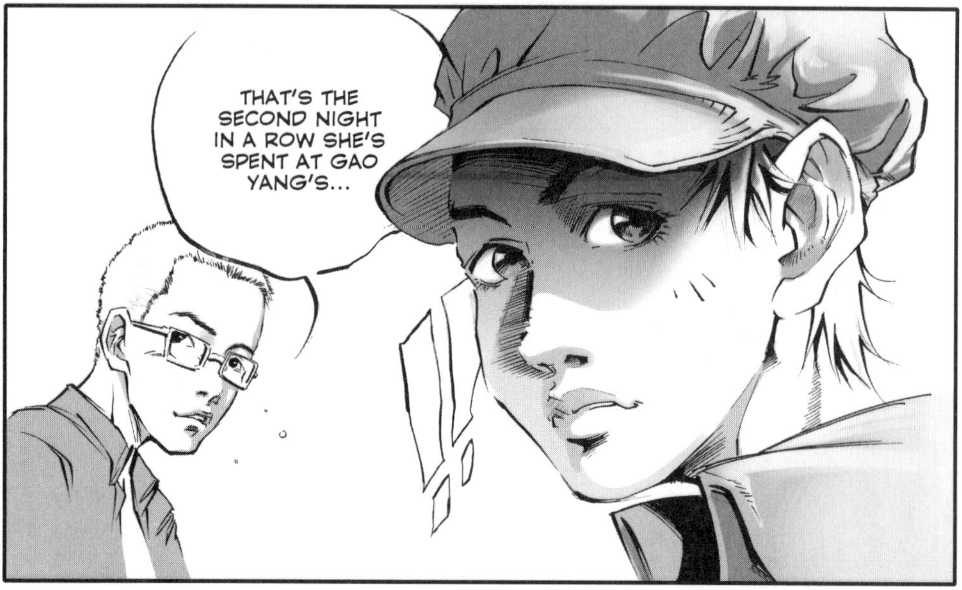
THAT'S THE SECOND NIGHT IN A ROW SHE'S SPENT AT GAO YANG'S...

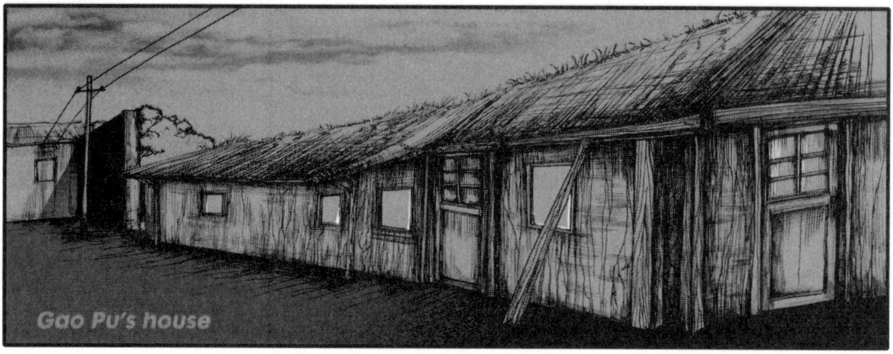
Gao Pu's house

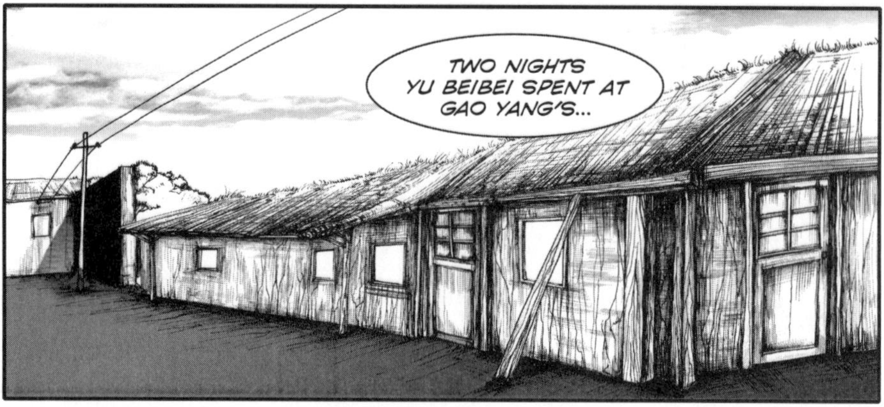
TWO NIGHTS YU BEIBEI SPENT AT GAO YANG'S...

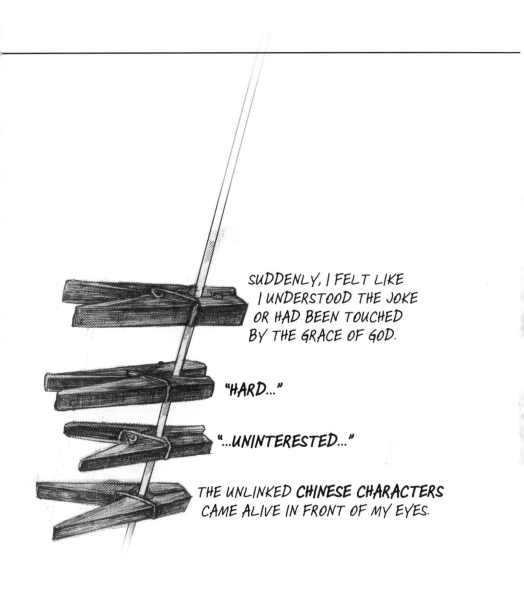

SUDDENLY, I FELT LIKE I UNDERSTOOD THE JOKE OR HAD BEEN TOUCHED BY THE GRACE OF GOD.

"HARD..."

"...UNINTERESTED..."

THE UNLINKED **CHINESE CHARACTERS** CAME ALIVE IN FRONT OF MY EYES.

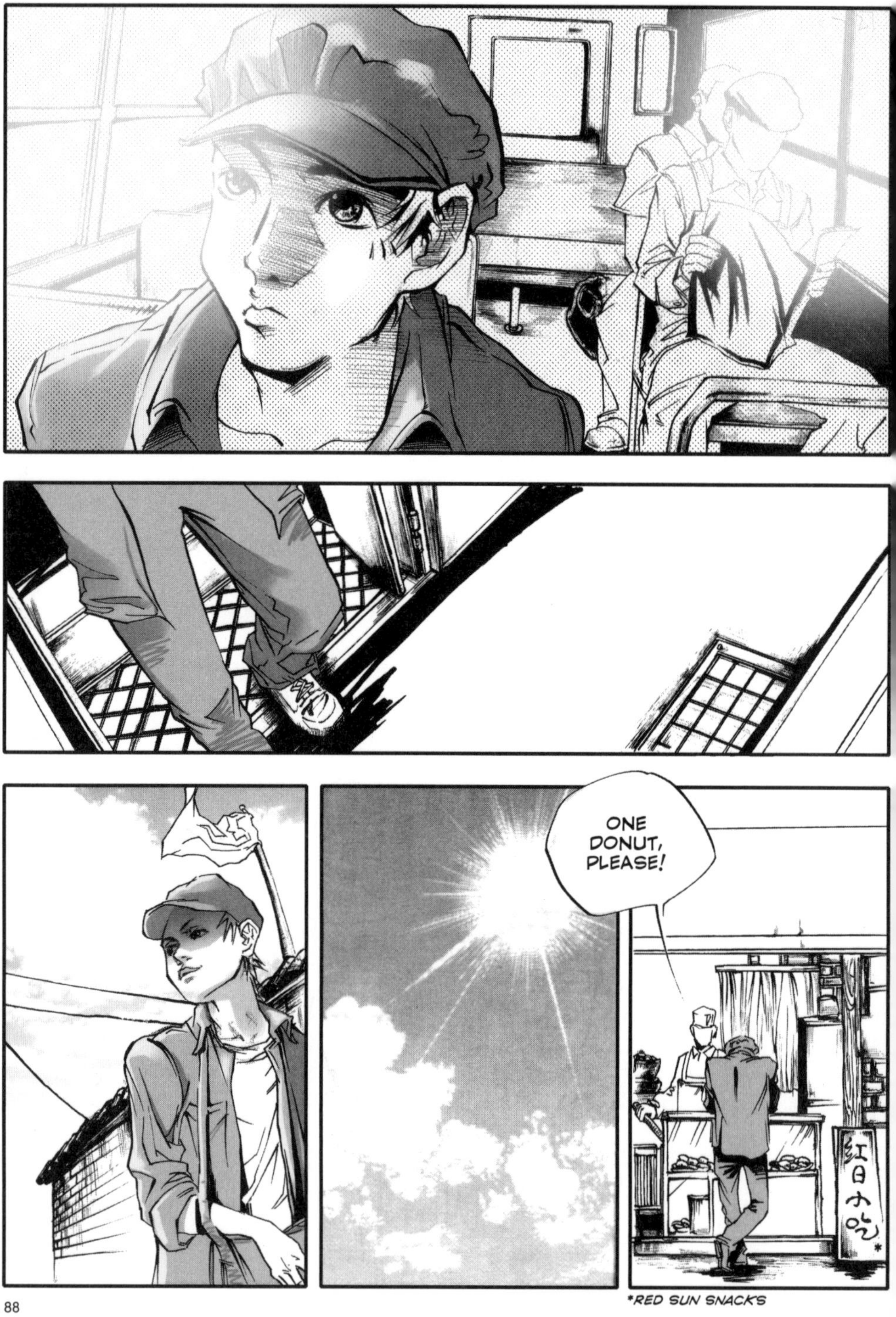
ONE DONUT, PLEASE!

*RED SUN SNACK'S

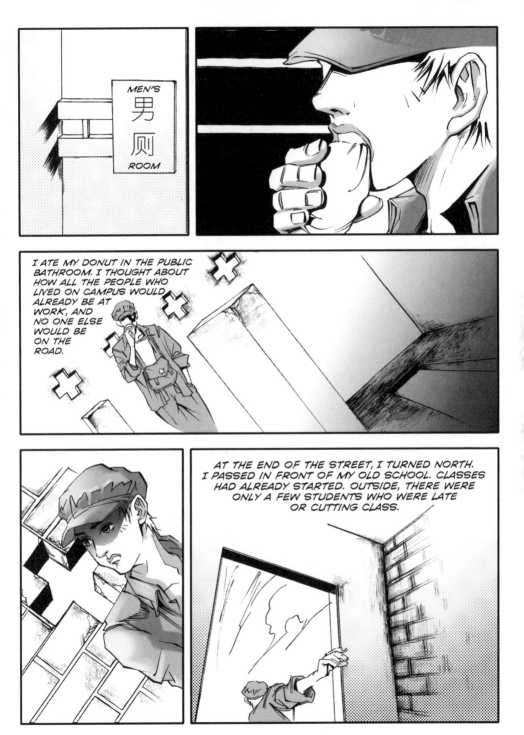

MEN'S
男厕
ROOM

I ATE MY DONUT IN THE PUBLIC BATHROOM. I THOUGHT ABOUT HOW ALL THE PEOPLE WHO LIVED ON CAMPUS WOULD ALREADY BE AT WORK, AND NO ONE ELSE WOULD BE ON THE ROAD.

AT THE END OF THE STREET, I TURNED NORTH. I PASSED IN FRONT OF MY OLD SCHOOL. CLASSES HAD ALREADY STARTED. OUTSIDE, THERE WERE ONLY A FEW STUDENTS WHO WERE LATE OR CUTTING CLASS.

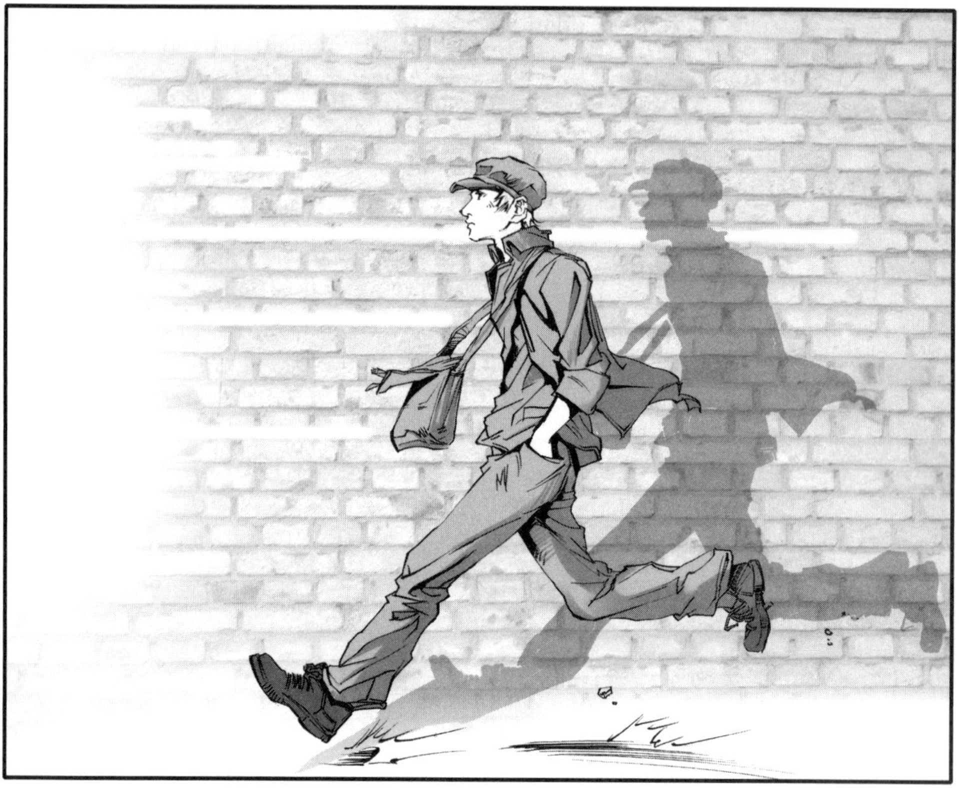
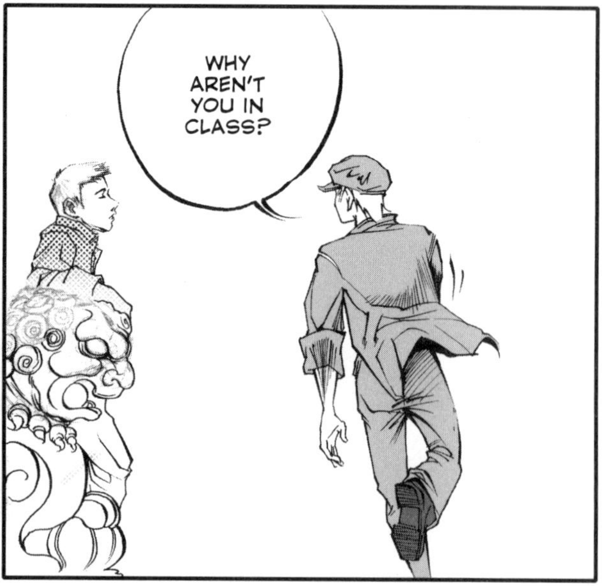
WHY AREN'T YOU IN CLASS?
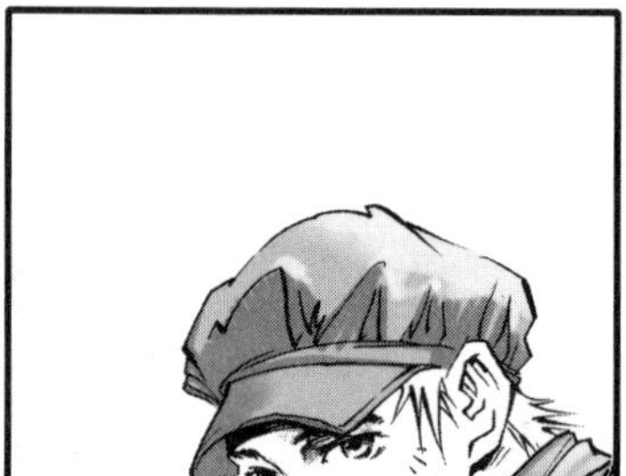
MA XIAO-JUN!

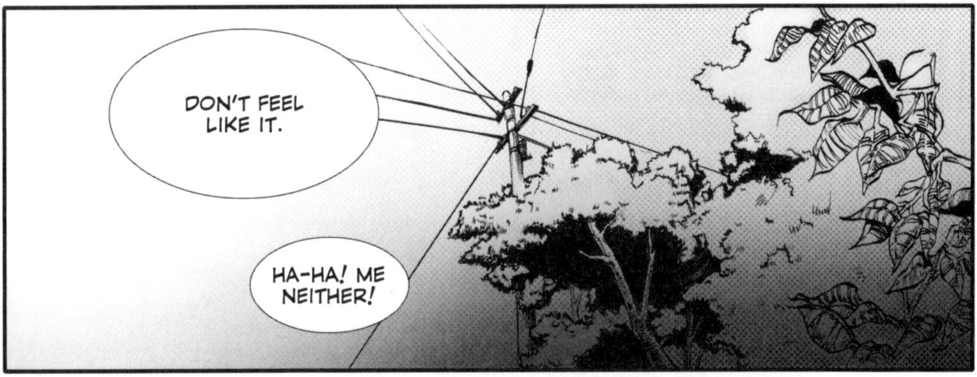
DON'T FEEL LIKE IT.
HA-HA! ME NEITHER!

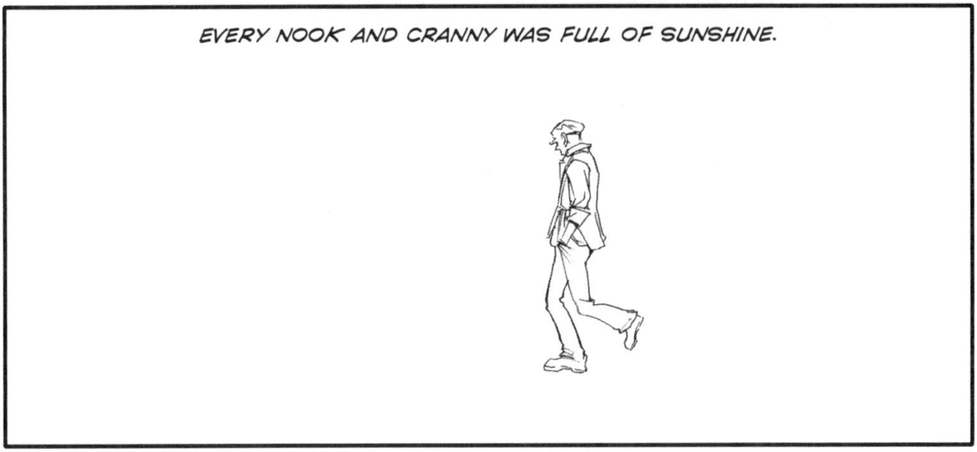
EVERY NOOK AND CRANNY WAS FULL OF SUNSHINE.

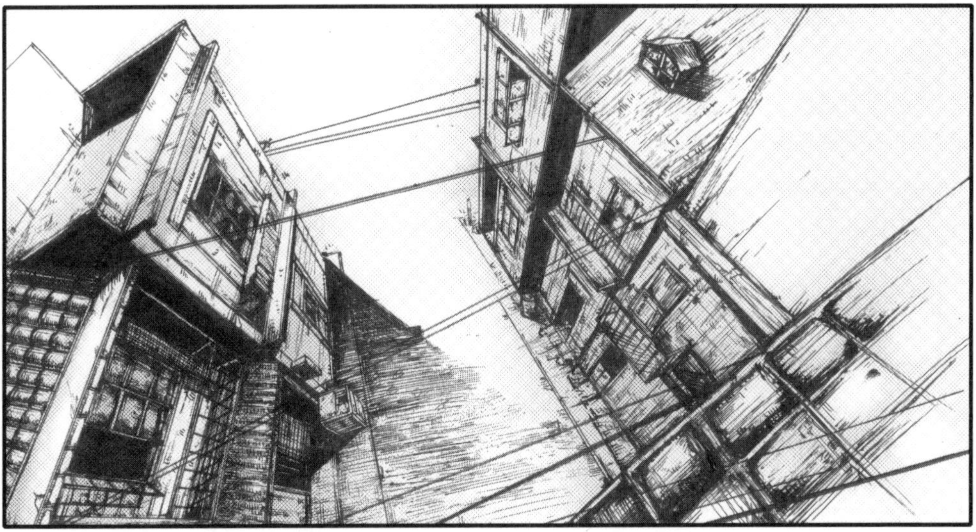

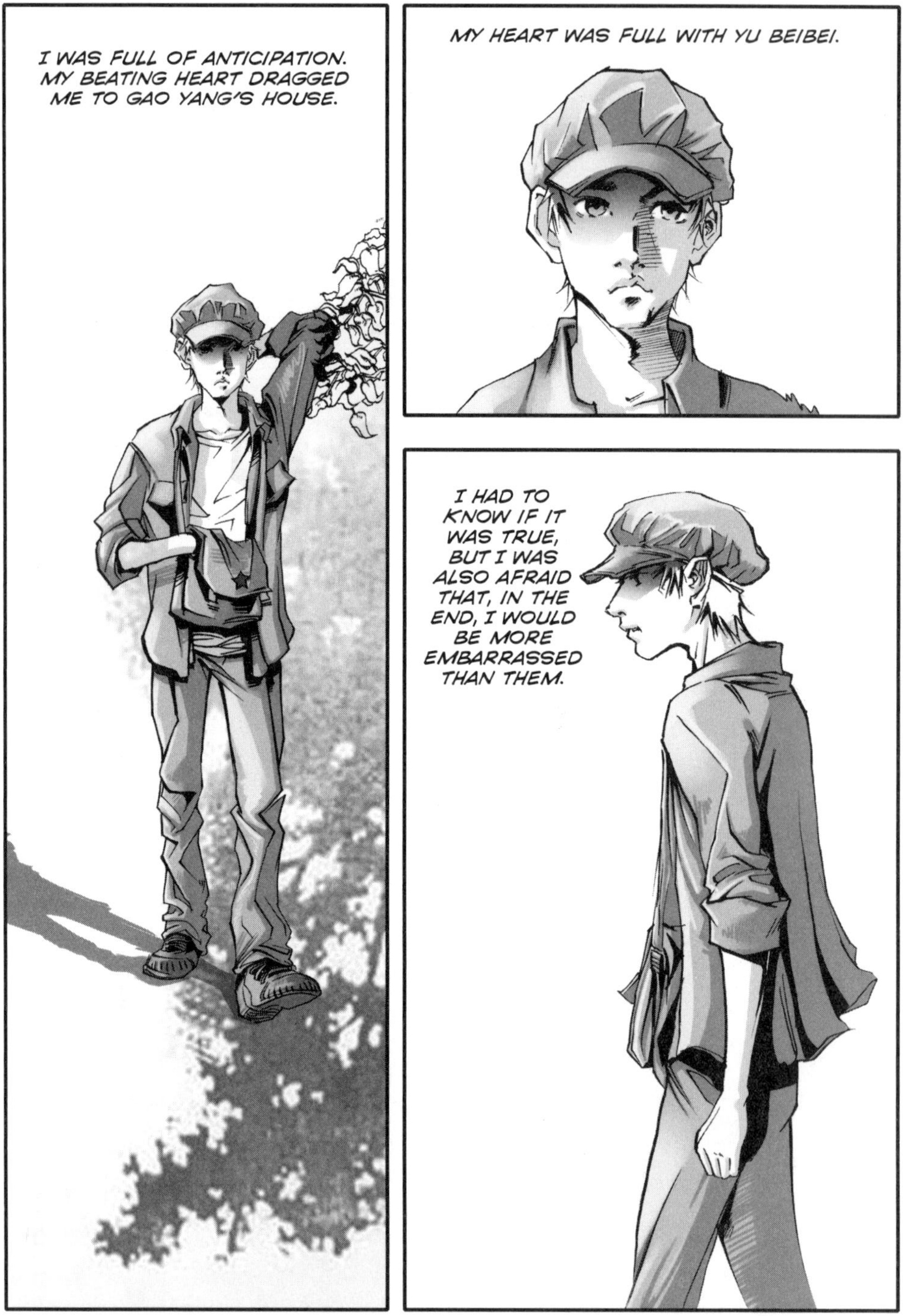
I WAS FULL OF ANTICIPATION. MY BEATING HEART DRAGGED ME TO GAO YANG'S HOUSE.
MY HEART WAS FULL WITH YU BEIBEI.
I HAD TO KNOW IF IT WAS TRUE, BUT I WAS ALSO AFRAID THAT, IN THE END, I WOULD BE MORE EMBARRASSED THAN THEM.

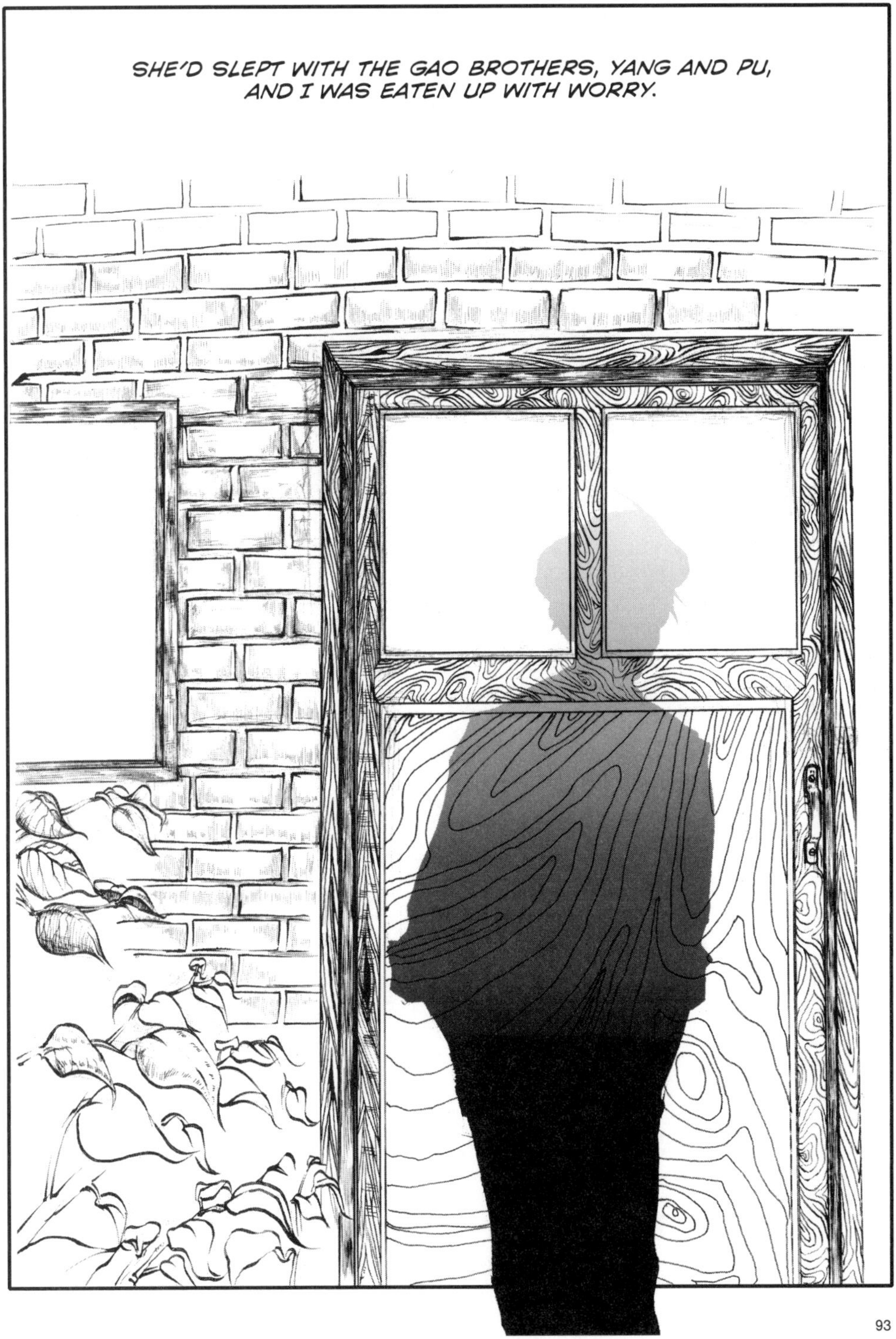
SHE'D SLEPT WITH THE GAO BROTHERS, YANG AND PU, AND I WAS EATEN UP WITH WORRY.

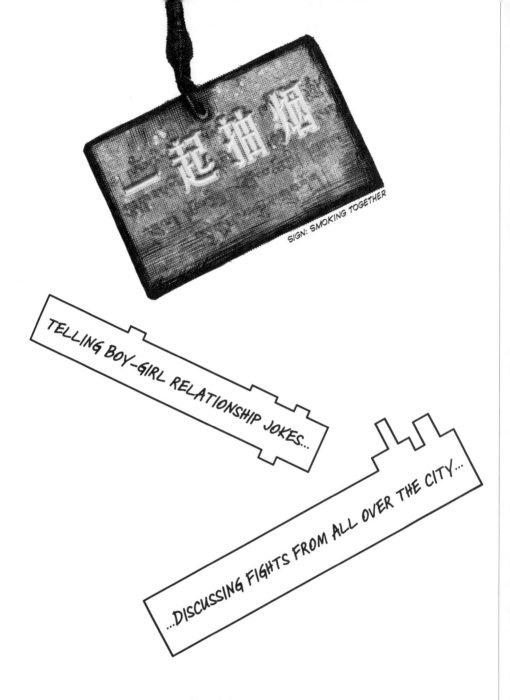

SIGN: SMOKING TOGETHER

TELLING BOY-GIRL RELATIONSHIP JOKES...

...DISCUSSING FIGHTS FROM ALL OVER THE CITY...

4 - Impressions

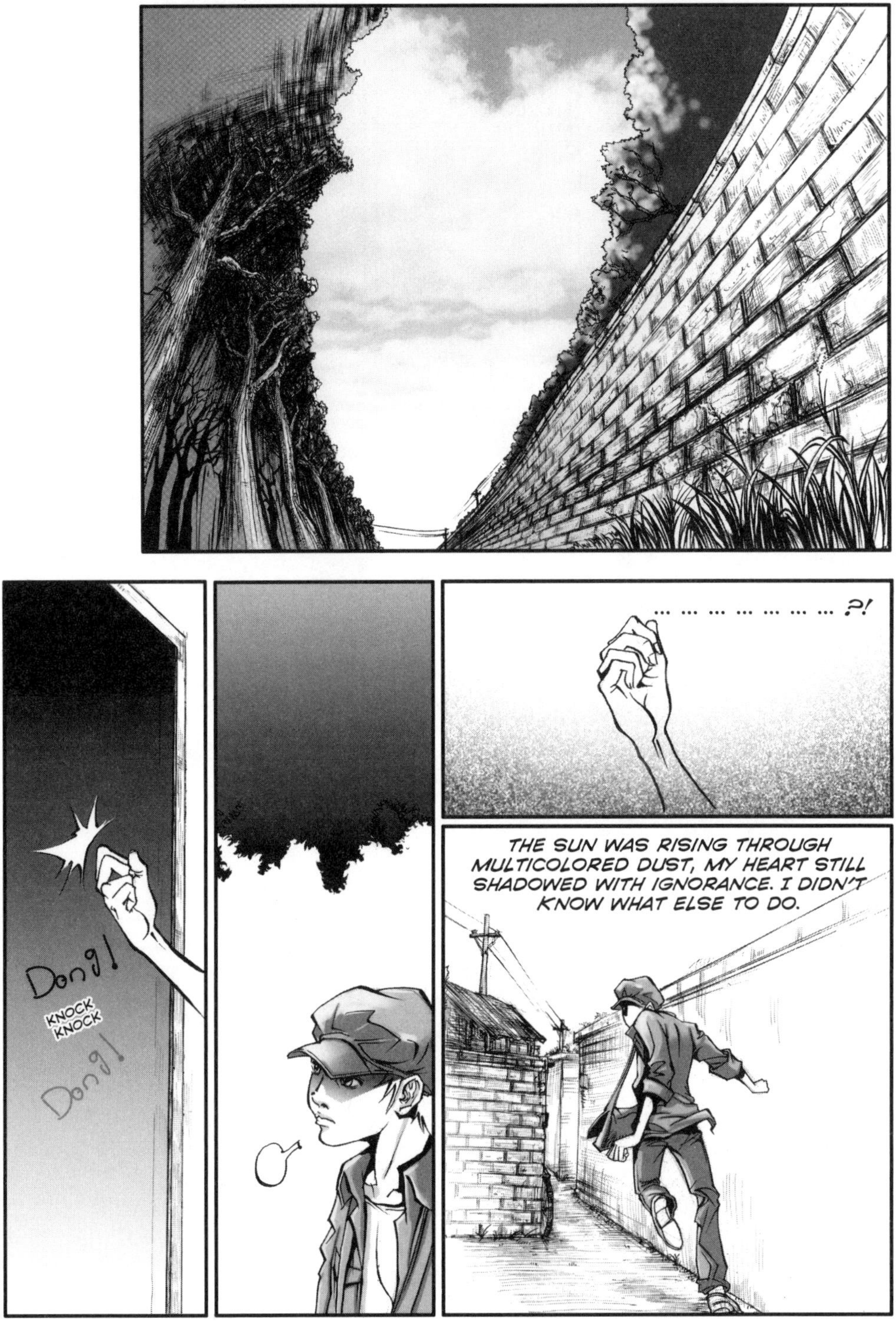
Dong!
KNOCK KNOCK
Dong!
… … … … … … … … ?!
THE SUN WAS RISING THROUGH MULTICOLORED DUST, MY HEART STILL SHADOWED WITH IGNORANCE. I DIDN'T KNOW WHAT ELSE TO DO.

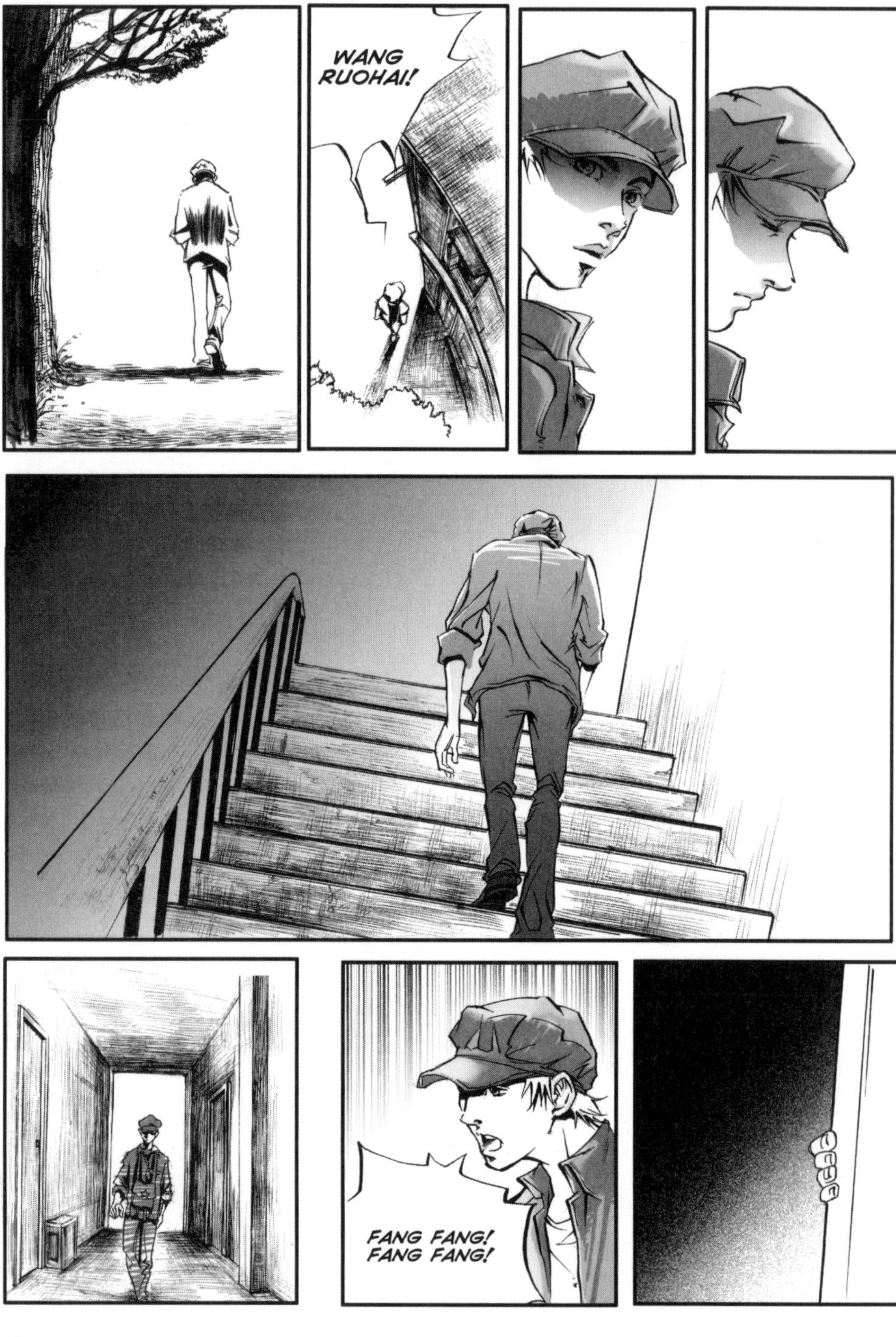
WANG RUOHAI!
FANG FANG! FANG FANG!

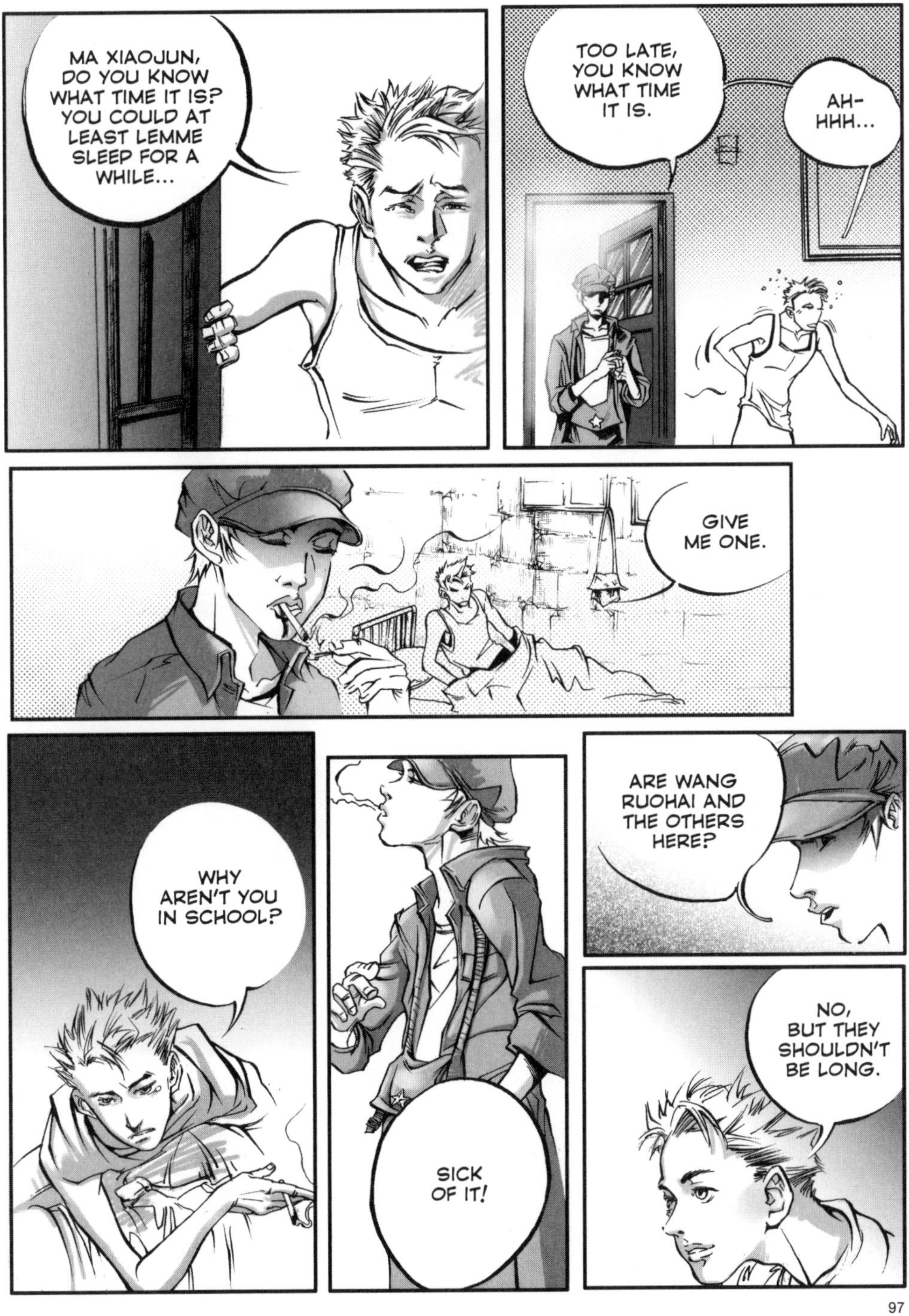
MA XIAOJUN, DO YOU KNOW WHAT TIME IT IS? YOU COULD AT LEAST LEMME SLEEP FOR A WHILE...
TOO LATE, YOU KNOW WHAT TIME IT IS.
AH-HHH...
GIVE ME ONE.
WHY AREN'T YOU IN SCHOOL?
SICK OF IT!
ARE WANG RUOHAI AND THE OTHERS HERE?
NO, BUT THEY SHOULDN'T BE LONG.

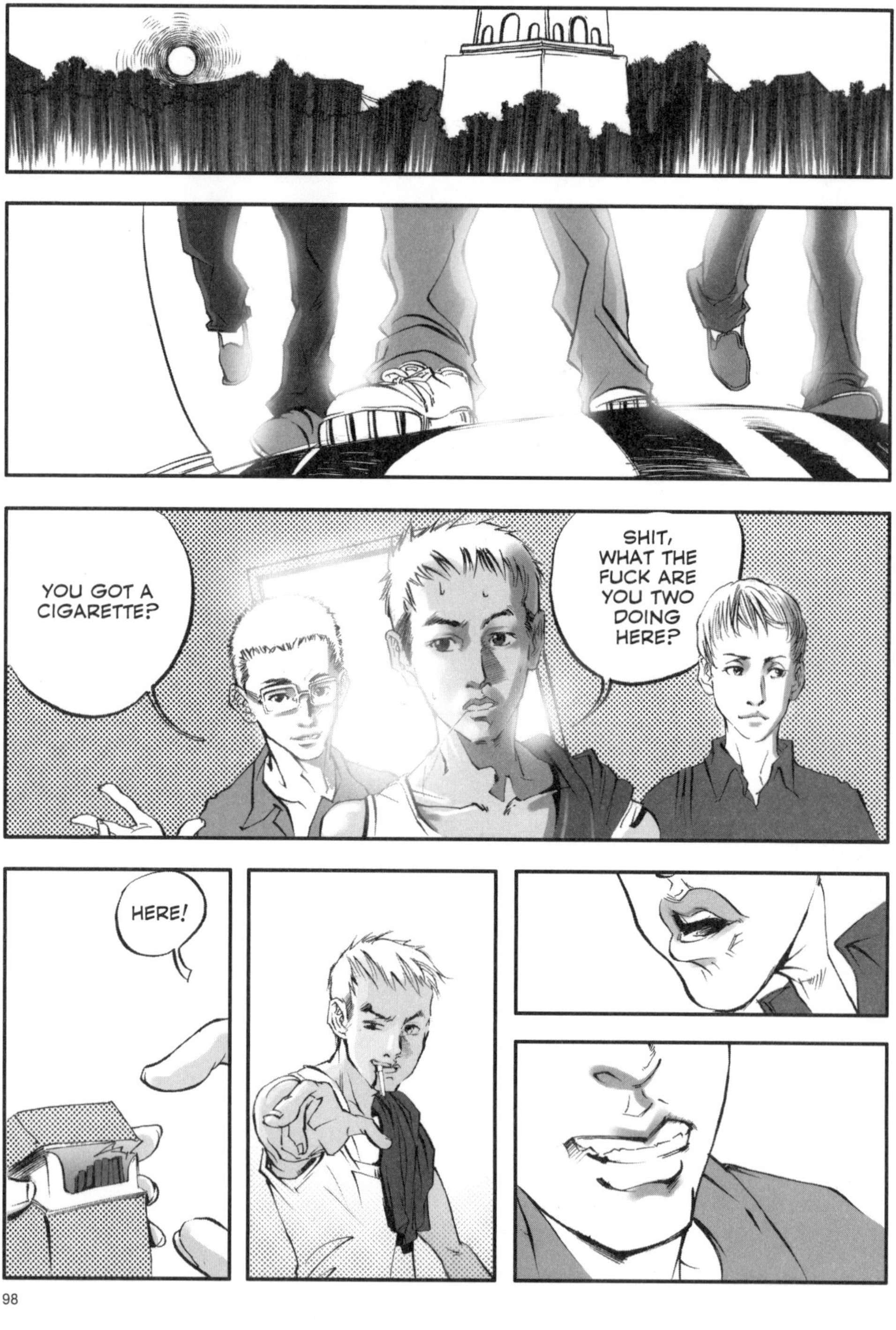
YOU GOT A CIGARETTE?
SHIT, WHAT THE FUCK ARE YOU TWO DOING HERE?
HERE!

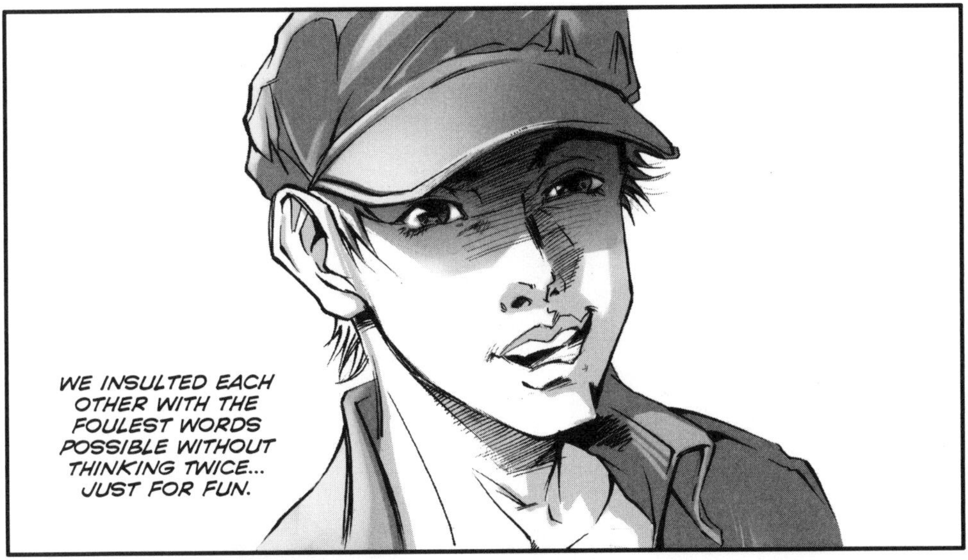
WE INSULTED EACH OTHER WITH THE FOULEST WORDS POSSIBLE WITHOUT THINKING TWICE... JUST FOR FUN.

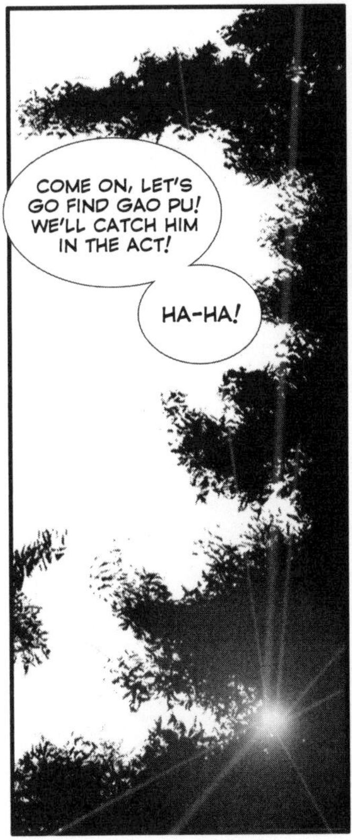
COME ON, LET'S GO FIND GAO PU! WE'LL CATCH HIM IN THE ACT!
HA-HA!

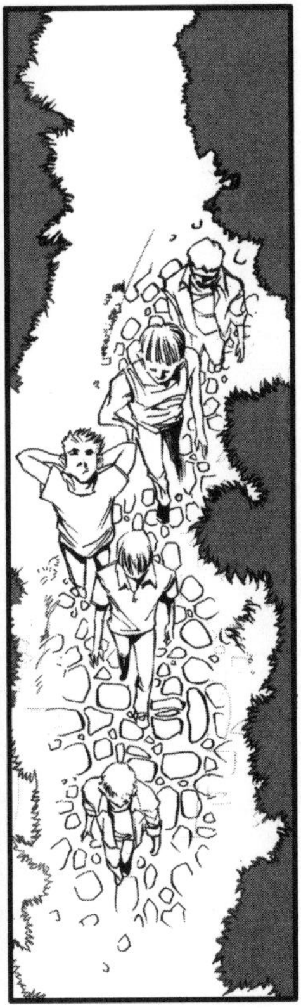

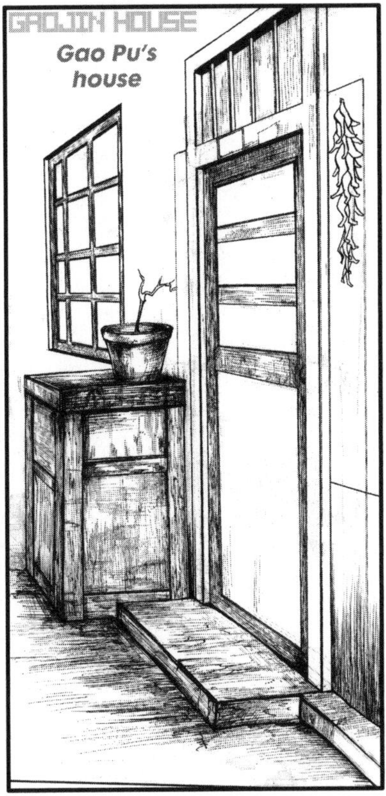
GAOJIN HOUSE
Gao Pu's house

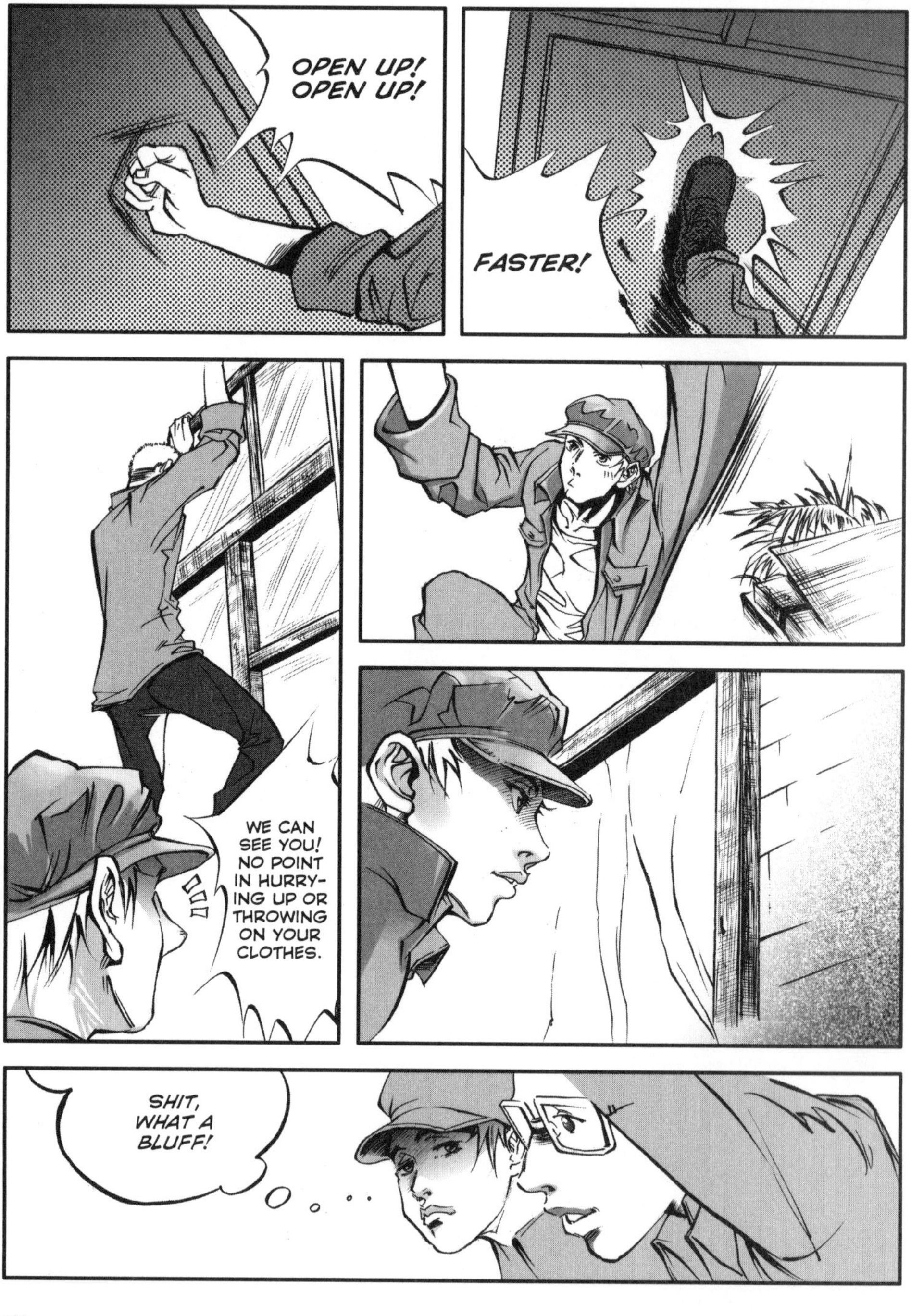
OPEN UP! OPEN UP!
FASTER!
WE CAN SEE YOU! NO POINT IN HURRYING UP OR THROWING ON YOUR CLOTHES.
SHIT, WHAT A BLUFF!

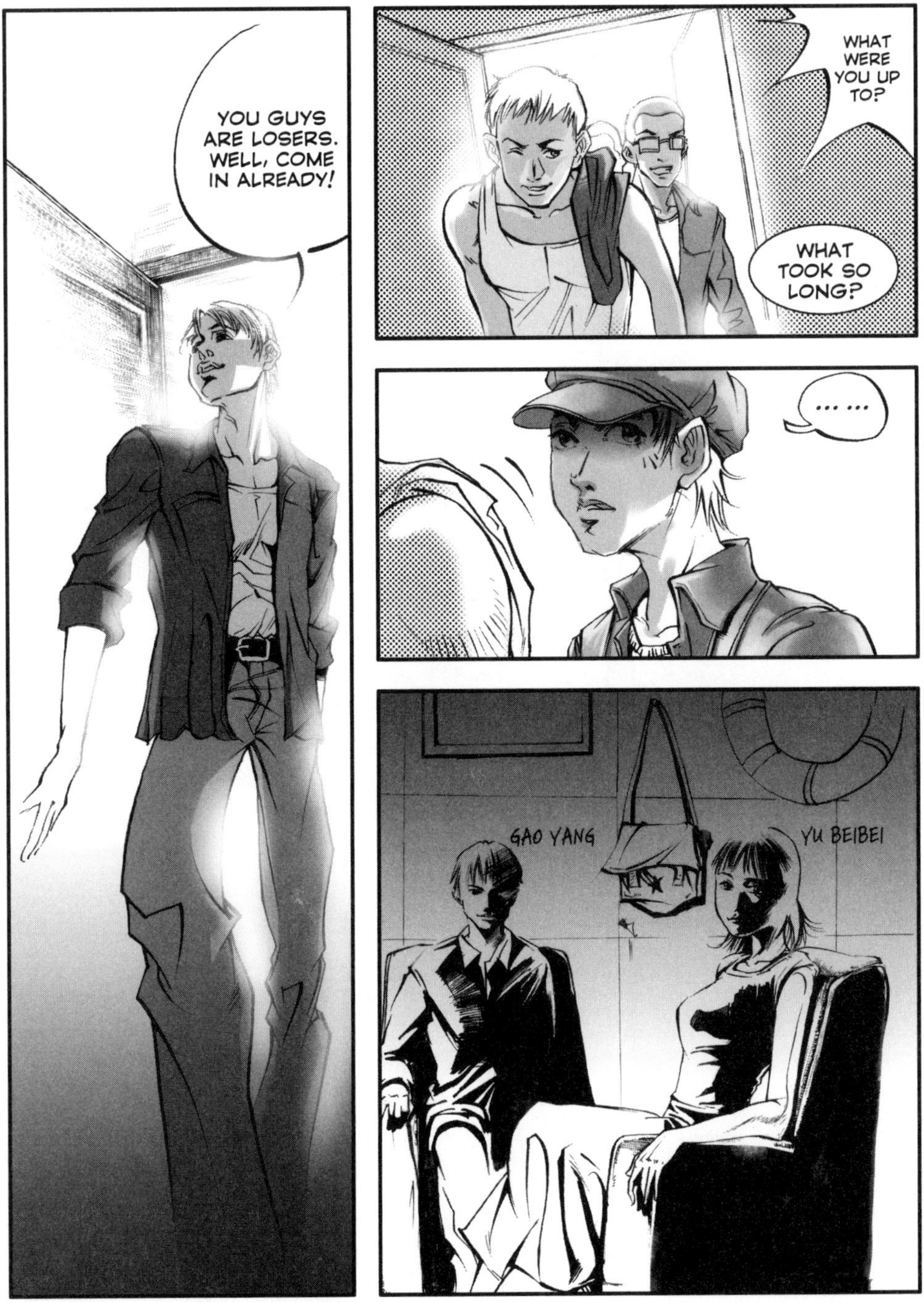
YOU GUYS ARE LOSERS. WELL, COME IN ALREADY!
WHAT WERE YOU UP TO?
WHAT TOOK SO LONG?
... ...
GAO YANG
YU BEIBEI

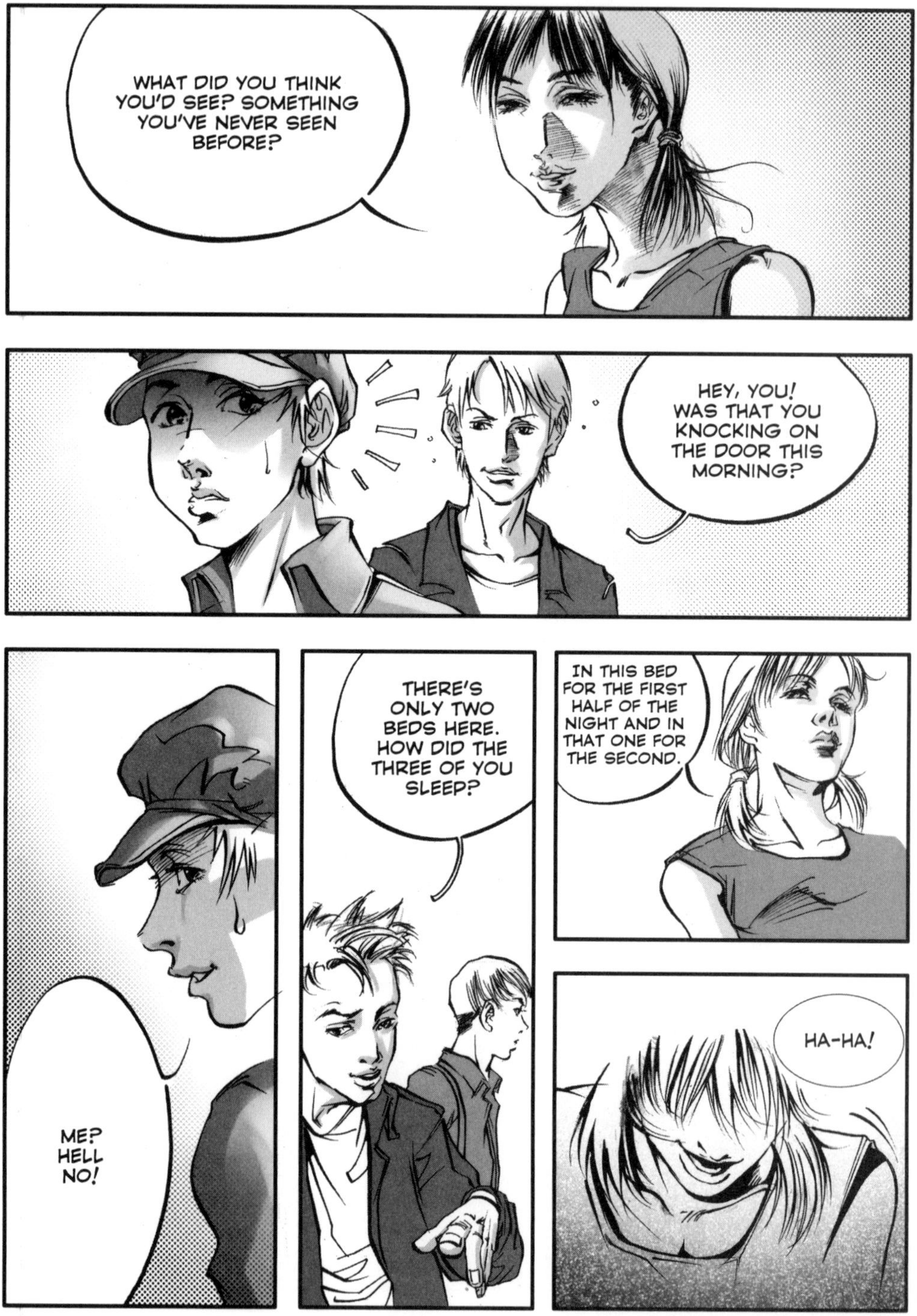
WHAT DID YOU THINK YOU'D SEE? SOMETHING YOU'VE NEVER SEEN BEFORE?
HEY, YOU! WAS THAT YOU KNOCKING ON THE DOOR THIS MORNING?
ME? HELL NO!
THERE'S ONLY TWO BEDS HERE. HOW DID THE THREE OF YOU SLEEP?
IN THIS BED FOR THE FIRST HALF OF THE NIGHT AND IN THAT ONE FOR THE SECOND.
HA-HA!

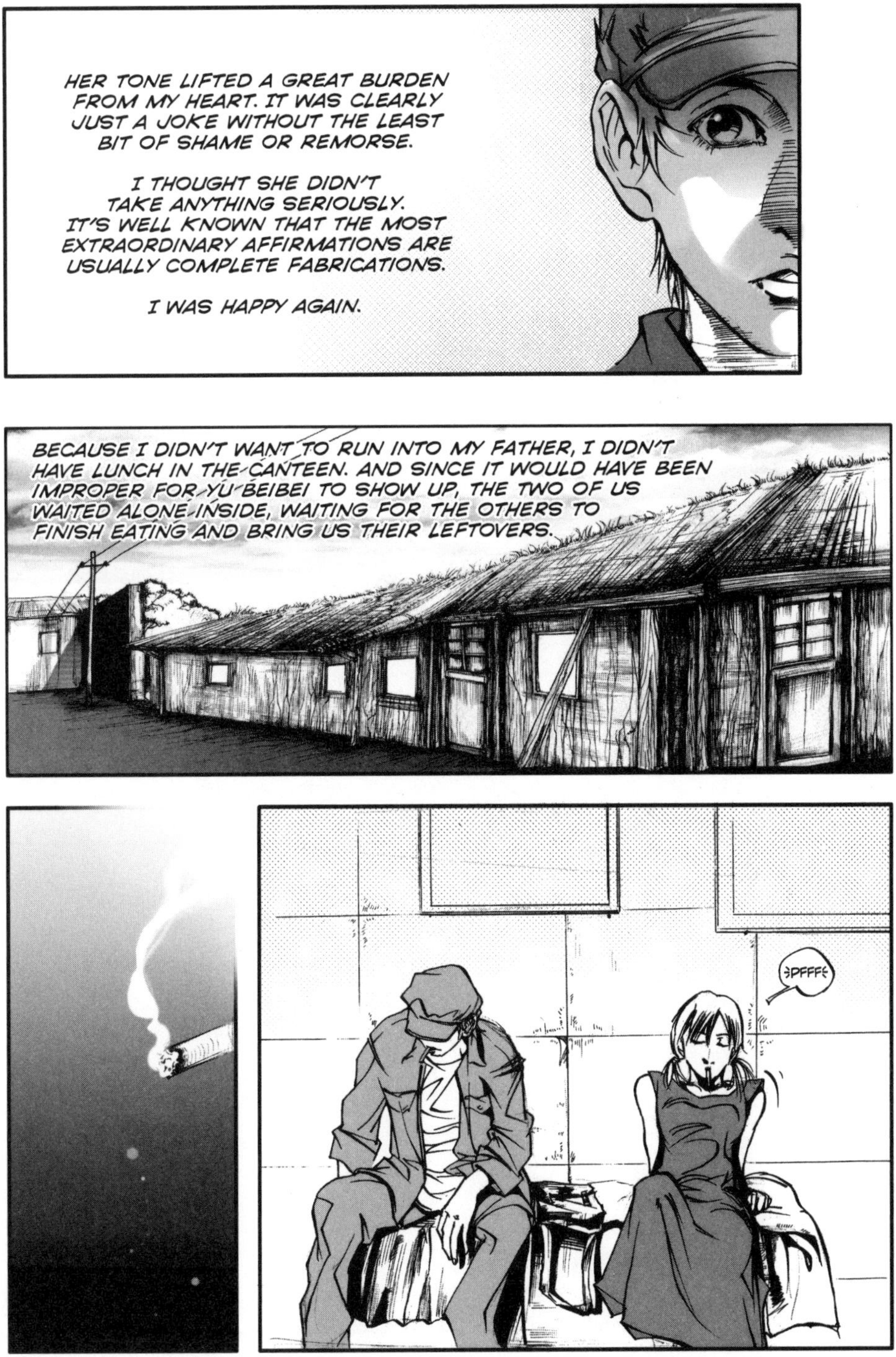
HER TONE LIFTED A GREAT BURDEN FROM MY HEART. IT WAS CLEARLY JUST A JOKE WITHOUT THE LEAST BIT OF SHAME OR REMORSE.
I THOUGHT SHE DIDN'T TAKE ANYTHING SERIOUSLY. IT'S WELL KNOWN THAT THE MOST EXTRAORDINARY AFFIRMATIONS ARE USUALLY COMPLETE FABRICATIONS.
I WAS HAPPY AGAIN.
BECAUSE I DIDN'T WANT TO RUN INTO MY FATHER, I DIDN'T HAVE LUNCH IN THE CANTEEN. AND SINCE IT WOULD HAVE BEEN IMPROPER FOR YU BEIBEI TO SHOW UP, THE TWO OF US WAITED ALONE INSIDE, WAITING FOR THE OTHERS TO FINISH EATING AND BRING US THEIR LEFTOVERS.
PFFF

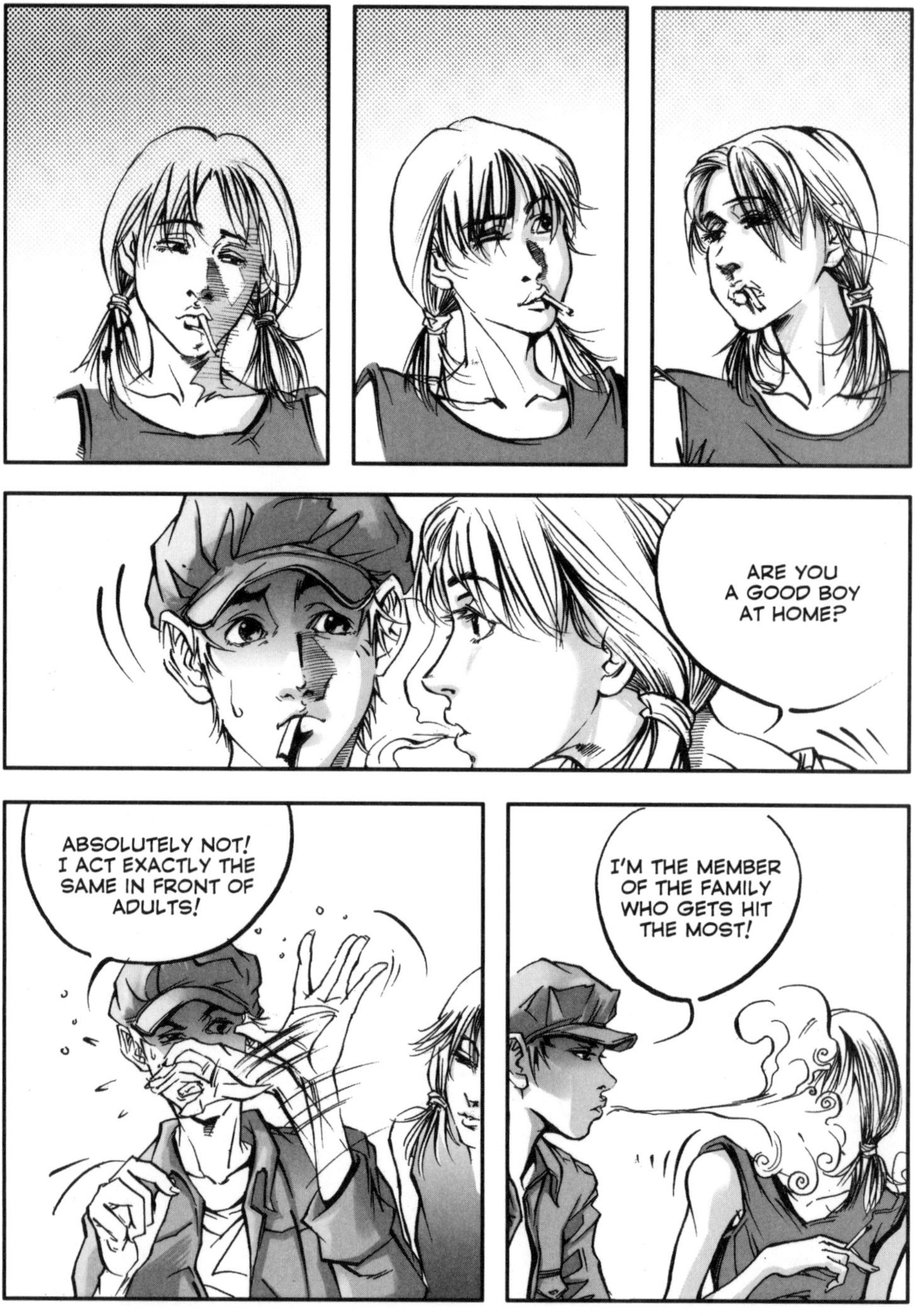

ARE YOU A GOOD BOY AT HOME?
ABSOLUTELY NOT! I ACT EXACTLY THE SAME IN FRONT OF ADULTS!
I'M THE MEMBER OF THE FAMILY WHO GETS HIT THE MOST!

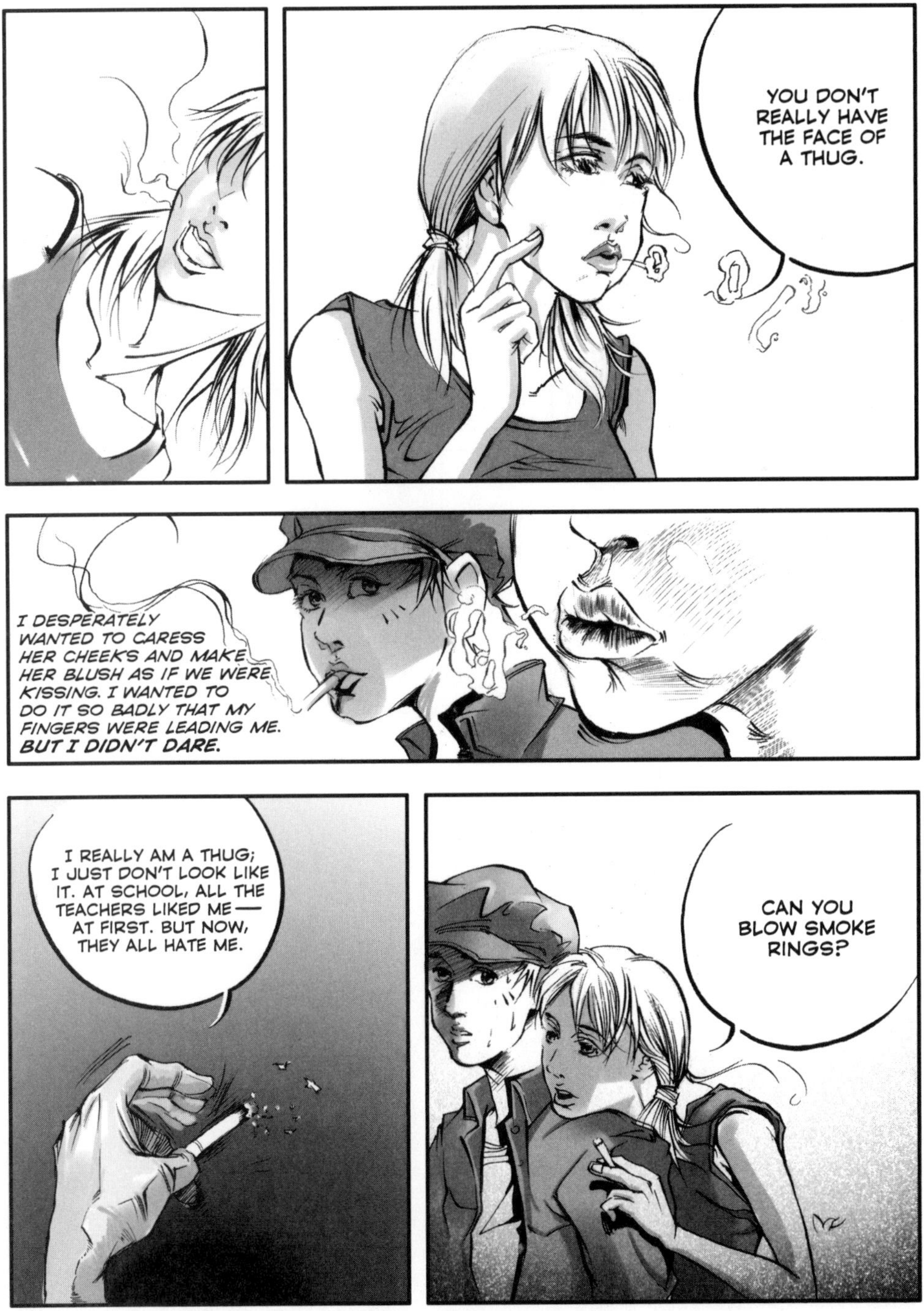
YOU DON'T REALLY HAVE THE FACE OF A THUG.
I DESPERATELY WANTED TO CARESS HER CHEEKS AND MAKE HER BLUSH AS IF WE WERE KISSING. I WANTED TO DO IT SO BADLY THAT MY FINGERS WERE LEADING ME. BUT I DIDN'T DARE.
I REALLY AM A THUG; I JUST DON'T LOOK LIKE IT. AT SCHOOL, ALL THE TEACHERS LIKED ME— AT FIRST. BUT NOW, THEY ALL HATE ME.
CAN YOU BLOW SMOKE RINGS?

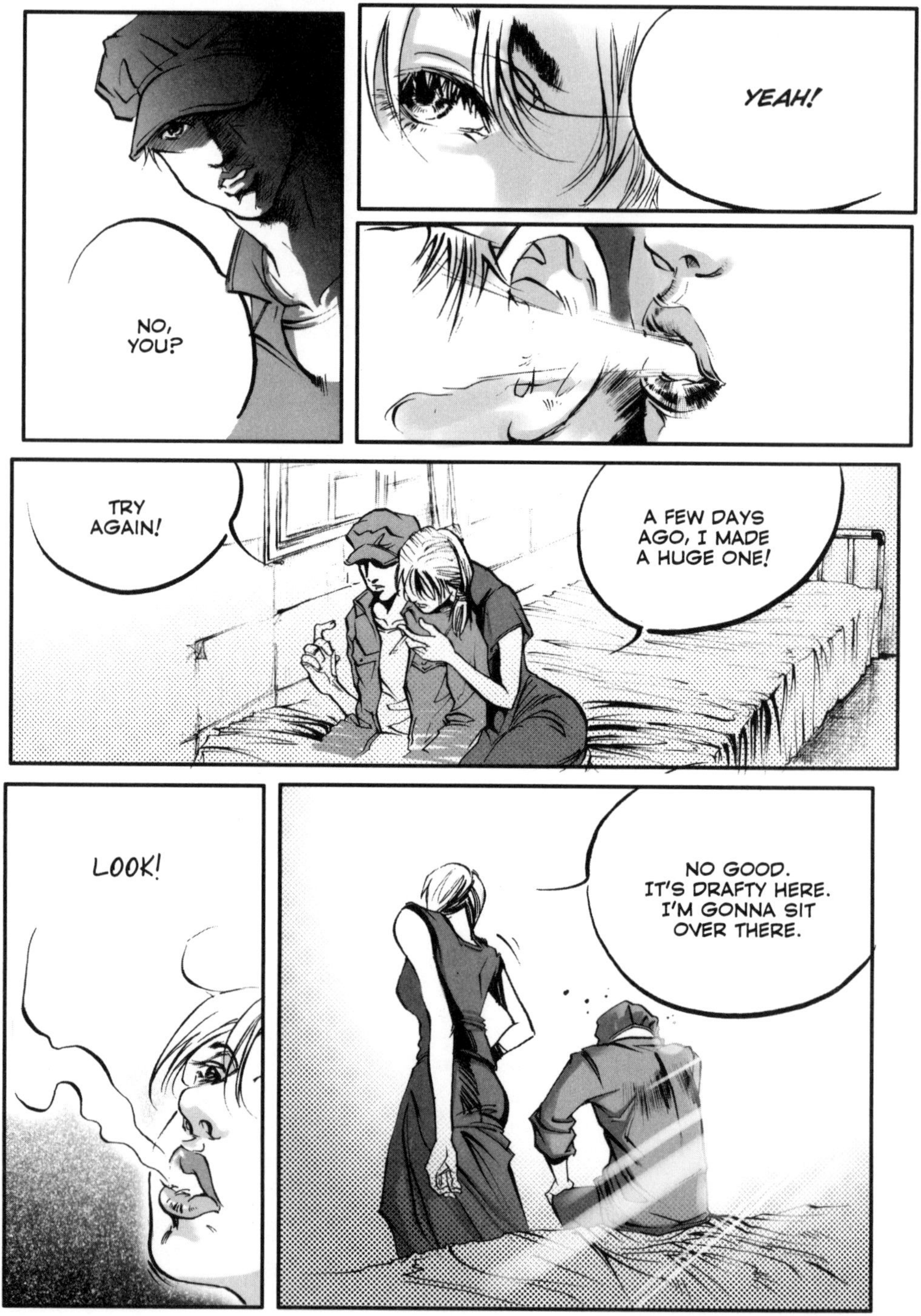
NO, YOU?
YEAH!
TRY AGAIN!
A FEW DAYS AGO, I MADE A HUGE ONE!
LOOK!
NO GOOD. IT'S DRAFTY HERE. I'M GONNA SIT OVER THERE.

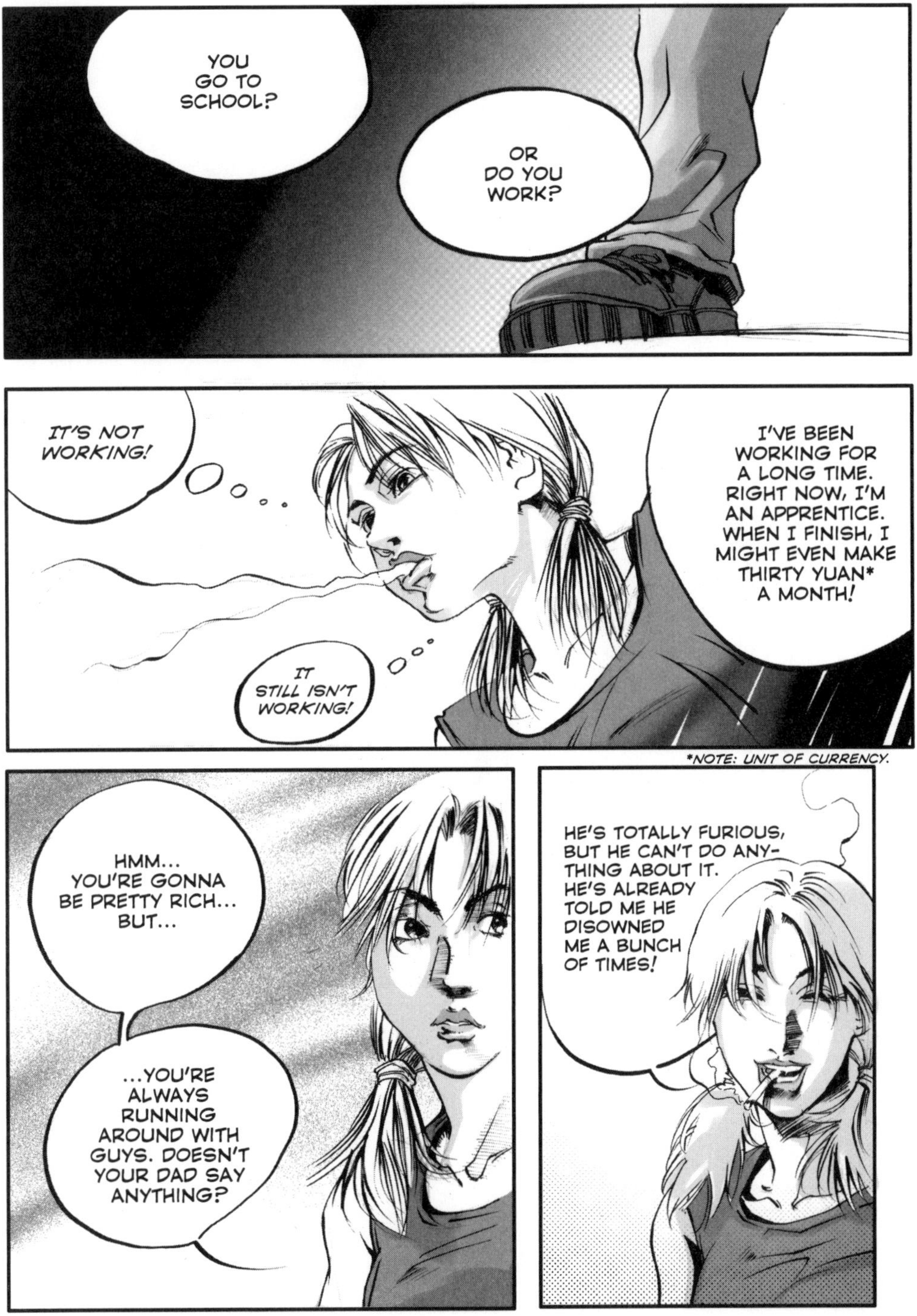
YOU GO TO SCHOOL?
OR DO YOU WORK?
IT'S NOT WORKING!
IT STILL ISN'T WORKING!
I'VE BEEN WORKING FOR A LONG TIME. RIGHT NOW, I'M AN APPRENTICE. WHEN I FINISH, I MIGHT EVEN MAKE THIRTY YUAN* A MONTH!
*NOTE: UNIT OF CURRENCY.
HMM... YOU'RE GONNA BE PRETTY RICH... BUT...
...YOU'RE ALWAYS RUNNING AROUND WITH GUYS. DOESN'T YOUR DAD SAY ANYTHING?
HE'S TOTALLY FURIOUS, BUT HE CAN'T DO ANYTHING ABOUT IT. HE'S ALREADY TOLD ME HE DISOWNED ME A BUNCH OF TIMES!

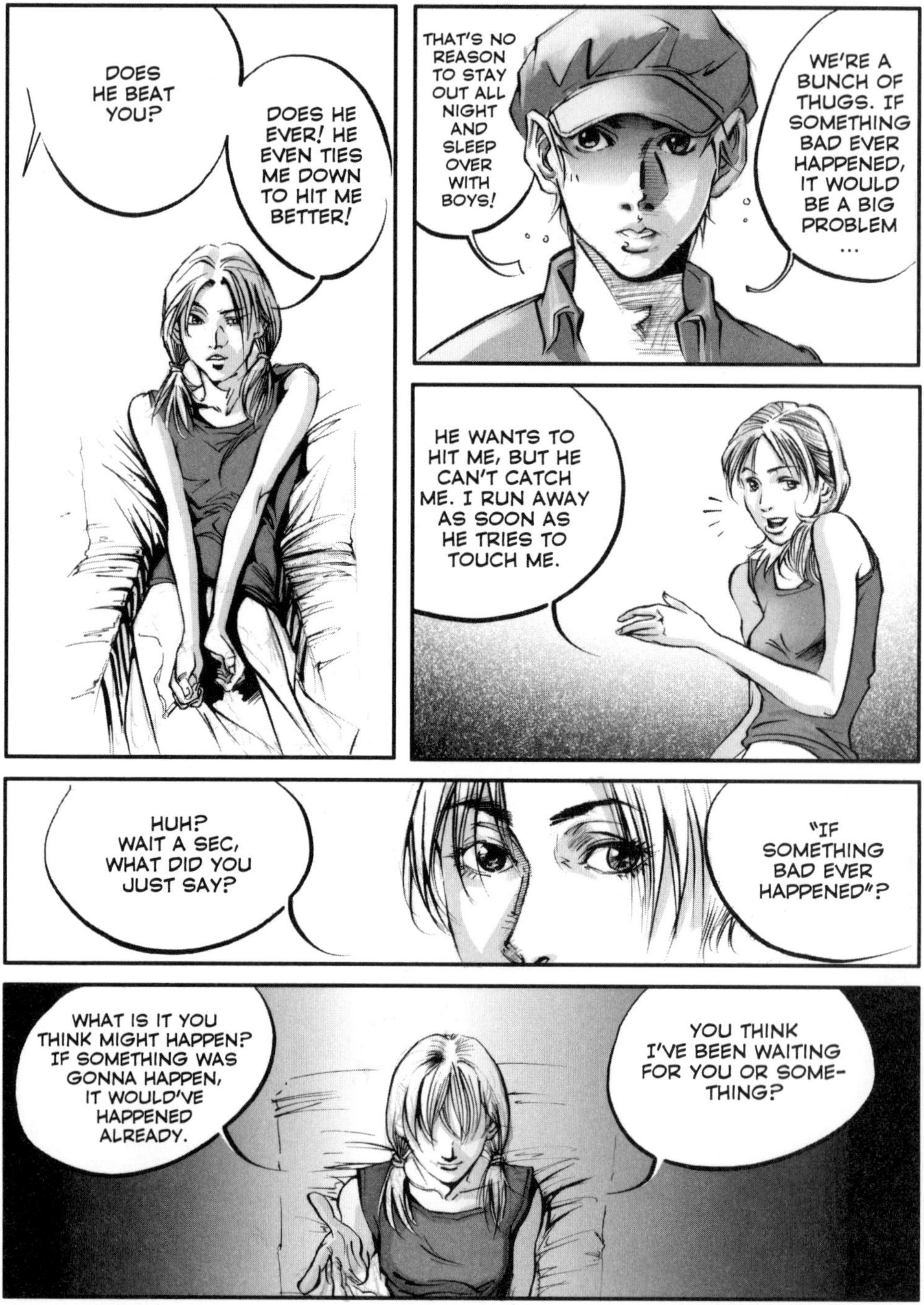
DOES HE BEAT YOU?
DOES HE EVER! HE EVEN TIES ME DOWN TO HIT ME BETTER!
THAT'S NO REASON TO STAY OUT ALL NIGHT AND SLEEP OVER WITH BOYS!
WE'RE A BUNCH OF THUGS. IF SOMETHING BAD EVER HAPPENED, IT WOULD BE A BIG PROBLEM ...
HE WANTS TO HIT ME, BUT HE CAN'T CATCH ME. I RUN AWAY AS SOON AS HE TRIES TO TOUCH ME.
HUH? WAIT A SEC, WHAT DID YOU JUST SAY?
"IF SOMETHING BAD EVER HAPPENED"?
WHAT IS IT YOU THINK MIGHT HAPPEN? IF SOMETHING WAS GONNA HAPPEN, IT WOULD'VE HAPPENED ALREADY.
YOU THINK I'VE BEEN WAITING FOR YOU OR SOME-THING?

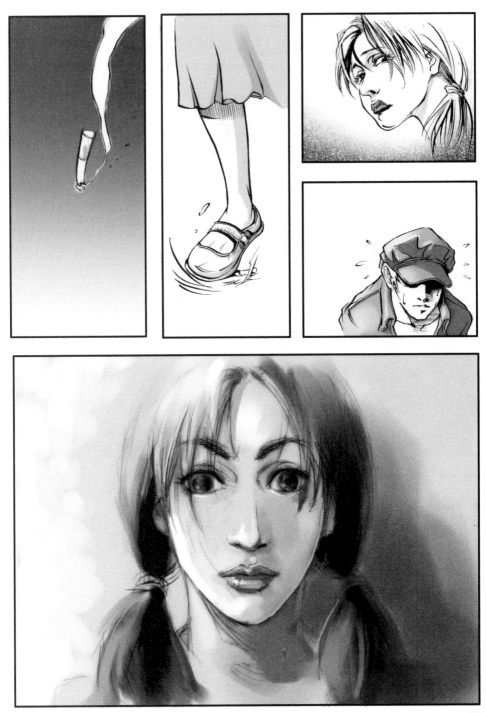

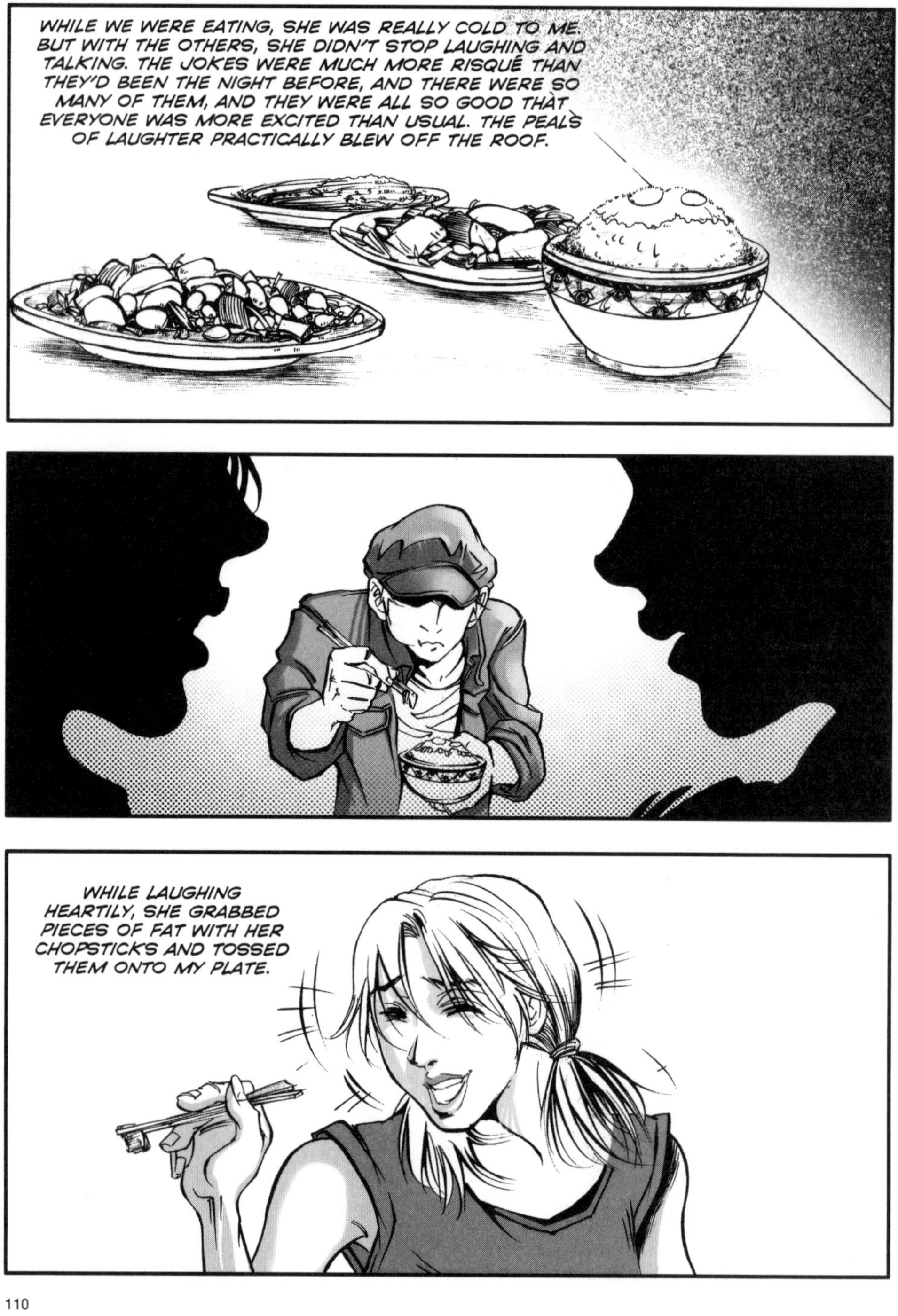
WHILE WE WERE EATING, SHE WAS REALLY COLD TO ME. BUT WITH THE OTHERS, SHE DIDN'T STOP LAUGHING AND TALKING. THE JOKES WERE MUCH MORE RISQUÉ THAN THEY'D BEEN THE NIGHT BEFORE, AND THERE WERE SO MANY OF THEM, AND THEY WERE ALL SO GOOD THAT EVERYONE WAS MORE EXCITED THAN USUAL. THE PEALS OF LAUGHTER PRACTICALLY BLEW OFF THE ROOF.
WHILE LAUGHING HEARTILY, SHE GRABBED PIECES OF FAT WITH HER CHOPSTICKS AND TOSSED THEM ONTO MY PLATE.

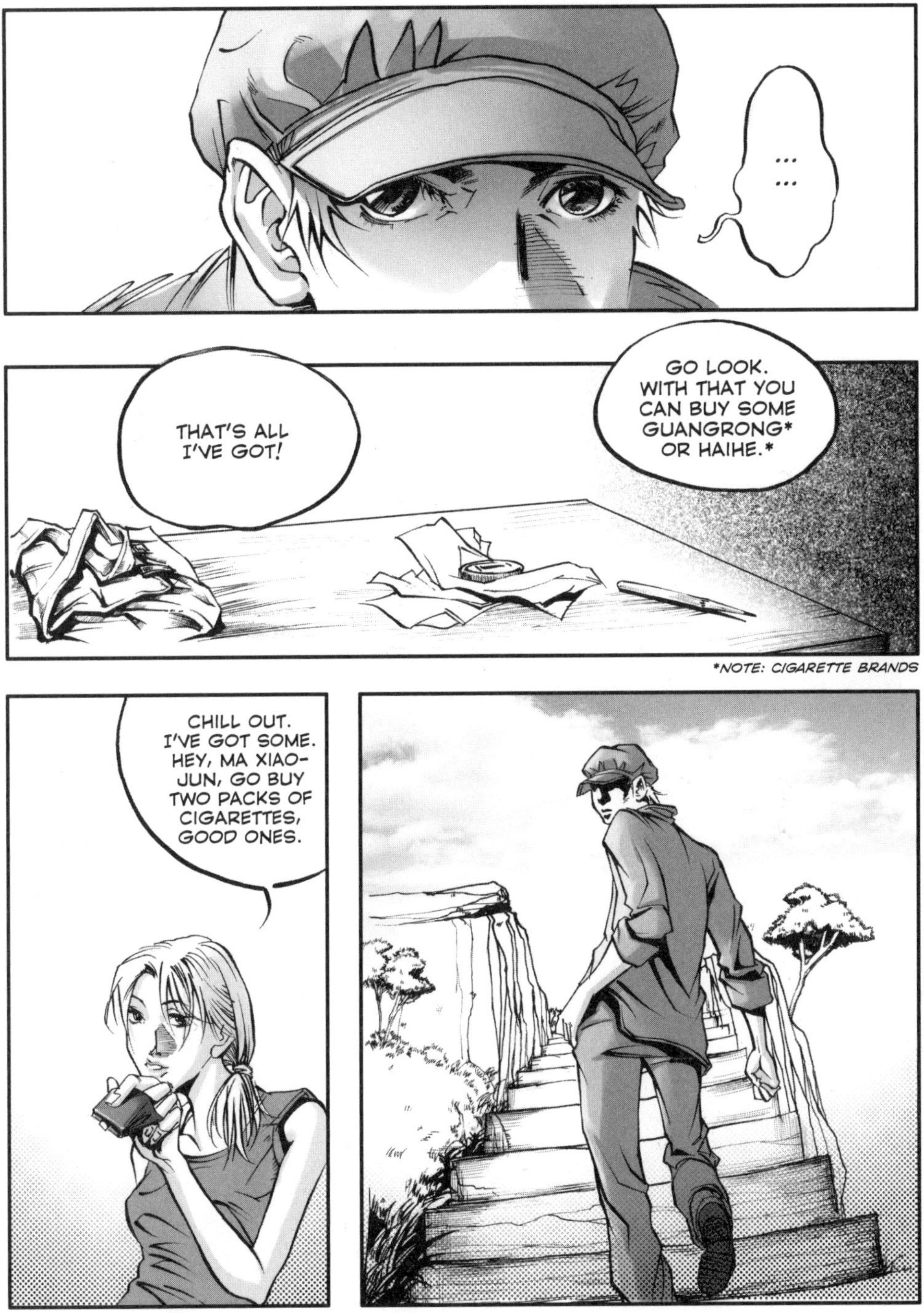
...
...
THAT'S ALL I'VE GOT!
GO LOOK. WITH THAT YOU CAN BUY SOME GUANGRONG* OR HAIHE.*
*NOTE: CIGARETTE BRANDS
CHILL OUT. I'VE GOT SOME. HEY, MA XIAO-JUN, GO BUY TWO PACKS OF CIGARETTES, GOOD ONES.

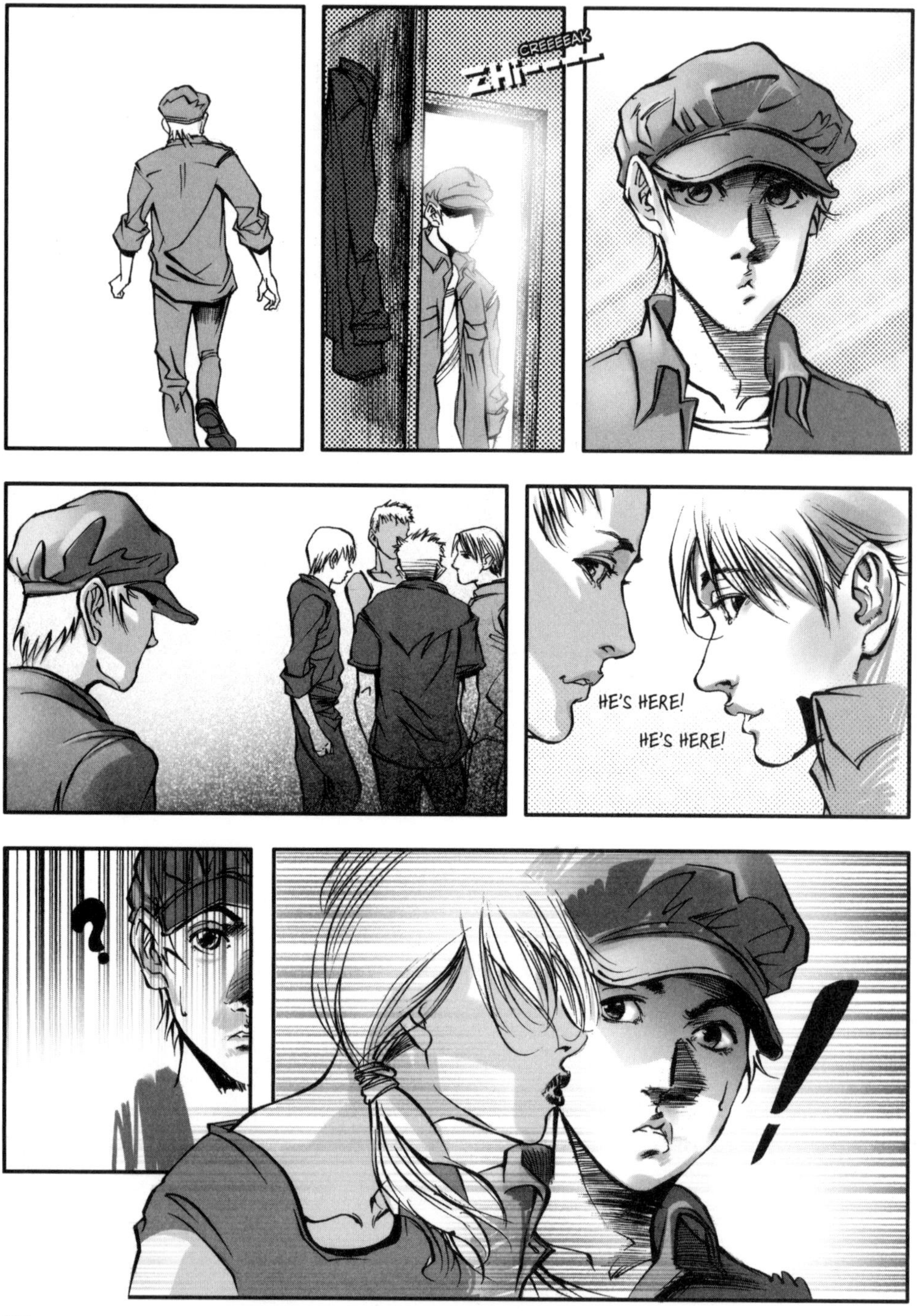
CREEEEAK
ZHI-----
HE'S HERE!
HE'S HERE!
?
!

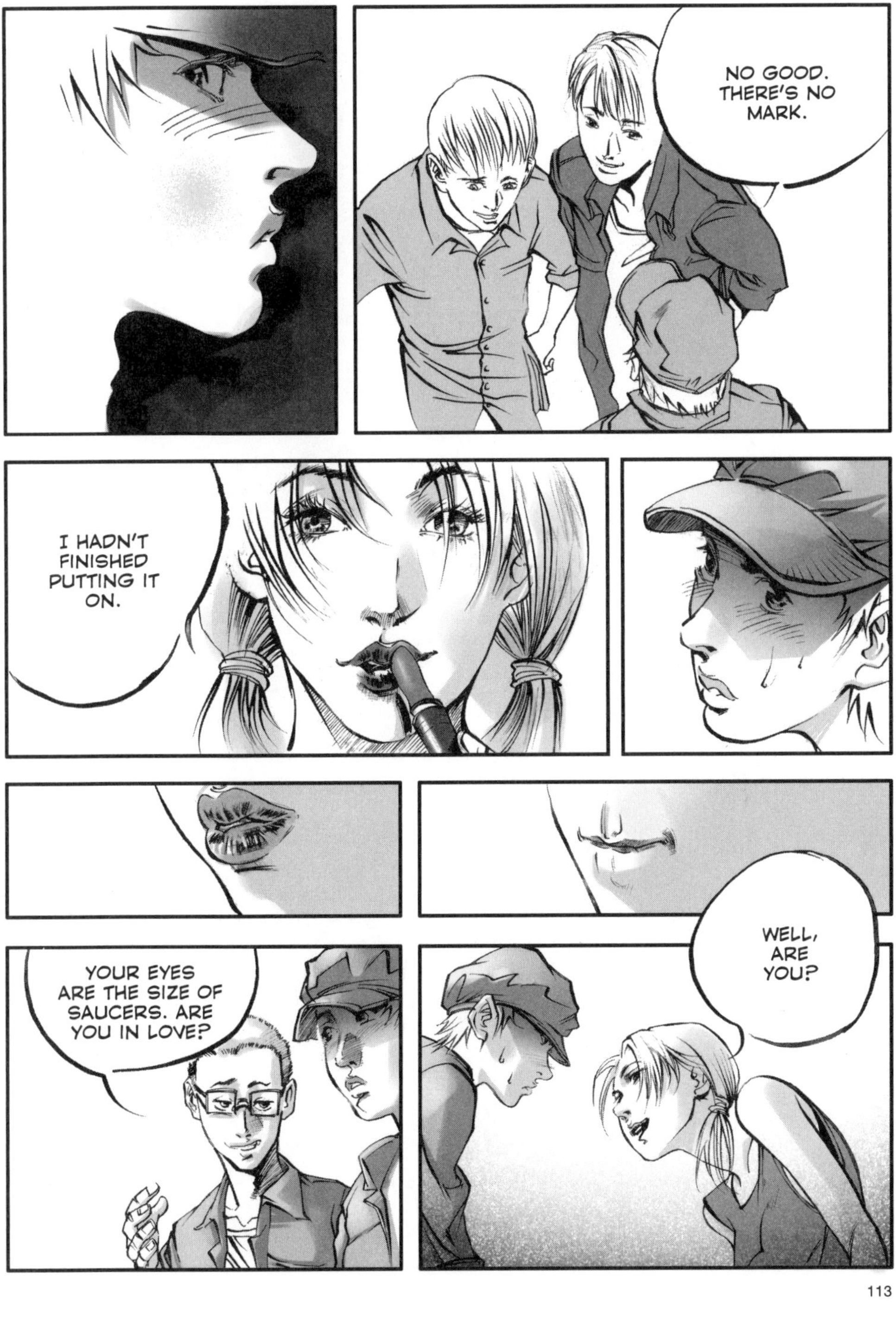
NO GOOD. THERE'S NO MARK.
I HADN'T FINISHED PUTTING IT ON.
YOUR EYES ARE THE SIZE OF SAUCERS. ARE YOU IN LOVE?
WELL, ARE YOU?

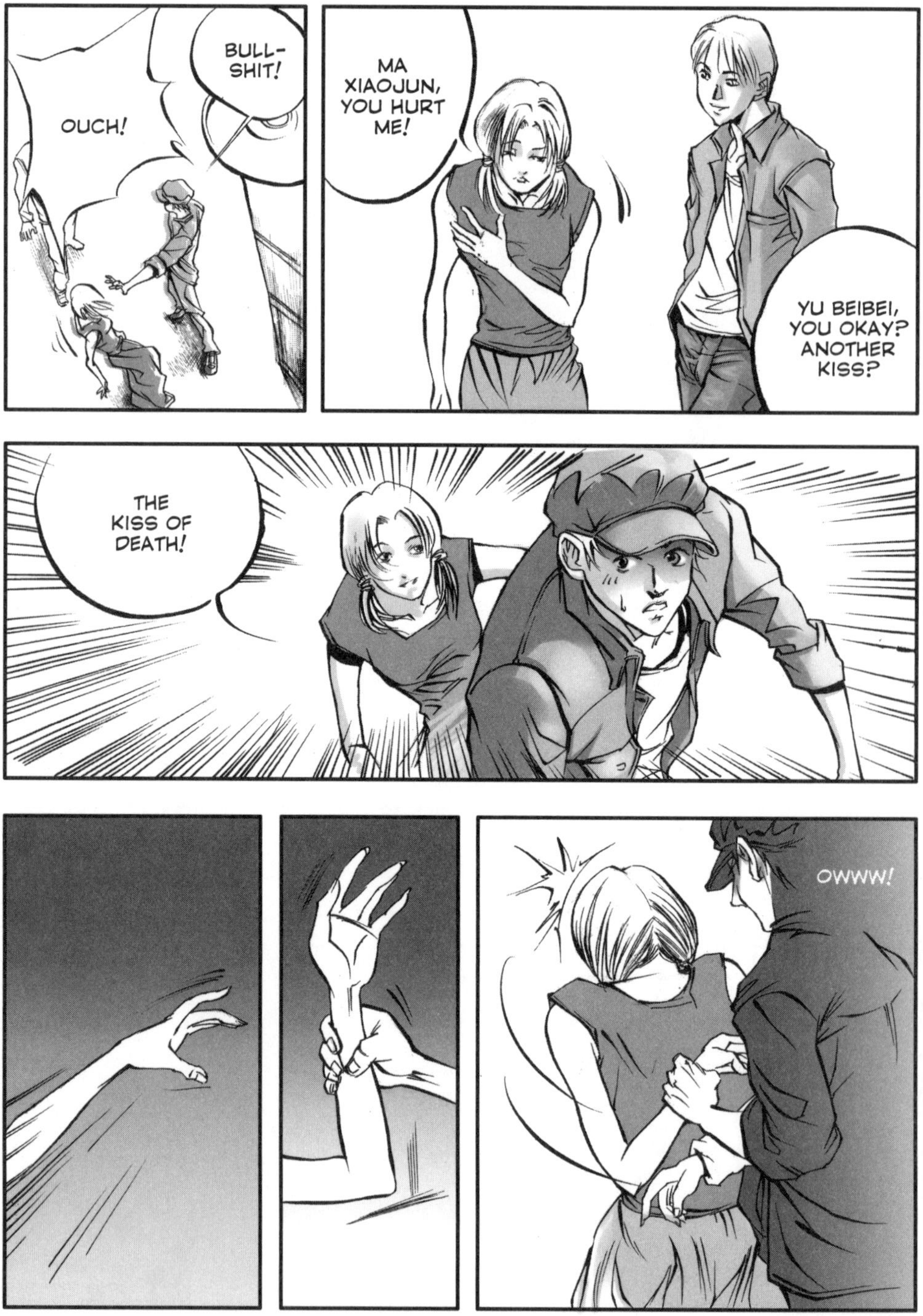
OUCH!
BULL-SHIT!
MA XIAOJUN, YOU HURT ME!
YU BEIBEI, YOU OKAY? ANOTHER KISS?
THE KISS OF DEATH!
OWWW!

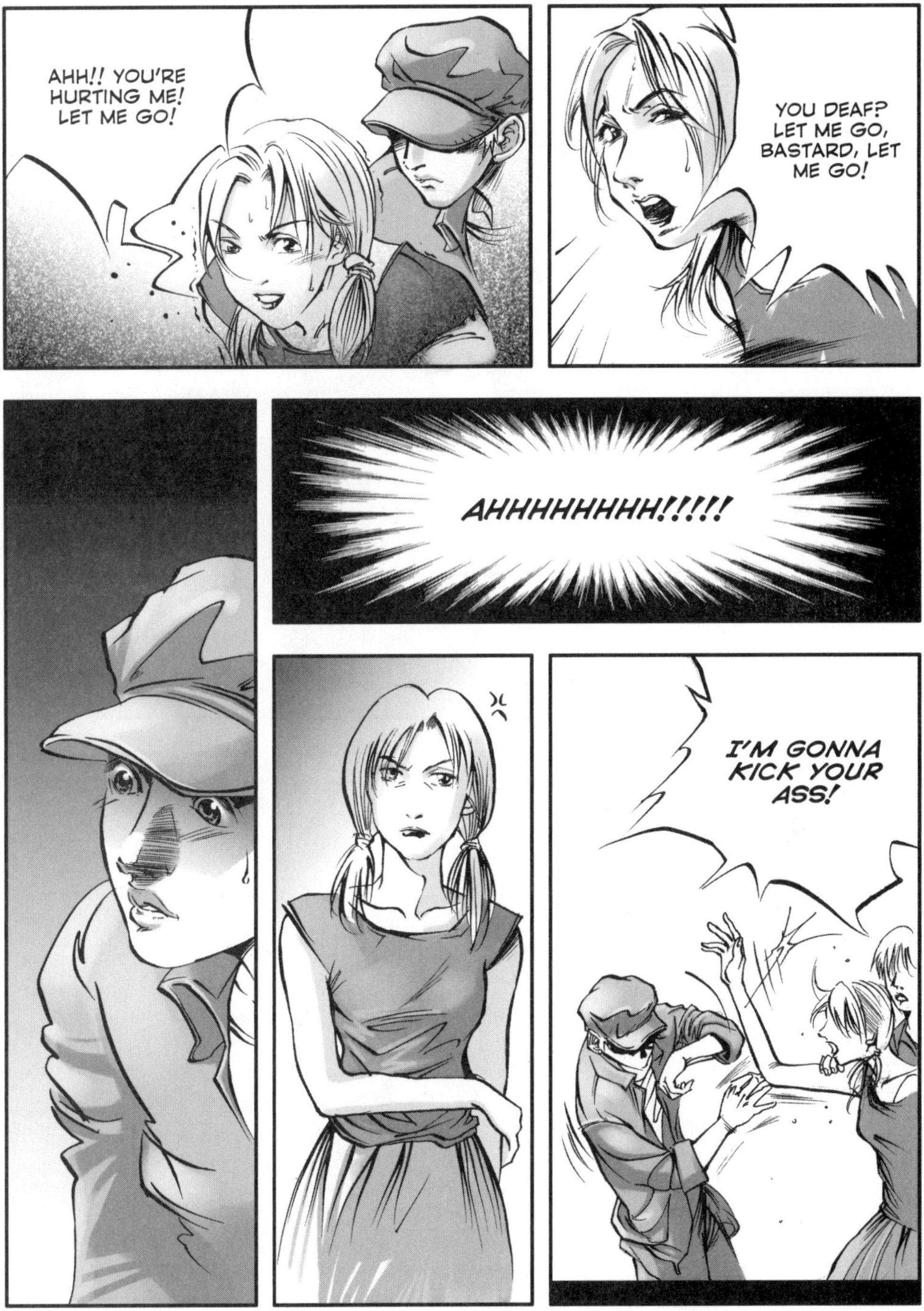
AHH!! YOU'RE HURTING ME! LET ME GO!
YOU DEAF? LET ME GO, BASTARD, LET ME GO!
AHHHHHHHH!!!!!
I'M GONNA KICK YOUR ASS!

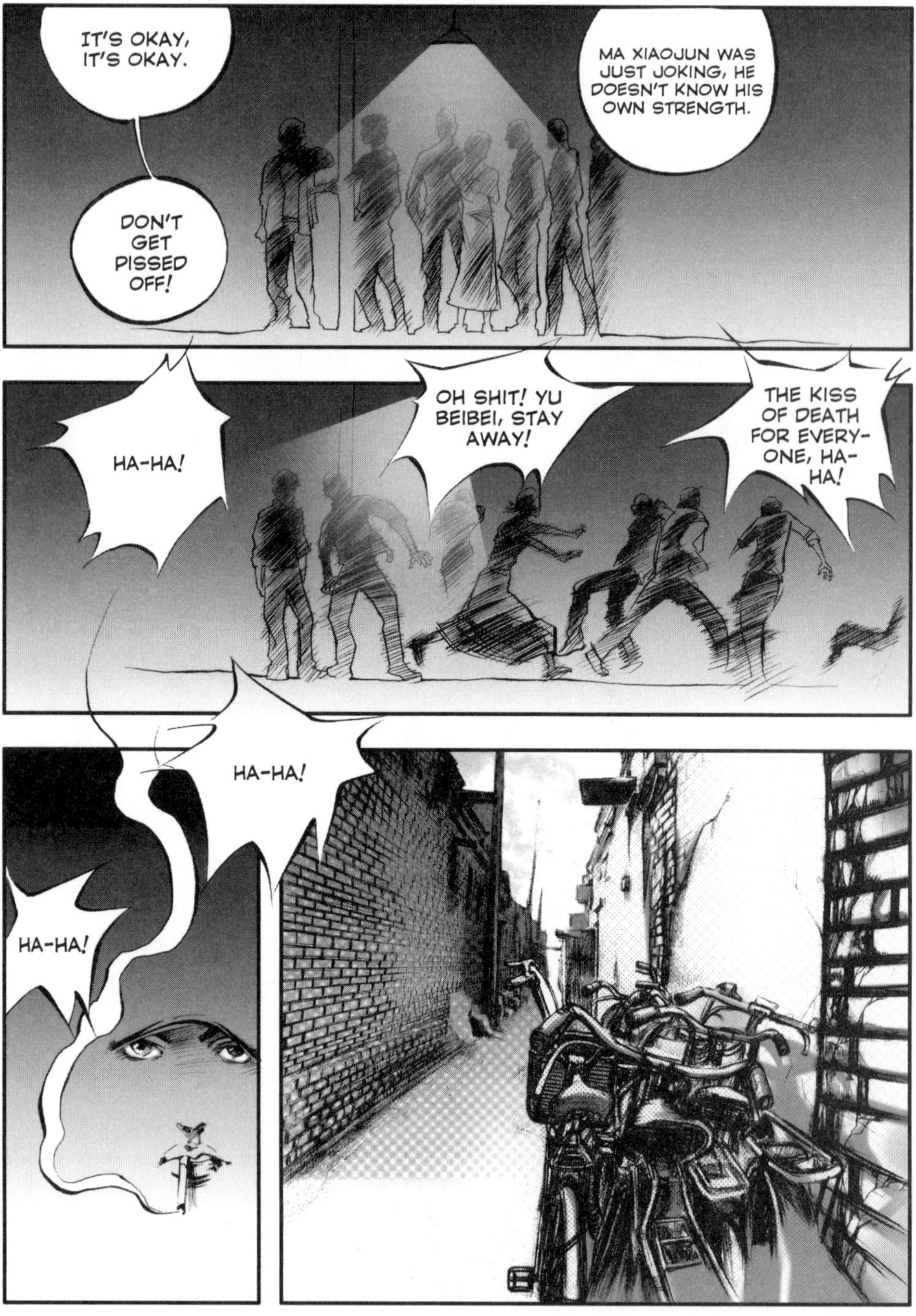
IT'S OKAY, IT'S OKAY.
DON'T GET PISSED OFF!
MA XIAOJUN WAS JUST JOKING, HE DOESN'T KNOW HIS OWN STRENGTH.
HA-HA!
OH SHIT! YU BEIBEI, STAY AWAY!
THE KISS OF DEATH FOR EVERY-ONE, HA-HA!
HA-HA!
HA-HA!

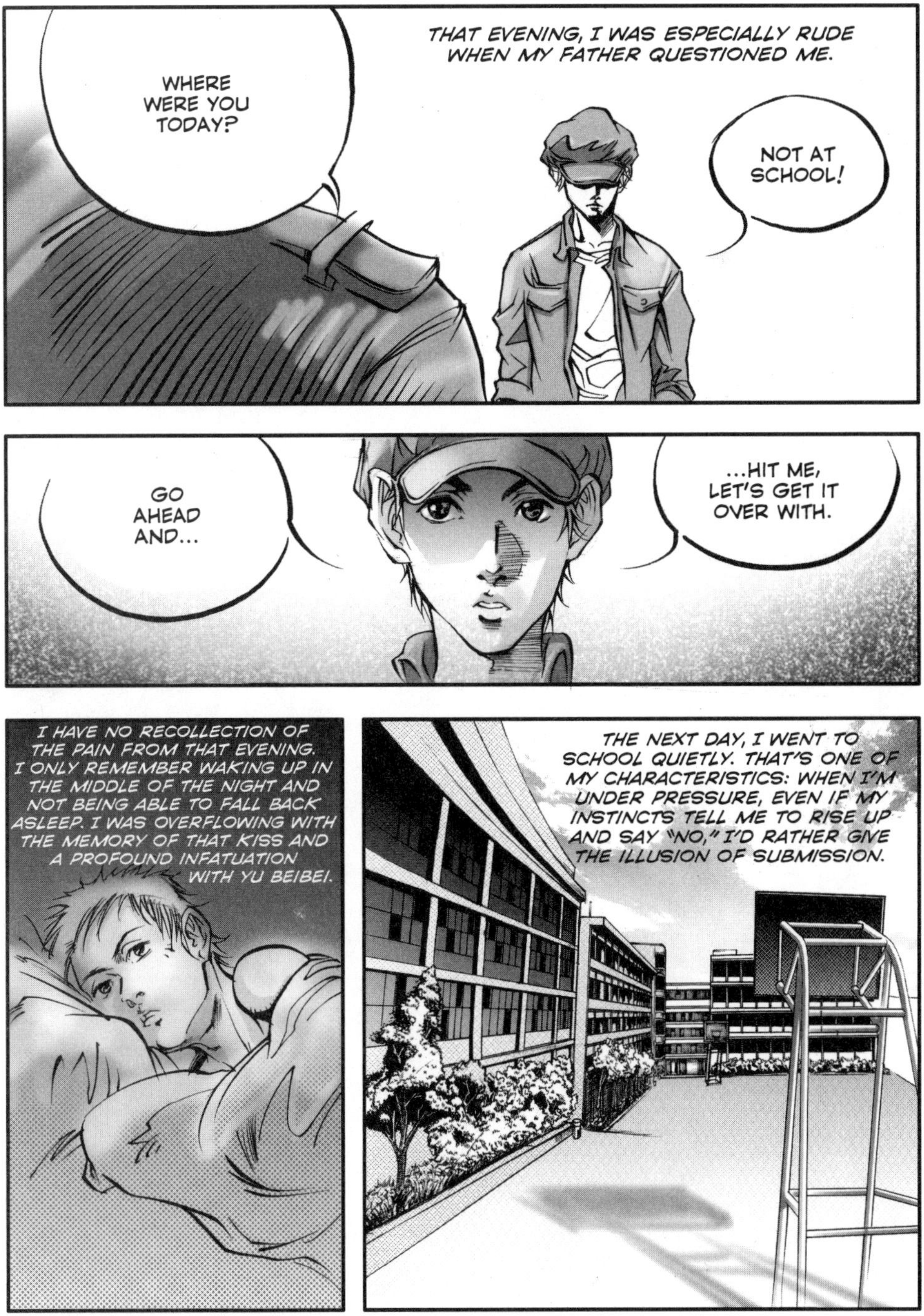
THAT EVENING, I WAS ESPECIALLY RUDE WHEN MY FATHER QUESTIONED ME.
WHERE WERE YOU TODAY?
NOT AT SCHOOL!
GO AHEAD AND...
...HIT ME, LET'S GET IT OVER WITH.
I HAVE NO RECOLLECTION OF THE PAIN FROM THAT EVENING. I ONLY REMEMBER WAKING UP IN THE MIDDLE OF THE NIGHT AND NOT BEING ABLE TO FALL BACK ASLEEP. I WAS OVERFLOWING WITH THE MEMORY OF THAT KISS AND A PROFOUND INFATUATION WITH YU BEIBEI.
THE NEXT DAY, I WENT TO SCHOOL QUIETLY. THAT'S ONE OF MY CHARACTERISTICS: WHEN I'M UNDER PRESSURE, EVEN IF MY INSTINCTS TELL ME TO RISE UP AND SAY "NO," I'D RATHER GIVE THE ILLUSION OF SUBMISSION.

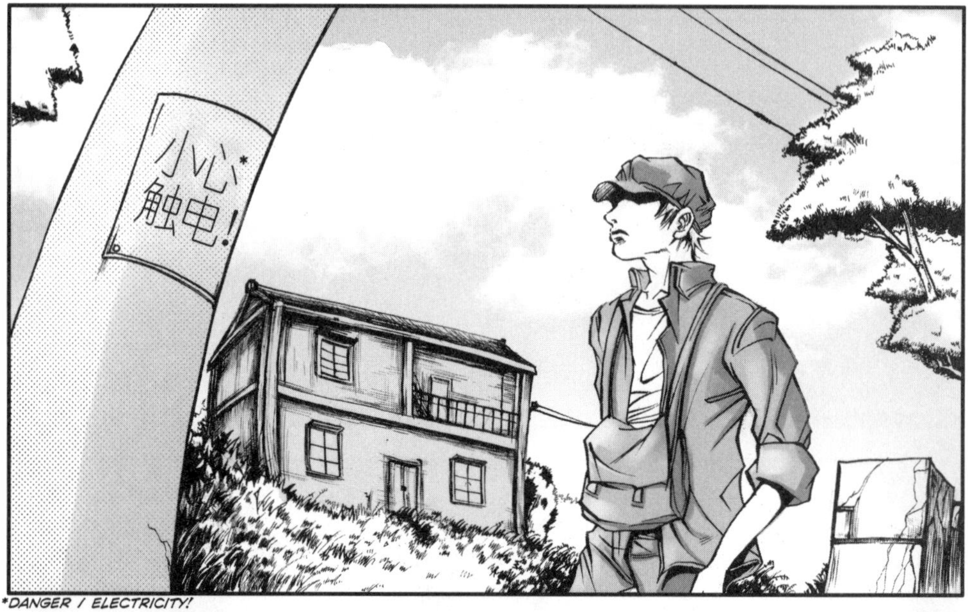
小心*
触电!
*DANGER / ELECTRICITY!

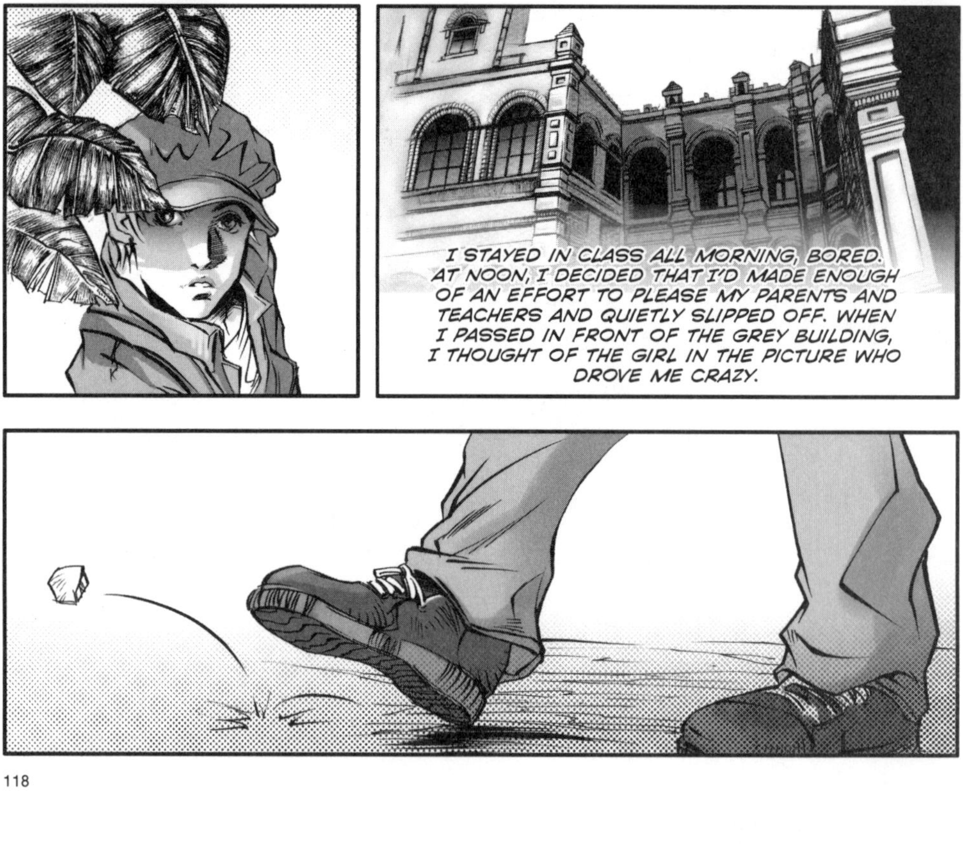
I STAYED IN CLASS ALL MORNING, BORED. AT NOON, I DECIDED THAT I'D MADE ENOUGH OF AN EFFORT TO PLEASE MY PARENTS AND TEACHERS AND QUIETLY SLIPPED OFF. WHEN I PASSED IN FRONT OF THE GREY BUILDING, I THOUGHT OF THE GIRL IN THE PICTURE WHO DROVE ME CRAZY.

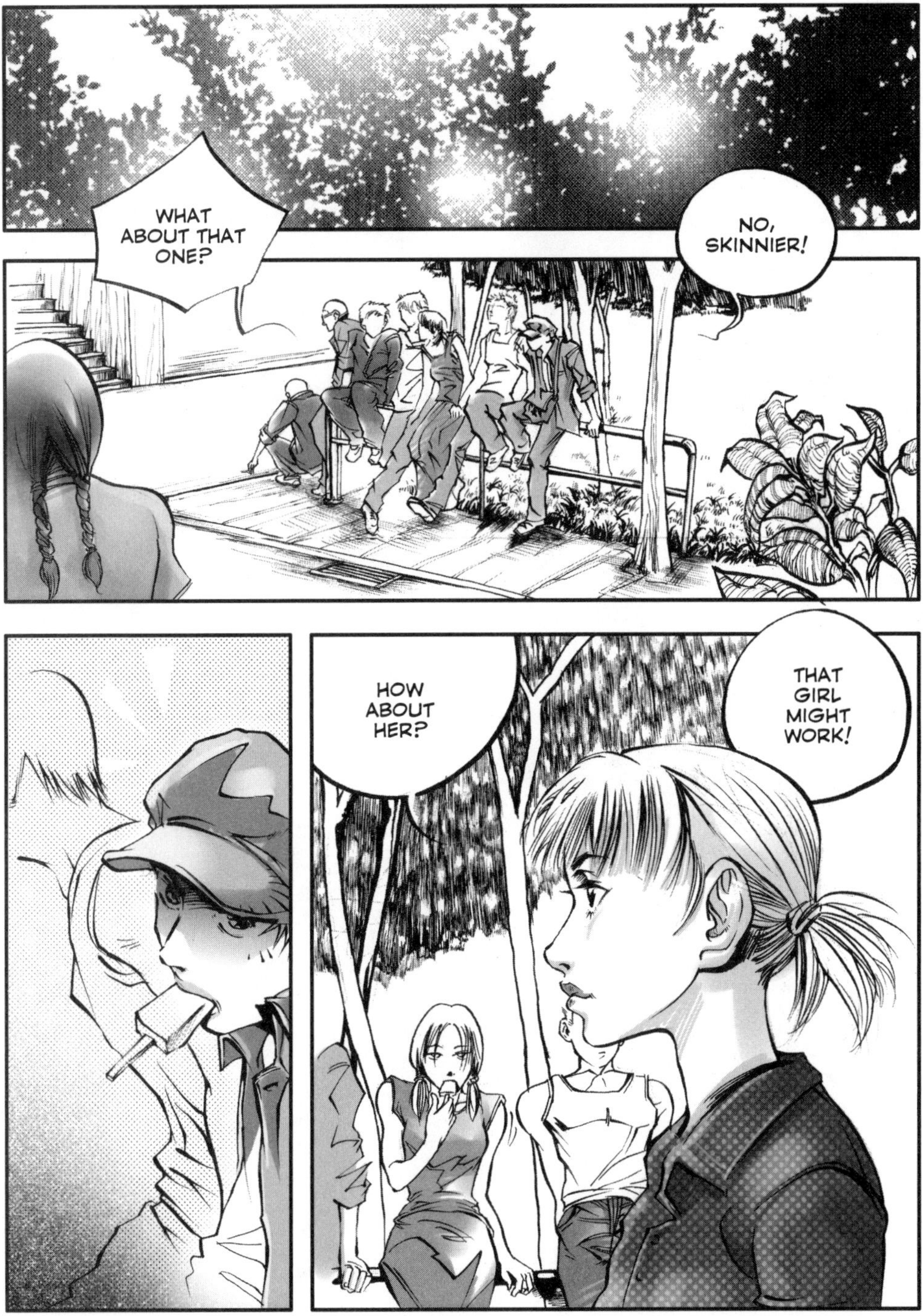
WHAT ABOUT THAT ONE?
NO, SKINNIER!
HOW ABOUT HER?
THAT GIRL MIGHT WORK!

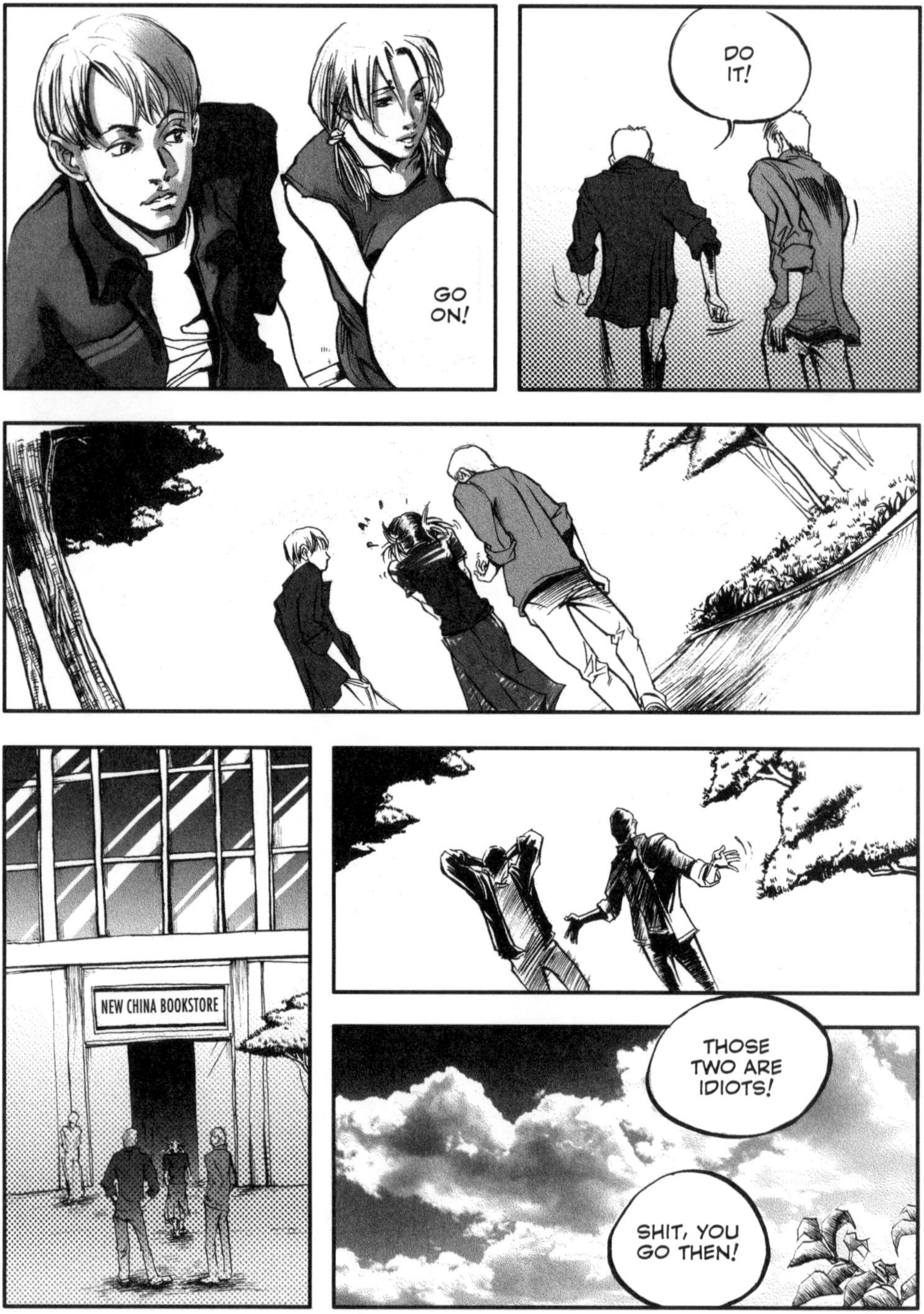
GO ON!
DO IT!
NEW CHINA BOOKSTORE
THOSE TWO ARE IDIOTS!
SHIT, YOU GO THEN!

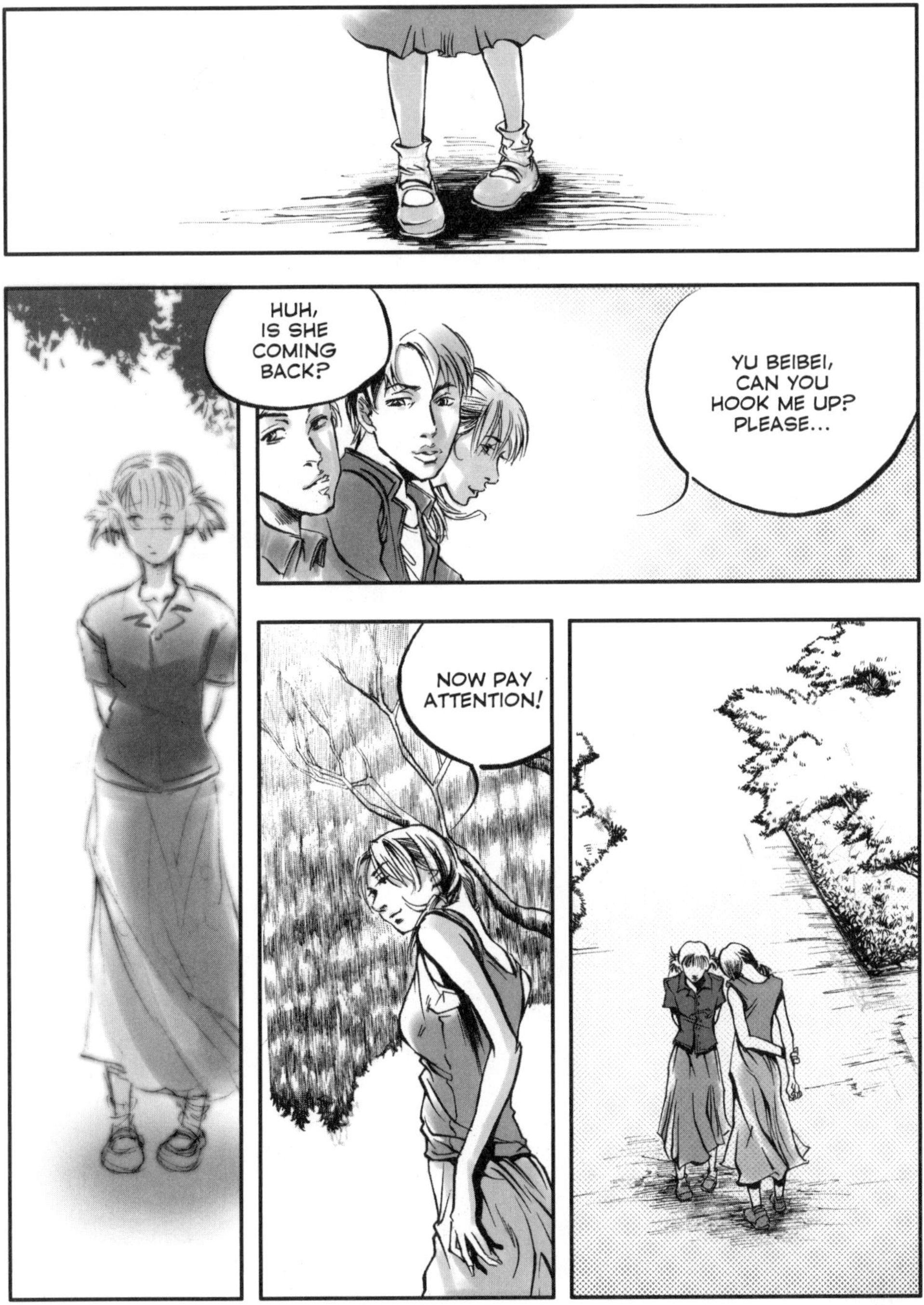
HUH, IS SHE COMING BACK?
YU BEIBEI, CAN YOU HOOK ME UP? PLEASE...
NOW PAY ATTENTION!

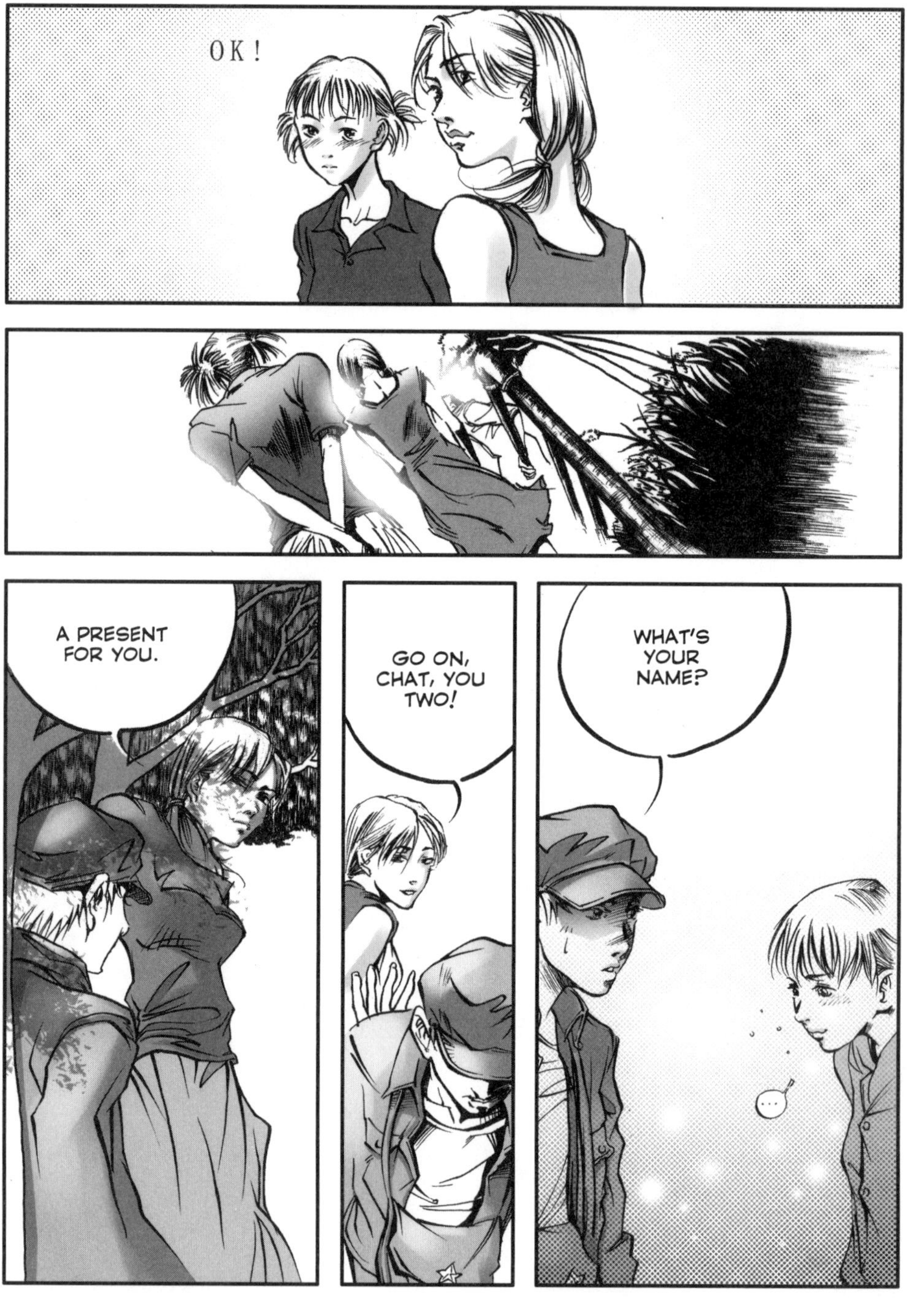
OK!
A PRESENT FOR YOU.
GO ON, CHAT, YOU TWO!
WHAT'S YOUR NAME?
...

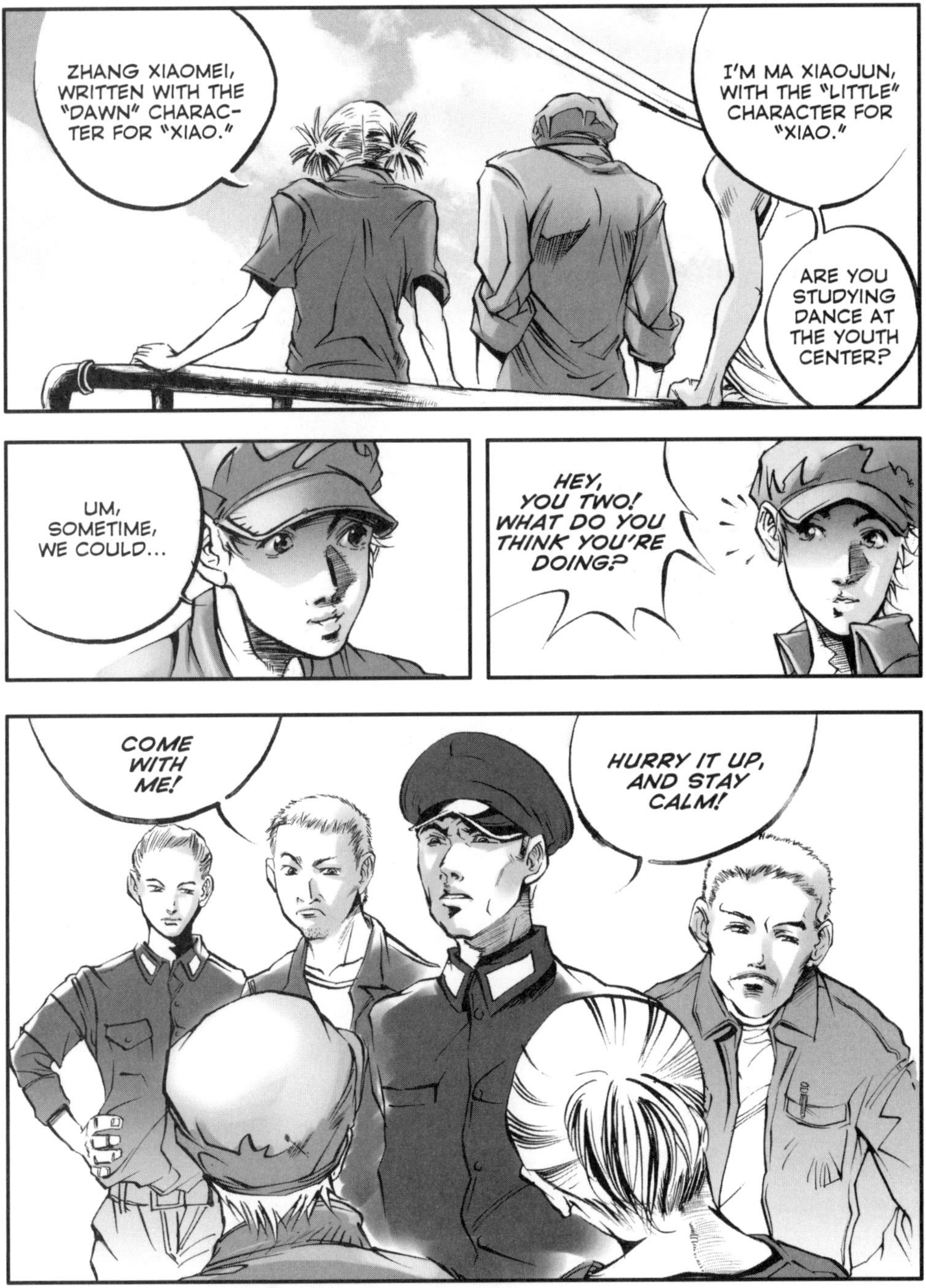
ZHANG XIAOMEI, WRITTEN WITH THE "DAWN" CHARACTER FOR "XIAO."
I'M MA XIAOJUN, WITH THE "LITTLE" CHARACTER FOR "XIAO."
ARE YOU STUDYING DANCE AT THE YOUTH CENTER?
UM, SOMETIME, WE COULD...
HEY, YOU TWO! WHAT DO YOU THINK YOU'RE DOING?
COME WITH ME!
HURRY IT UP, AND STAY CALM!

5 - the fight with the kids from 6th Street

I RAN THROUGH THE STREETS
UNTIL I WAS OUT OF BREATH...

...UNDER THE SUNSET AND
THE YELLOW LAMPLIGHT.

THE GROUND WAS COVERED
WITH THE BROWN DEBRIS OF
BRICKS THAT HAD BROKEN
INTO THOUSANDS OF PIECES.

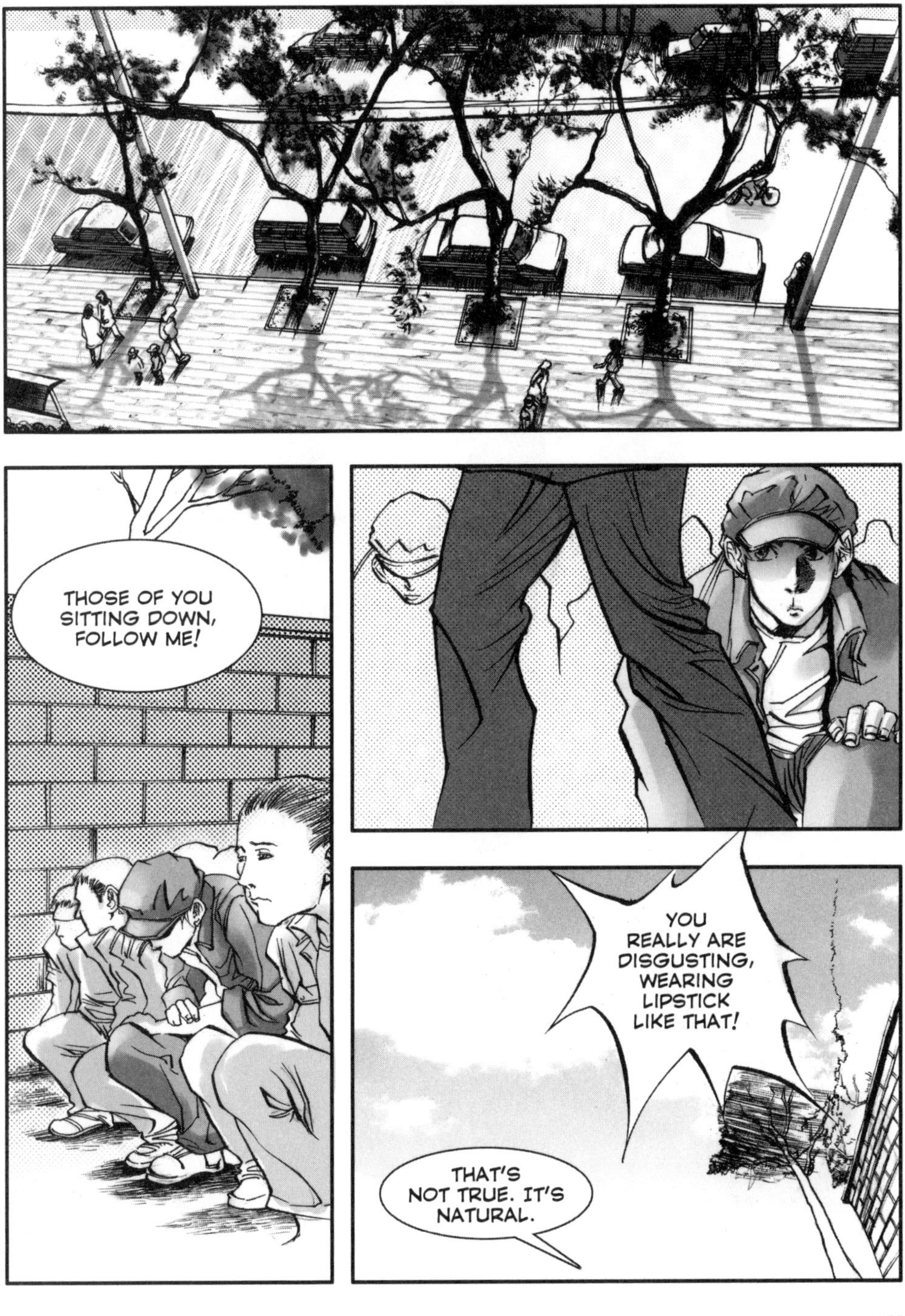
THOSE OF YOU SITTING DOWN, FOLLOW ME!
YOU REALLY ARE DISGUSTING, WEARING LIPSTICK LIKE THAT!
THAT'S NOT TRUE. IT'S NATURAL.

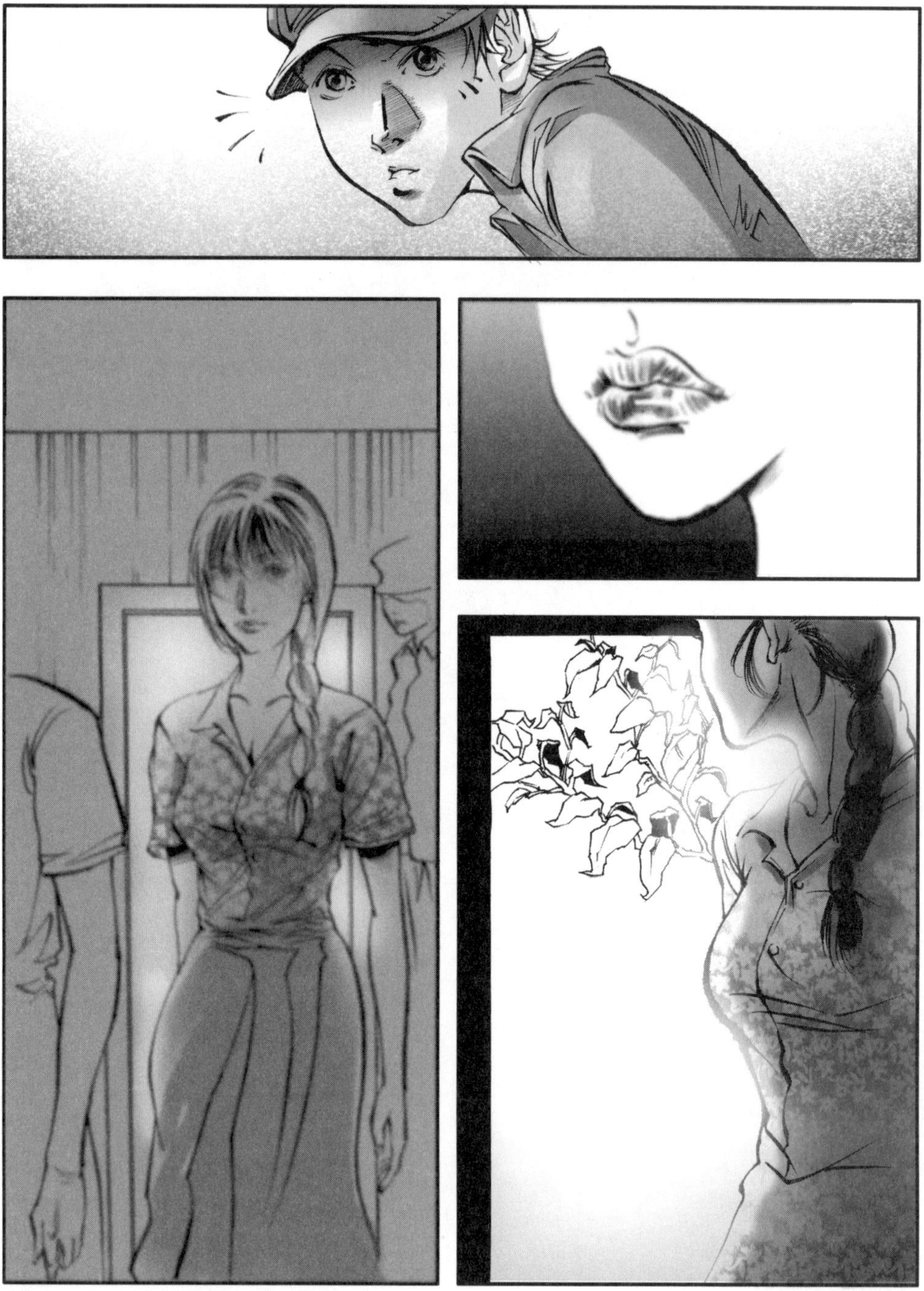

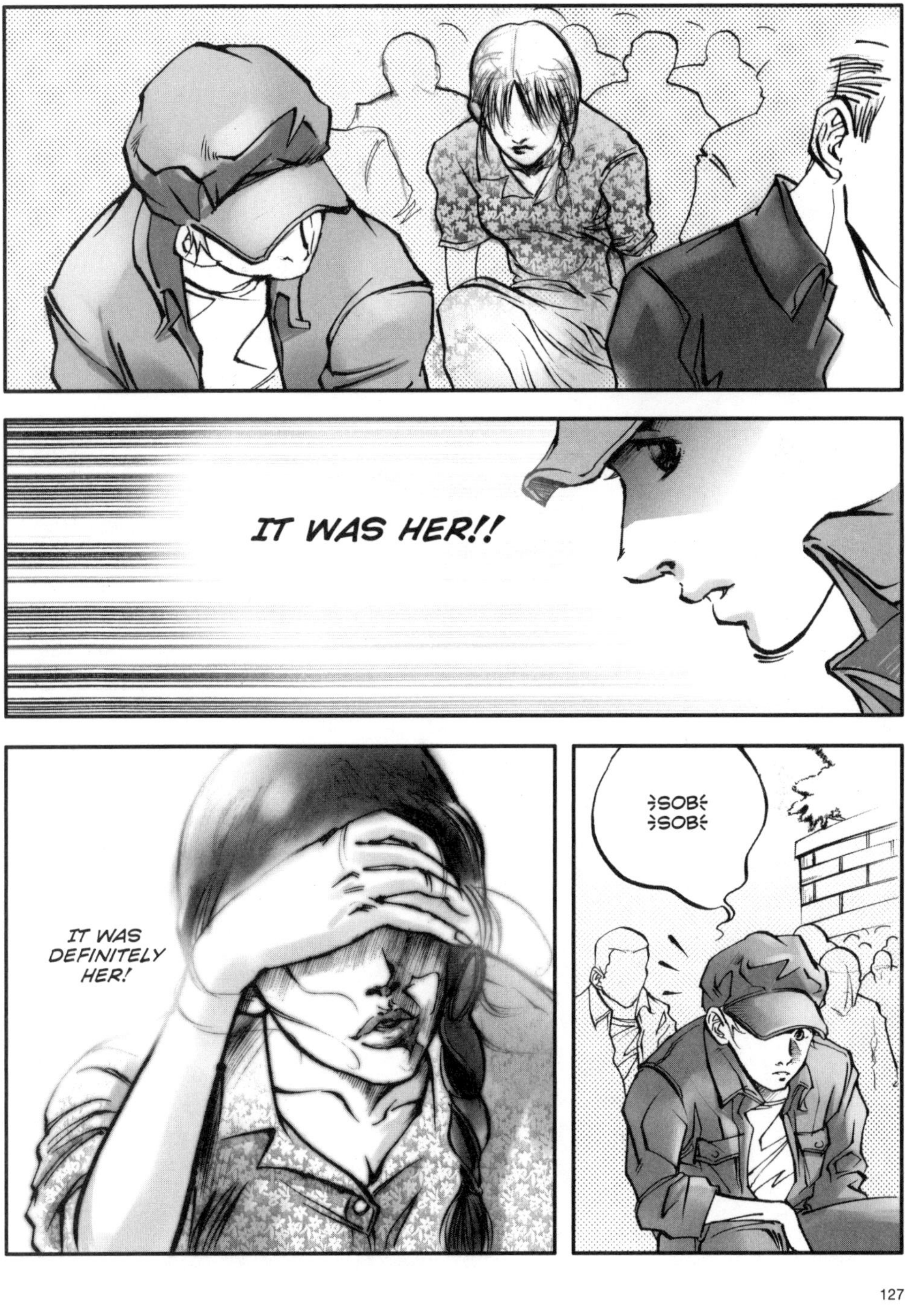
IT WAS HER!!
IT WAS DEFINITELY HER!
SOB SOB

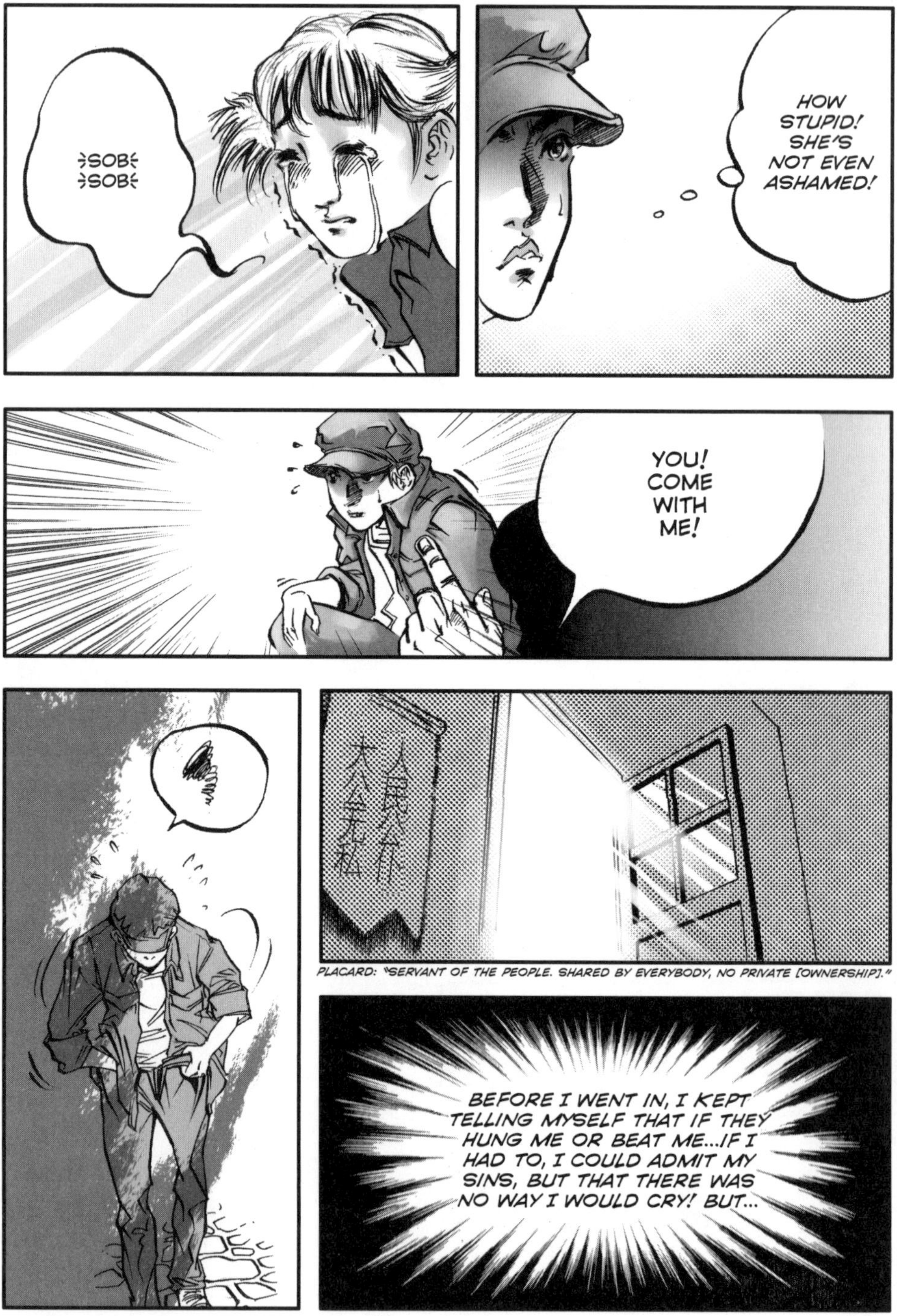

⪢SOB⪡ ⪢SOB⪡
HOW STUPID! SHE'S NOT EVEN ASHAMED!
YOU! COME WITH ME!
PLACARD: "SERVANT OF THE PEOPLE. SHARED BY EVERYBODY, NO PRIVATE [OWNERSHIP]."
BEFORE I WENT IN, I KEPT TELLING MYSELF THAT IF THEY HUNG ME OR BEAT ME...IF I HAD TO, I COULD ADMIT MY SINS, BUT THAT THERE WAS NO WAY I WOULD CRY! BUT...

...I SNIVELED LIKE A BABY...

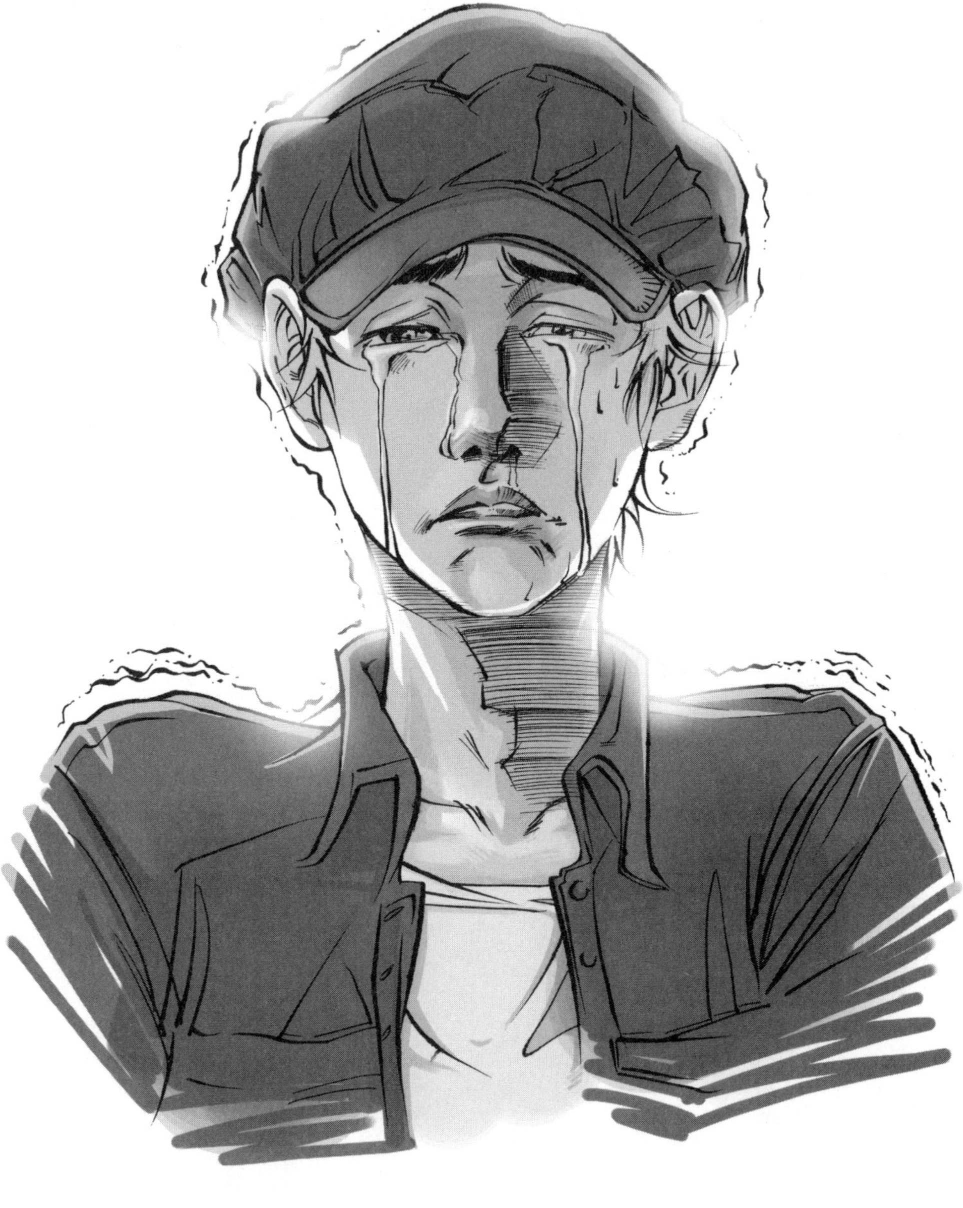

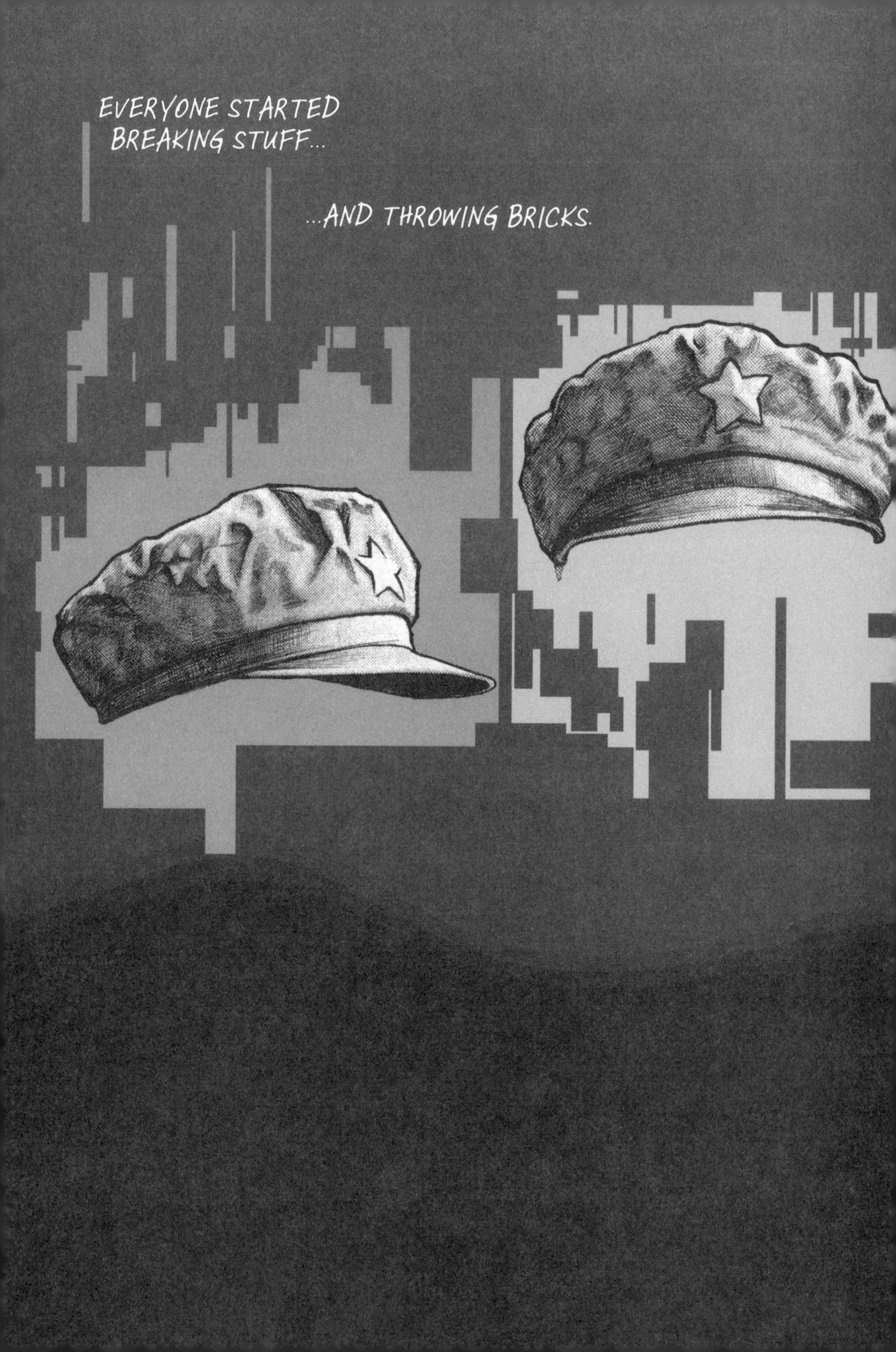
EVERYONE STARTED BREAKING STUFF...
...AND THROWING BRICKS.

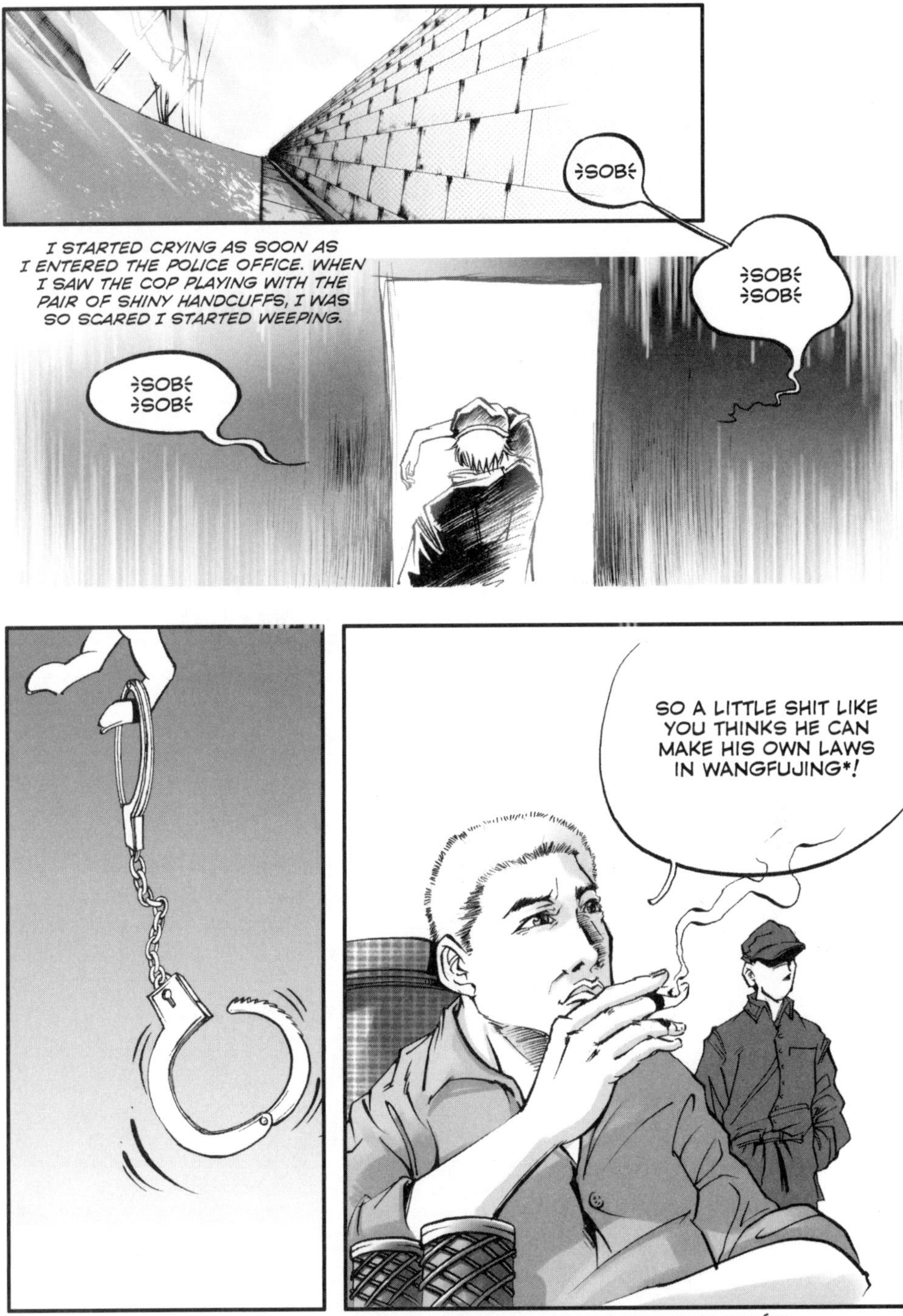

SOB
I STARTED CRYING AS SOON AS I ENTERED THE POLICE OFFICE. WHEN I SAW THE COP PLAYING WITH THE PAIR OF SHINY HANDCUFFS, I WAS SO SCARED I STARTED WEEPING.
SOB SOB
SOB SOB
SO A LITTLE SHIT LIKE YOU THINKS HE CAN MAKE HIS OWN LAWS IN WANGFUJING*!

*NOTE: THE PEKING EQUIVALENT OF THE CHAMPS-ELYSÉES IN PARIS, FRANCE OR FIFTH AVENUE IN NEW YORK CITY.

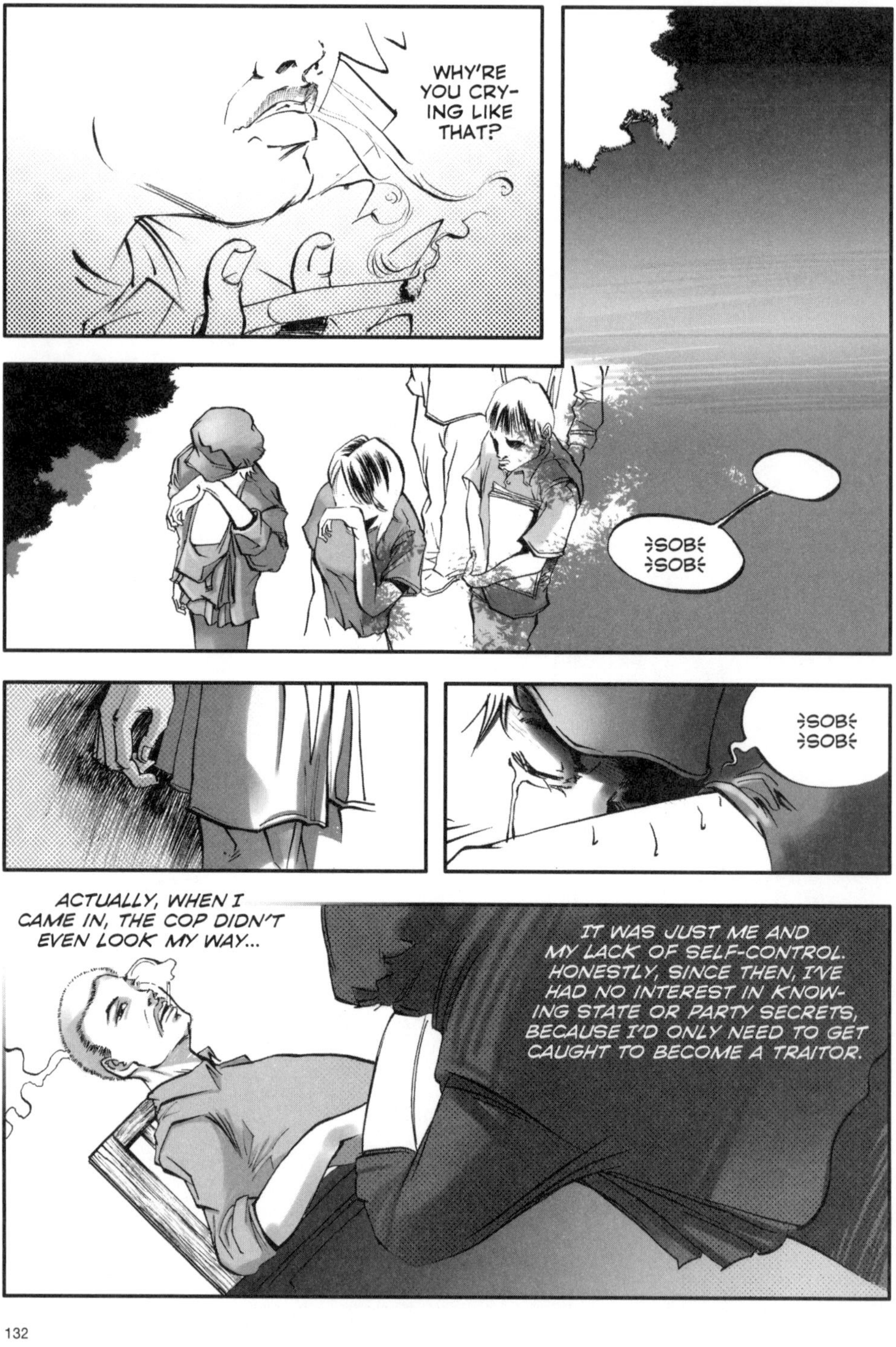
WHY'RE YOU CRY-ING LIKE THAT?
SOB SOB
SOB SOB
ACTUALLY, WHEN I CAME IN, THE COP DIDN'T EVEN LOOK MY WAY...
IT WAS JUST ME AND MY LACK OF SELF-CONTROL. HONESTLY, SINCE THEN, I'VE HAD NO INTEREST IN KNOWING STATE OR PARTY SECRETS, BECAUSE I'D ONLY NEED TO GET CAUGHT TO BECOME A TRAITOR.

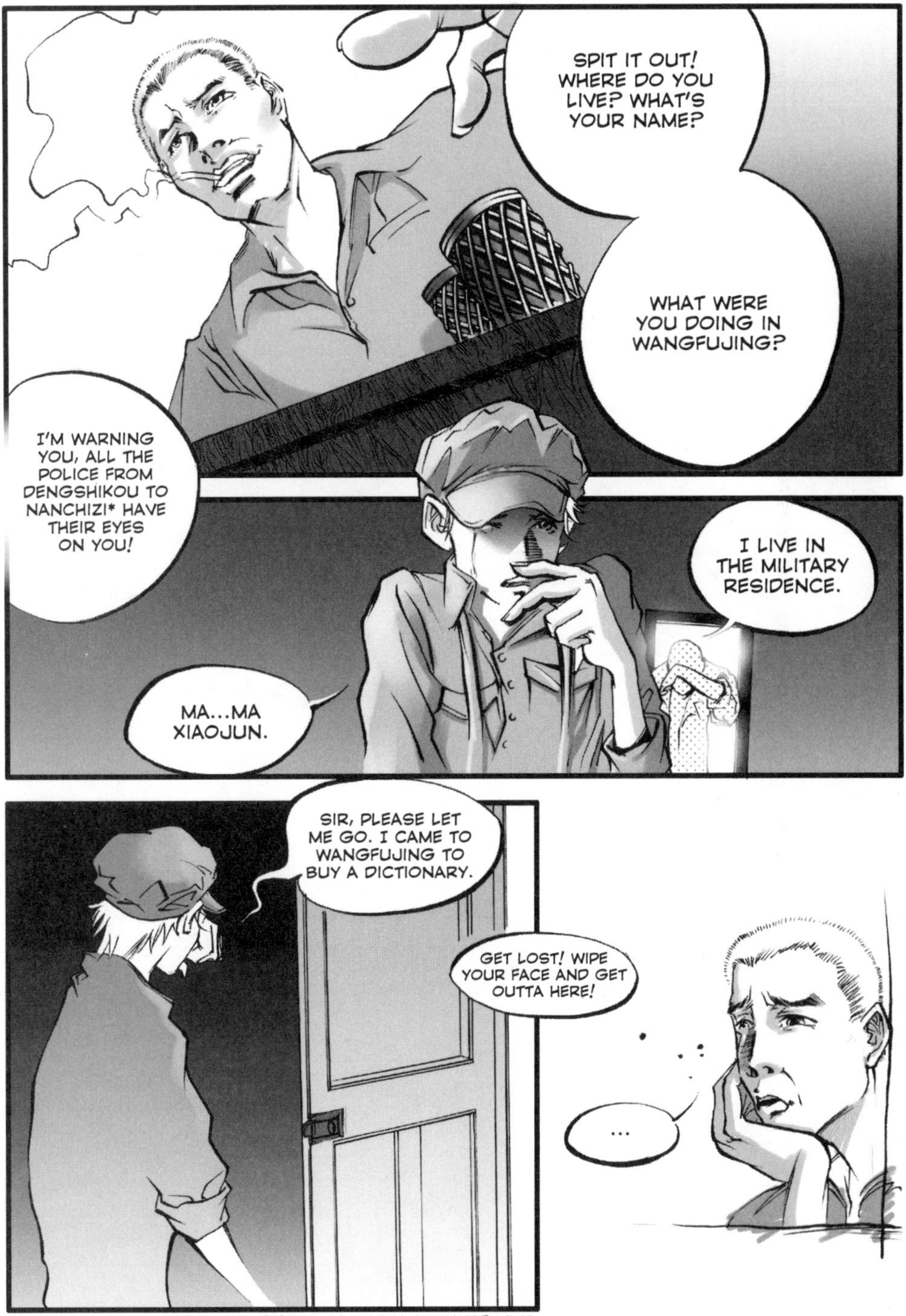
SPIT IT OUT! WHERE DO YOU LIVE? WHAT'S YOUR NAME?
WHAT WERE YOU DOING IN WANGFUJING?
I'M WARNING YOU, ALL THE POLICE FROM DENGSHIKOU TO NANCHIZI* HAVE THEIR EYES ON YOU!
I LIVE IN THE MILITARY RESIDENCE.
MA...MA XIAOJUN.
SIR, PLEASE LET ME GO. I CAME TO WANGFUJING TO BUY A DICTIONARY.
GET LOST! WIPE YOUR FACE AND GET OUTTA HERE!
...

NOTE: TWO NEIGHBORHOODS IN PEKING, ADJACENT TO WANGFUJING.

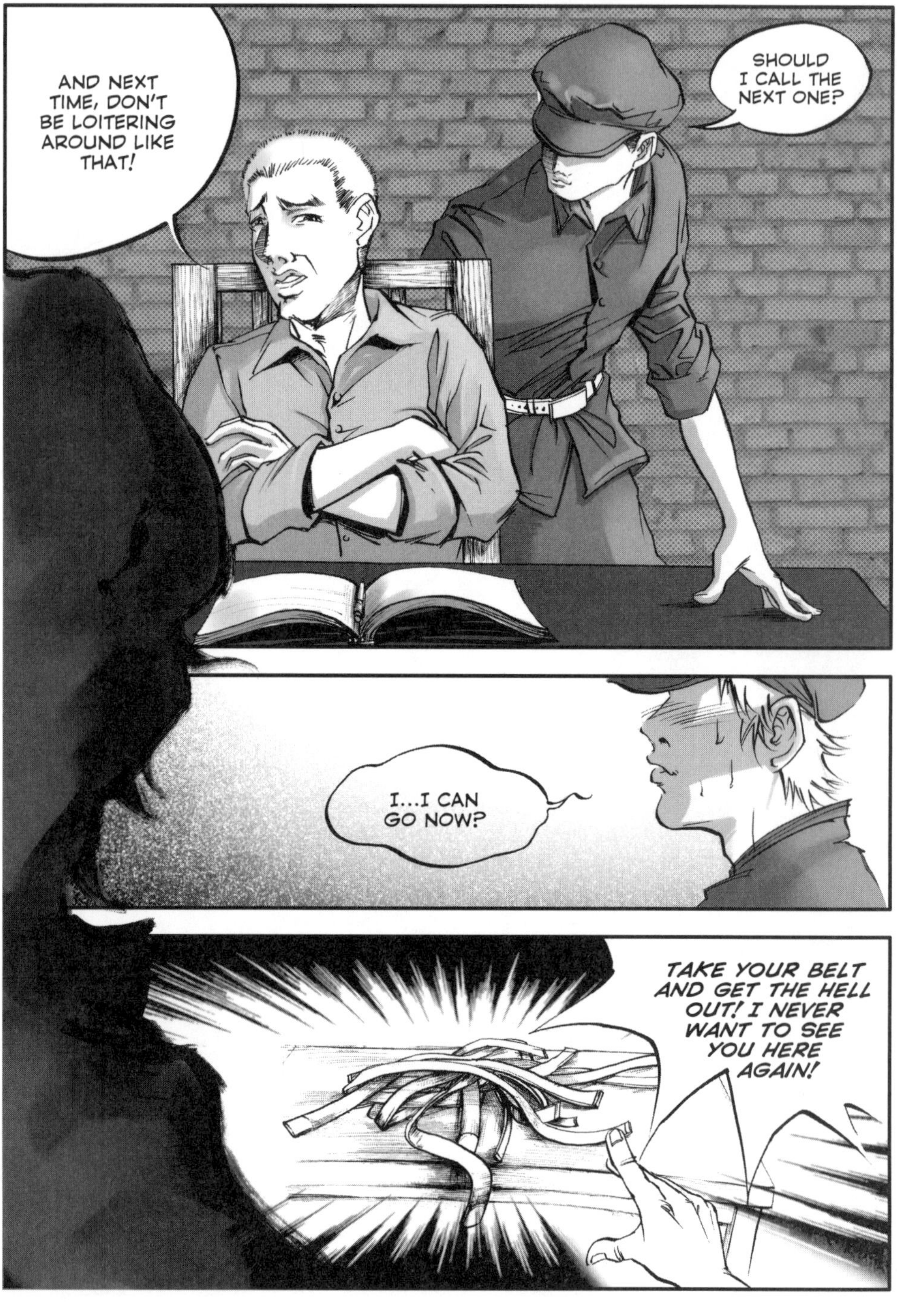
AND NEXT TIME, DON'T BE LOITERING AROUND LIKE THAT!
SHOULD I CALL THE NEXT ONE?
I...I CAN GO NOW?
TAKE YOUR BELT AND GET THE HELL OUT! I NEVER WANT TO SEE YOU HERE AGAIN!

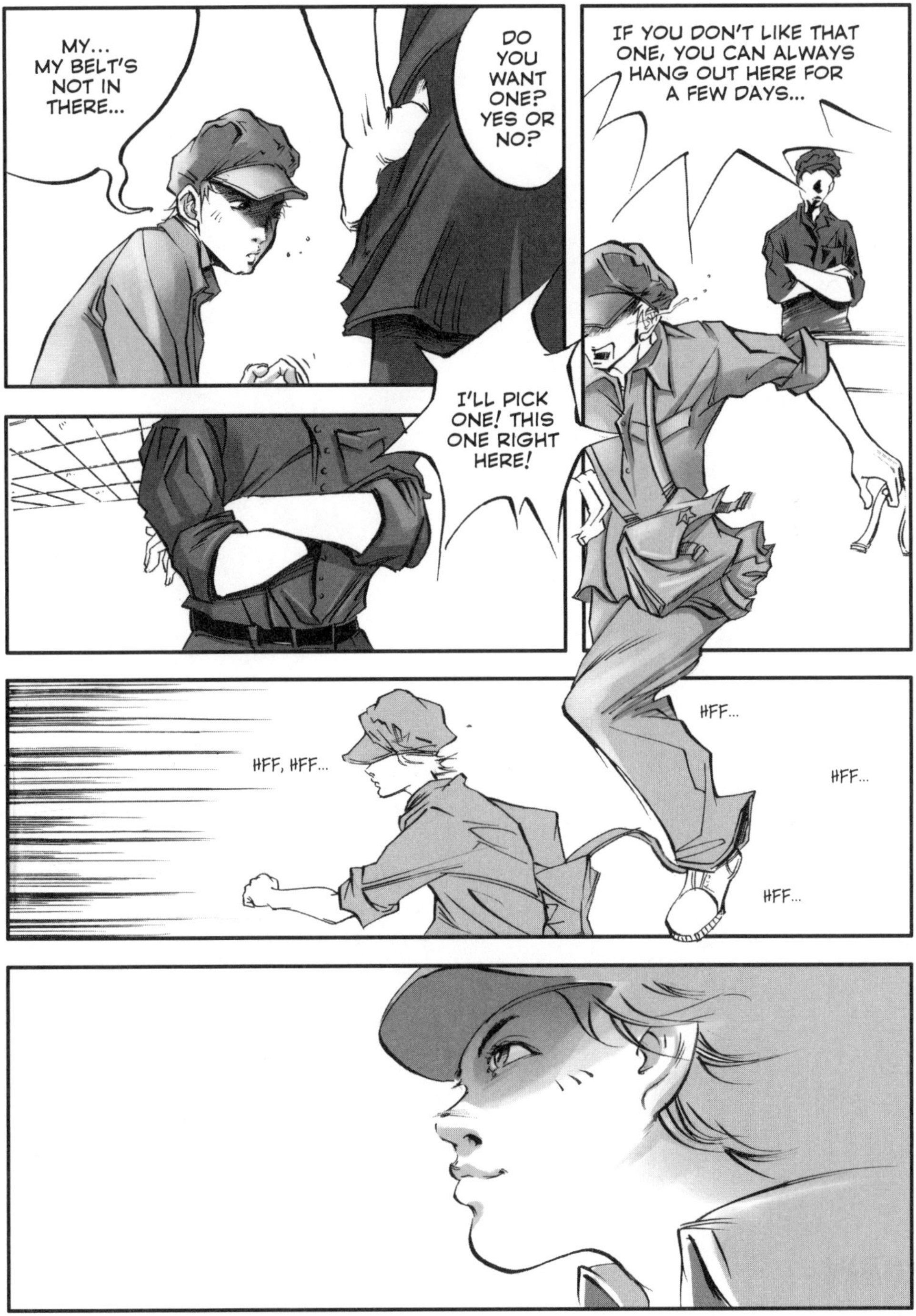
MY... MY BELT'S NOT IN THERE...
DO YOU WANT ONE? YES OR NO?
IF YOU DON'T LIKE THAT ONE, YOU CAN ALWAYS HANG OUT HERE FOR A FEW DAYS...
I'LL PICK ONE! THIS ONE RIGHT HERE!
HFF, HFF...
HFF...
HFF...
HFF...

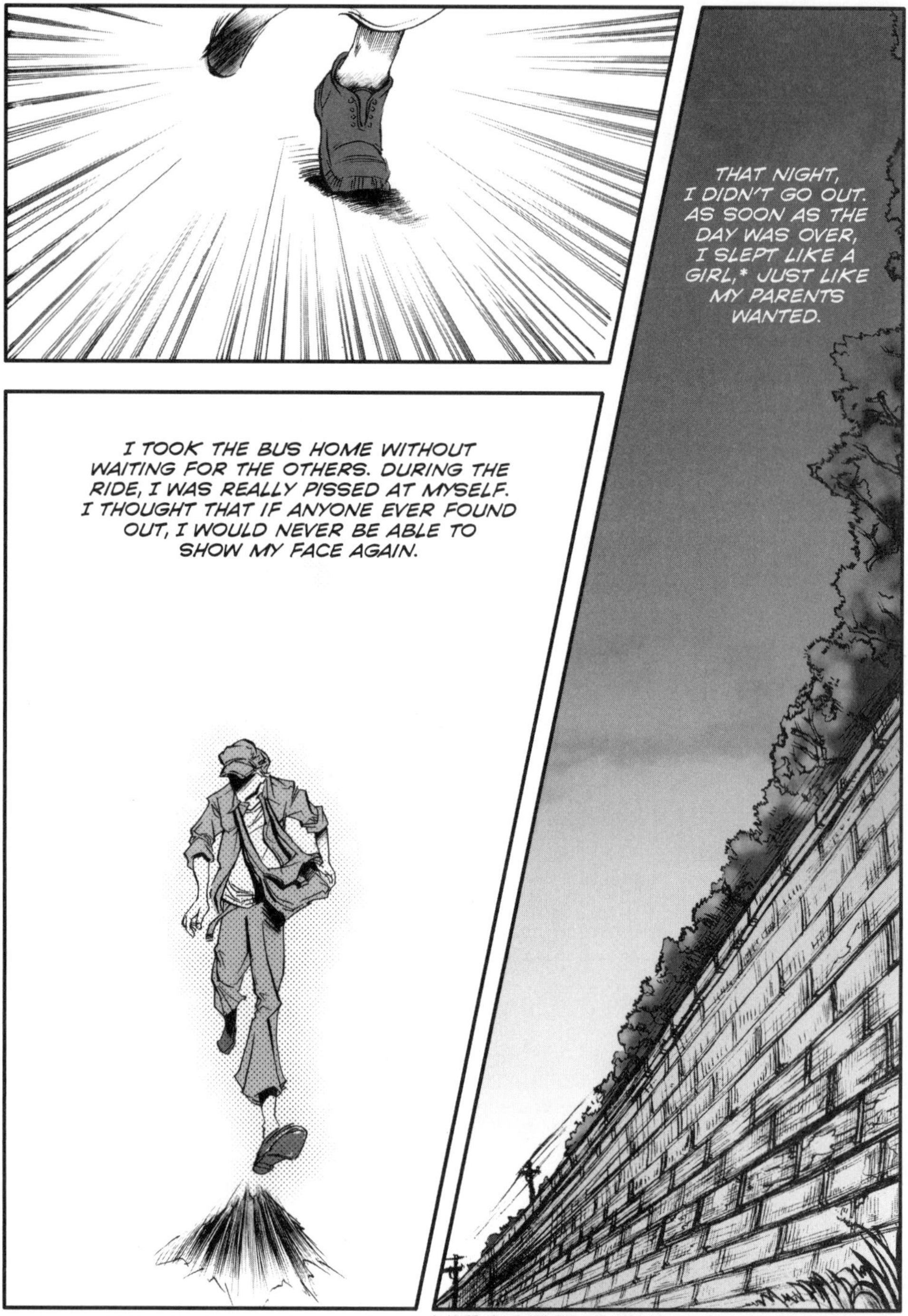
I TOOK THE BUS HOME WITHOUT WAITING FOR THE OTHERS. DURING THE RIDE, I WAS REALLY PISSED AT MYSELF. I THOUGHT THAT IF ANYONE EVER FOUND OUT, I WOULD NEVER BE ABLE TO SHOW MY FACE AGAIN.
THAT NIGHT, I DIDN'T GO OUT. AS SOON AS THE DAY WAS OVER, I SLEPT LIKE A GIRL,* JUST LIKE MY PARENTS WANTED.

*NOTE: IN ENGLISH, WE WOULD SAY "I SLEPT LIKE A LOG," OR "I SLEPT LIKE A BABY."

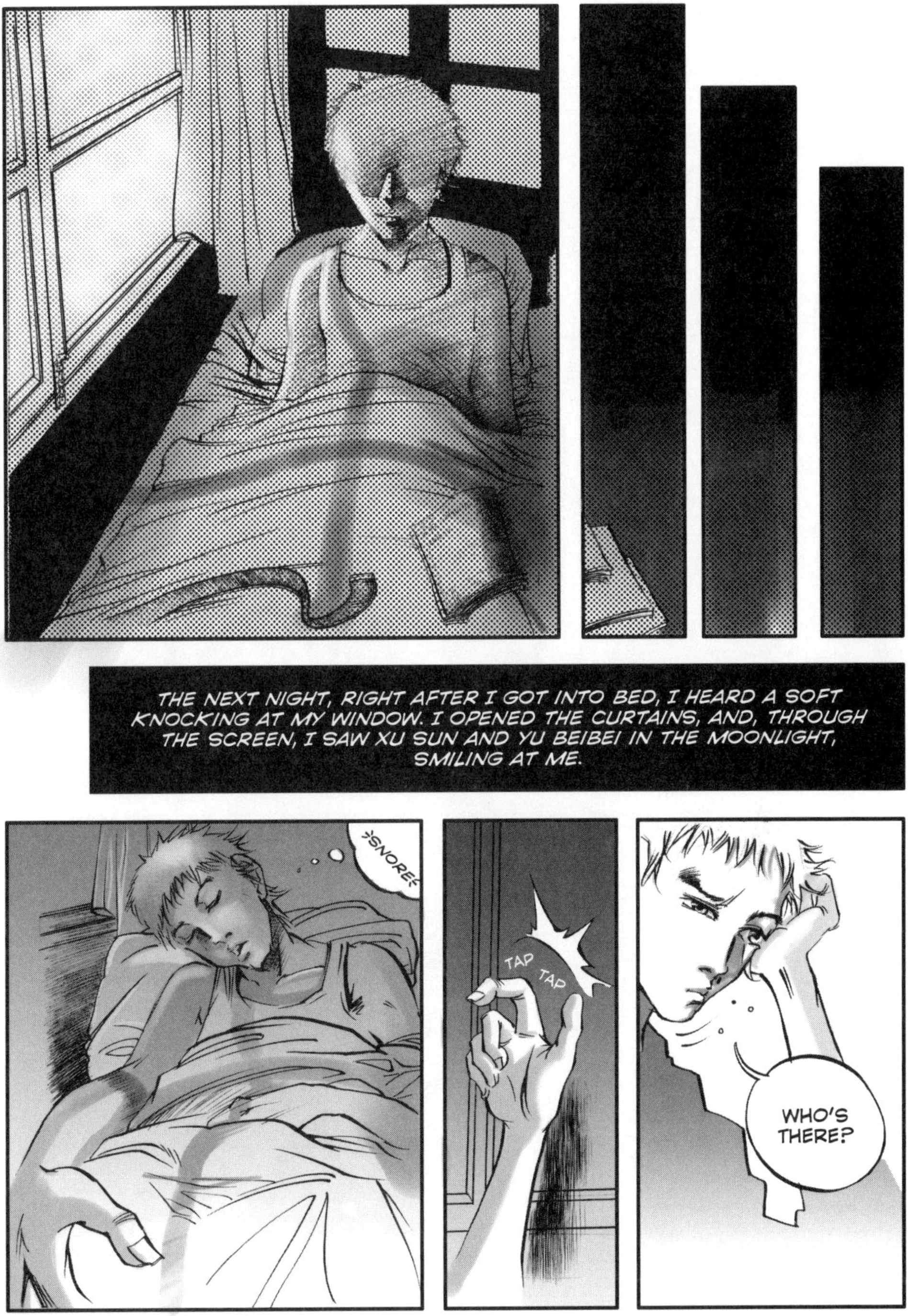
THE NEXT NIGHT, RIGHT AFTER I GOT INTO BED, I HEARD A SOFT KNOCKING AT MY WINDOW. I OPENED THE CURTAINS, AND, THROUGH THE SCREEN, I SAW XU SUN AND YU BEIBEI IN THE MOONLIGHT, SMILING AT ME.
SNORE
TAP TAP
WHO'S THERE?

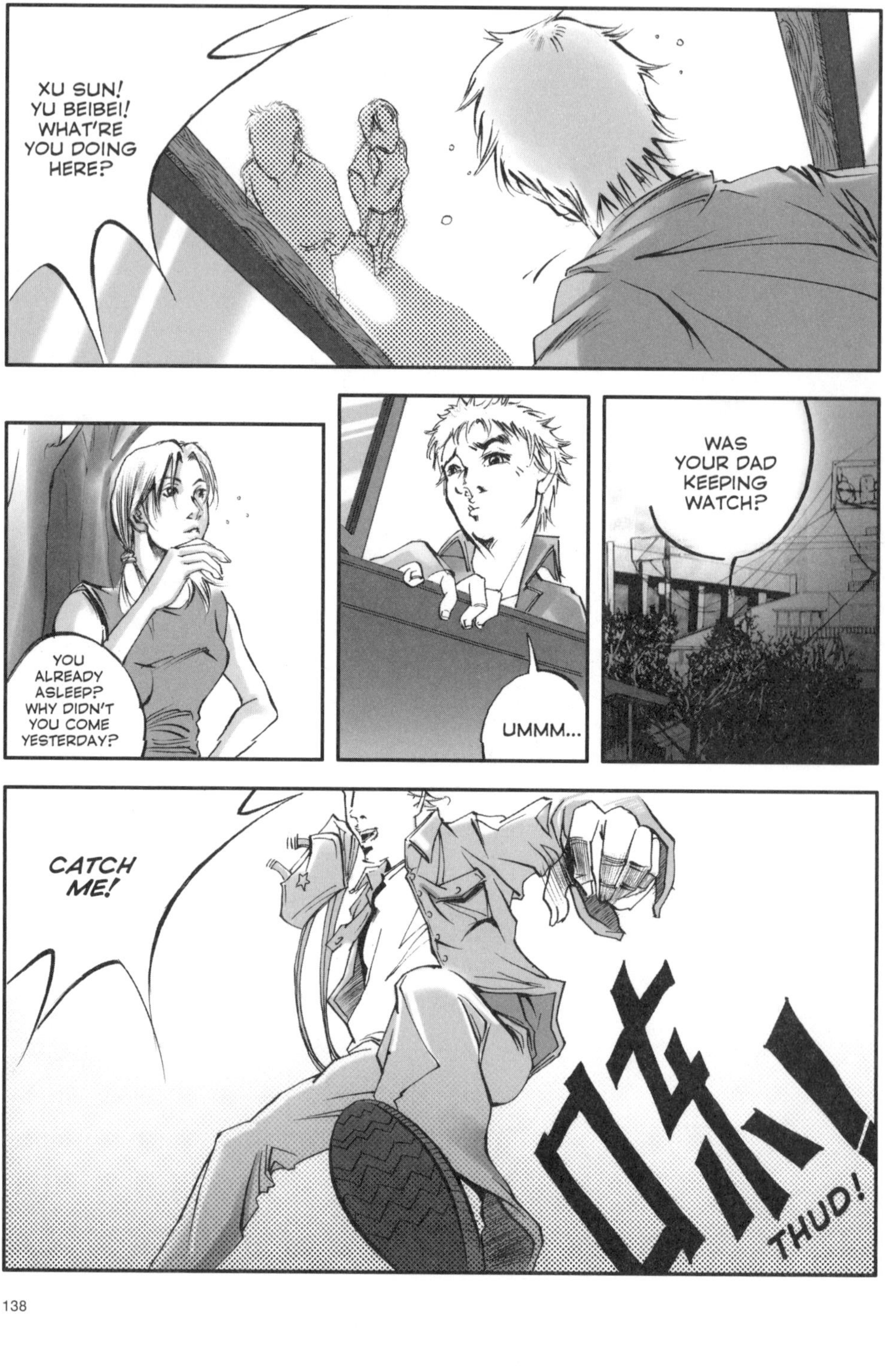
XU SUN! YU BEIBEI! WHAT'RE YOU DOING HERE?
YOU ALREADY ASLEEP? WHY DIDN'T YOU COME YESTERDAY?
UMMM...
WAS YOUR DAD KEEPING WATCH?
CATCH ME!
THUD!

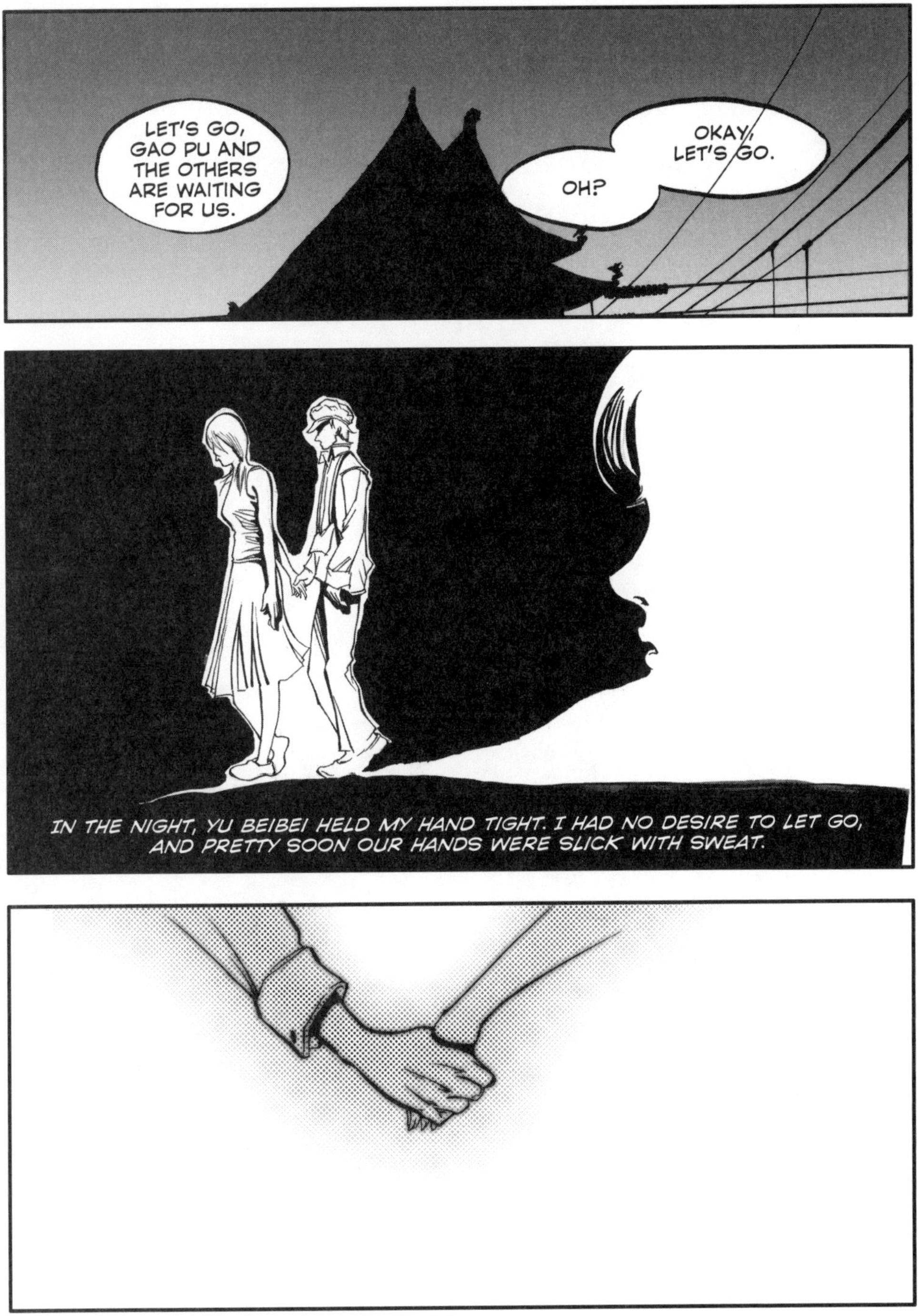
LET'S GO, GAO PU AND THE OTHERS ARE WAITING FOR US.
OH?
OKAY, LET'S GO.
IN THE NIGHT, YU BEIBEI HELD MY HAND TIGHT. I HAD NO DESIRE TO LET GO, AND PRETTY SOON OUR HANDS WERE SLICK WITH SWEAT.

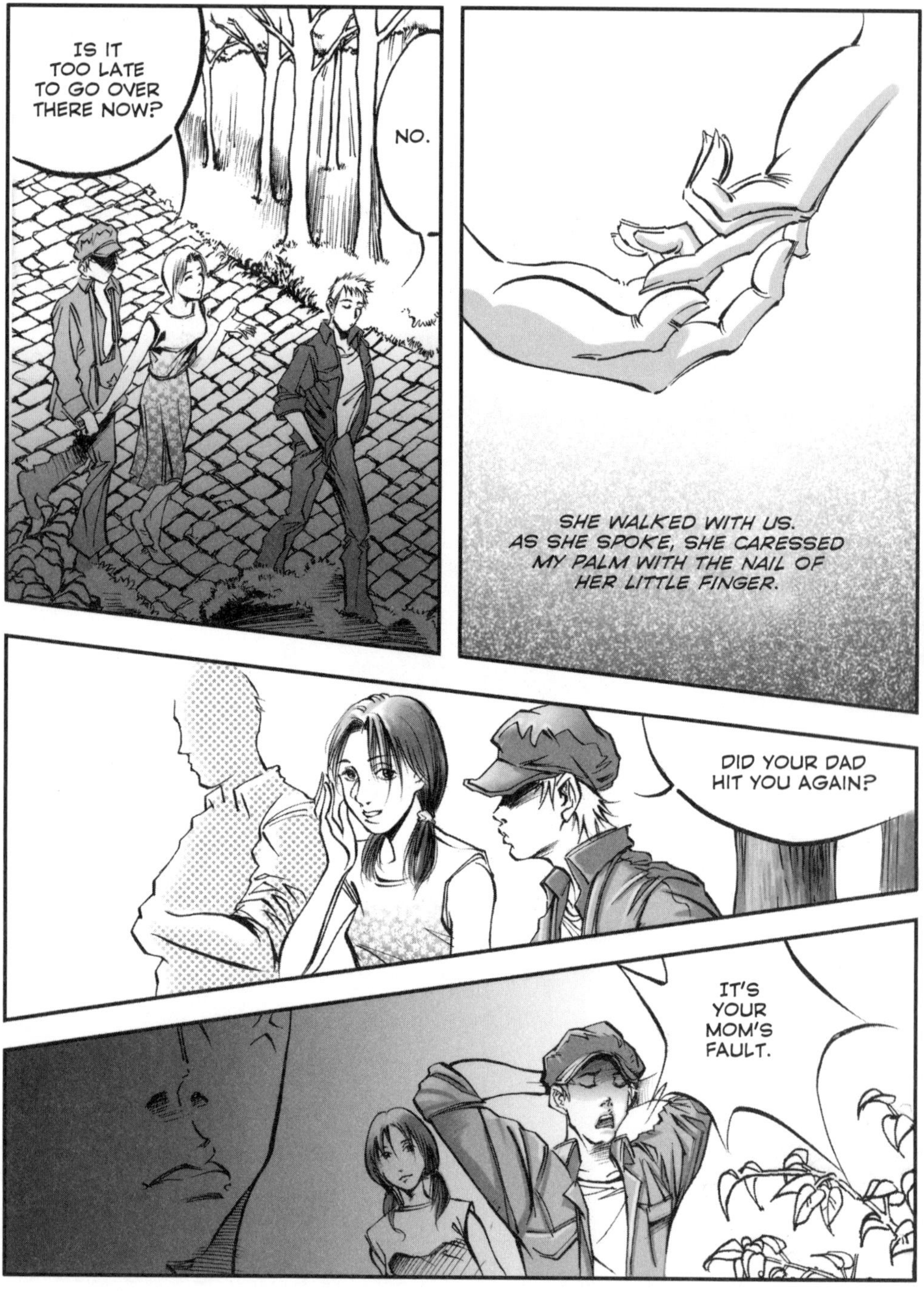
IS IT TOO LATE TO GO OVER THERE NOW?
NO.
SHE WALKED WITH US. AS SHE SPOKE, SHE CARESSED MY PALM WITH THE NAIL OF HER LITTLE FINGER.
DID YOUR DAD HIT YOU AGAIN?
IT'S YOUR MOM'S FAULT.

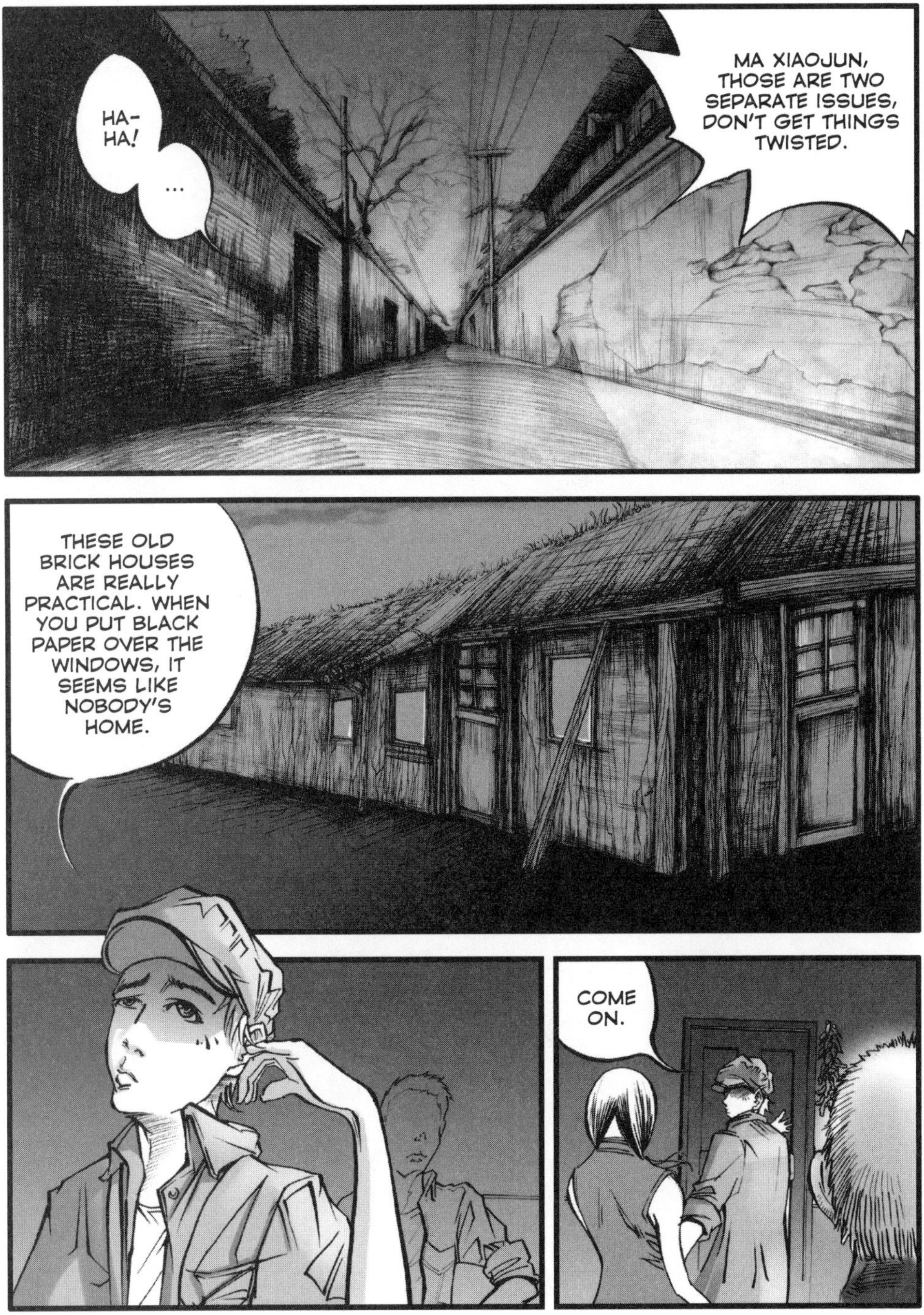
HA-HA!
...
MA XIAOJUN, THOSE ARE TWO SEPARATE ISSUES, DON'T GET THINGS TWISTED.
THESE OLD BRICK HOUSES ARE REALLY PRACTICAL. WHEN YOU PUT BLACK PAPER OVER THE WINDOWS, IT SEEMS LIKE NOBODY'S HOME.
COME ON.

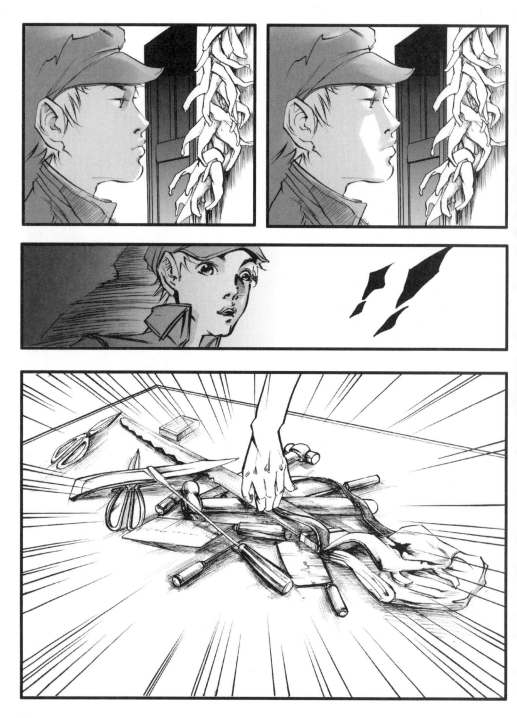

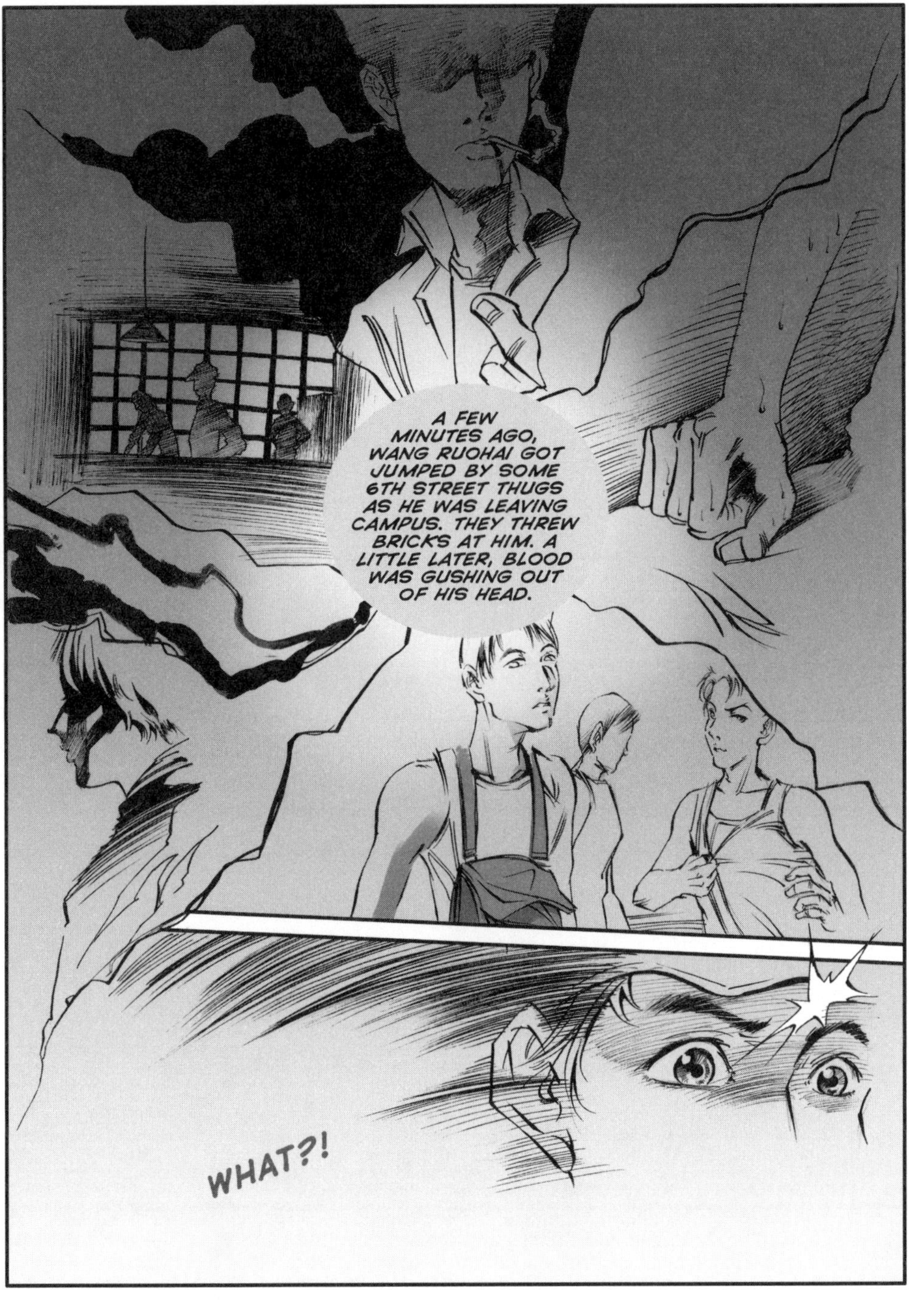
A FEW MINUTES AGO, WANG RUOHAI GOT JUMPED BY SOME 6TH STREET THUGS AS HE WAS LEAVING CAMPUS. THEY THREW BRICKS AT HIM. A LITTLE LATER, BLOOD WAS GUSHING OUT OF HIS HEAD.
WHAT?!

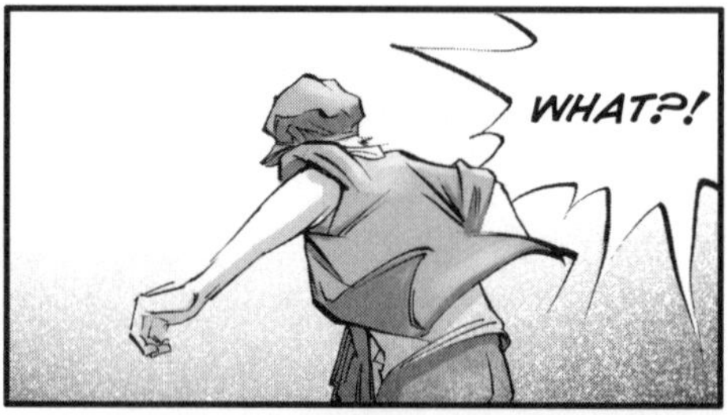
WHAT?!

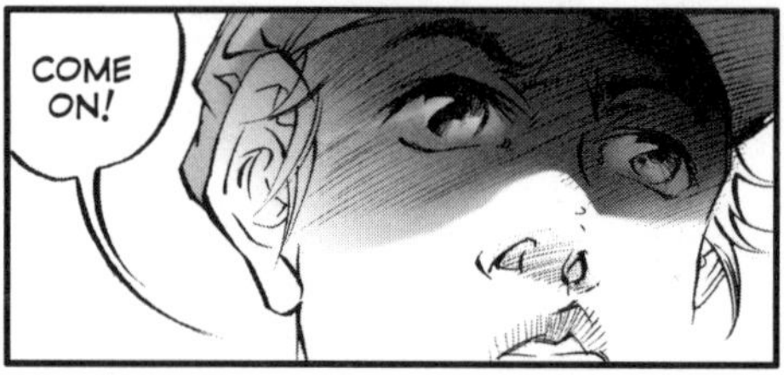
COME ON!

WE ENLISTED SOME KIDS FROM GRADE SCHOOL WHO LIVED ON CAMPUS. THEY WERE SO PROUD TO HAVE BEEN TRUSTED BY THE OLDER KIDS TO HELP OUT IN THIS GLORIOUS BATTLE THAT THEY WERE SHAKING WITH EXCITEMENT.

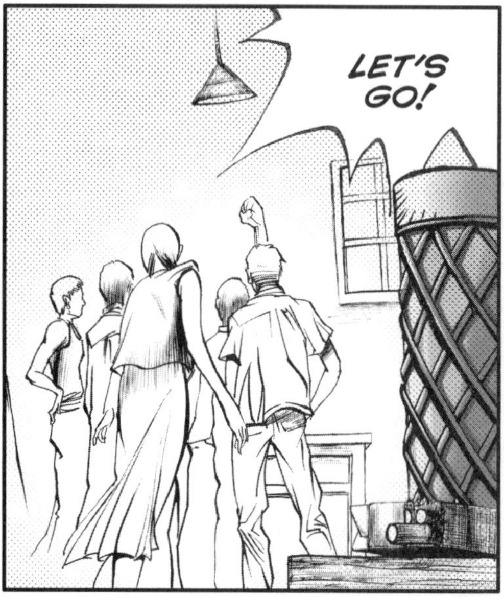
LET'S GO!

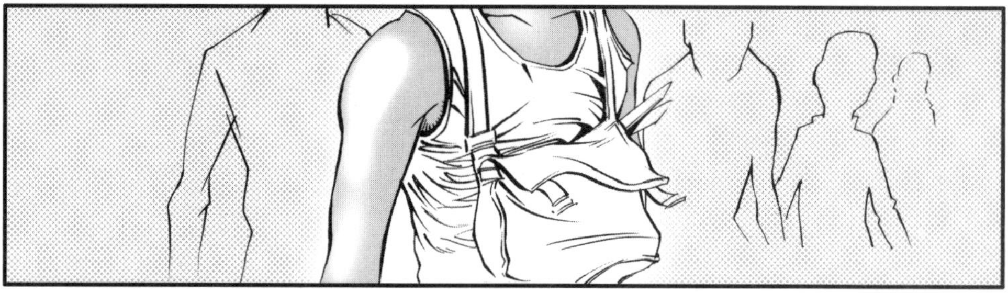

I SAW GAO PU PUT A JAPANESE TYPE-38 RIFLE BAYONET IN THE MILITARY BAG HANGING FROM HIS NECK. AT THE TIME, IT WAS A VERY COVETED WEAPON.

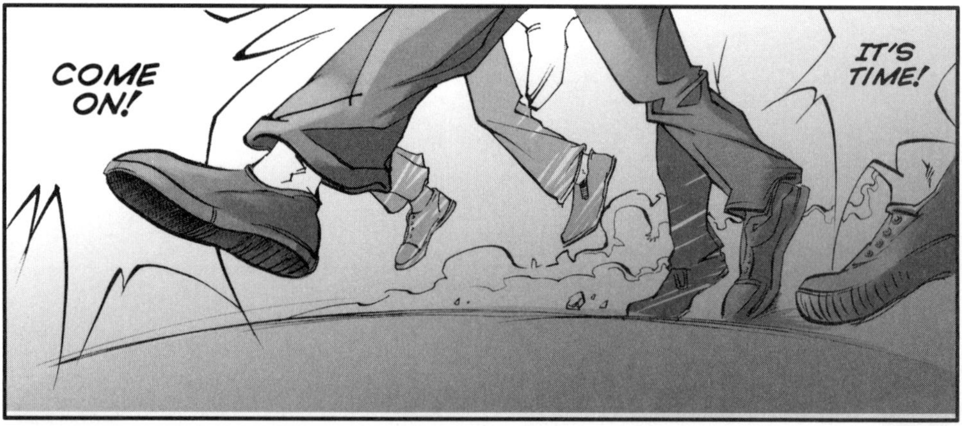
COME ON!
IT'S TIME!

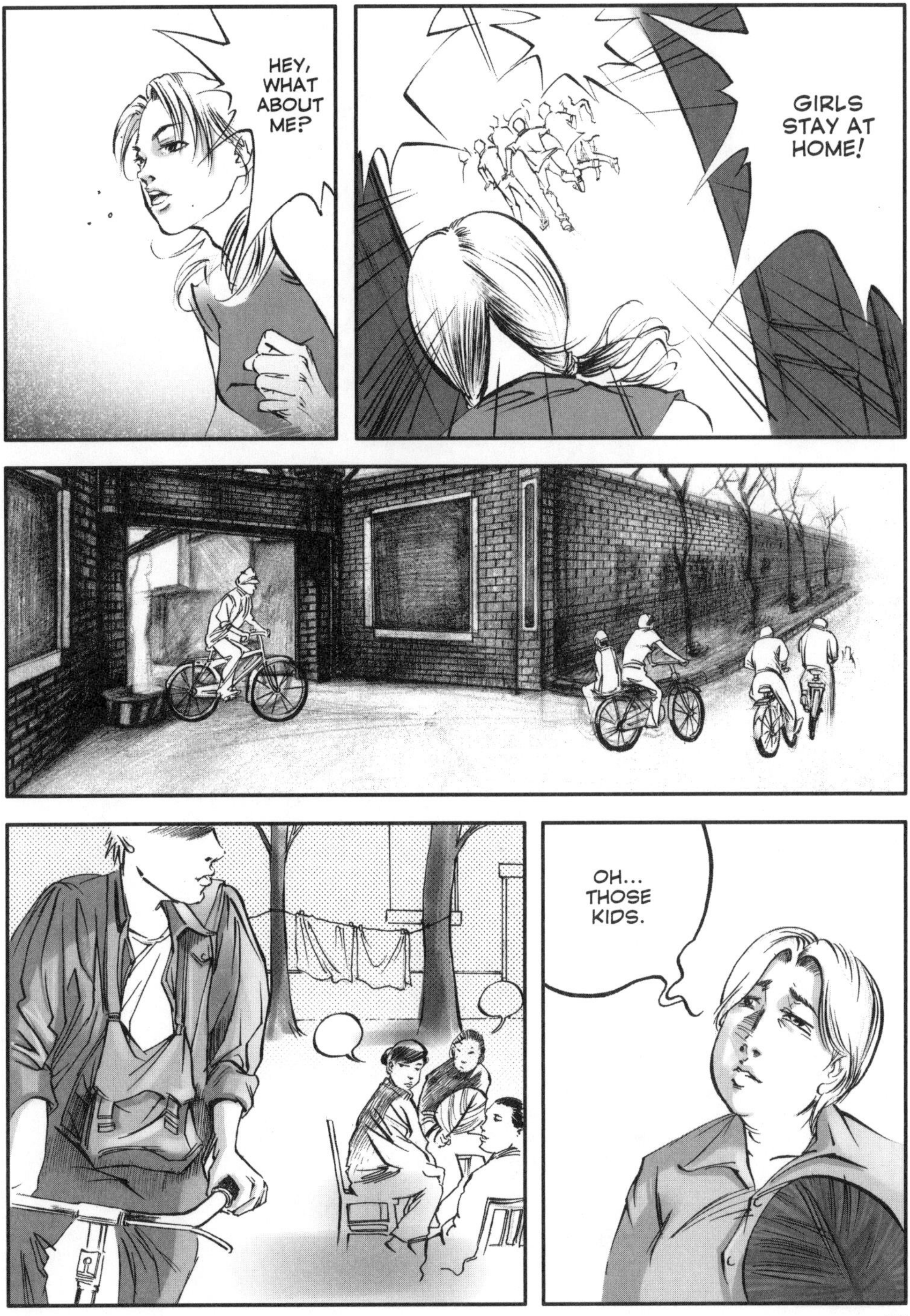

HEY, WHAT ABOUT ME?
GIRLS STAY AT HOME!
OH... THOSE KIDS.

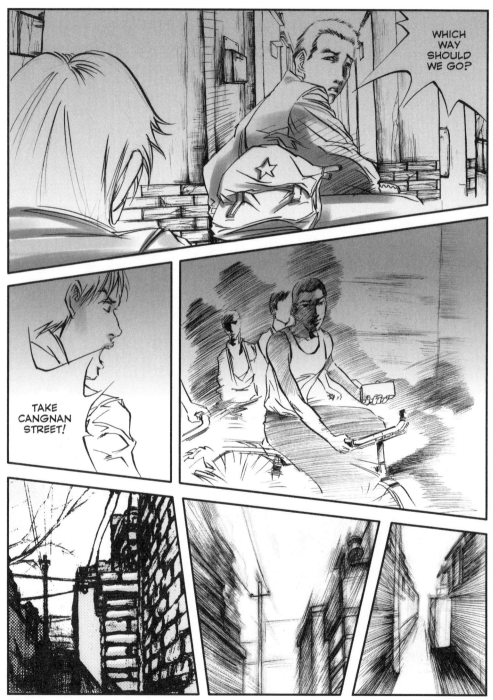

WHICH WAY SHOULD WE GO?

TAKE CANGNAN STREET!

146

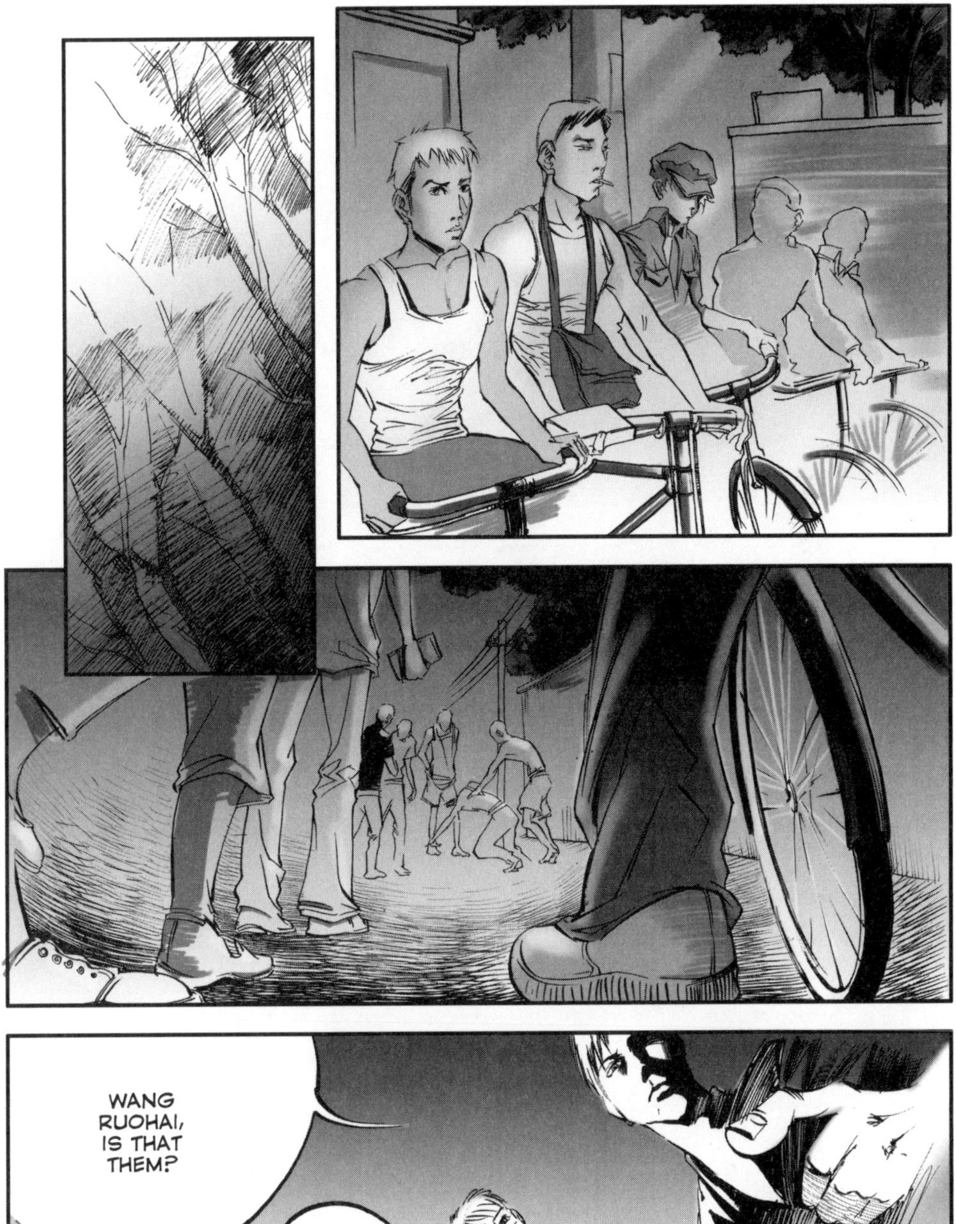
WANG RUOHAI, IS THAT THEM?
YEAH, THOSE GUYS!

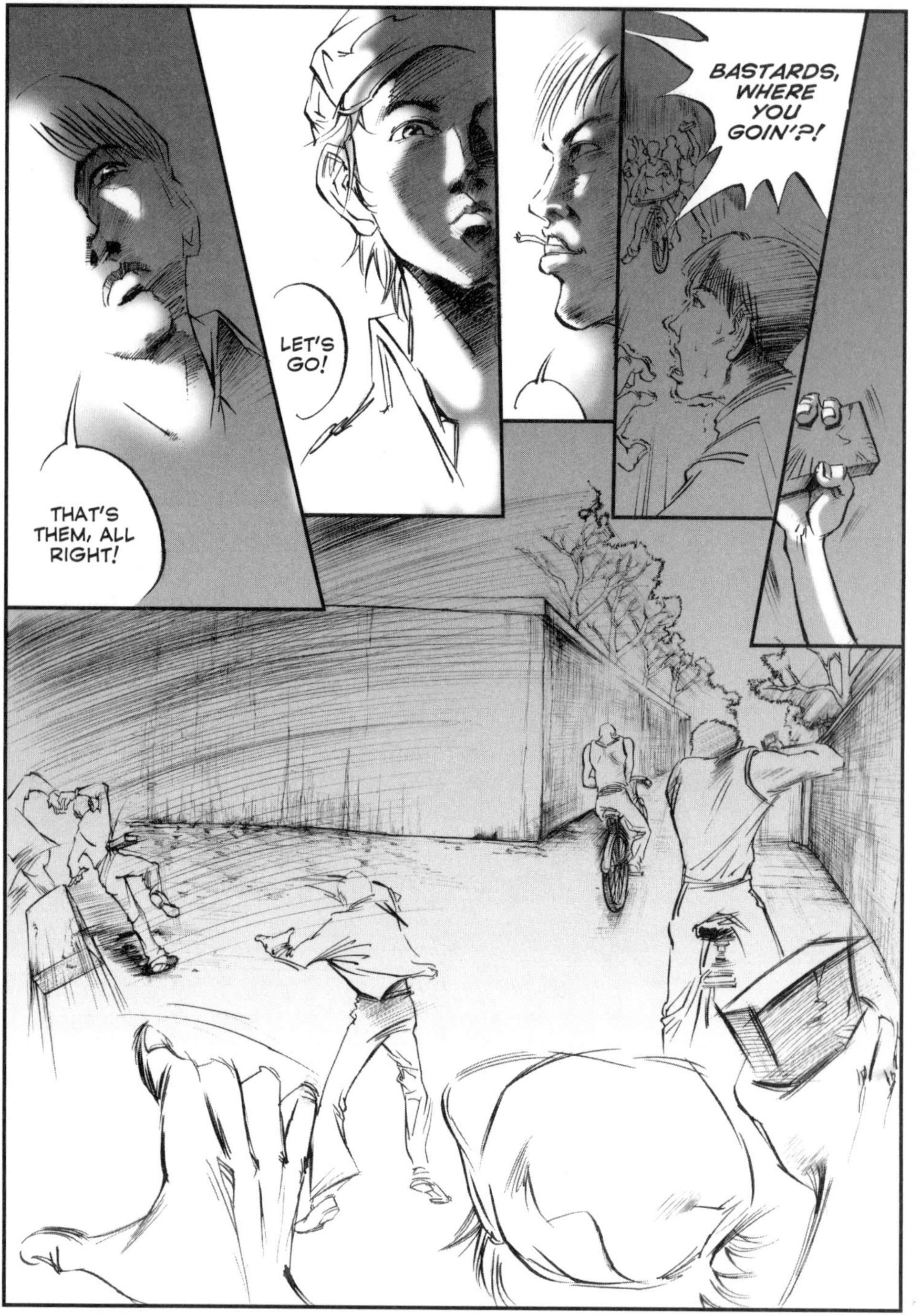
THAT'S THEM, ALL RIGHT!
LET'S GO!
BASTARDS, WHERE YOU GOIN'?!

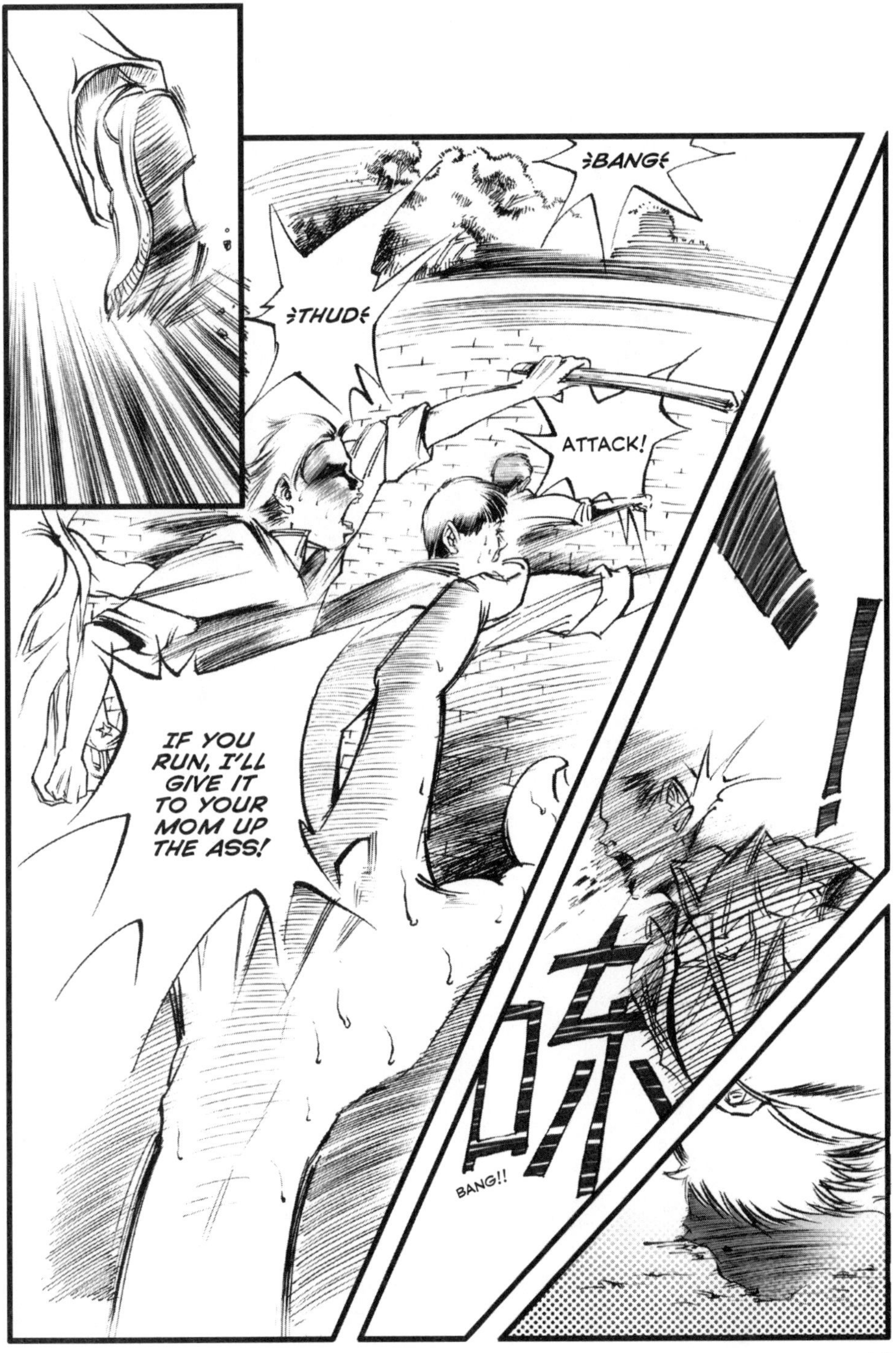

BANG
THUD
ATTACK!
IF YOU RUN, I'LL GIVE IT TO YOUR MOM UP THE ASS!
BANG!!

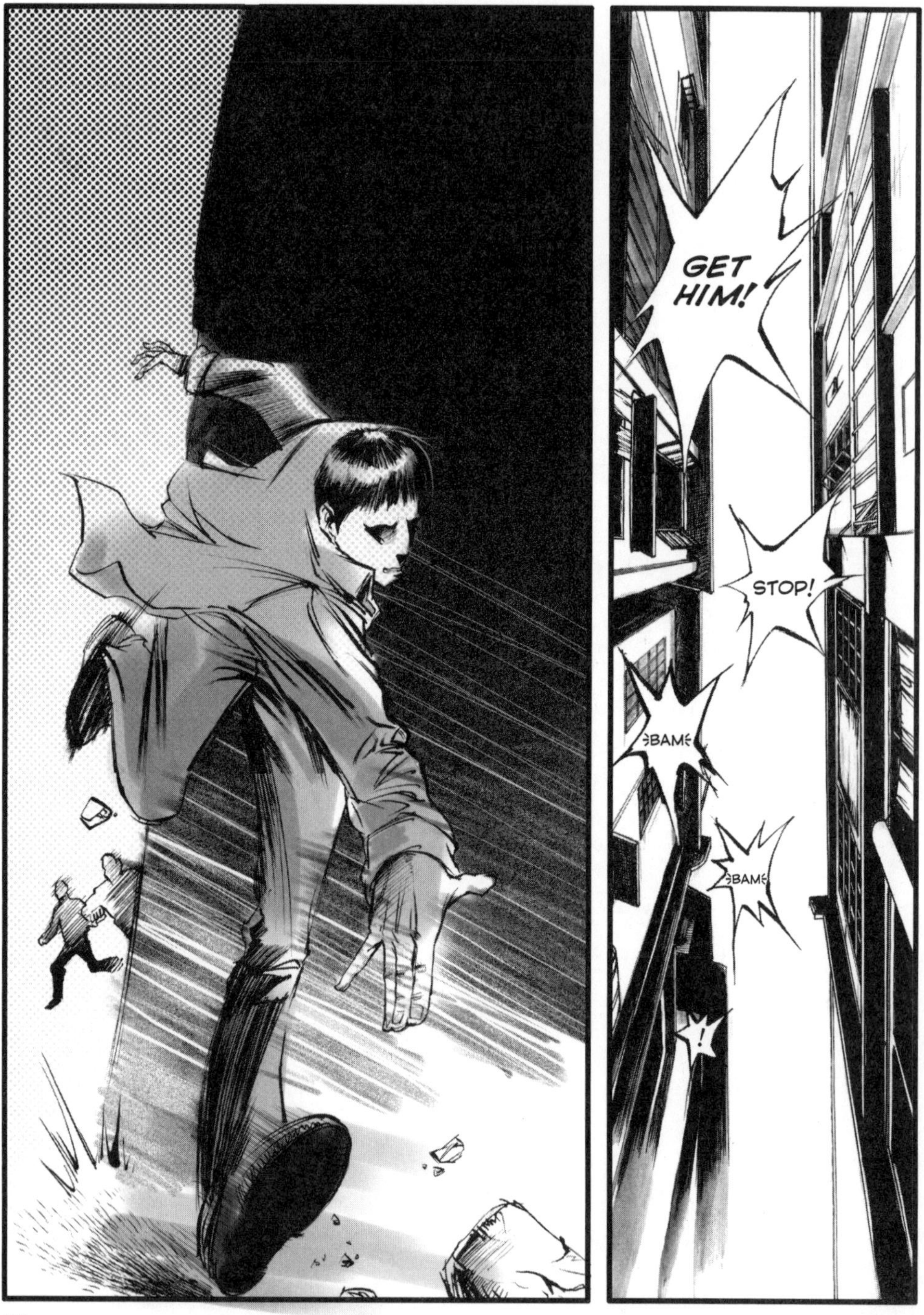
GET HIM!
STOP!
BAM
BAM
!

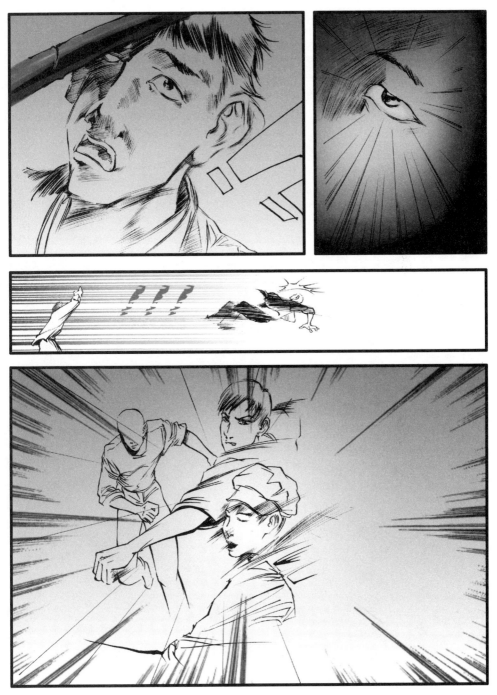

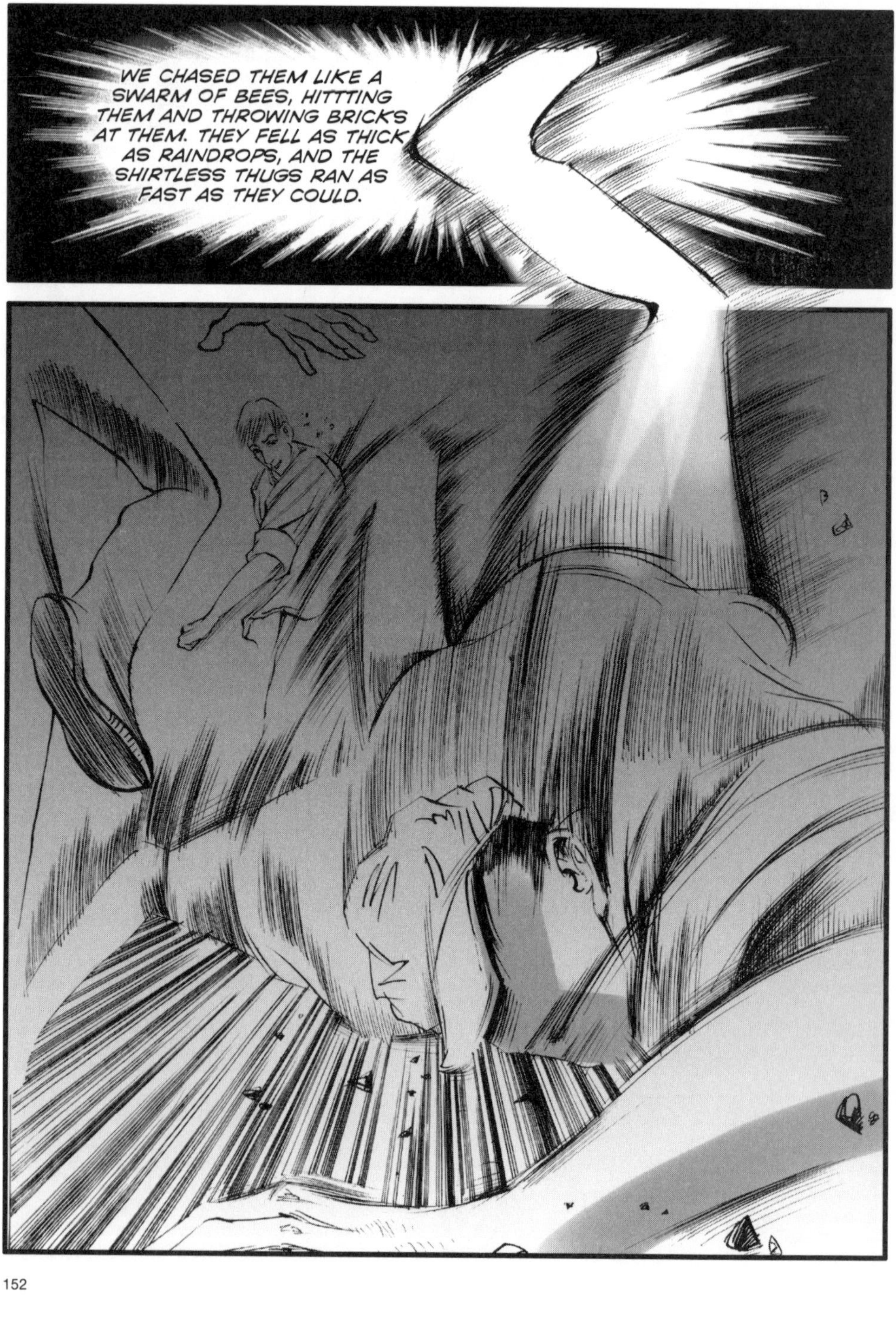
WE CHASED THEM LIKE A SWARM OF BEES, HITTTING THEM AND THROWING BRICKS AT THEM. THEY FELL AS THICK AS RAINDROPS, AND THE SHIRTLESS THUGS RAN AS FAST AS THEY COULD.

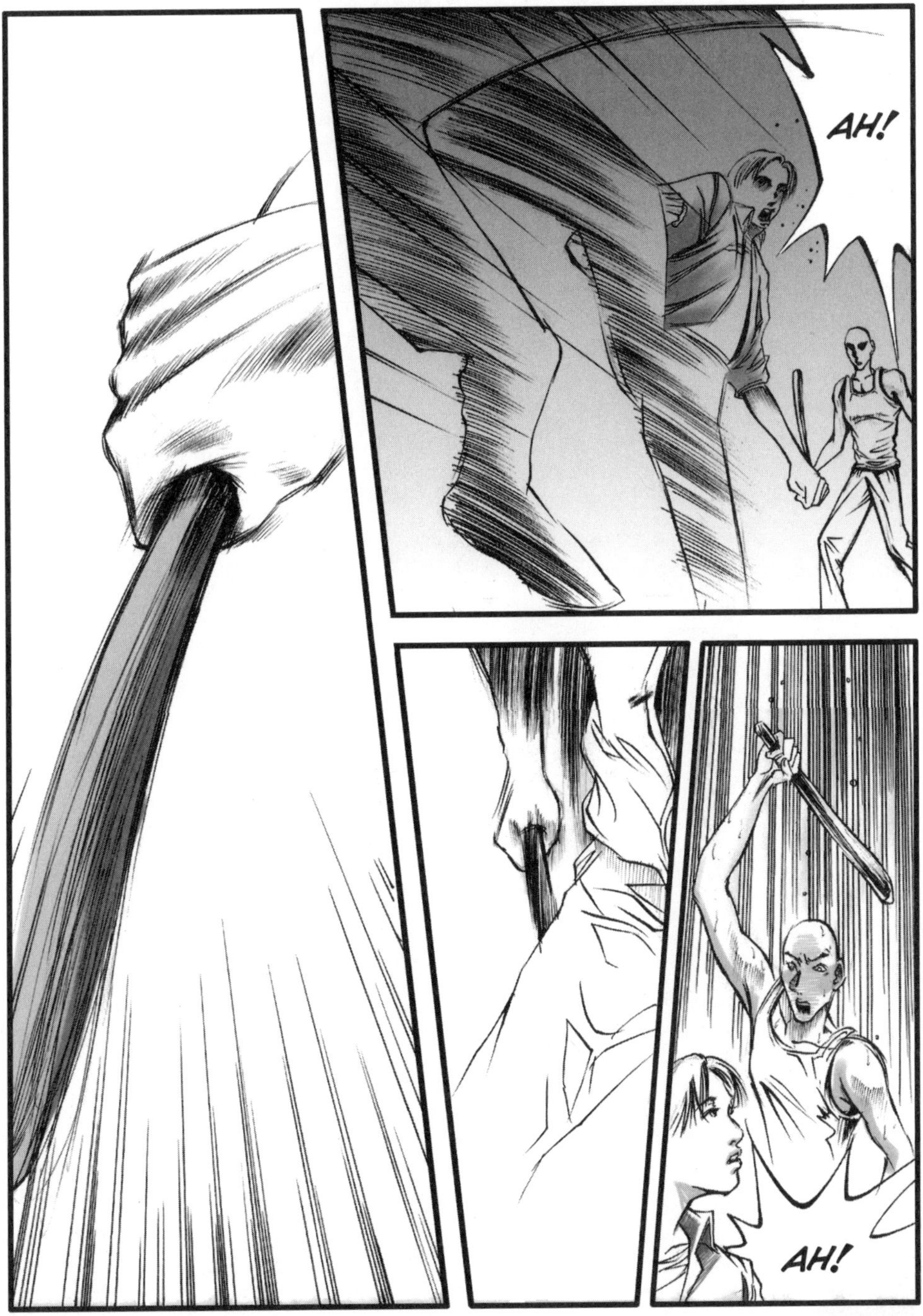
AH!
AH!

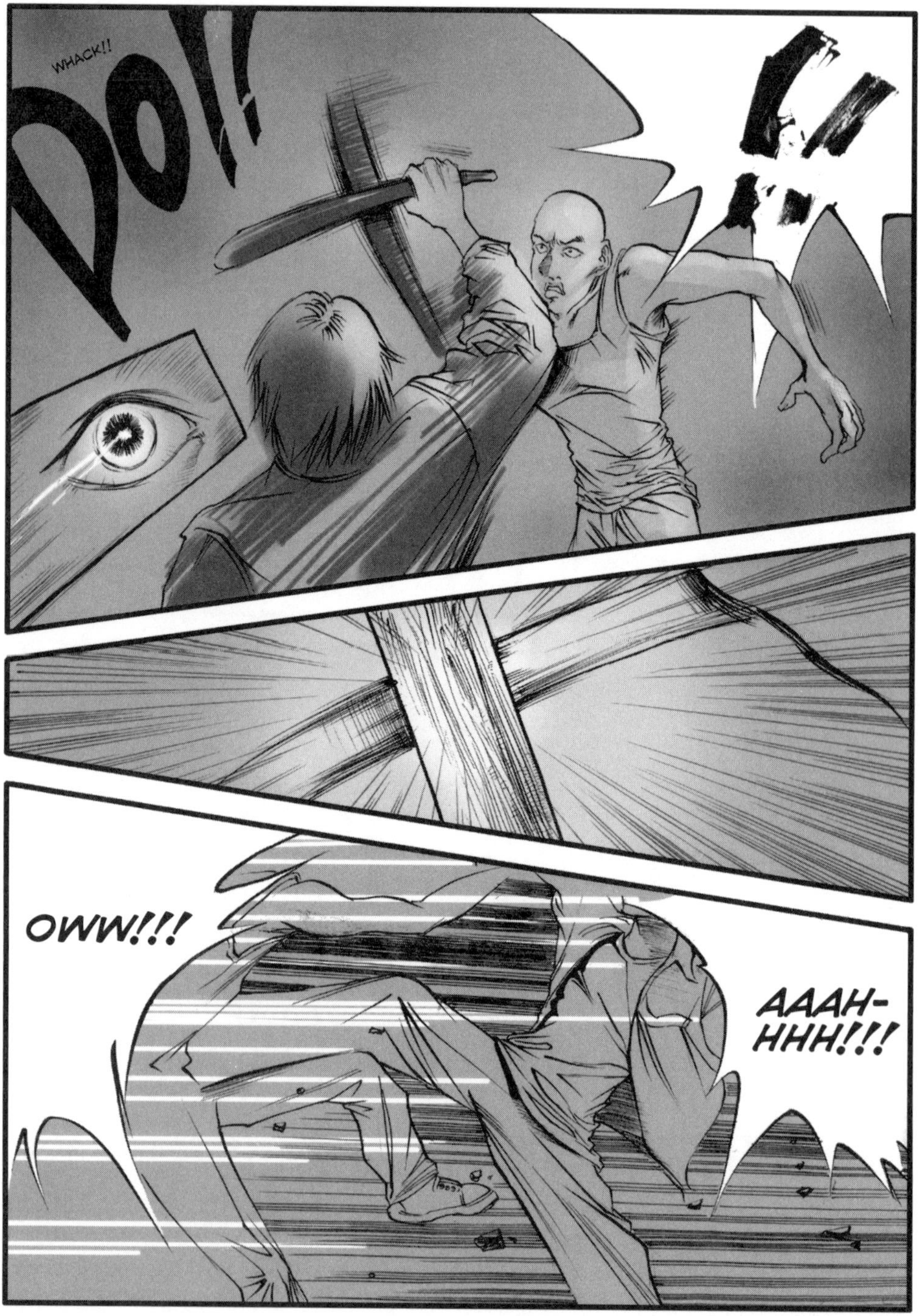
WHACK!!
DO!!
OWW!!!
AAAH-
HHH!!!

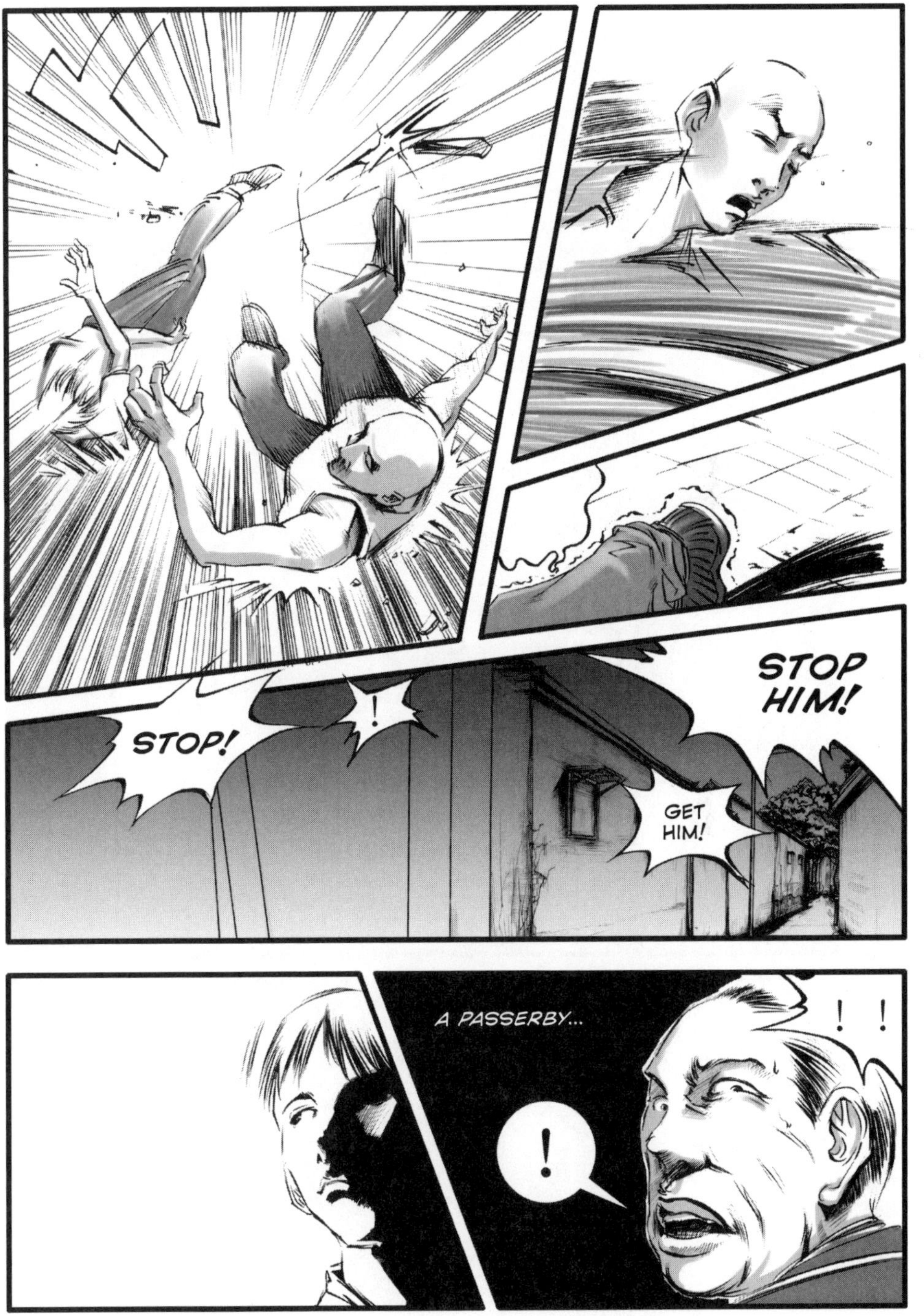
STOP HIM!
STOP!
!
GET HIM!
A PASSERBY...
! !
!

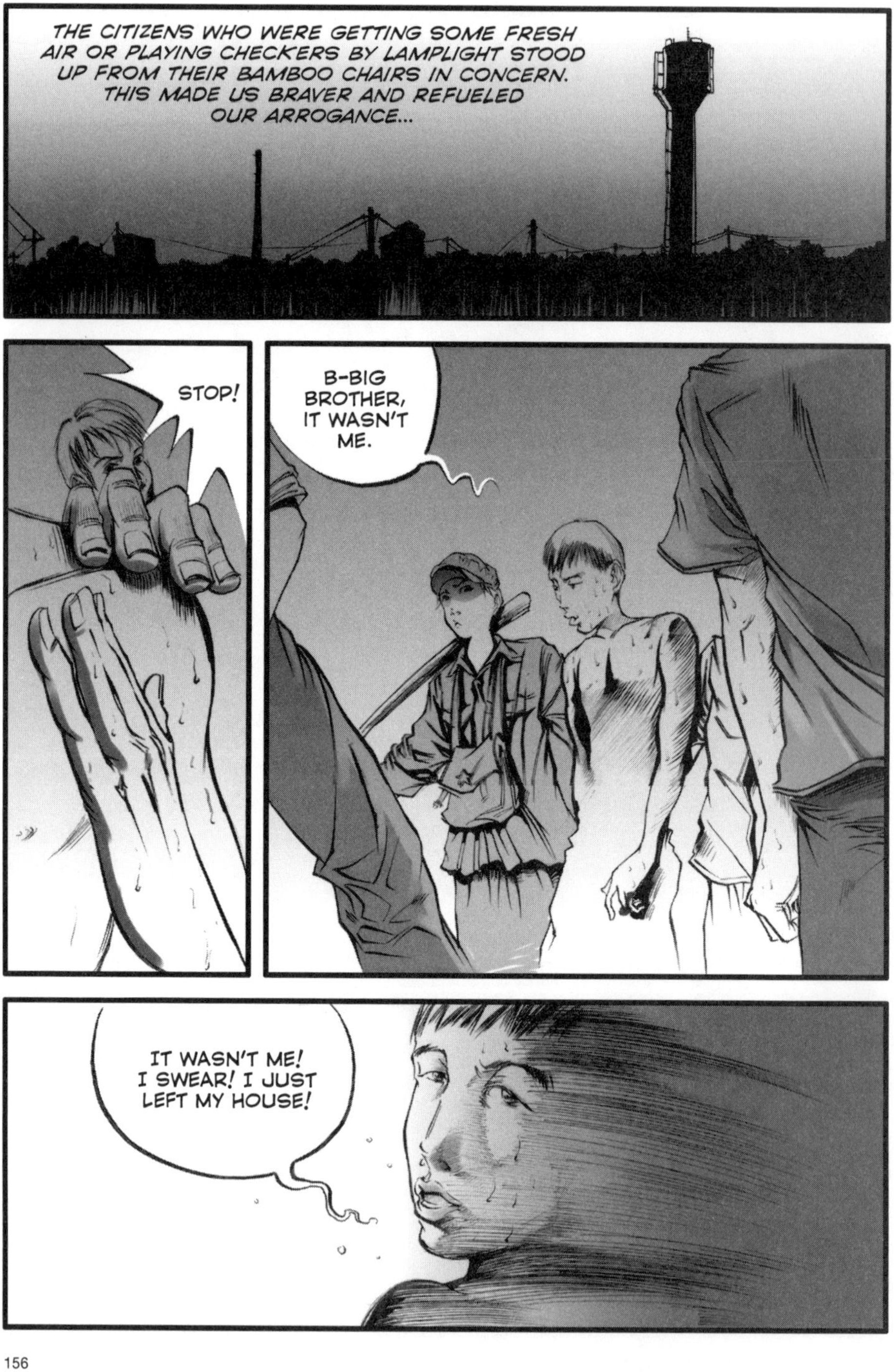
THE CITIZENS WHO WERE GETTING SOME FRESH AIR OR PLAYING CHECKERS BY LAMPLIGHT STOOD UP FROM THEIR BAMBOO CHAIRS IN CONCERN. THIS MADE US BRAVER AND REFUELED OUR ARROGANCE...
STOP!
B-BIG BROTHER, IT WASN'T ME.
IT WASN'T ME! I SWEAR! I JUST LEFT MY HOUSE!

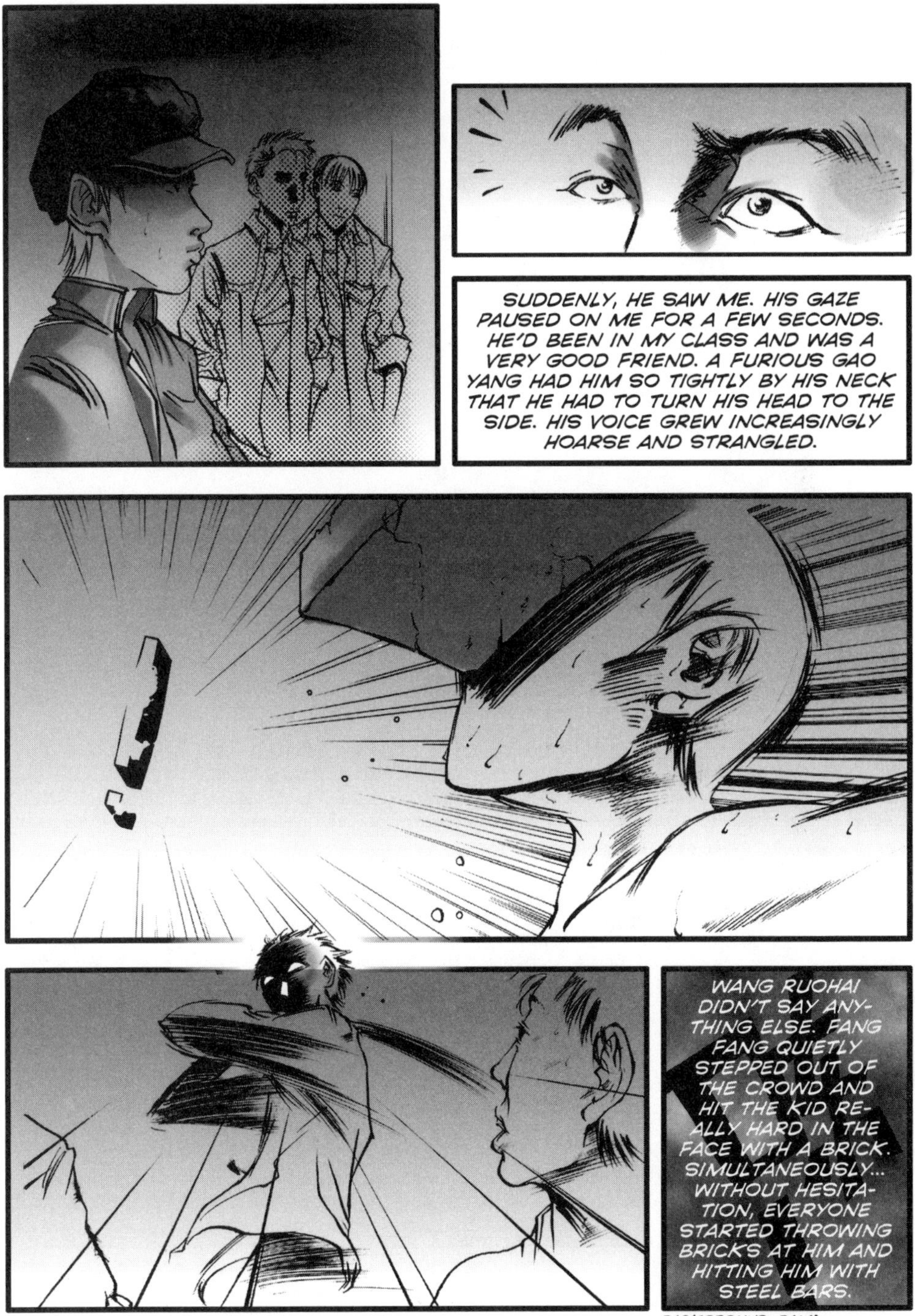
SUDDENLY, HE SAW ME. HIS GAZE PAUSED ON ME FOR A FEW SECONDS. HE'D BEEN IN MY CLASS AND WAS A VERY GOOD FRIEND. A FURIOUS GAO YANG HAD HIM SO TIGHTLY BY HIS NECK THAT HE HAD TO TURN HIS HEAD TO THE SIDE. HIS VOICE GREW INCREASINGLY HOARSE AND STRANGLED.
WANG RUOHAI DIDN'T SAY ANYTHING ELSE. FANG FANG QUIETLY STEPPED OUT OF THE CROWD AND HIT THE KID REALLY HARD IN THE FACE WITH A BRICK. SIMULTANEOUSLY... WITHOUT HESITATION, EVERYONE STARTED THROWING BRICKS AT HIM AND HITTING HIM WITH STEEL BARS.
BACKGROUND: BAM!

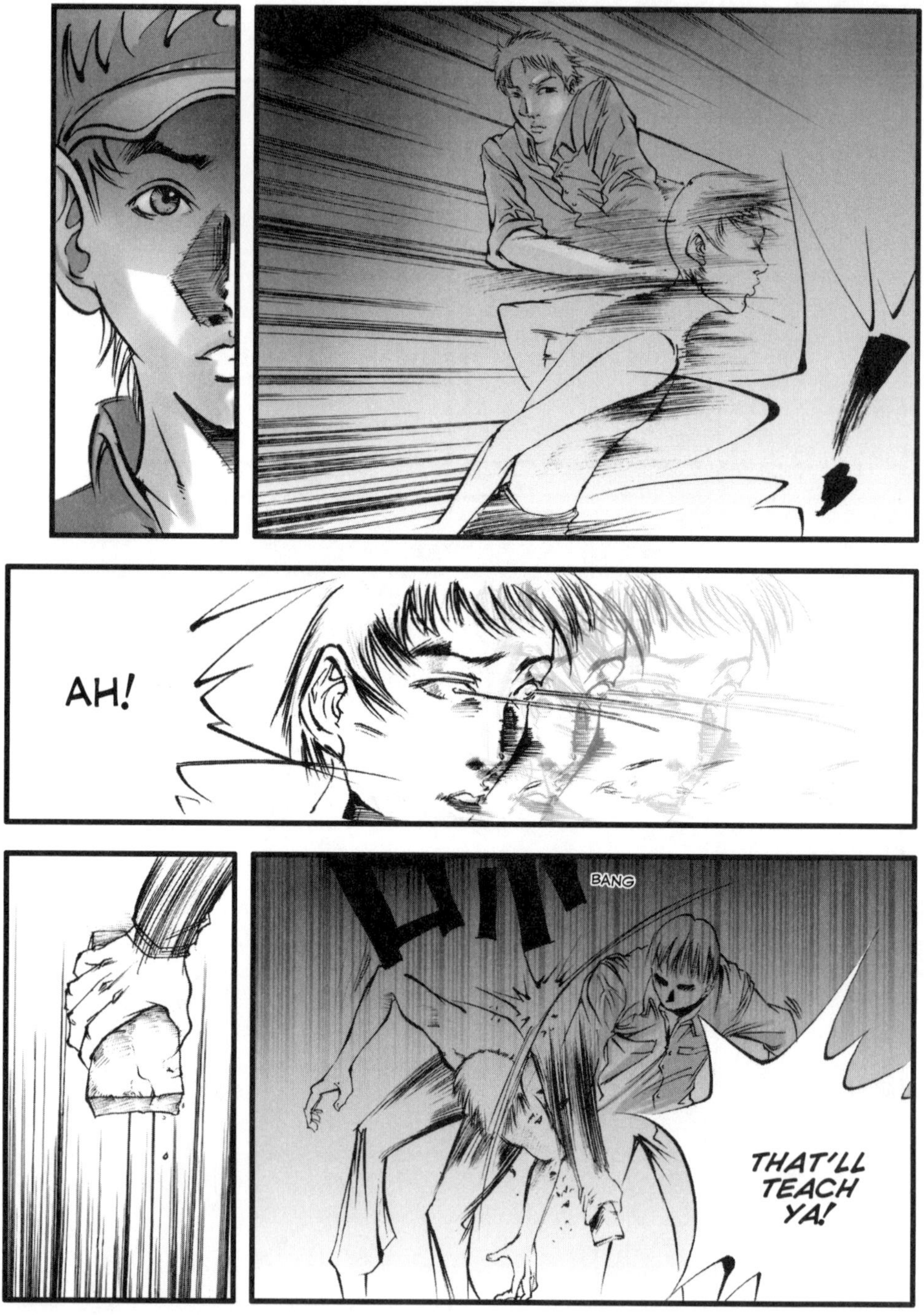
AH!
BANG
THAT'LL TEACH YA!

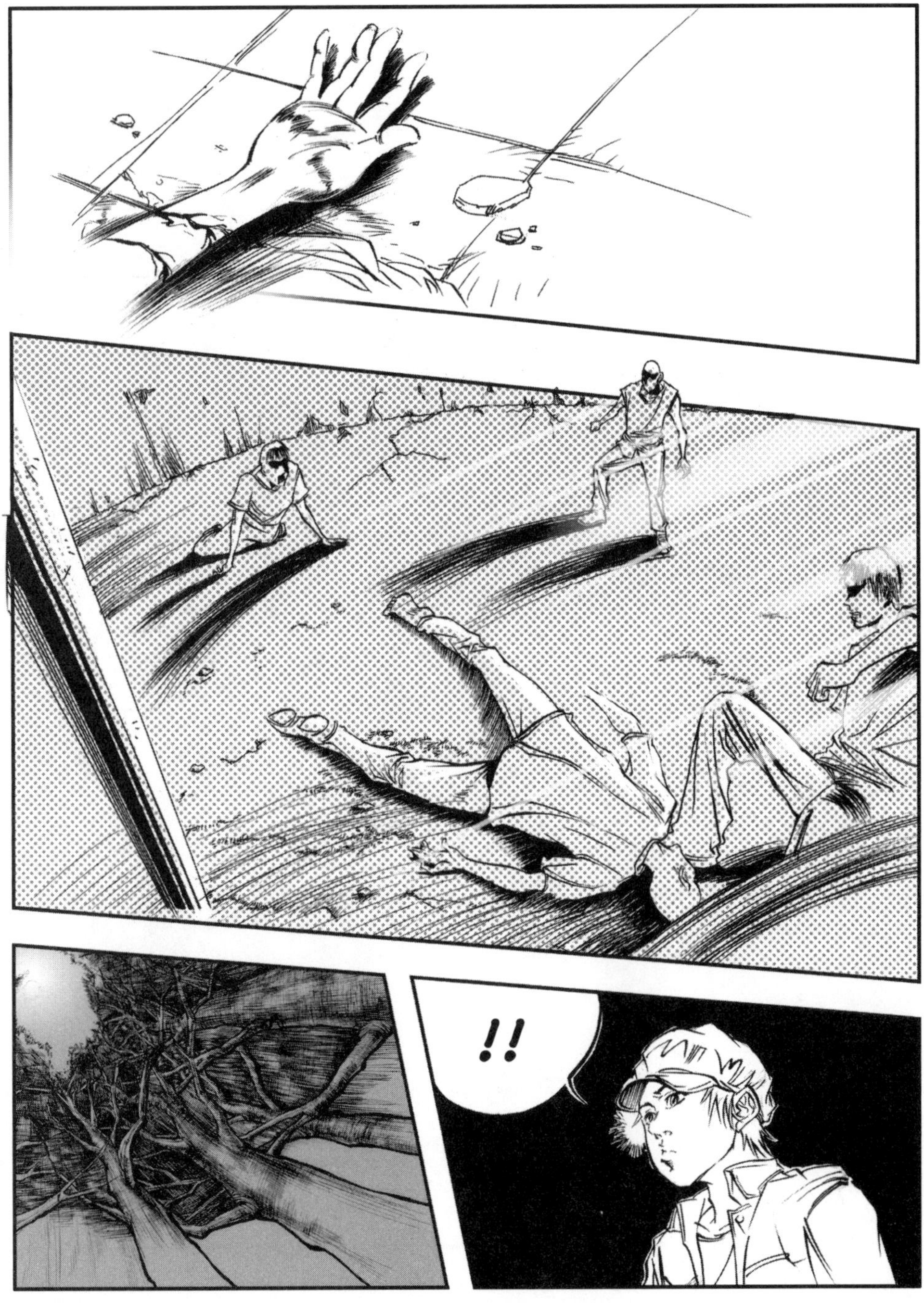
!!

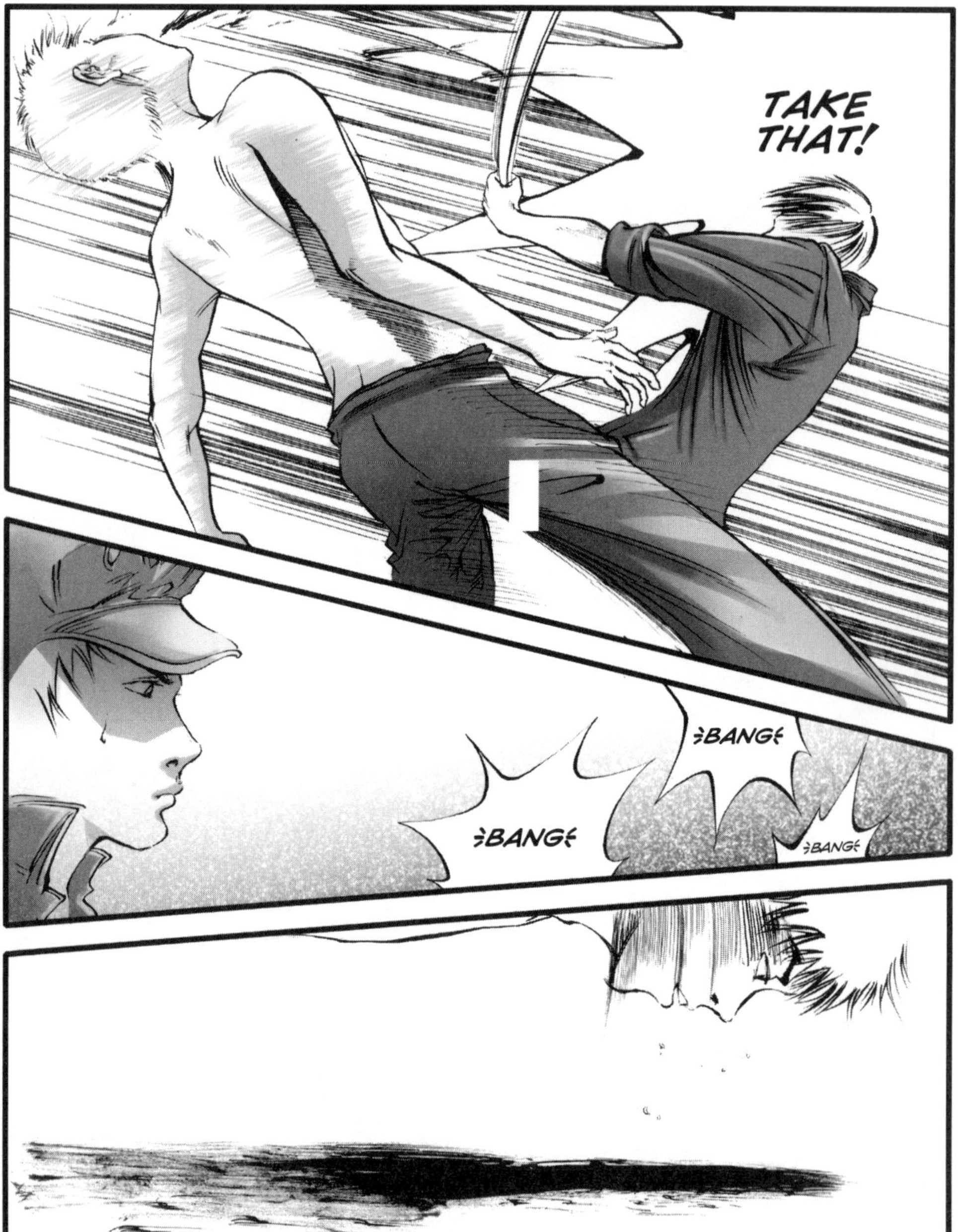
TAKE THAT!
BANG
BANG
BANG

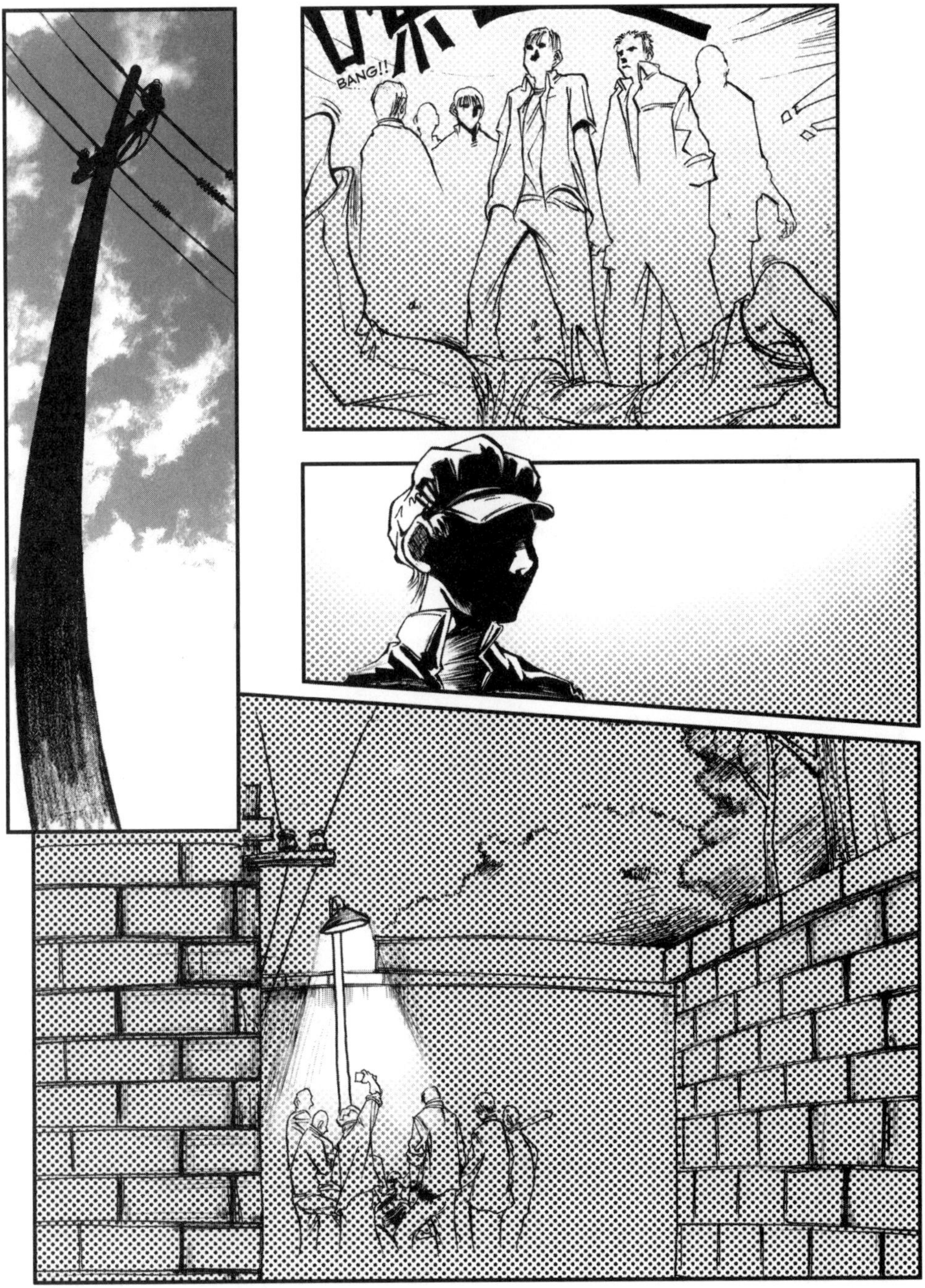
BANG!!

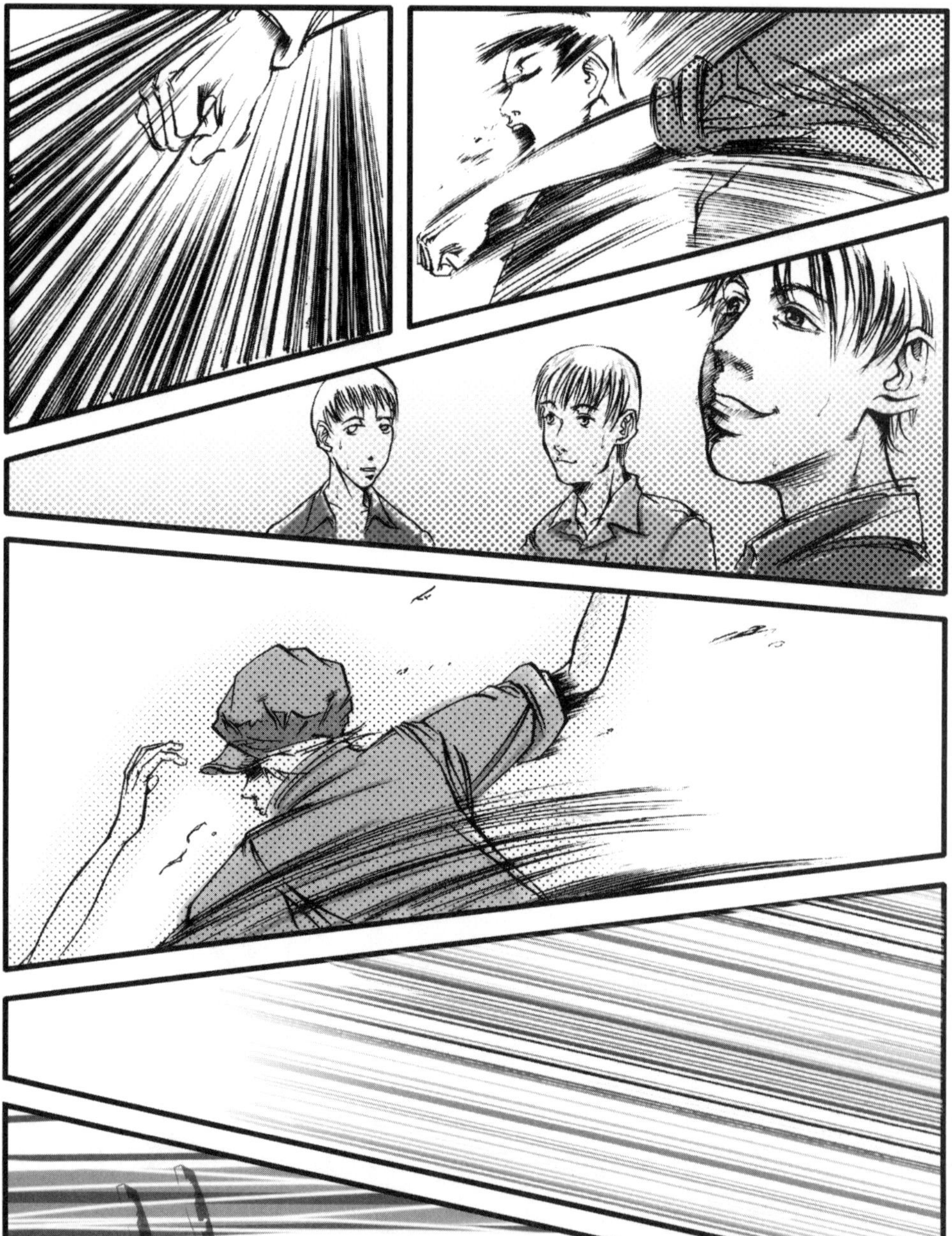

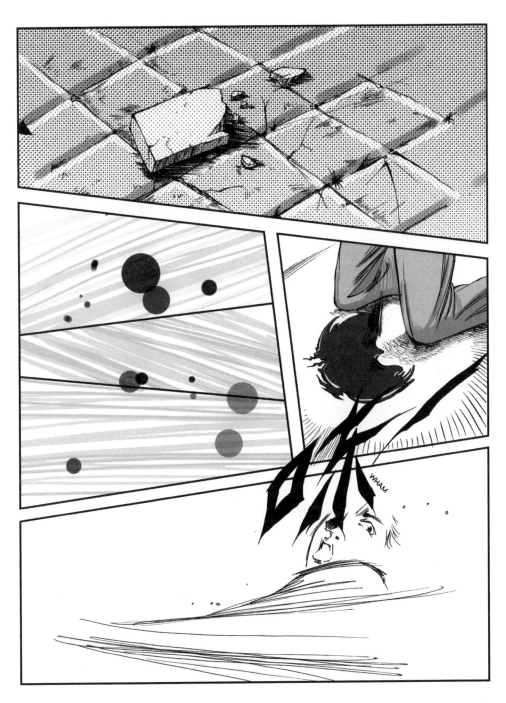

WHAM

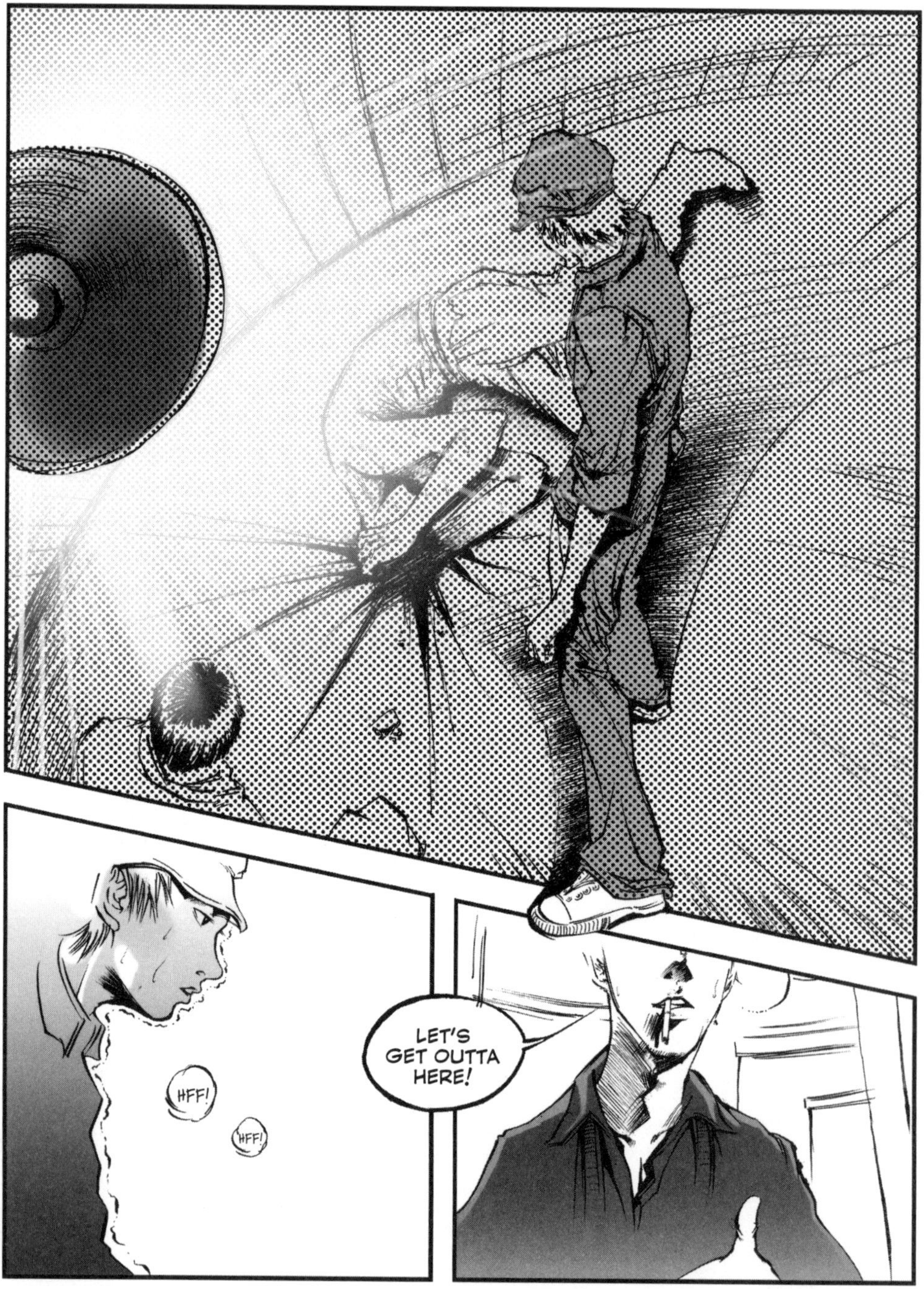
HFF!
HFF!
LET'S GET OUTTA HERE!

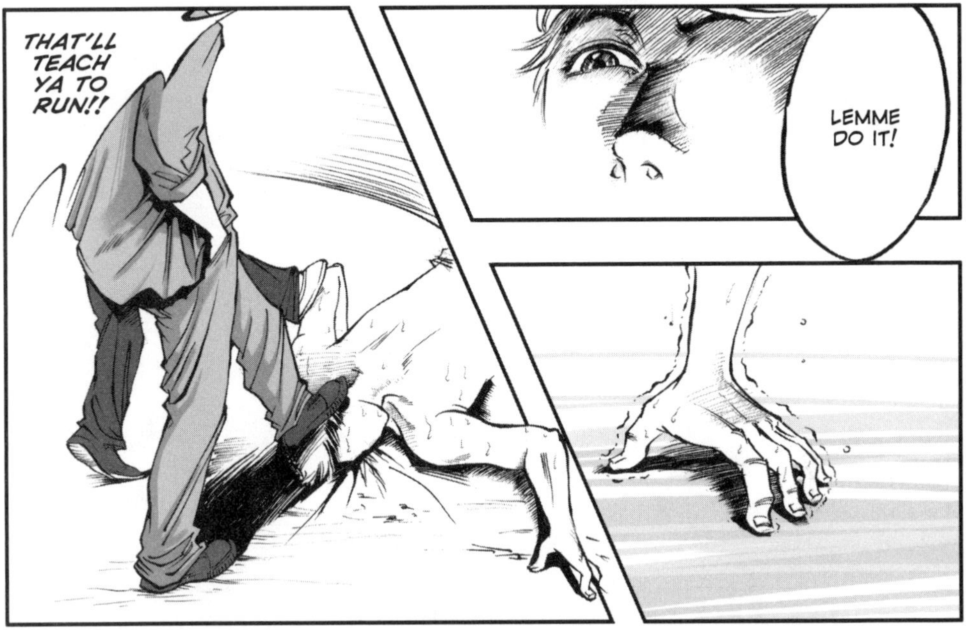
THAT'LL TEACH YA TO RUN!!
LEMME DO IT!

IN DEAD SILENCE, I STARTED HITTING HIM VICIOUSLY WITH A BRICK, AND EVEN AFTER THE OTHERS HAD LEFT, I KEPT ON PUMMELING HIM. ONLY AFTER THROWING ANOTHER BLOOD-SOAKED BRICK AT HIS HEAD DID I FINALLY RUN AWAY.

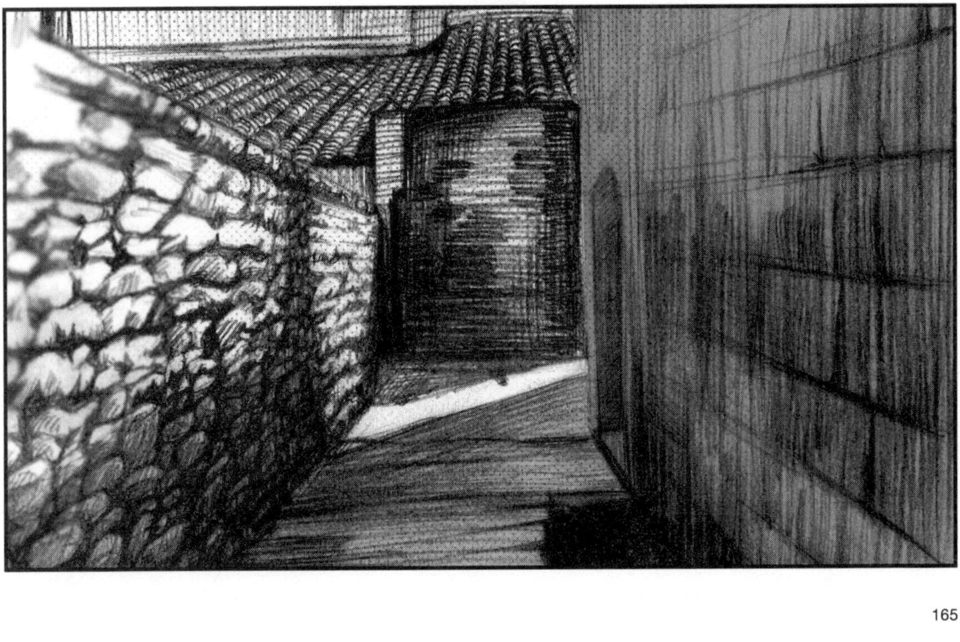

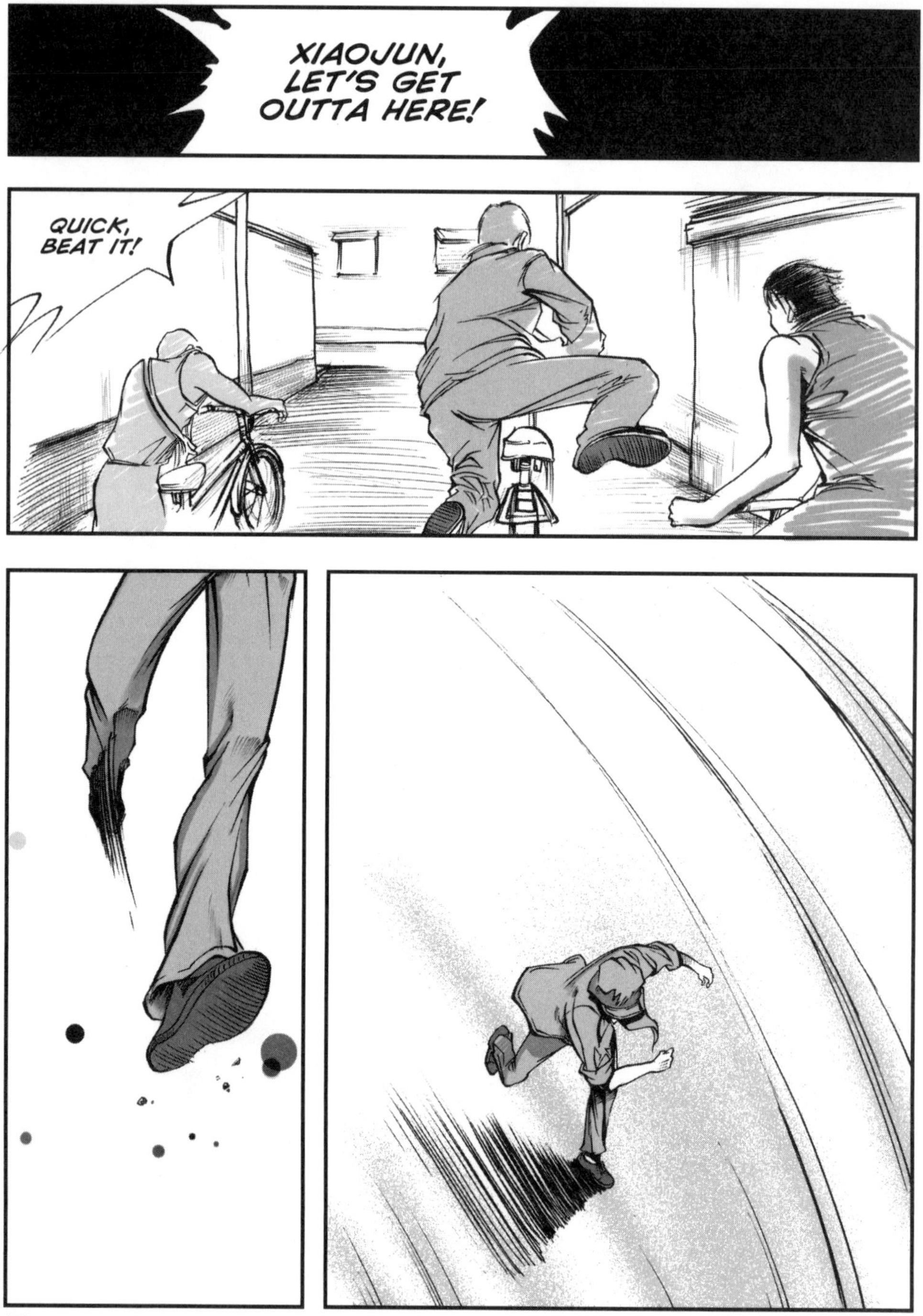
XIAOJUN, LET'S GET OUTTA HERE!
QUICK, BEAT IT!

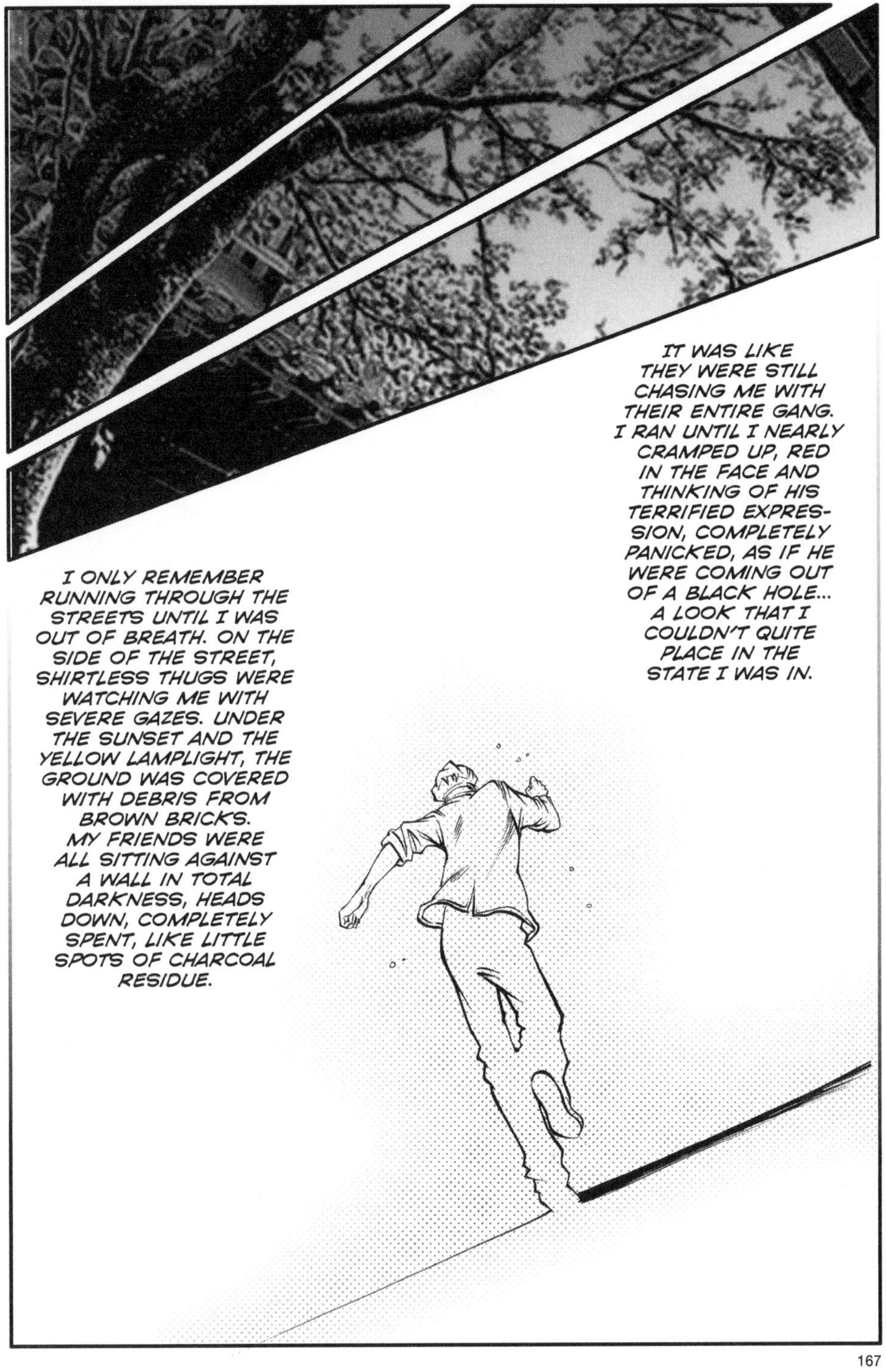
IT WAS LIKE THEY WERE STILL CHASING ME WITH THEIR ENTIRE GANG. I RAN UNTIL I NEARLY CRAMPED UP, RED IN THE FACE AND THINKING OF HIS TERRIFIED EXPRES-SION, COMPLETELY PANICKED, AS IF HE WERE COMING OUT OF A BLACK HOLE... A LOOK THAT I COULDN'T QUITE PLACE IN THE STATE I WAS IN.
I ONLY REMEMBER RUNNING THROUGH THE STREETS UNTIL I WAS OUT OF BREATH. ON THE SIDE OF THE STREET, SHIRTLESS THUGS WERE WATCHING ME WITH SEVERE GAZES. UNDER THE SUNSET AND THE YELLOW LAMPLIGHT, THE GROUND WAS COVERED WITH DEBRIS FROM BROWN BRICKS.
MY FRIENDS WERE ALL SITTING AGAINST A WALL IN TOTAL DARKNESS, HEADS DOWN, COMPLETELY SPENT, LIKE LITTLE SPOTS OF CHARCOAL RESIDUE.

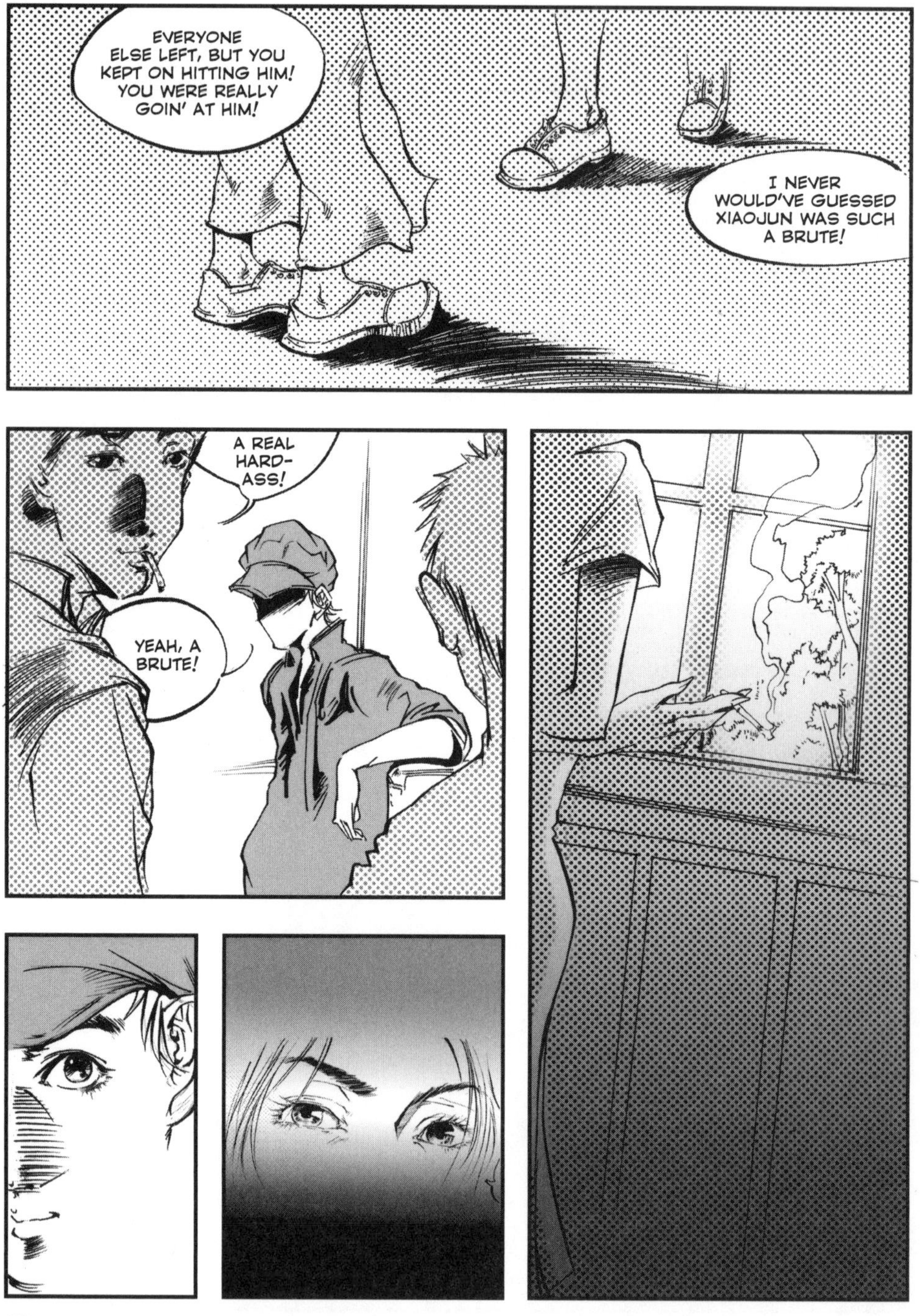
EVERYONE ELSE LEFT, BUT YOU KEPT ON HITTING HIM! YOU WERE REALLY GOIN' AT HIM!
I NEVER WOULD'VE GUESSED XIAOJUN WAS SUCH A BRUTE!
A REAL HARD-ASS!
YEAH, A BRUTE!

IT WAS THE LOGICAL OUTCOME OF
THE MOST FORCEFUL POLITICAL
IDEOLOGY I'D EVER HAD.

THEN I WENT TO SLEEP.

YU BEIBEI WAS SILENTLY
ASLEEP AGAINST THE WALL,
A BLANKET COVERING HER BODY.

BEFORE I KNEW IT,
IT WAS ALREADY
DAYTIME!

YU BEIBEI'S LAUGH MADE ME OVERFLOW WITH PRIDE. CONSIDERING HOW WE WERE DESCRIBING OUR MILITARY EXPLOITS, ANYONE WOULD HAVE THOUGHT THAT THE GUY GOT KILLED.

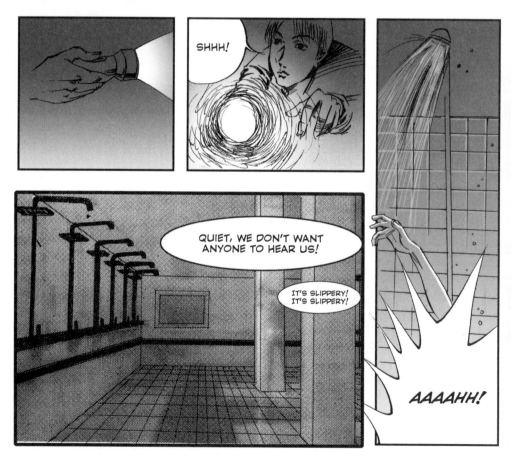

SHHH!

QUIET, WE DON'T WANT ANYONE TO HEAR US!

IT'S SLIPPERY! IT'S SLIPPERY!

AAAAHH!

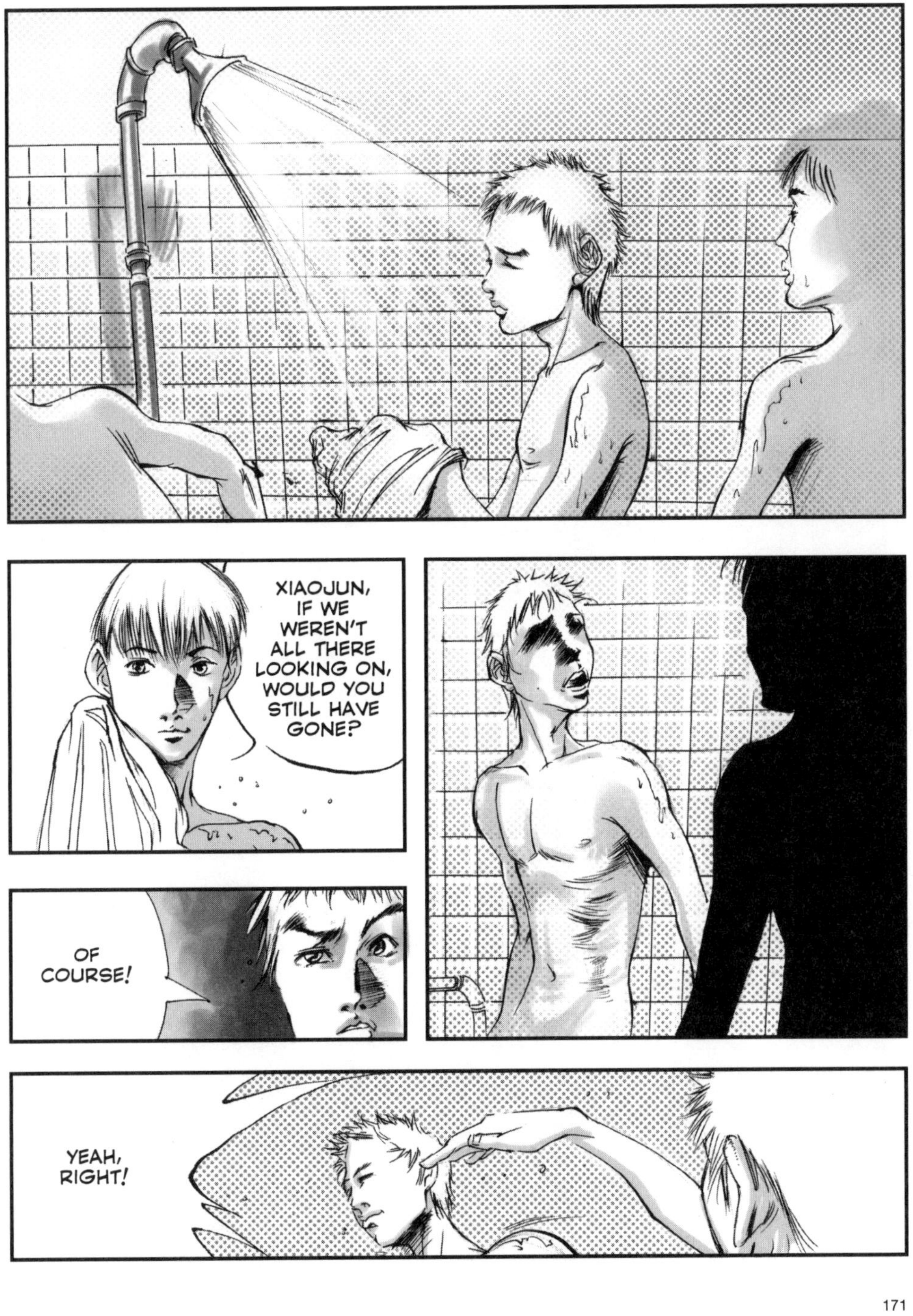
XIAOJUN, IF WE WEREN'T ALL THERE LOOKING ON, WOULD YOU STILL HAVE GONE?
OF COURSE!
YEAH, RIGHT!

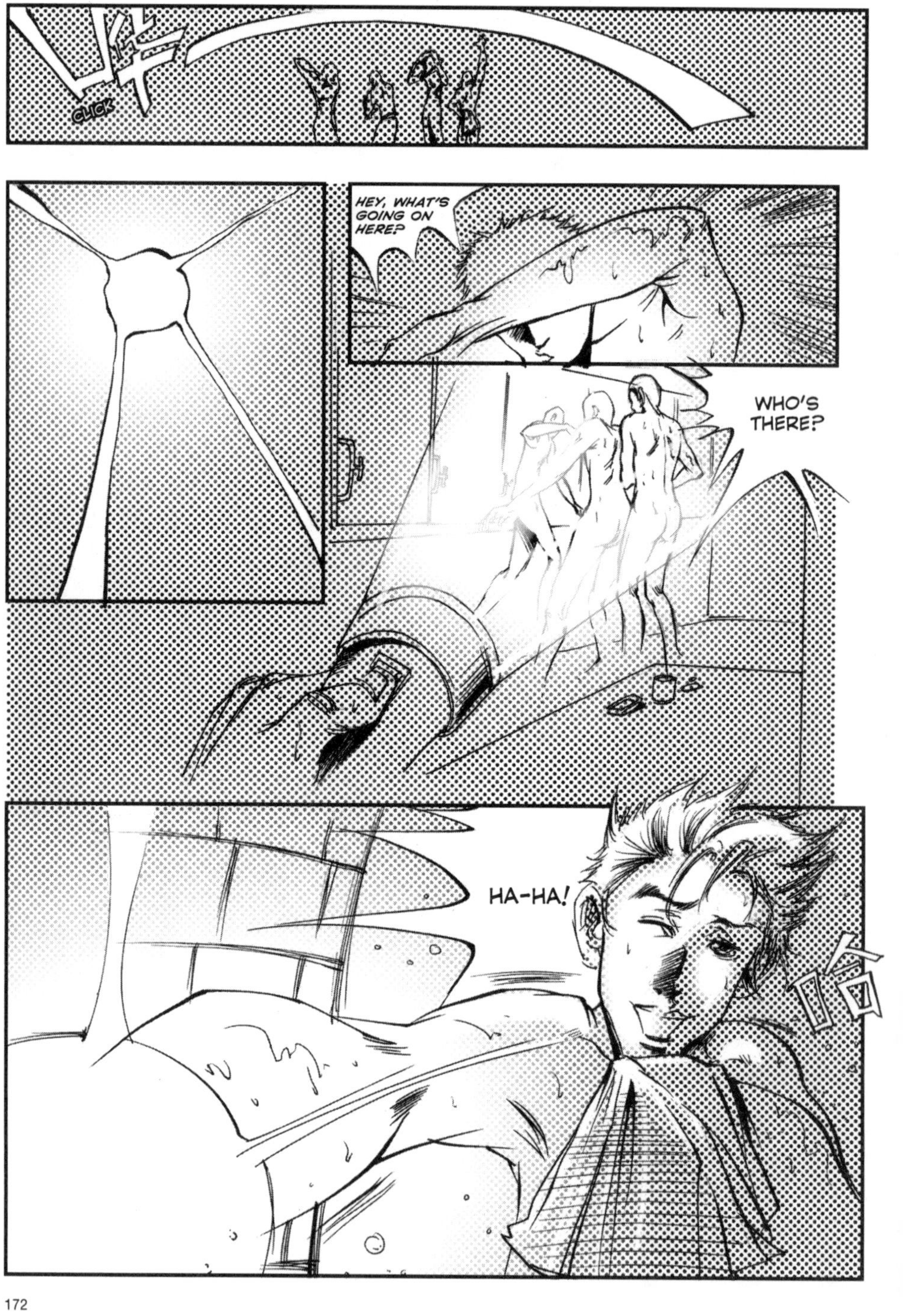
CLICK
HEY, WHAT'S GOING ON HERE?
WHO'S THERE?
HA-HA!

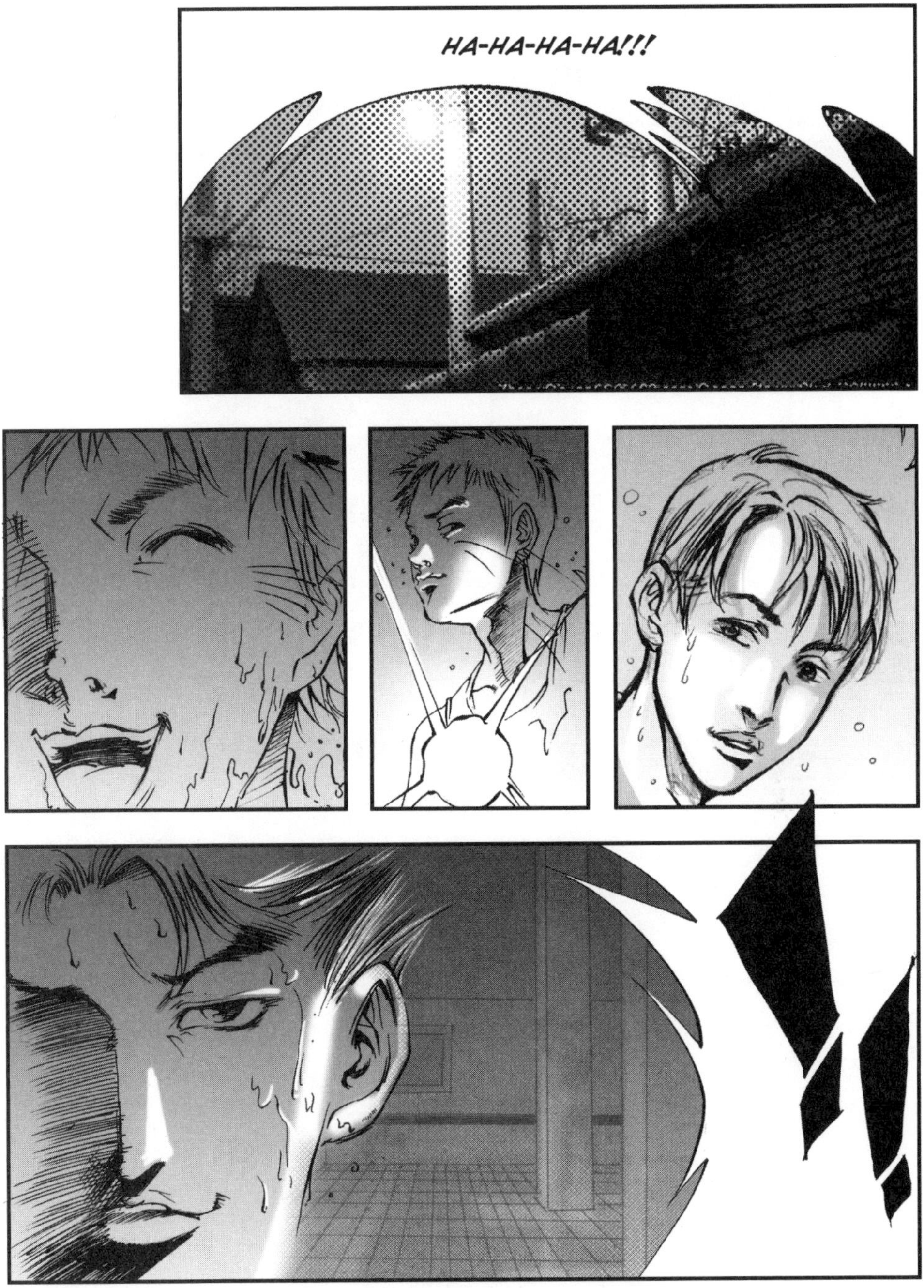
HA-HA-HA-HA!!!

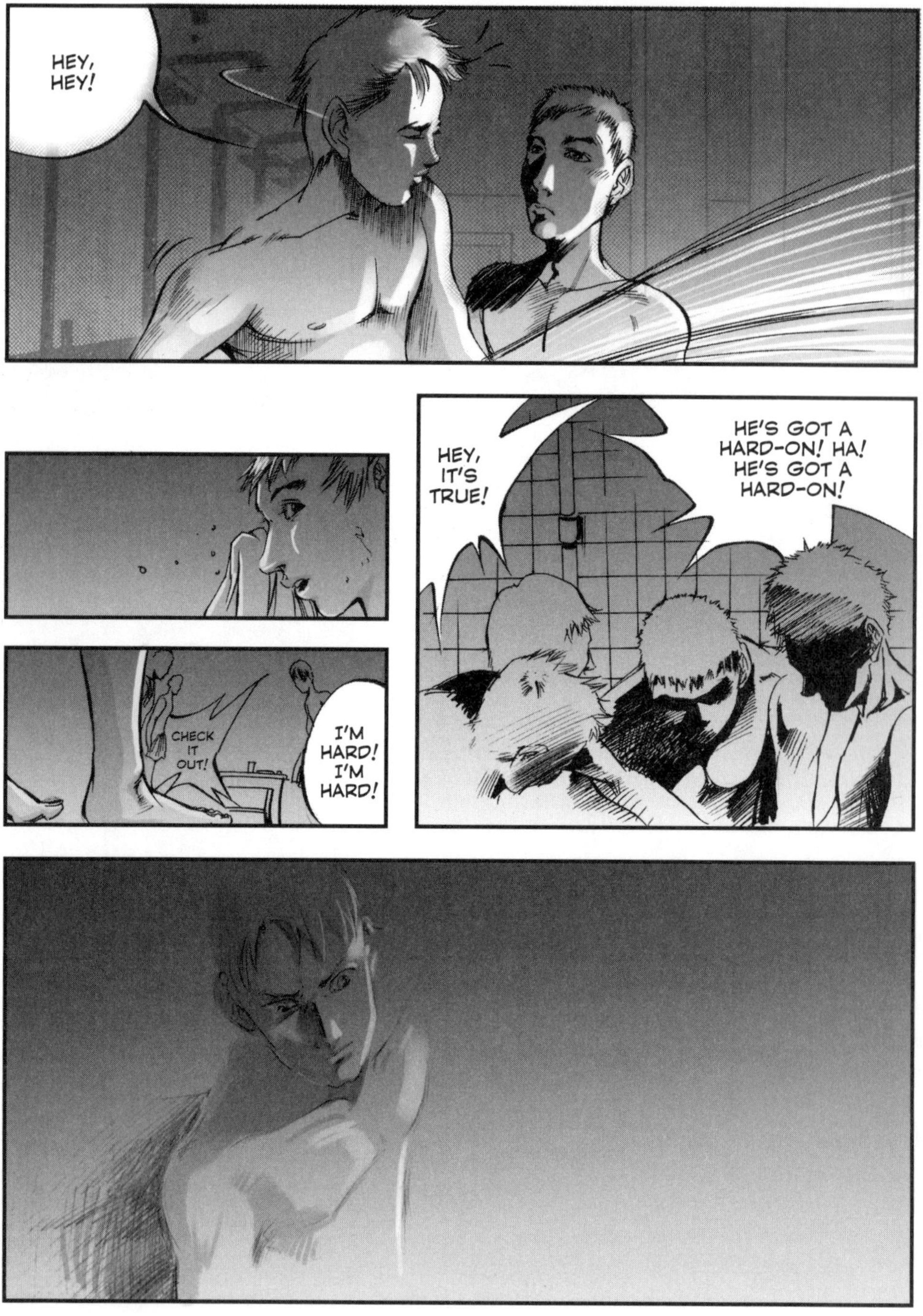
HEY, HEY!
CHECK IT OUT!
I'M HARD! I'M HARD!
HEY, IT'S TRUE!
HE'S GOT A HARD-ON! HA! HE'S GOT A HARD-ON!

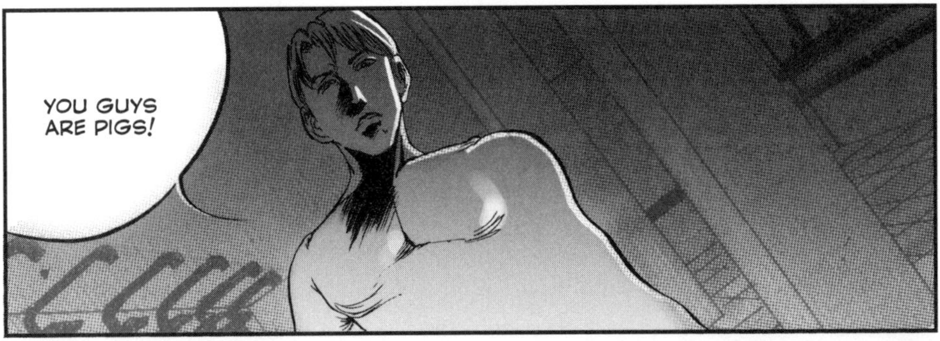
YOU GUYS ARE PIGS!

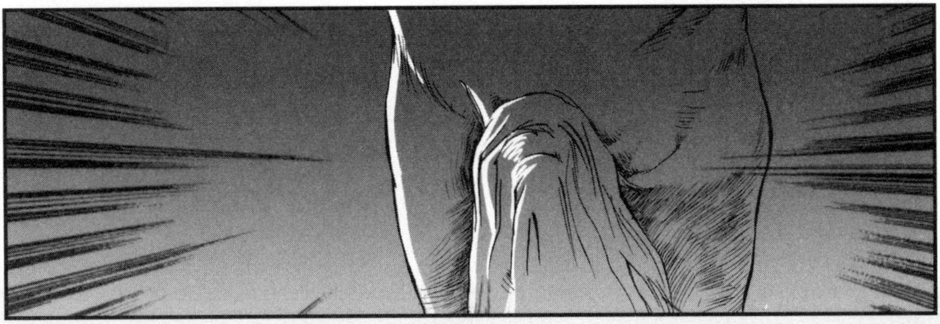

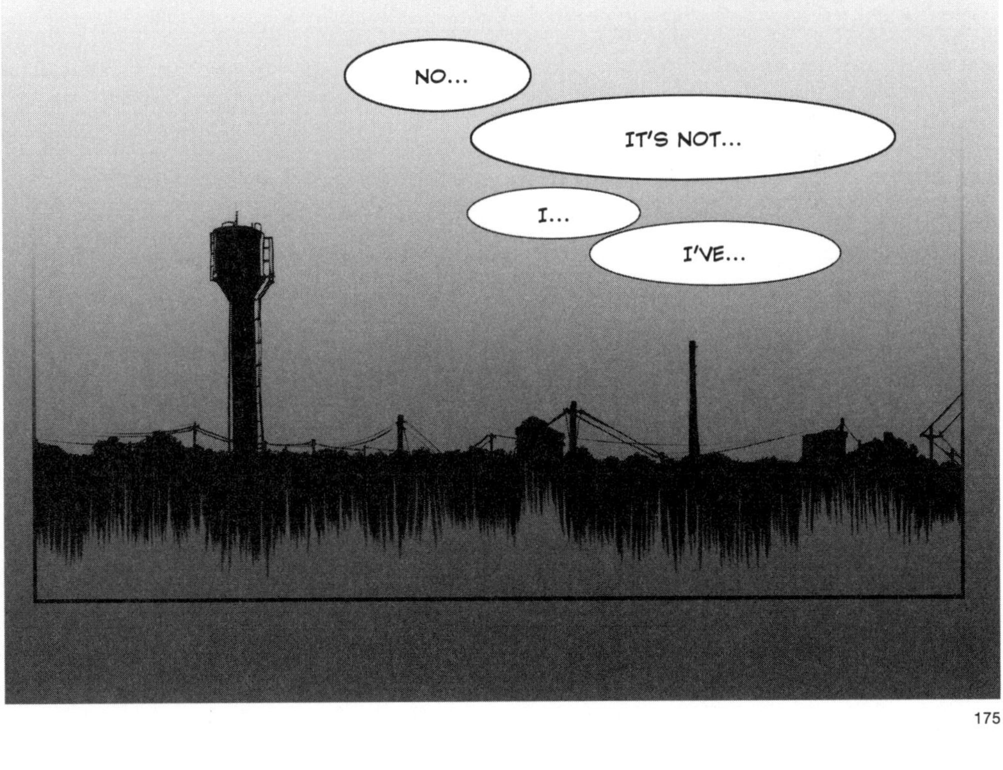
NO...
IT'S NOT...
I...
I'VE...

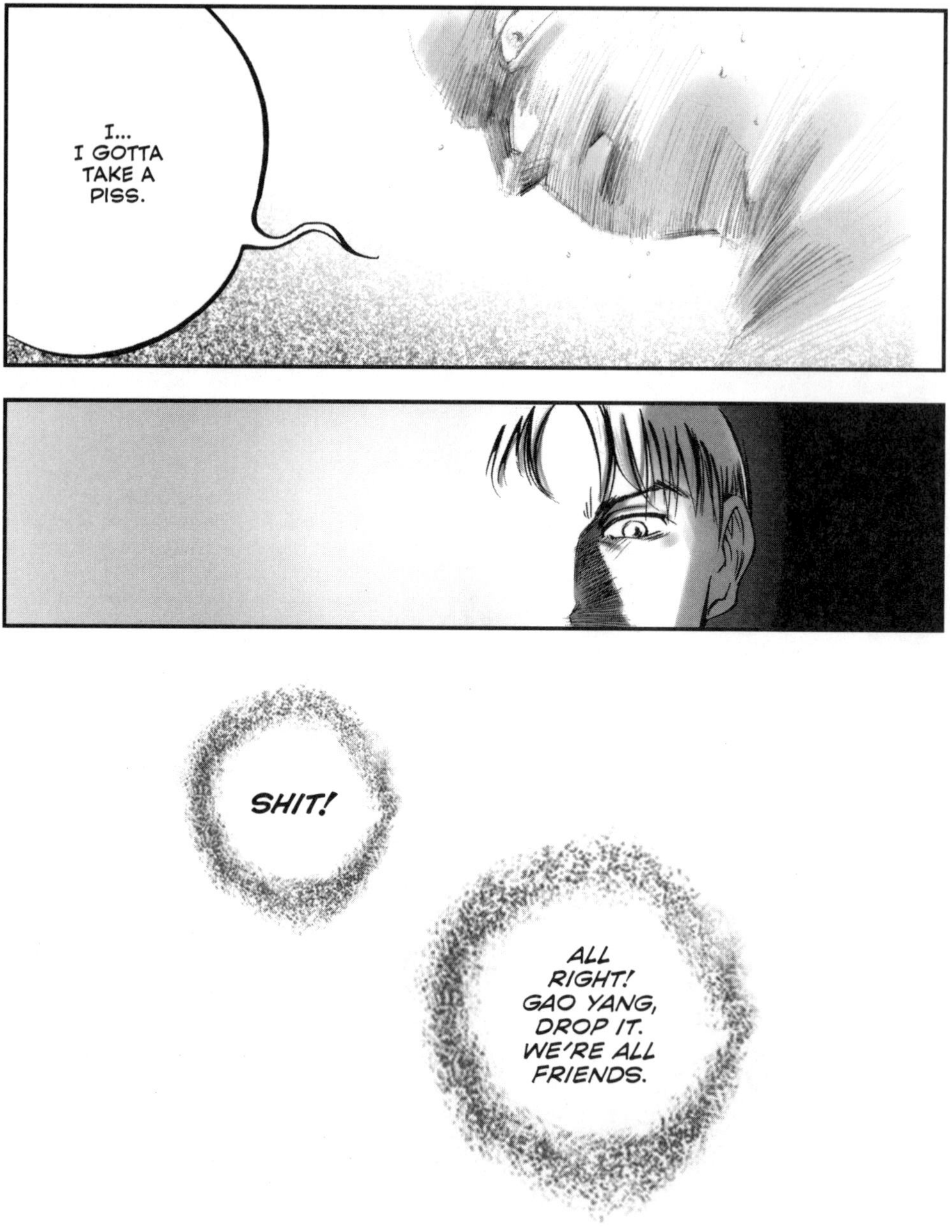
I... I GOTTA TAKE A PISS.
SHIT!
ALL RIGHT! GAO YANG, DROP IT. WE'RE ALL FRIENDS.

6 - mi lan and me

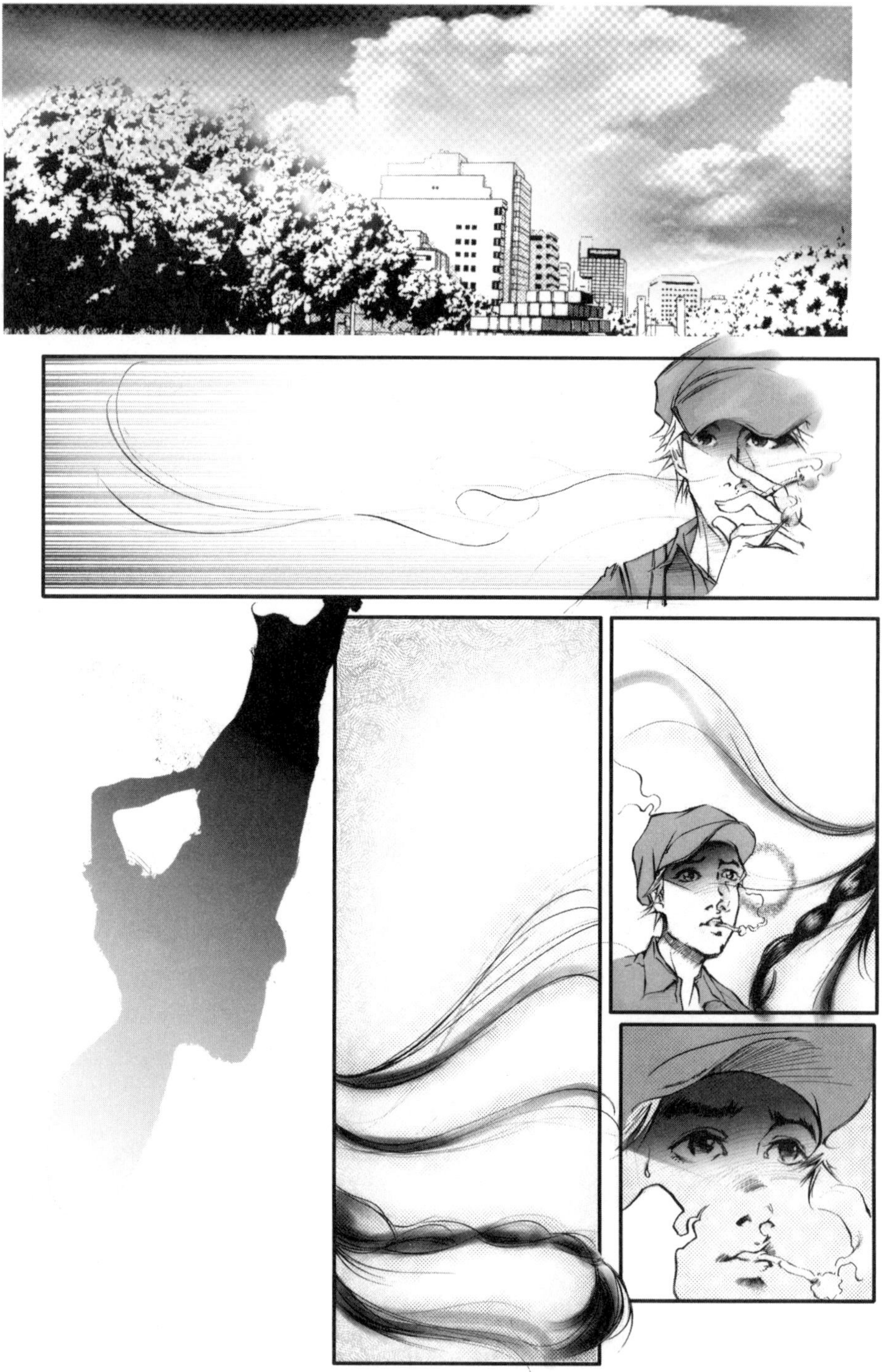

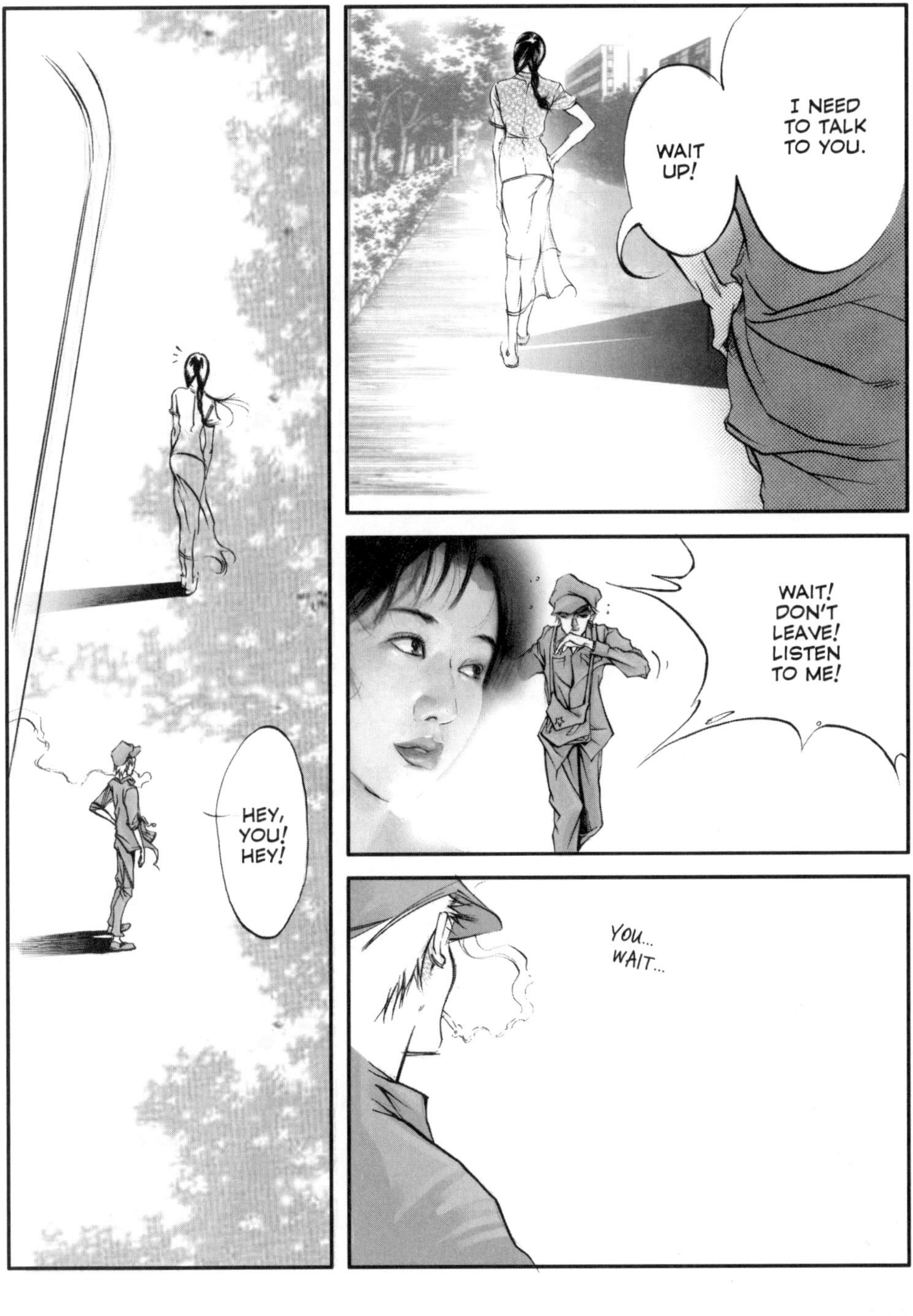
I NEED TO TALK TO YOU.
WAIT UP!
HEY, YOU! HEY!
WAIT! DON'T LEAVE! LISTEN TO ME!
YOU... WAIT...

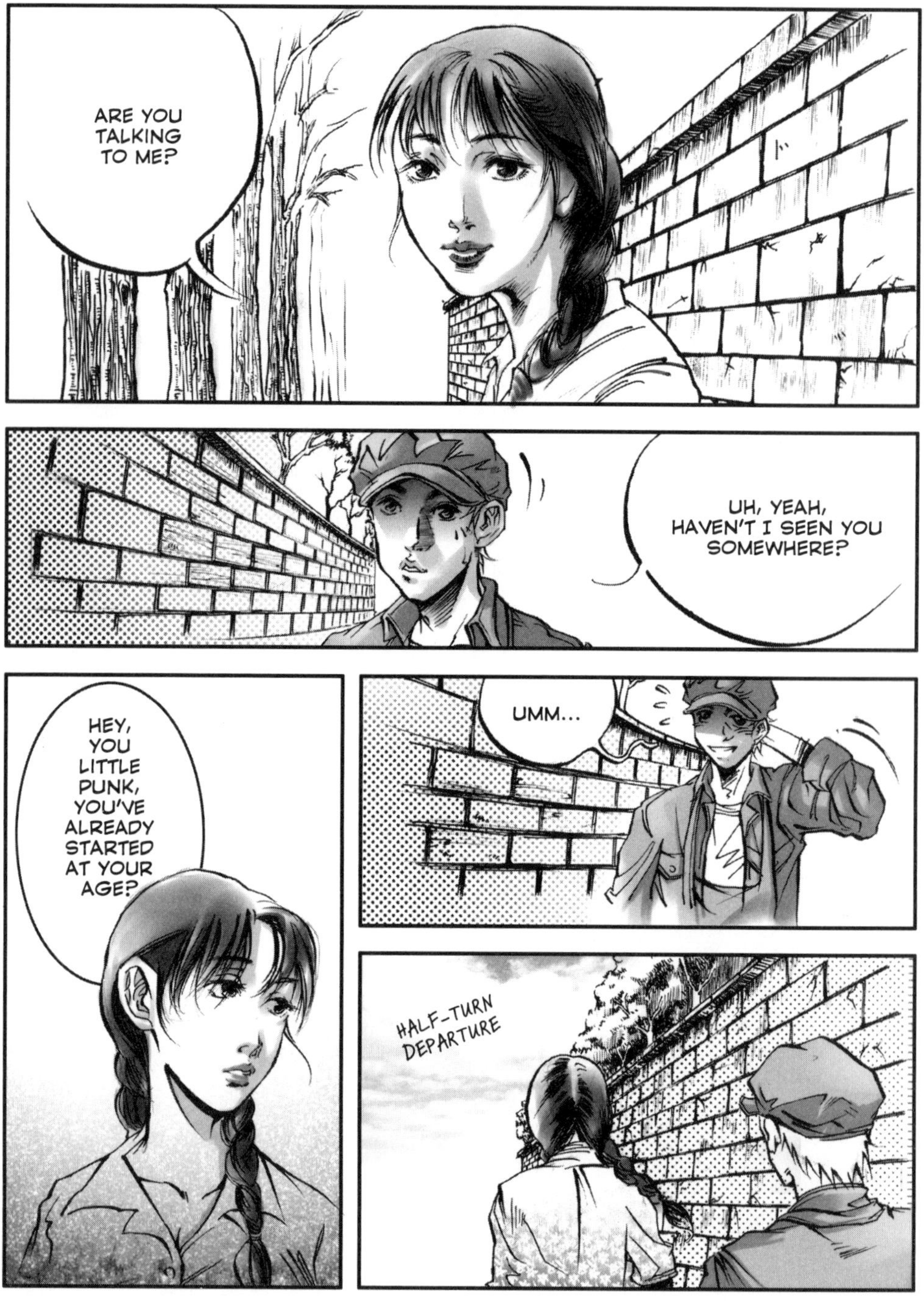
ARE YOU TALKING TO ME?
UH, YEAH, HAVEN'T I SEEN YOU SOMEWHERE?
HEY, YOU LITTLE PUNK, YOU'VE ALREADY STARTED AT YOUR AGE?
UMM...
HALF-TURN DEPARTURE

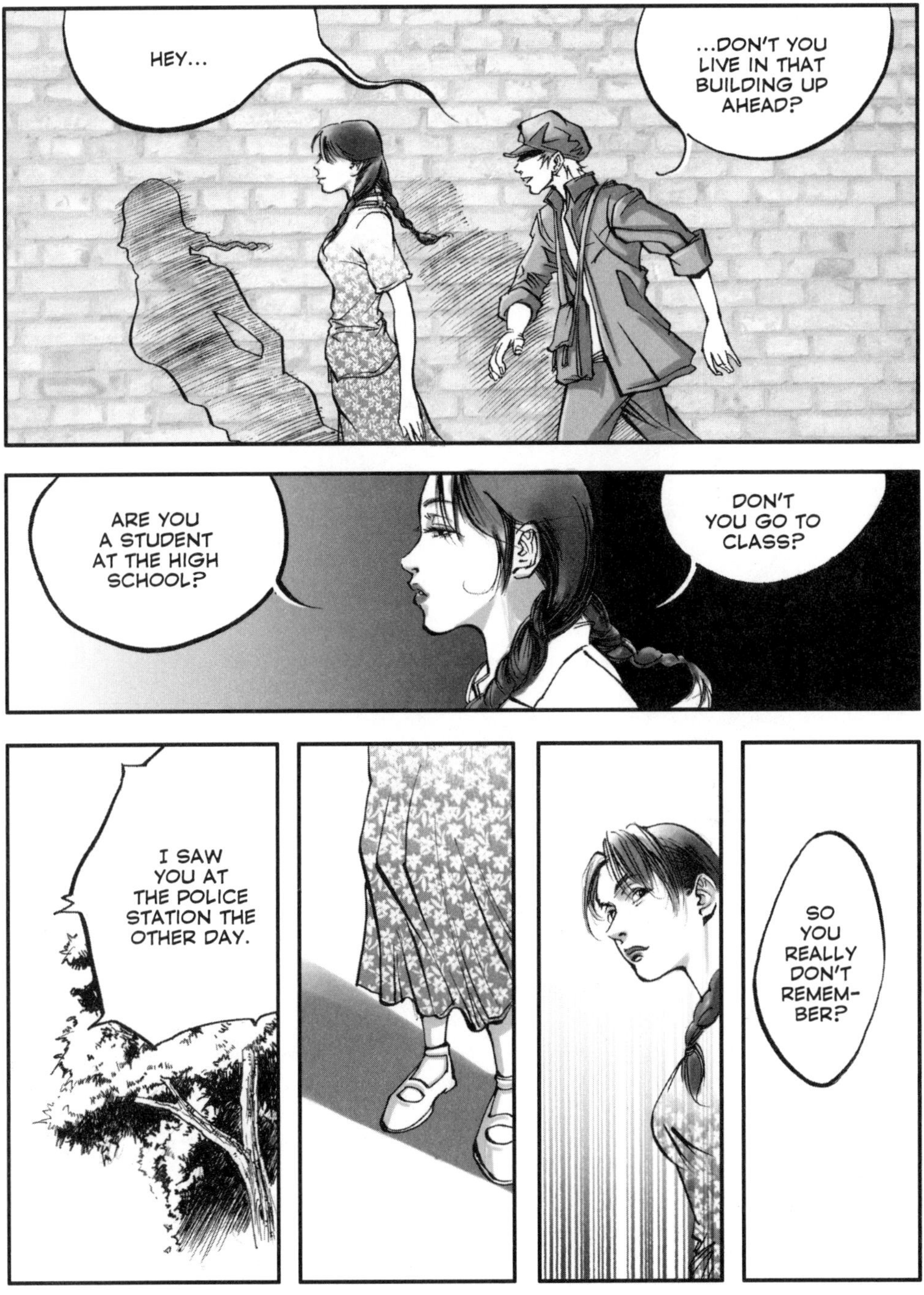
HEY...
...DON'T YOU LIVE IN THAT BUILDING UP AHEAD?
ARE YOU A STUDENT AT THE HIGH SCHOOL?
DON'T YOU GO TO CLASS?
I SAW YOU AT THE POLICE STATION THE OTHER DAY.
SO YOU REALLY DON'T REMEM-BER?

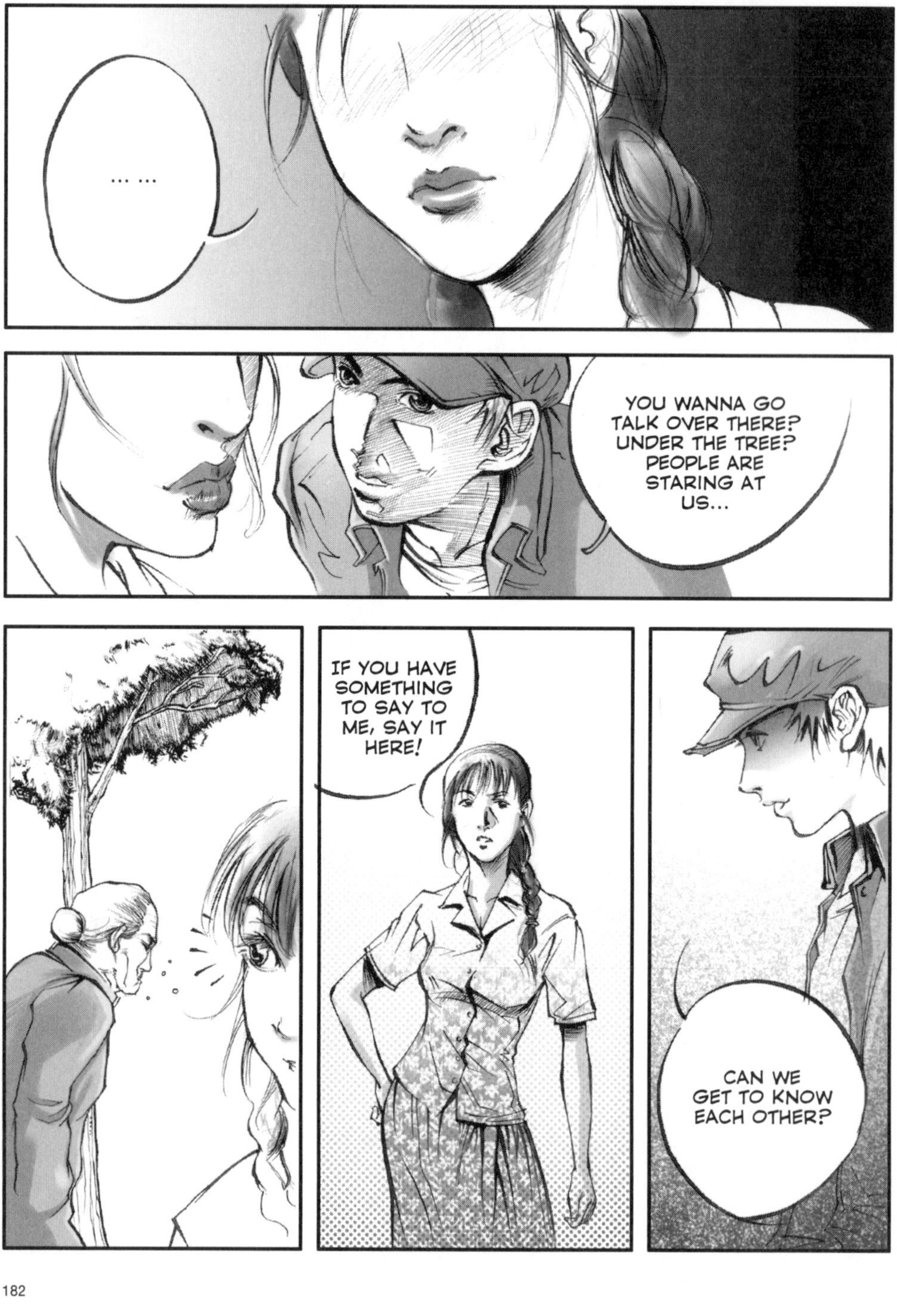
... ...
YOU WANNA GO TALK OVER THERE? UNDER THE TREE? PEOPLE ARE STARING AT US...
IF YOU HAVE SOMETHING TO SAY TO ME, SAY IT HERE!
CAN WE GET TO KNOW EACH OTHER?

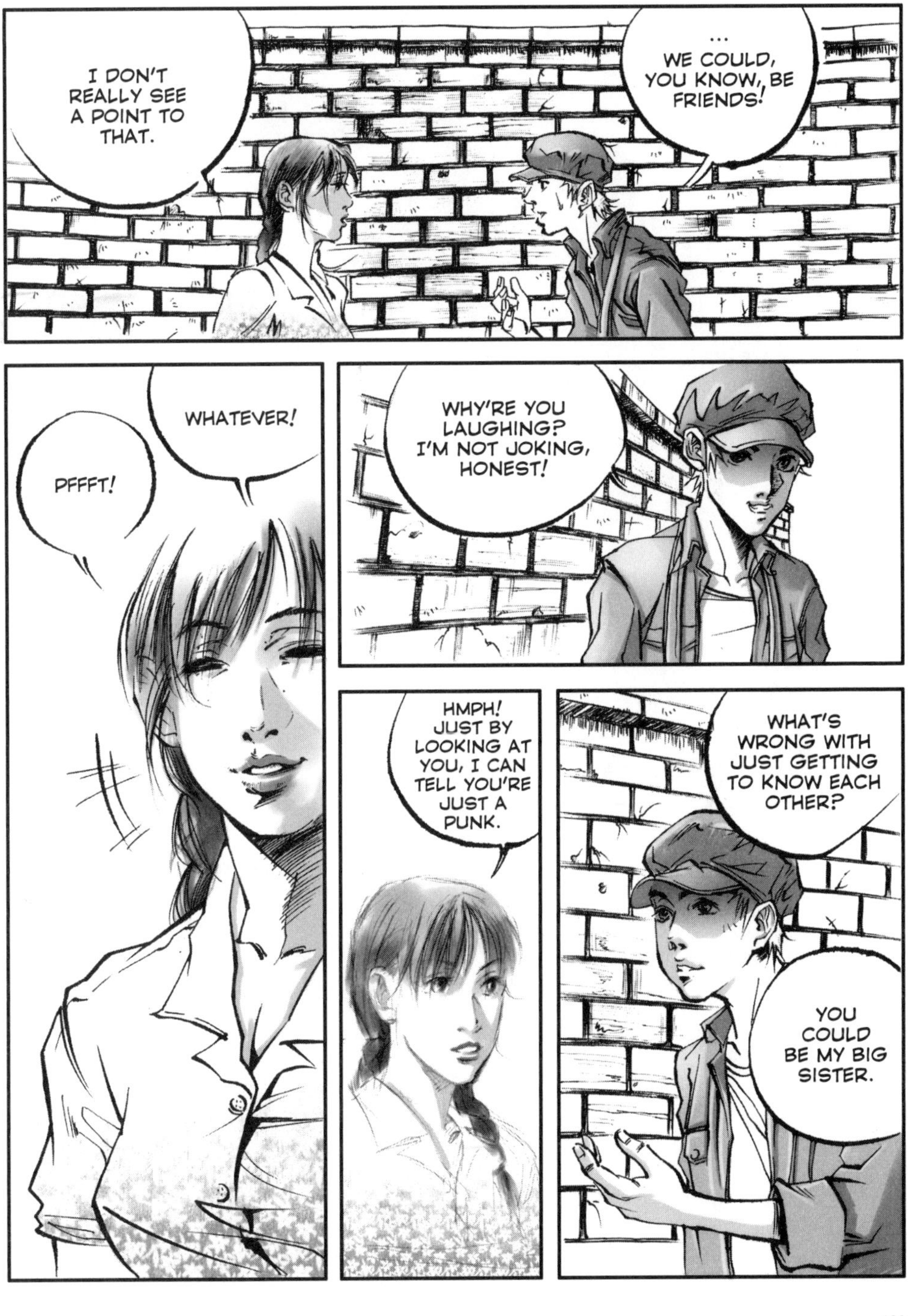
I DON'T REALLY SEE A POINT TO THAT.
... WE COULD, YOU KNOW, BE FRIENDS!
PFFFT!
WHATEVER!
WHY'RE YOU LAUGHING? I'M NOT JOKING, HONEST!
HMPH! JUST BY LOOKING AT YOU, I CAN TELL YOU'RE JUST A PUNK.
WHAT'S WRONG WITH JUST GETTING TO KNOW EACH OTHER?
YOU COULD BE MY BIG SISTER.

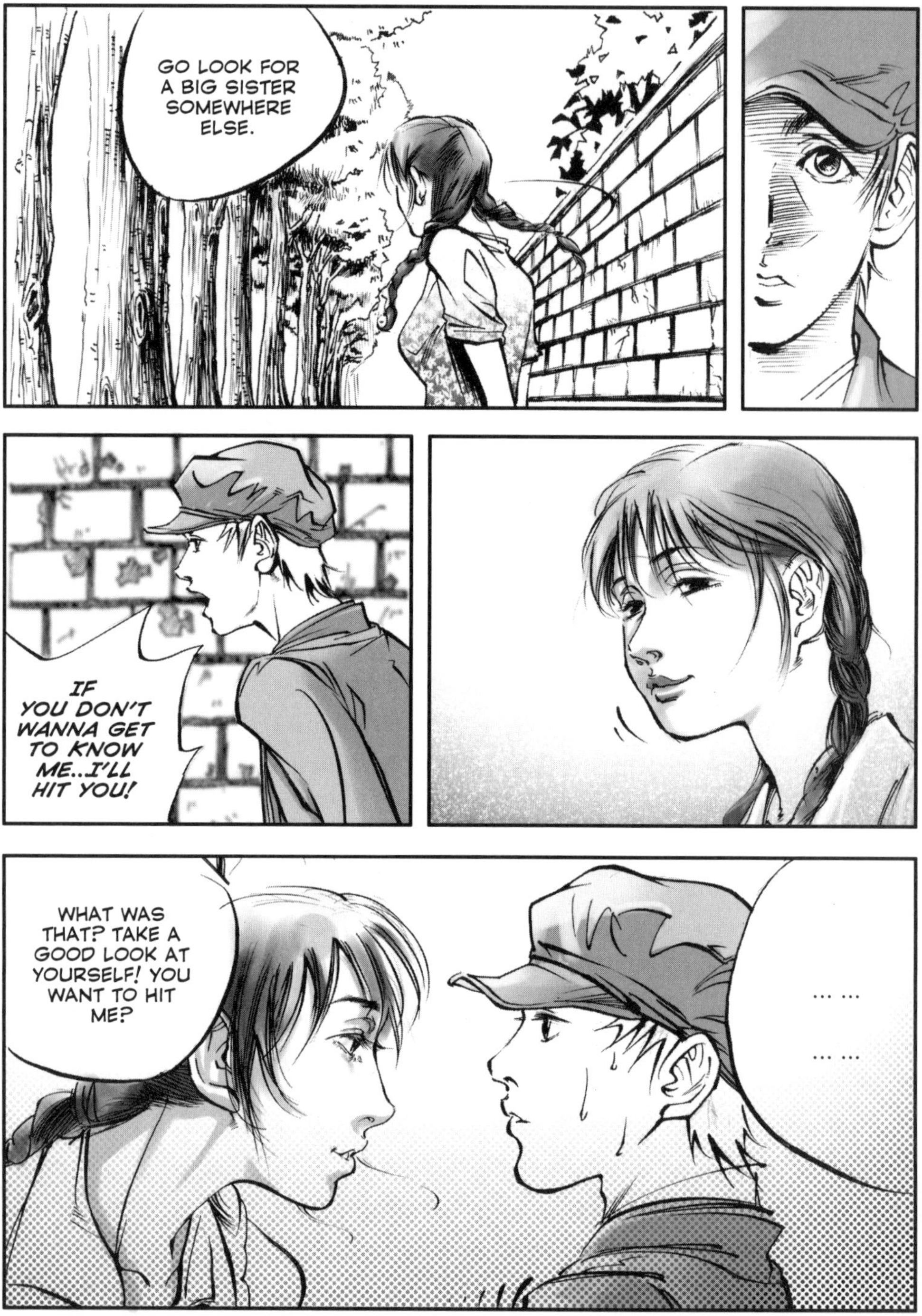
GO LOOK FOR A BIG SISTER SOMEWHERE ELSE.
IF YOU DON'T WANNA GET TO KNOW ME..I'LL HIT YOU!
WHAT WAS THAT? TAKE A GOOD LOOK AT YOURSELF! YOU WANT TO HIT ME?
... ...
... ...

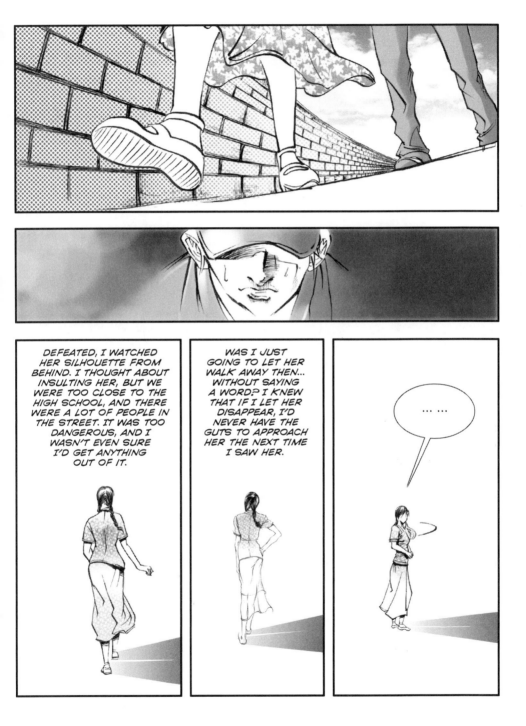

DEFEATED, I WATCHED HER SILHOUETTE FROM BEHIND. I THOUGHT ABOUT INSULTING HER, BUT WE WERE TOO CLOSE TO THE HIGH SCHOOL, AND THERE WERE A LOT OF PEOPLE IN THE STREET. IT WAS TOO DANGEROUS, AND I WASN'T EVEN SURE I'D GET ANYTHING OUT OF IT.

WAS I JUST GOING TO LET HER WALK AWAY THEN... WITHOUT SAYING A WORD? I KNEW THAT IF I LET HER DISAPPEAR, I'D NEVER HAVE THE GUTS TO APPROACH HER THE NEXT TIME I SAW HER.

....

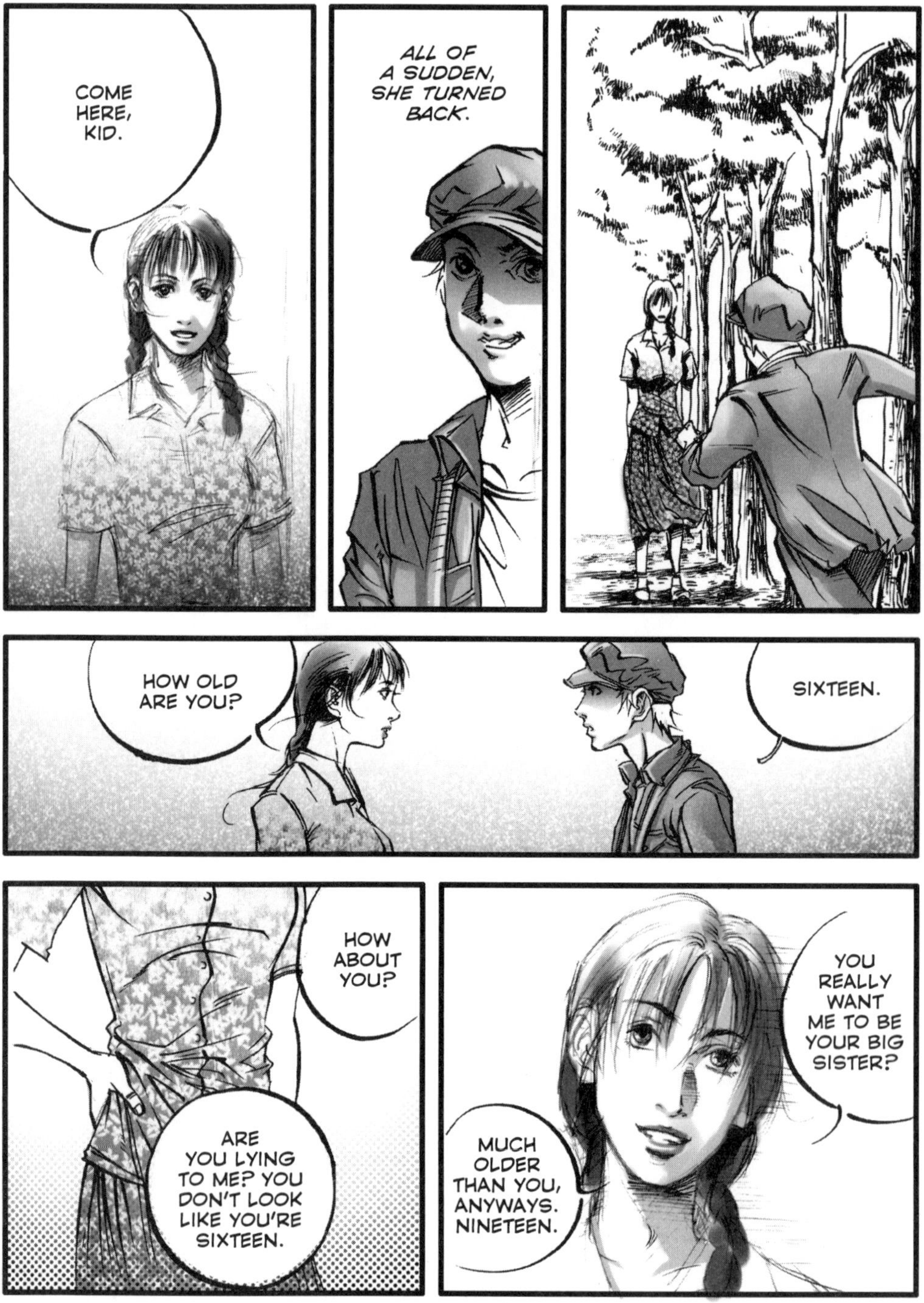
COME HERE, KID.
ALL OF A SUDDEN, SHE TURNED BACK.
HOW OLD ARE YOU?
SIXTEEN.
HOW ABOUT YOU?
ARE YOU LYING TO ME? YOU DON'T LOOK LIKE YOU'RE SIXTEEN.
YOU REALLY WANT ME TO BE YOUR BIG SISTER?
MUCH OLDER THAN YOU, ANYWAYS. NINETEEN.

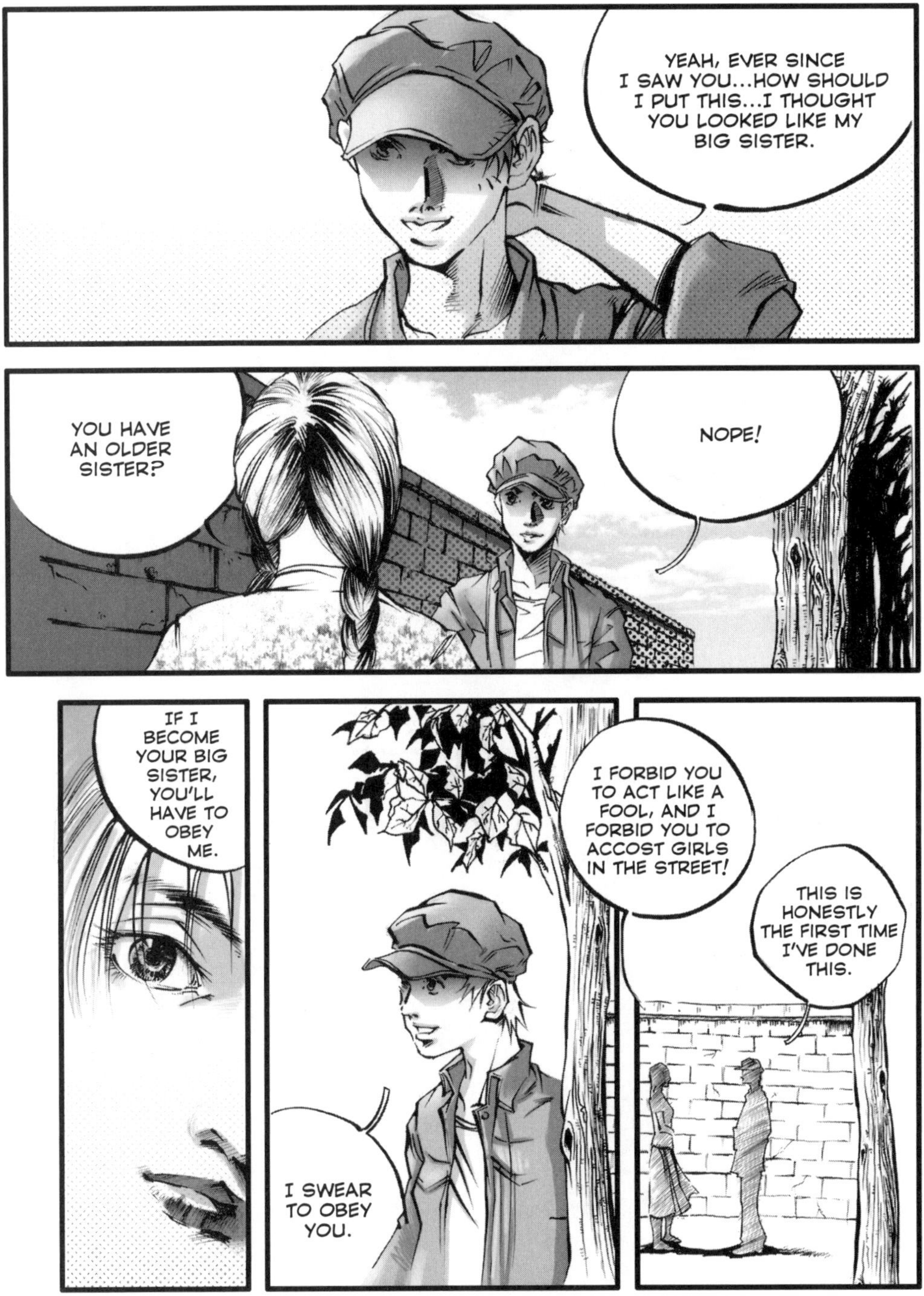
YEAH, EVER SINCE I SAW YOU...HOW SHOULD I PUT THIS...I THOUGHT YOU LOOKED LIKE MY BIG SISTER.
YOU HAVE AN OLDER SISTER?
NOPE!
IF I BECOME YOUR BIG SISTER, YOU'LL HAVE TO OBEY ME.
I FORBID YOU TO ACT LIKE A FOOL, AND I FORBID YOU TO ACCOST GIRLS IN THE STREET!
I SWEAR TO OBEY YOU.
THIS IS HONESTLY THE FIRST TIME I'VE DONE THIS.

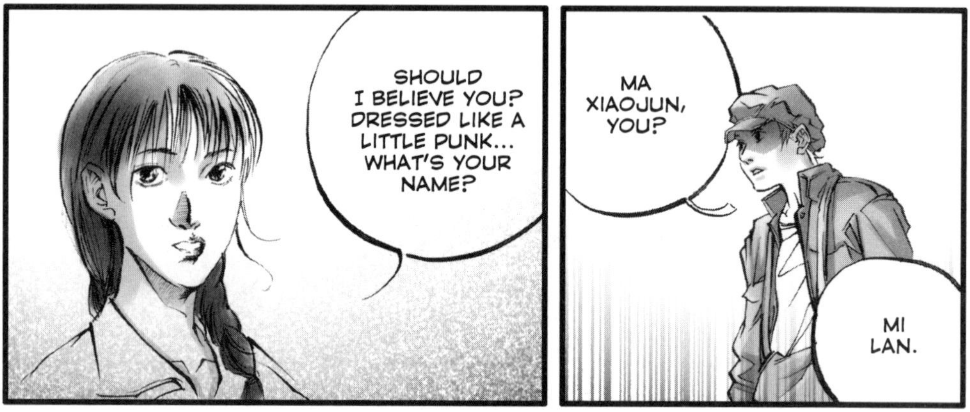
SHOULD I BELIEVE YOU? DRESSED LIKE A LITTLE PUNK... WHAT'S YOUR NAME?
MA XIAOJUN, YOU?
MI LAN.

I DIDN'T MAKE THE CONNECTION WITH THE NAME YU BEIBEI HAD SAID. AT THAT AGE, I LIKED TO BE THE ONE WHO COULD DO ANYTHING AND KNEW IT ALL.

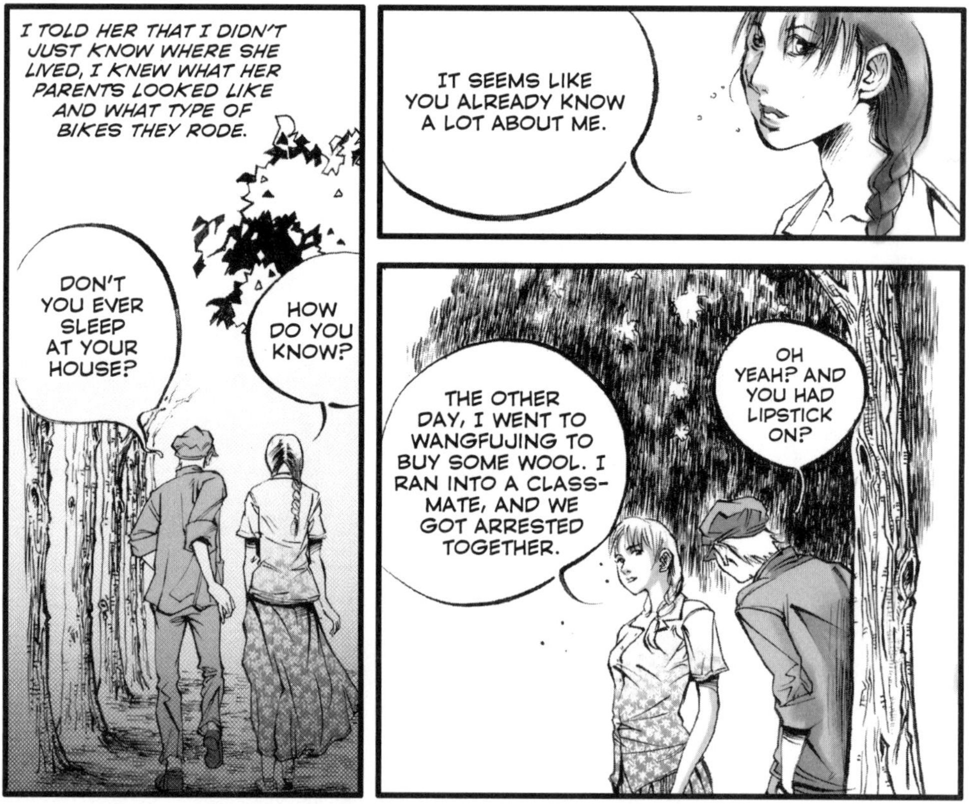
I TOLD HER THAT I DIDN'T JUST KNOW WHERE SHE LIVED, I KNEW WHAT HER PARENTS LOOKED LIKE AND WHAT TYPE OF BIKES THEY RODE.
DON'T YOU EVER SLEEP AT YOUR HOUSE?
HOW DO YOU KNOW?
IT SEEMS LIKE YOU ALREADY KNOW A LOT ABOUT ME.
THE OTHER DAY, I WENT TO WANGFUJING TO BUY SOME WOOL. I RAN INTO A CLASS-MATE, AND WE GOT ARRESTED TOGETHER.
OH YEAH? AND YOU HAD LIPSTICK ON?

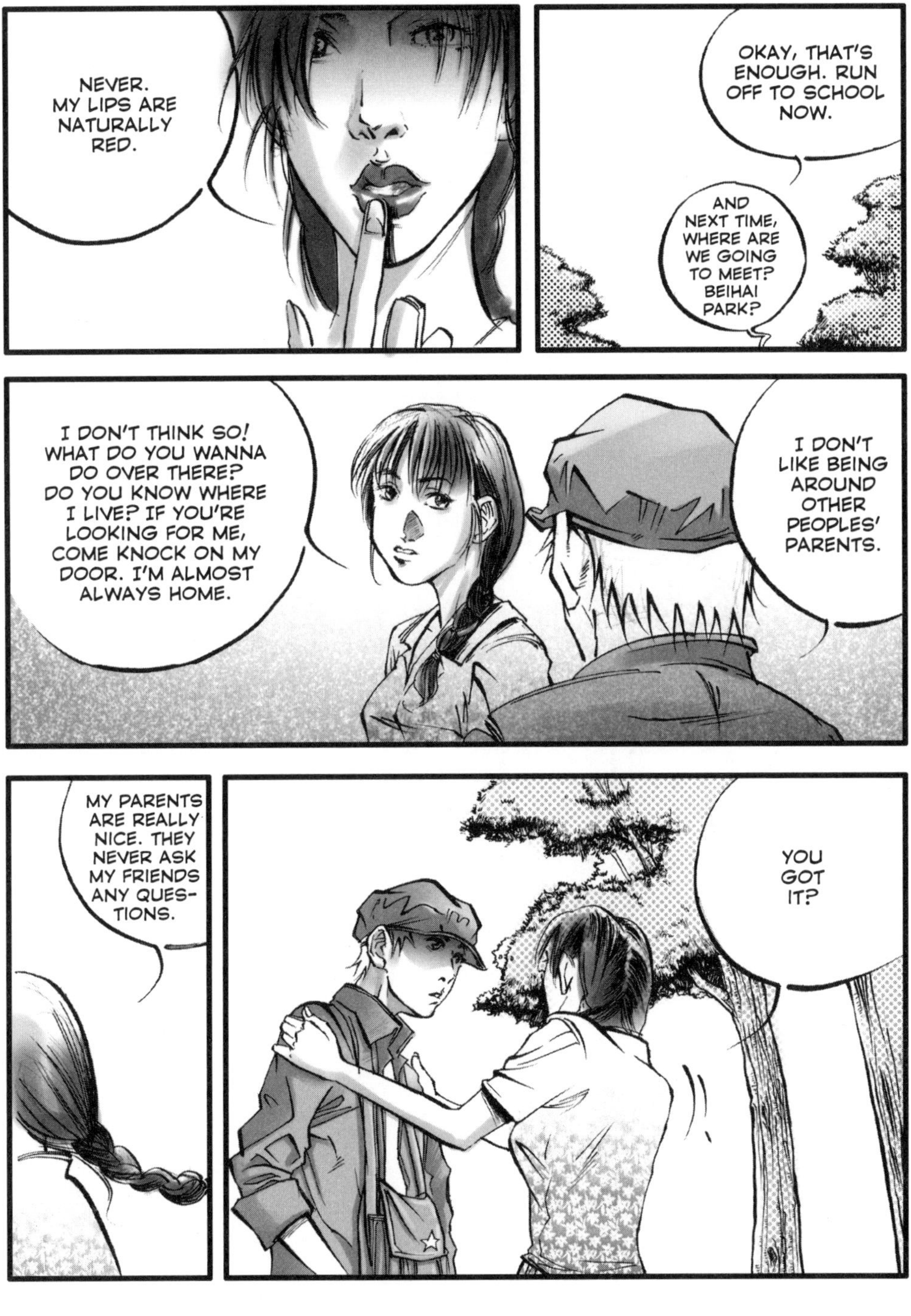
NEVER. MY LIPS ARE NATURALLY RED.
OKAY, THAT'S ENOUGH. RUN OFF TO SCHOOL NOW.
AND NEXT TIME, WHERE ARE WE GOING TO MEET? BEIHAI PARK?
I DON'T THINK SO! WHAT DO YOU WANNA DO OVER THERE? DO YOU KNOW WHERE I LIVE? IF YOU'RE LOOKING FOR ME, COME KNOCK ON MY DOOR. I'M ALMOST ALWAYS HOME.
I DON'T LIKE BEING AROUND OTHER PEOPLES' PARENTS.
MY PARENTS ARE REALLY NICE. THEY NEVER ASK MY FRIENDS ANY QUES-TIONS.
YOU GOT IT?

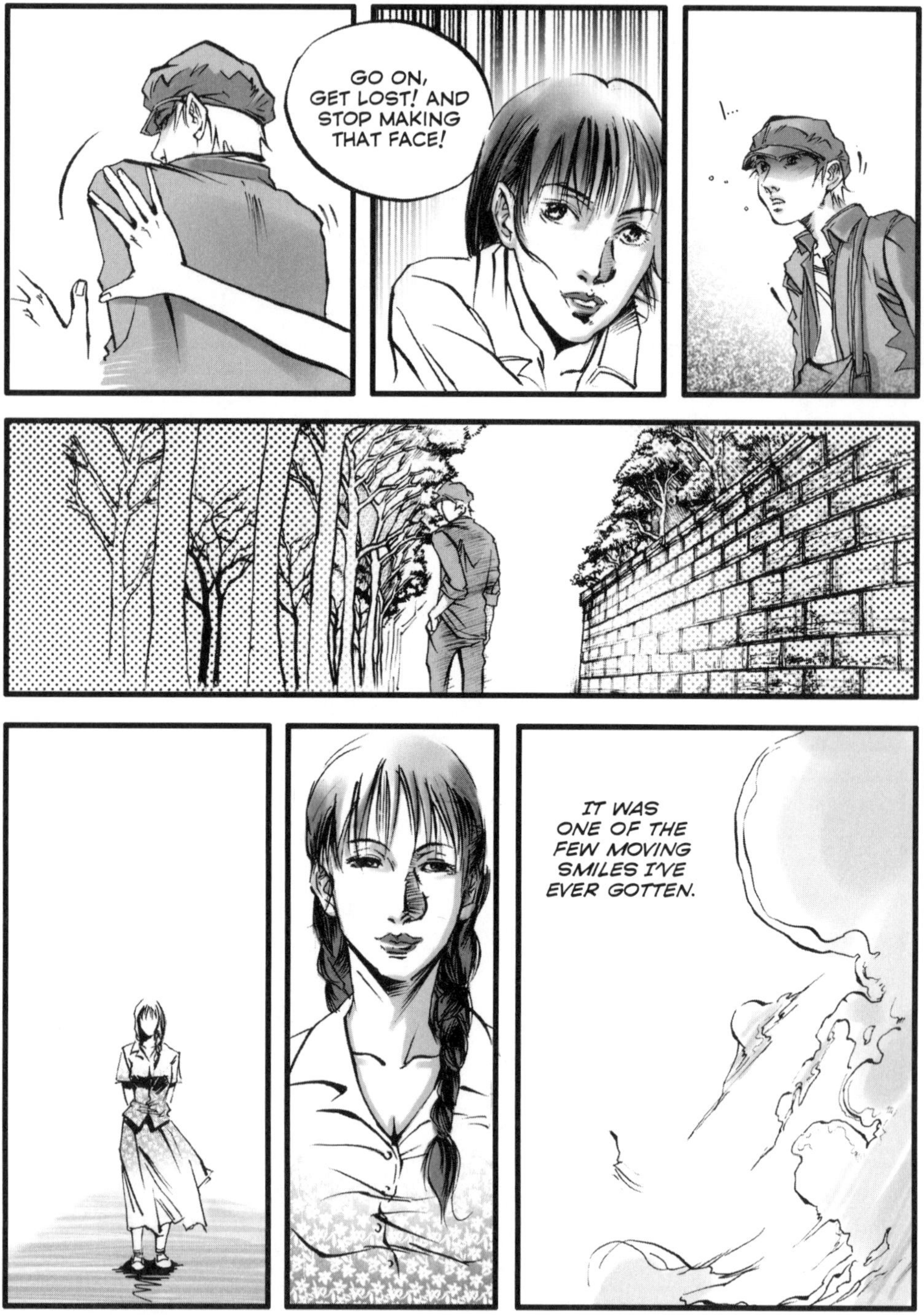
GO ON, GET LOST! AND STOP MAKING THAT FACE!
I...
IT WAS ONE OF THE FEW MOVING SMILES I'VE EVER GOTTEN.

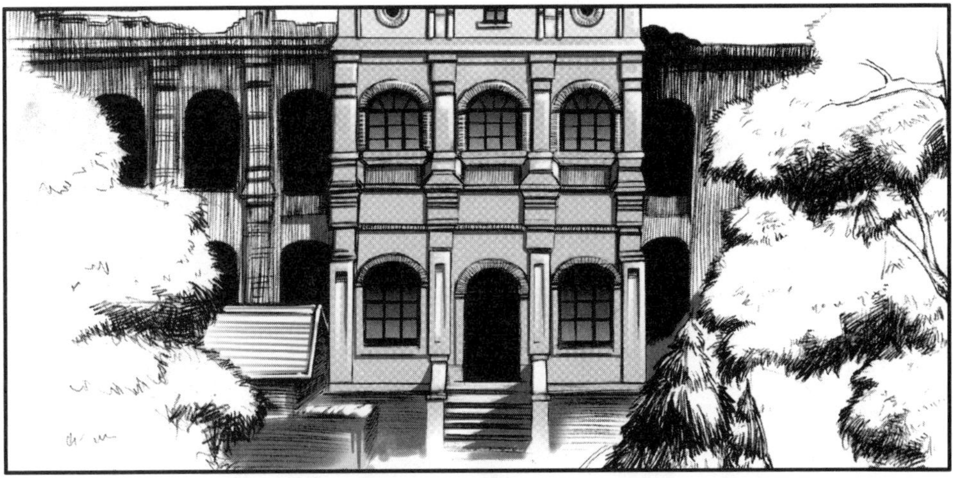

ON EACH OCCASION, I TOOK THE STEPS FOUR AT A TIME AS FAST AS I COULD—MY HEART BEATING WITH HAPPINESS—TO KNOCK ON HER DOOR. BUT EITHER NO ONE WAS HOME, OR I HEARD THE VOICE OF HER PARENTS SAYING...

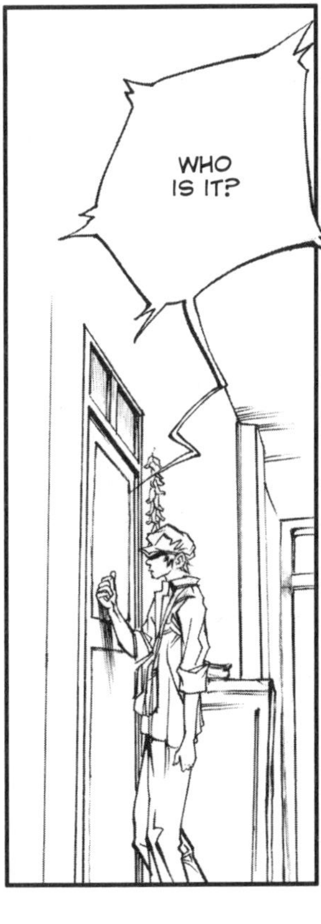
WHO IS IT?

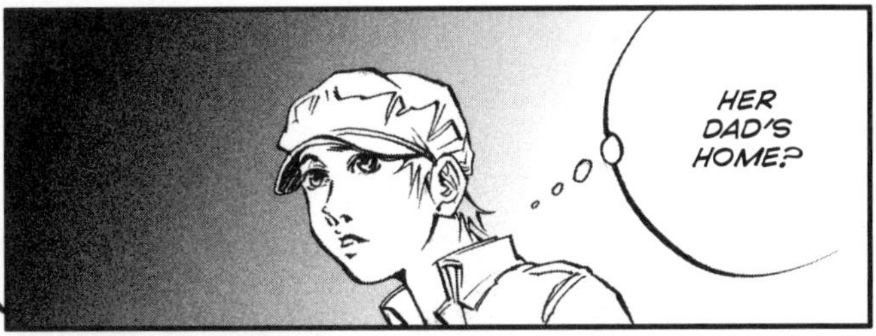
HER DAD'S HOME?

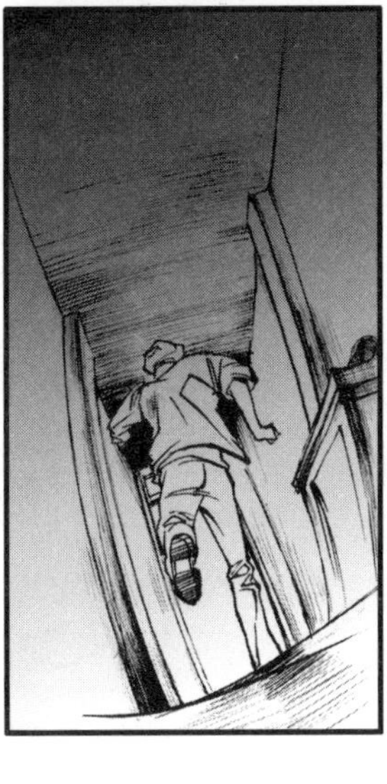

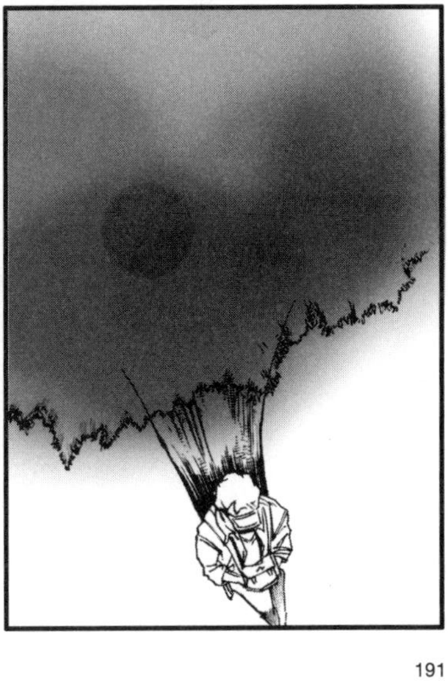

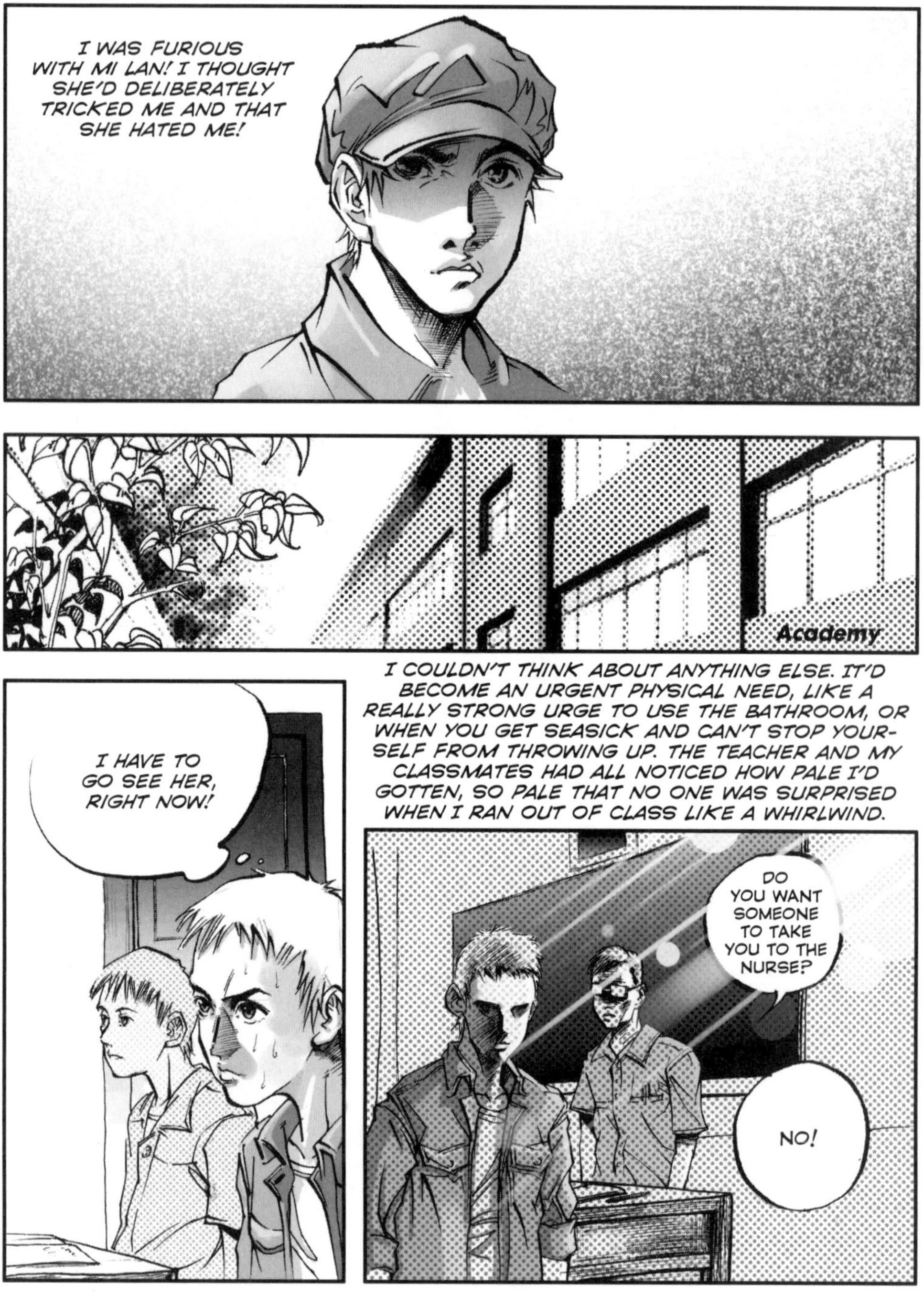
I WAS FURIOUS WITH MI LAN! I THOUGHT SHE'D DELIBERATELY TRICKED ME AND THAT SHE HATED ME!
Academy
I HAVE TO GO SEE HER, RIGHT NOW!
I COULDN'T THINK ABOUT ANYTHING ELSE. IT'D BECOME AN URGENT PHYSICAL NEED, LIKE A REALLY STRONG URGE TO USE THE BATHROOM, OR WHEN YOU GET SEASICK AND CAN'T STOP YOURSELF FROM THROWING UP. THE TEACHER AND MY CLASSMATES HAD ALL NOTICED HOW PALE I'D GOTTEN, SO PALE THAT NO ONE WAS SURPRISED WHEN I RAN OUT OF CLASS LIKE A WHIRLWIND.
DO YOU WANT SOMEONE TO TAKE YOU TO THE NURSE?
NO!

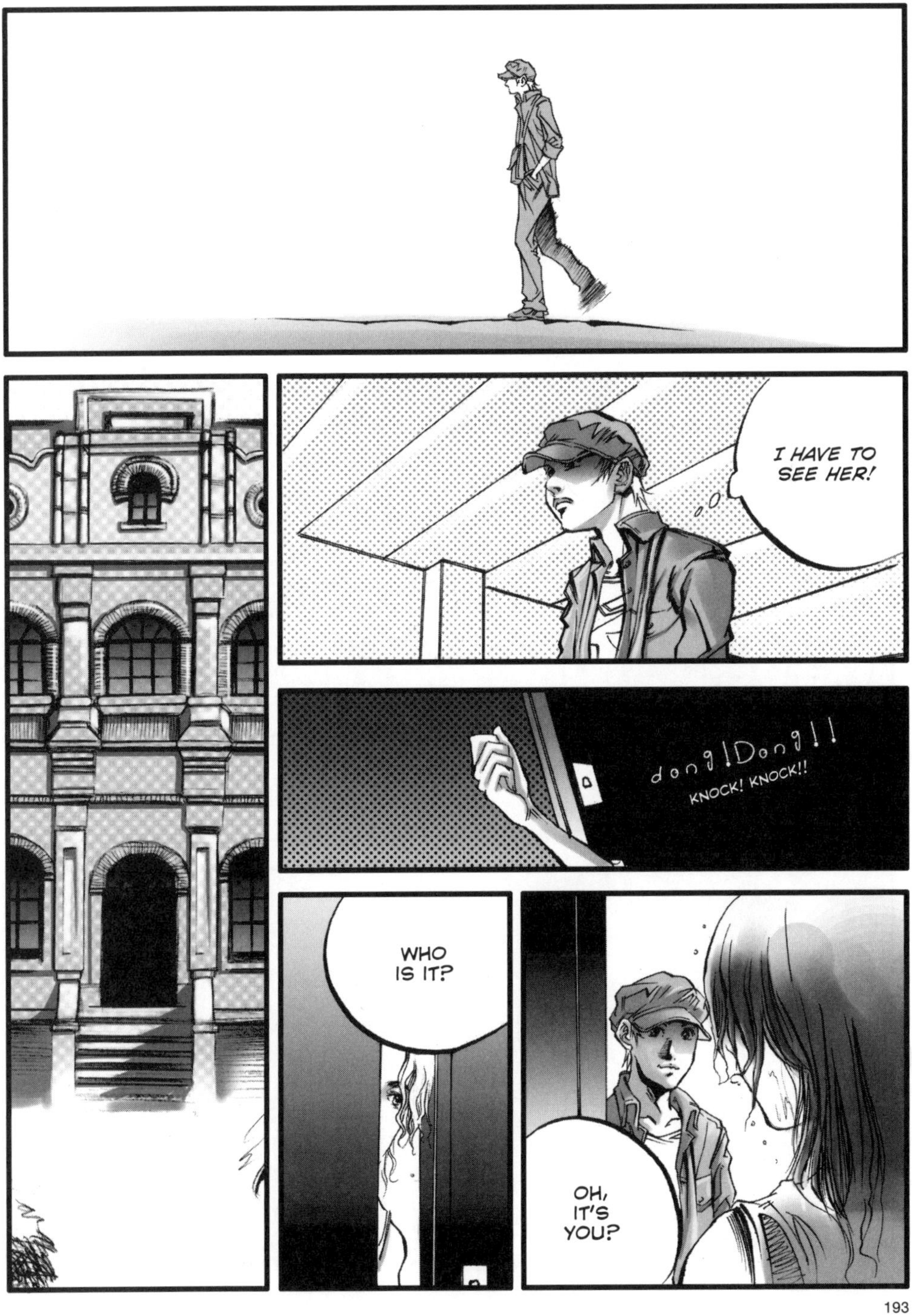
I HAVE TO SEE HER!
dong!Dong!!
KNOCK! KNOCK!!
WHO IS IT?
OH, IT'S YOU?

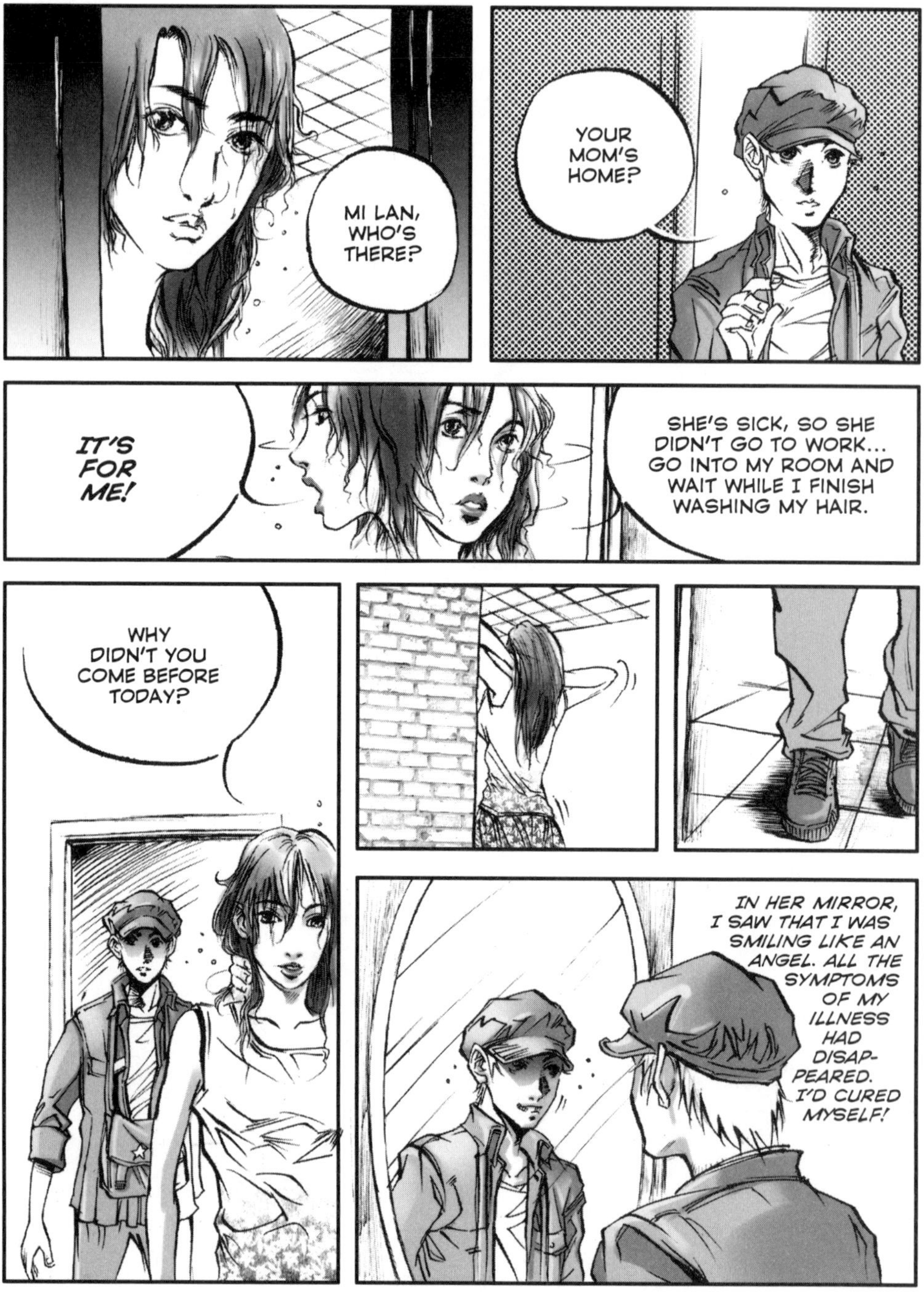
MI LAN, WHO'S THERE?
YOUR MOM'S HOME?
IT'S FOR ME!
SHE'S SICK, SO SHE DIDN'T GO TO WORK... GO INTO MY ROOM AND WAIT WHILE I FINISH WASHING MY HAIR.
WHY DIDN'T YOU COME BEFORE TODAY?
IN HER MIRROR, I SAW THAT I WAS SMILING LIKE AN ANGEL. ALL THE SYMPTOMS OF MY ILLNESS HAD DISAP-PEARED. I'D CURED MYSELF!

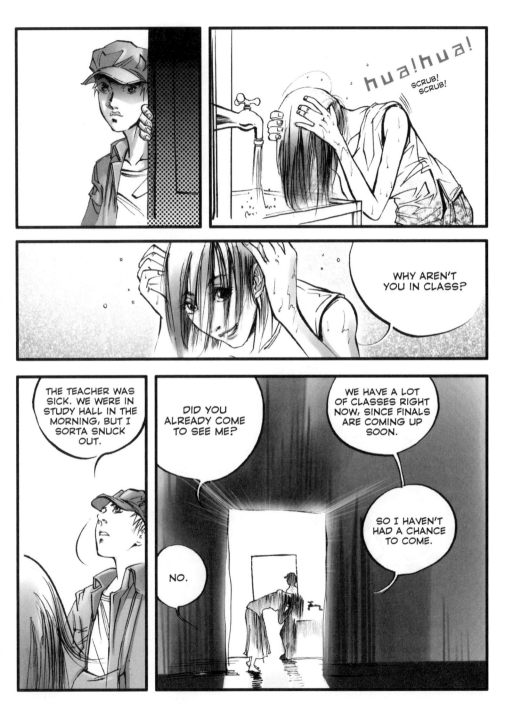

hua!hua!

SCRUB!
SCRUB!

WHY AREN'T YOU IN CLASS?

THE TEACHER WAS SICK. WE WERE IN STUDY HALL IN THE MORNING, BUT I SORTA SNUCK OUT.

DID YOU ALREADY COME TO SEE ME?

WE HAVE A LOT OF CLASSES RIGHT NOW, SINCE FINALS ARE COMING UP SOON.

SO I HAVEN'T HAD A CHANCE TO COME.

NO.

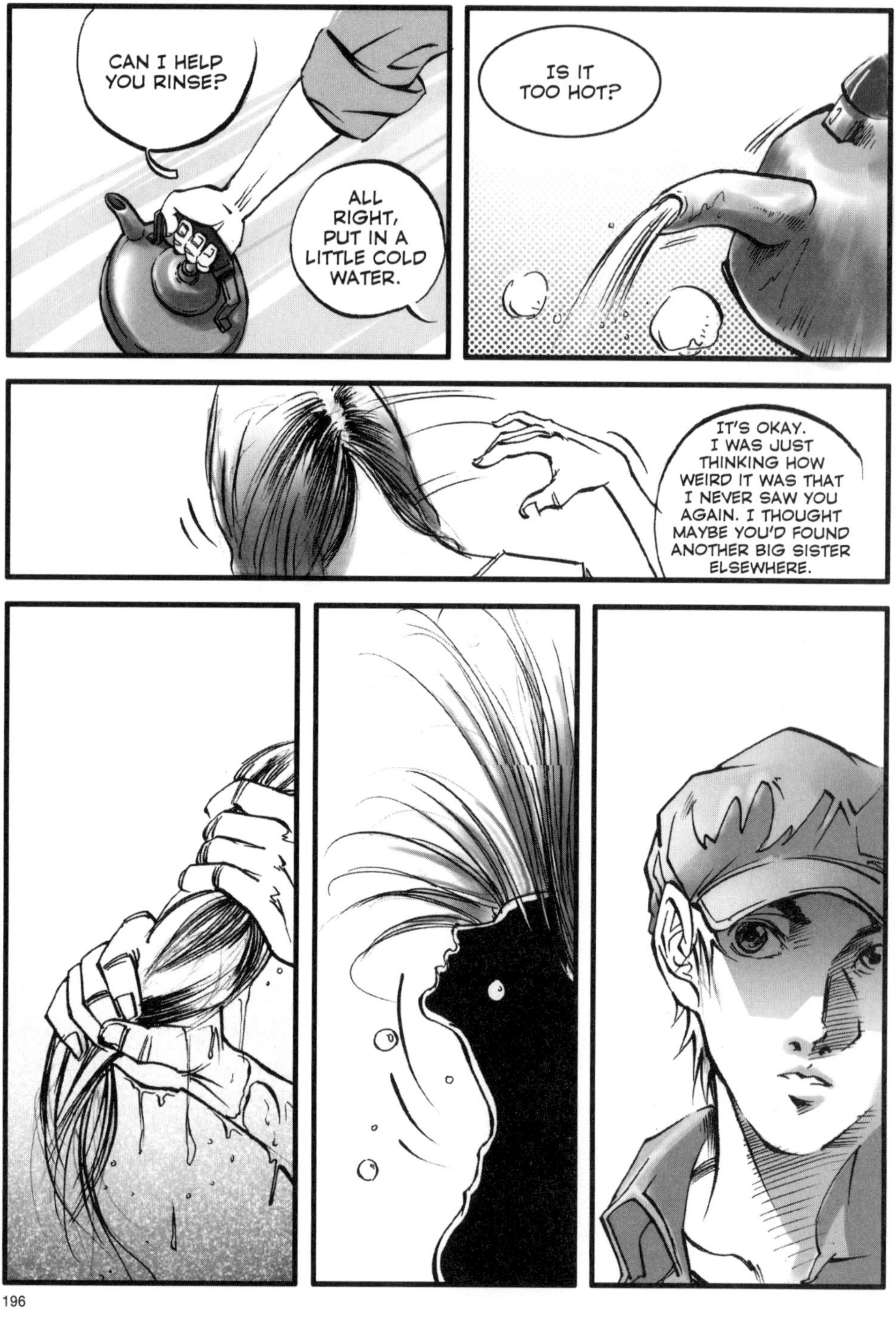
CAN I HELP YOU RINSE?
ALL RIGHT, PUT IN A LITTLE COLD WATER.
IS IT TOO HOT?
IT'S OKAY. I WAS JUST THINKING HOW WEIRD IT WAS THAT I NEVER SAW YOU AGAIN. I THOUGHT MAYBE YOU'D FOUND ANOTHER BIG SISTER ELSEWHERE.

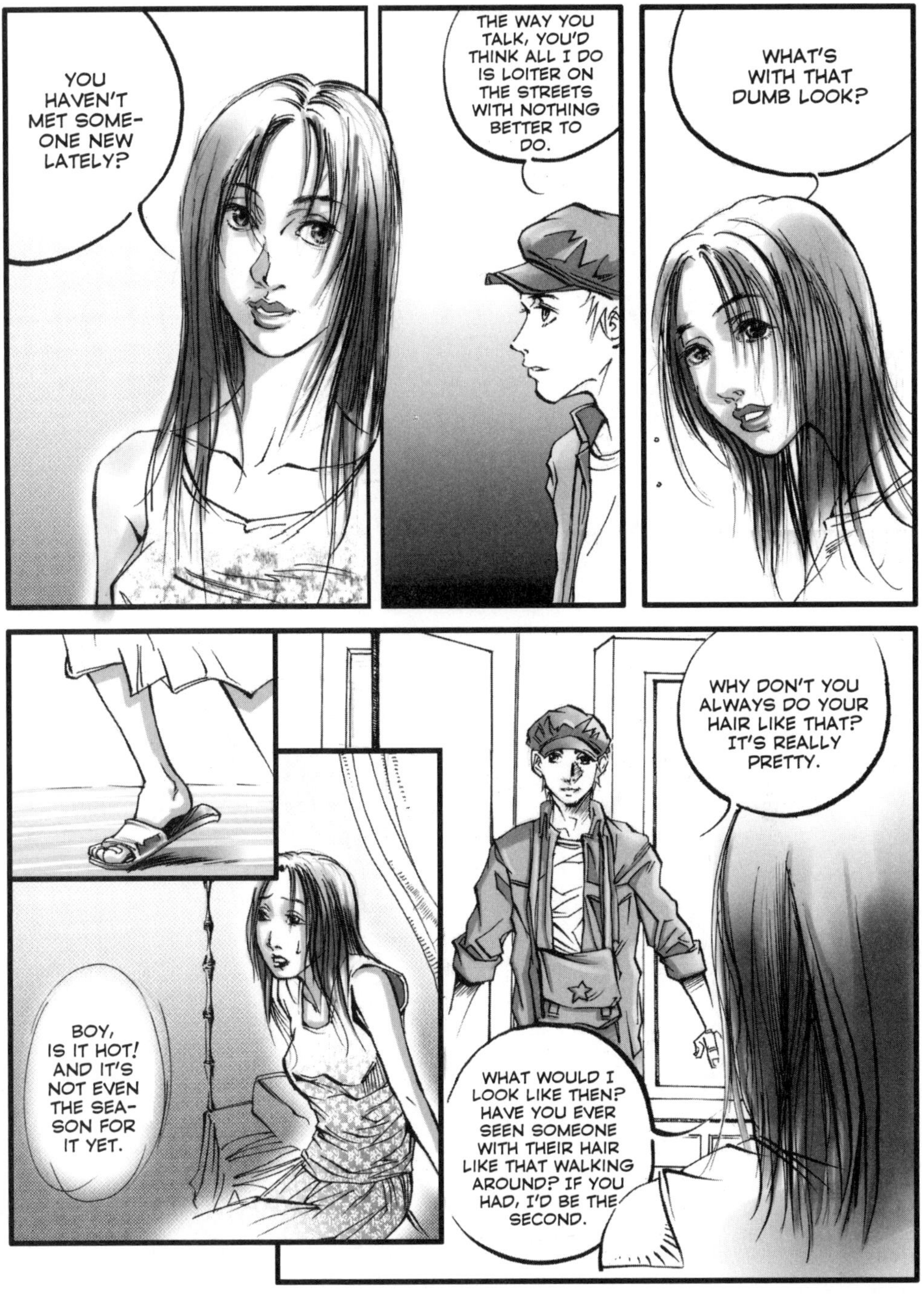
YOU HAVEN'T MET SOME-ONE NEW LATELY?
THE WAY YOU TALK, YOU'D THINK ALL I DO IS LOITER ON THE STREETS WITH NOTHING BETTER TO DO.
WHAT'S WITH THAT DUMB LOOK?
BOY, IS IT HOT! AND IT'S NOT EVEN THE SEA-SON FOR IT YET.
WHY DON'T YOU ALWAYS DO YOUR HAIR LIKE THAT? IT'S REALLY PRETTY.
WHAT WOULD I LOOK LIKE THEN? HAVE YOU EVER SEEN SOMEONE WITH THEIR HAIR LIKE THAT WALKING AROUND? IF YOU HAD, I'D BE THE SECOND.

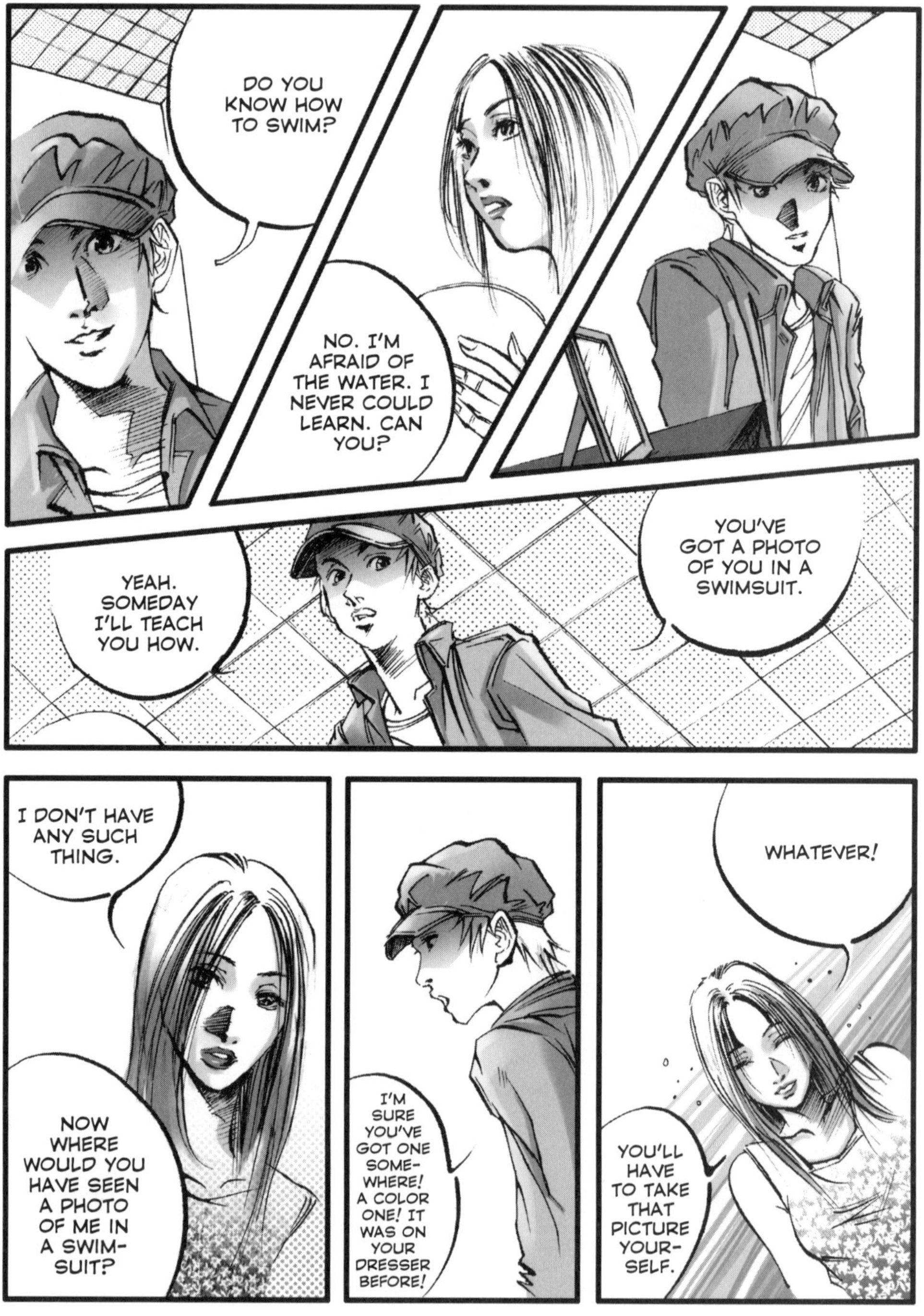
DO YOU KNOW HOW TO SWIM?
NO. I'M AFRAID OF THE WATER. I NEVER COULD LEARN. CAN YOU?
YEAH. SOMEDAY I'LL TEACH YOU HOW.
YOU'VE GOT A PHOTO OF YOU IN A SWIMSUIT.
I DON'T HAVE ANY SUCH THING.
NOW WHERE WOULD YOU HAVE SEEN A PHOTO OF ME IN A SWIM-SUIT?
I'M SURE YOU'VE GOT ONE SOME-WHERE! A COLOR ONE! IT WAS ON YOUR DRESSER BEFORE!
WHATEVER!
YOU'LL HAVE TO TAKE THAT PICTURE YOUR-SELF.

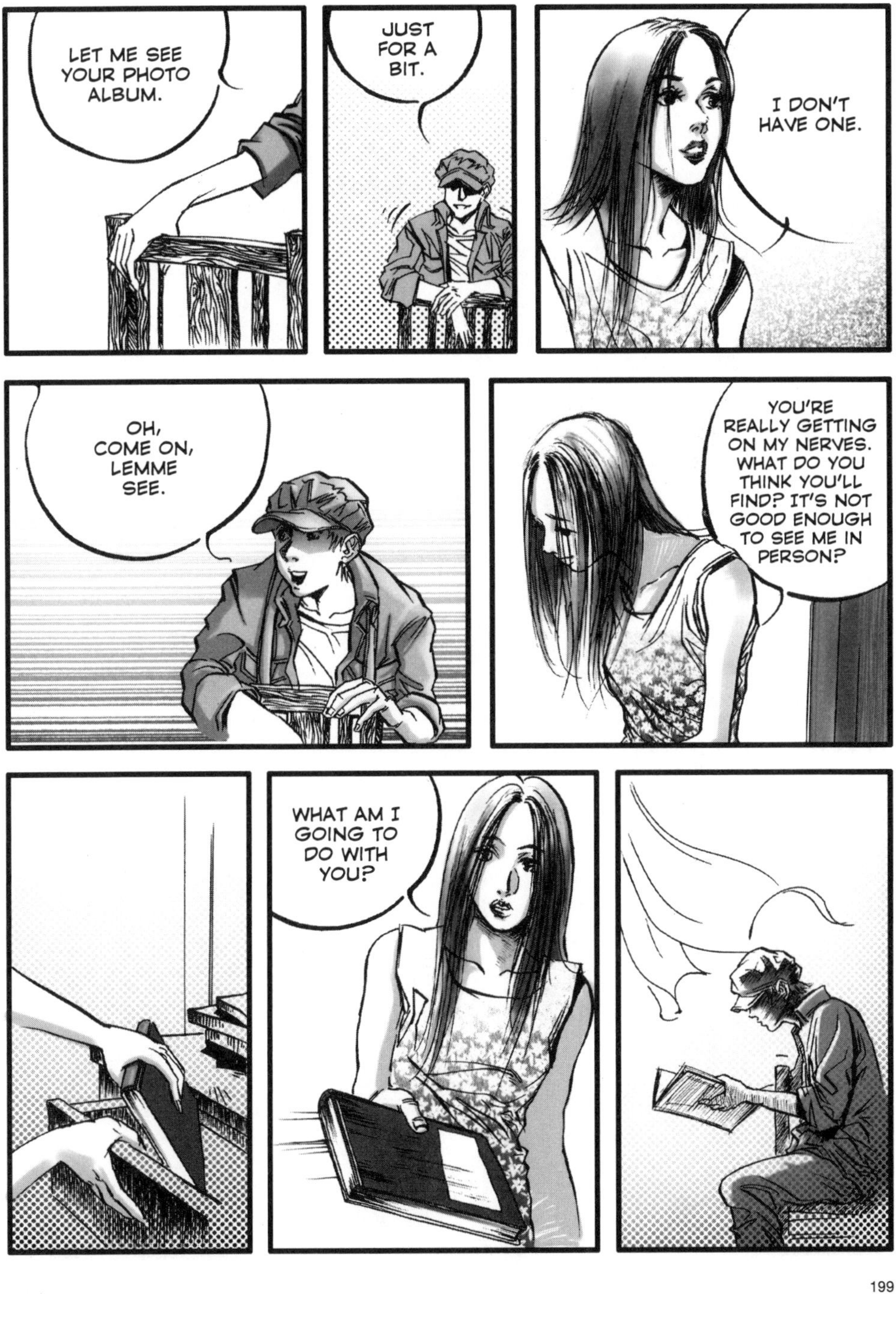
LET ME SEE YOUR PHOTO ALBUM.
JUST FOR A BIT.
I DON'T HAVE ONE.
OH, COME ON, LEMME SEE.
YOU'RE REALLY GETTING ON MY NERVES. WHAT DO YOU THINK YOU'LL FIND? IT'S NOT GOOD ENOUGH TO SEE ME IN PERSON?
WHAT AM I GOING TO DO WITH YOU?

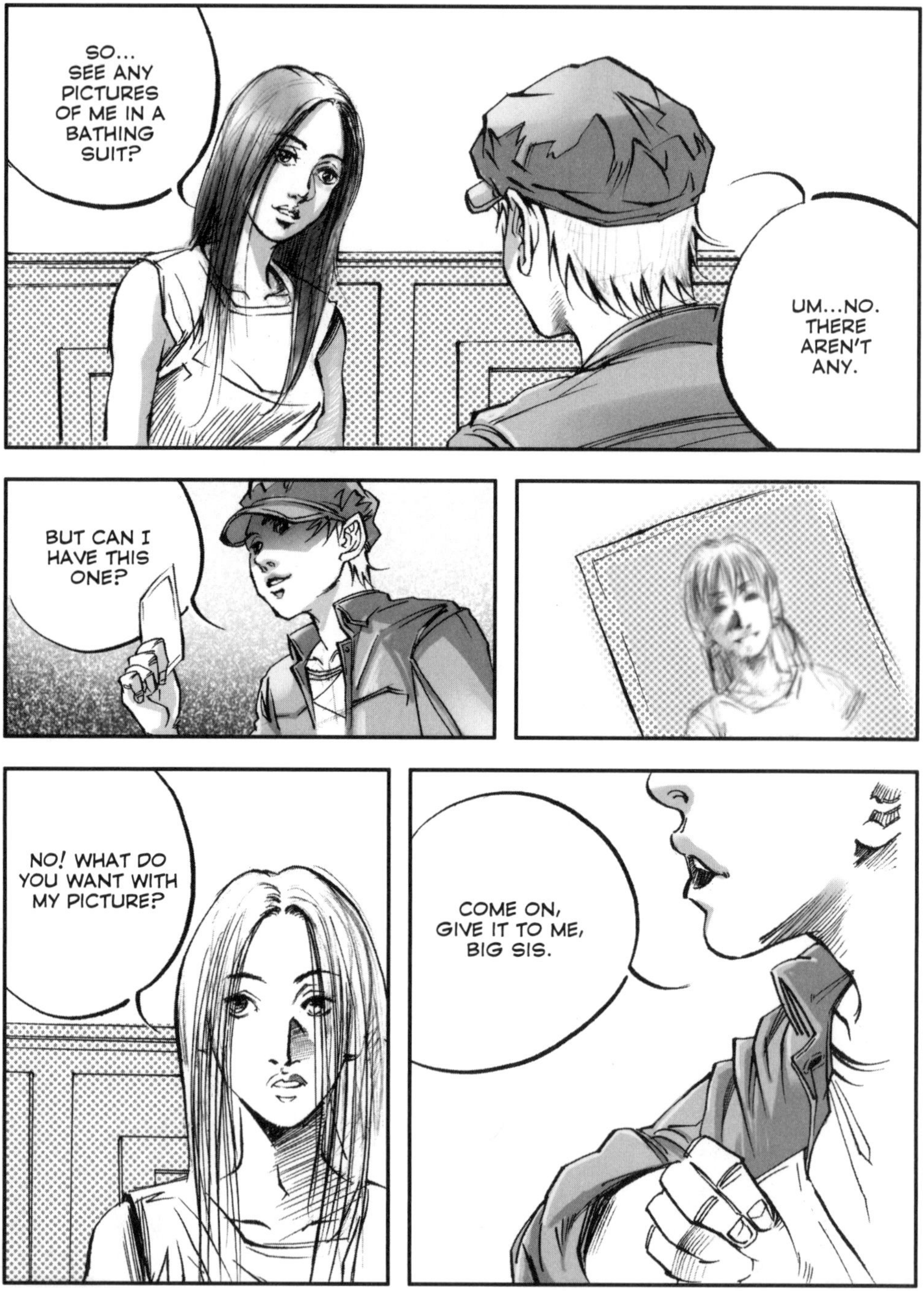

SO... SEE ANY PICTURES OF ME IN A BATHING SUIT?
UM...NO. THERE AREN'T ANY.
BUT CAN I HAVE THIS ONE?
NO! WHAT DO YOU WANT WITH MY PICTURE?
COME ON, GIVE IT TO ME, BIG SIS.

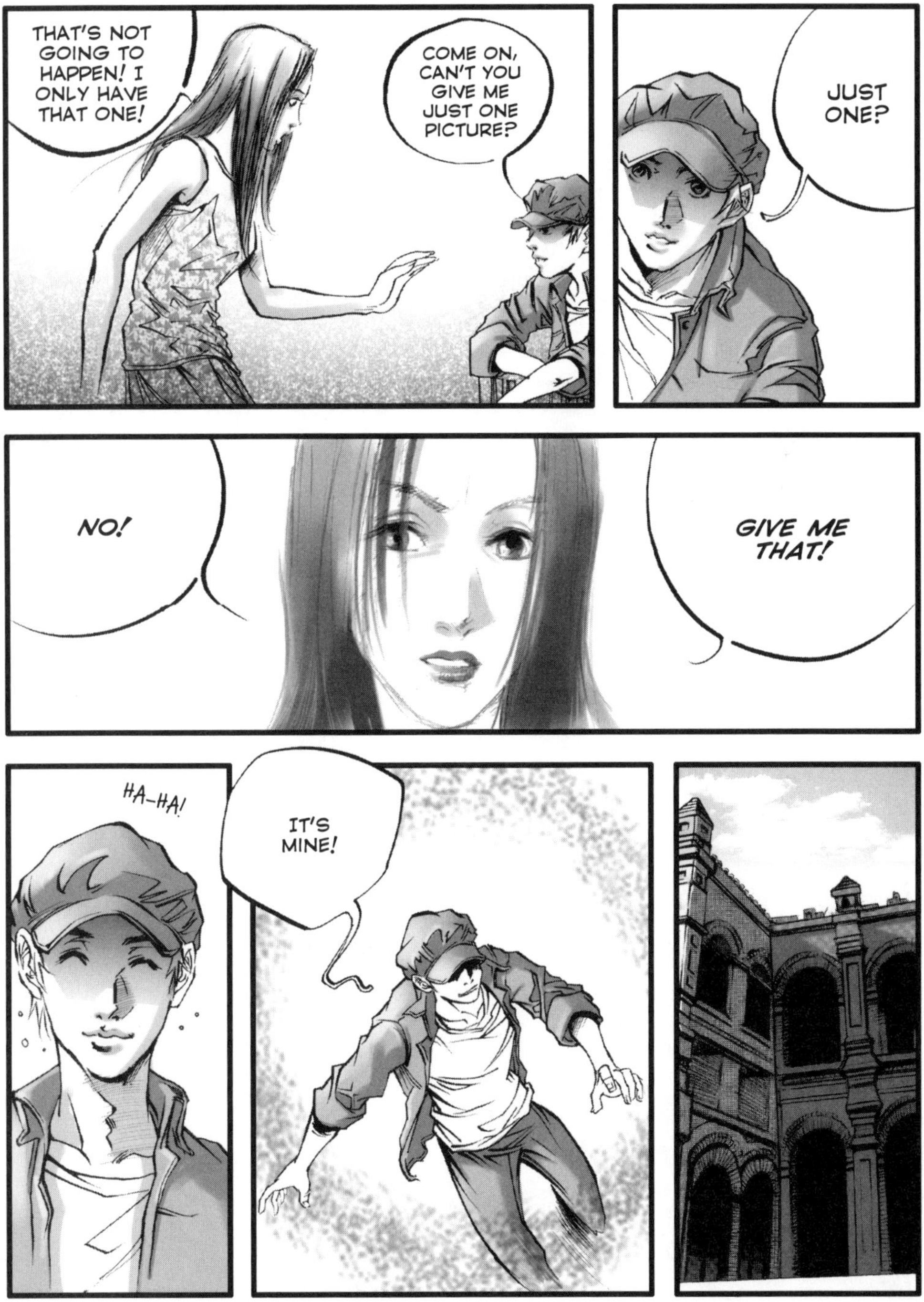
THAT'S NOT GOING TO HAPPEN! I ONLY HAVE THAT ONE!
COME ON, CAN'T YOU GIVE ME JUST ONE PICTURE?
JUST ONE?
NO!
GIVE ME THAT!
HA-HA!
IT'S MINE!

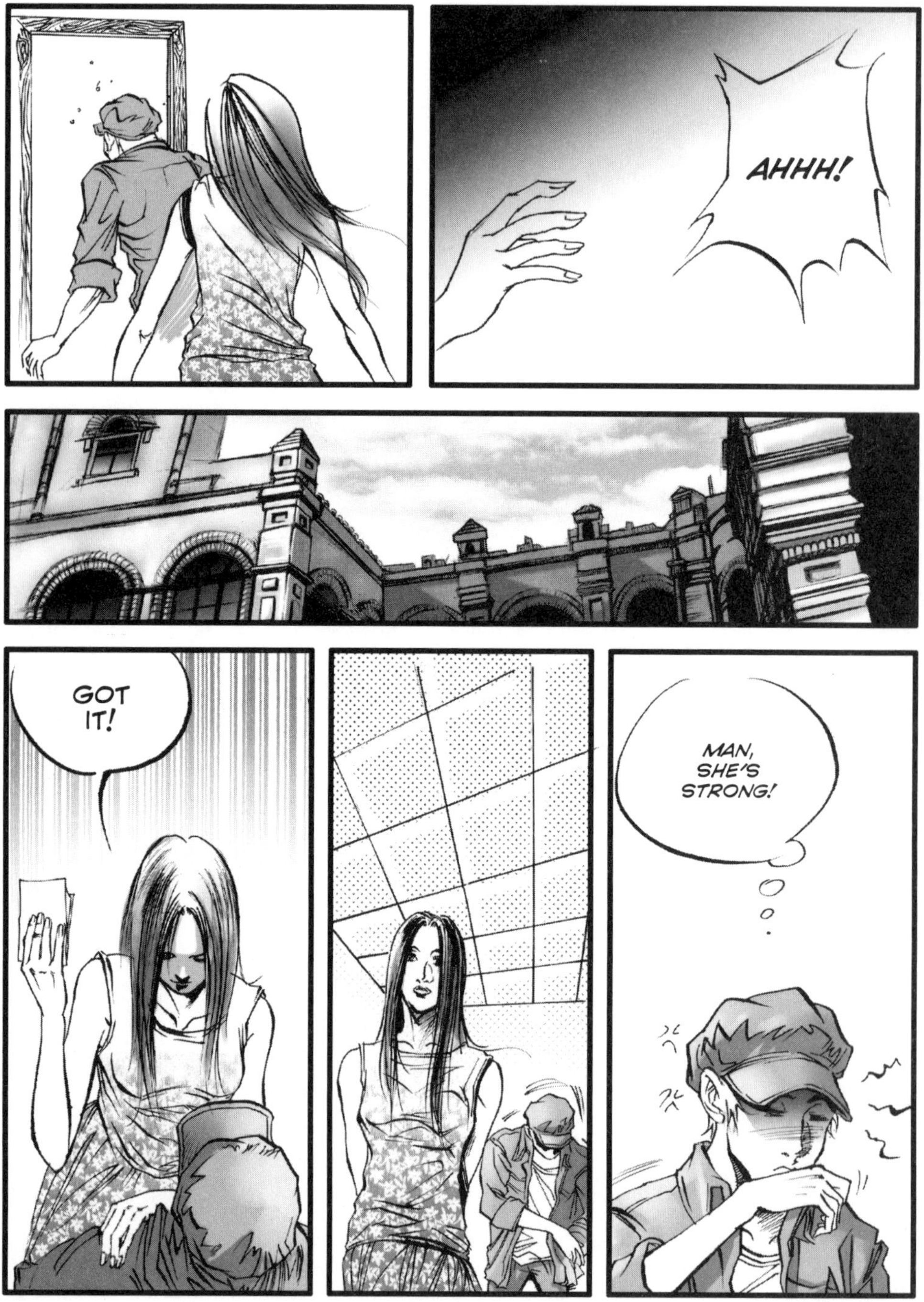
AHHH!
GOT IT!
MAN, SHE'S STRONG!

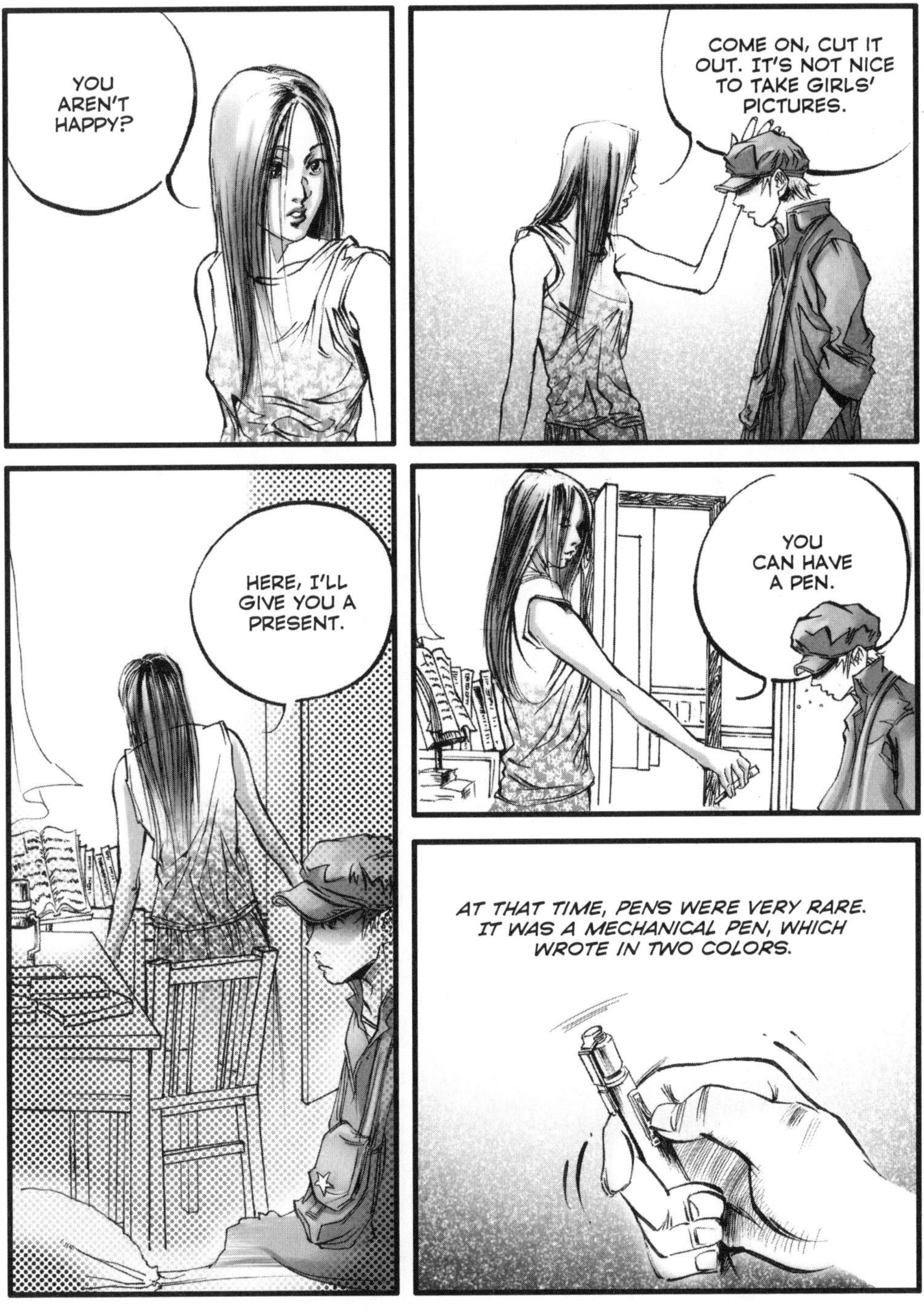
YOU AREN'T HAPPY?
COME ON, CUT IT OUT. IT'S NOT NICE TO TAKE GIRLS' PICTURES.
HERE, I'LL GIVE YOU A PRESENT.
YOU CAN HAVE A PEN.
AT THAT TIME, PENS WERE VERY RARE. IT WAS A MECHANICAL PEN, WHICH WROTE IN TWO COLORS.

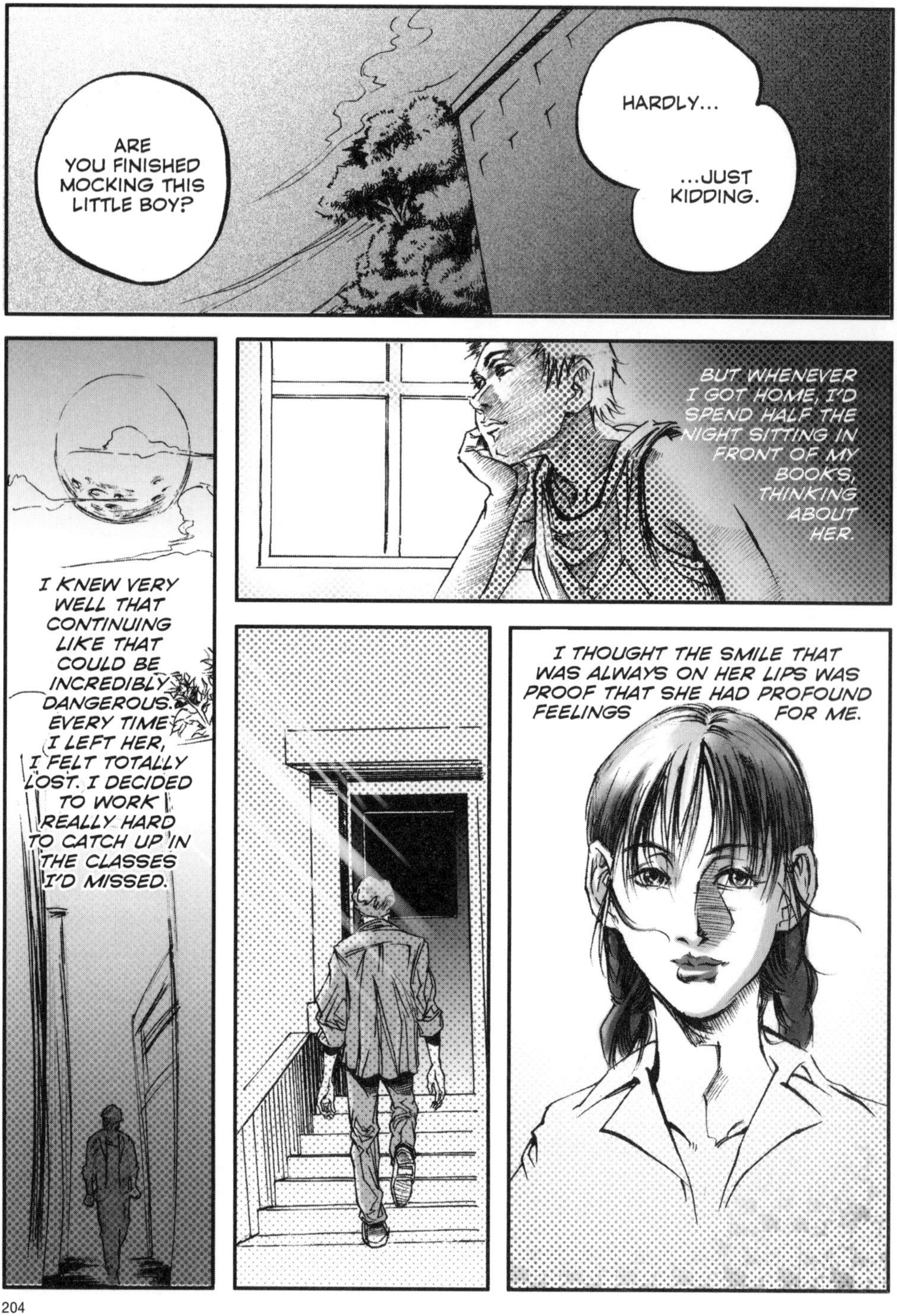
ARE YOU FINISHED MOCKING THIS LITTLE BOY?
HARDLY...
...JUST KIDDING.
BUT WHENEVER I GOT HOME, I'D SPEND HALF THE NIGHT SITTING IN FRONT OF MY BOOKS, THINKING ABOUT HER.
I KNEW VERY WELL THAT CONTINUING LIKE THAT COULD BE INCREDIBLY DANGEROUS. EVERY TIME I LEFT HER, I FELT TOTALLY LOST. I DECIDED TO WORK REALLY HARD TO CATCH UP IN THE CLASSES I'D MISSED.
I THOUGHT THE SMILE THAT WAS ALWAYS ON HER LIPS WAS PROOF THAT SHE HAD PROFOUND FEELINGS FOR ME.

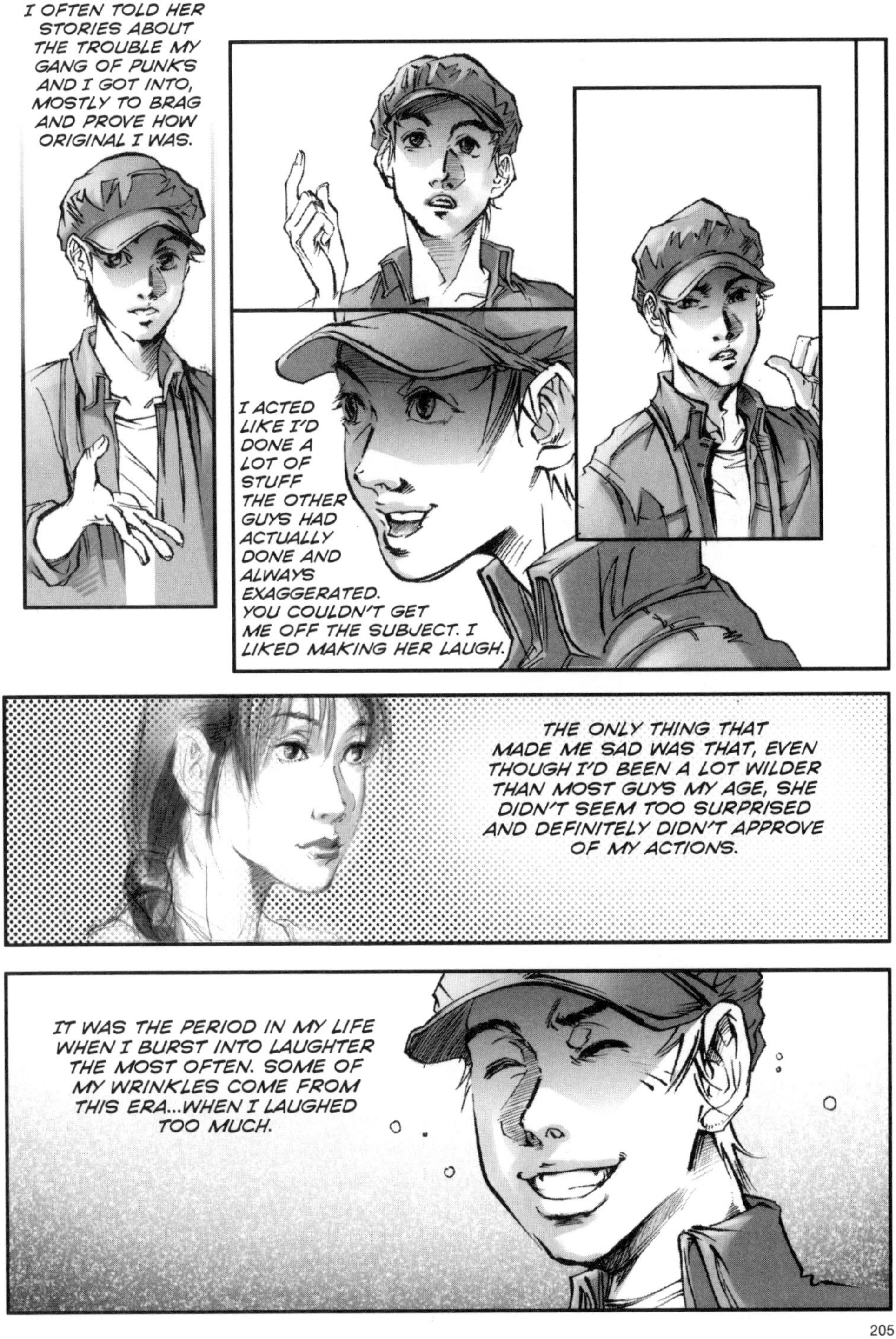
I OFTEN TOLD HER STORIES ABOUT THE TROUBLE MY GANG OF PUNKS AND I GOT INTO, MOSTLY TO BRAG AND PROVE HOW ORIGINAL I WAS.
I ACTED LIKE I'D DONE A LOT OF STUFF THE OTHER GUYS HAD ACTUALLY DONE AND ALWAYS EXAGGERATED. YOU COULDN'T GET ME OFF THE SUBJECT. I LIKED MAKING HER LAUGH.
THE ONLY THING THAT MADE ME SAD WAS THAT, EVEN THOUGH I'D BEEN A LOT WILDER THAN MOST GUYS MY AGE, SHE DIDN'T SEEM TOO SURPRISED AND DEFINITELY DIDN'T APPROVE OF MY ACTIONS.
IT WAS THE PERIOD IN MY LIFE WHEN I BURST INTO LAUGHTER THE MOST OFTEN. SOME OF MY WRINKLES COME FROM THIS ERA...WHEN I LAUGHED TOO MUCH.

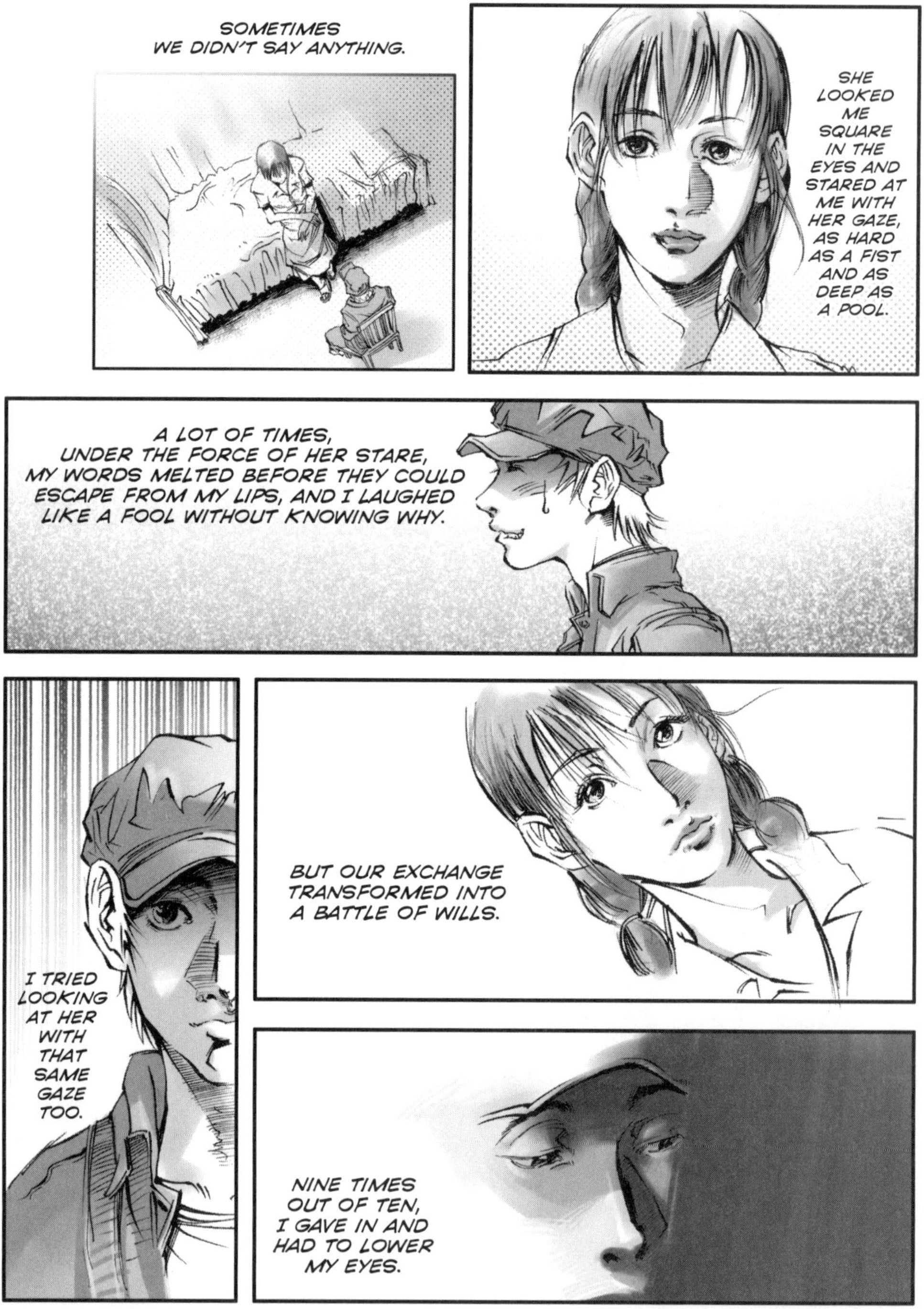
SOMETIMES WE DIDN'T SAY ANYTHING.
SHE LOOKED ME SQUARE IN THE EYES AND STARED AT ME WITH HER GAZE, AS HARD AS A FIST AND AS DEEP AS A POOL.
A LOT OF TIMES, UNDER THE FORCE OF HER STARE, MY WORDS MELTED BEFORE THEY COULD ESCAPE FROM MY LIPS, AND I LAUGHED LIKE A FOOL WITHOUT KNOWING WHY.
I TRIED LOOKING AT HER WITH THAT SAME GAZE TOO.
BUT OUR EXCHANGE TRANSFORMED INTO A BATTLE OF WILLS.
NINE TIMES OUT OF TEN, I GAVE IN AND HAD TO LOWER MY EYES.

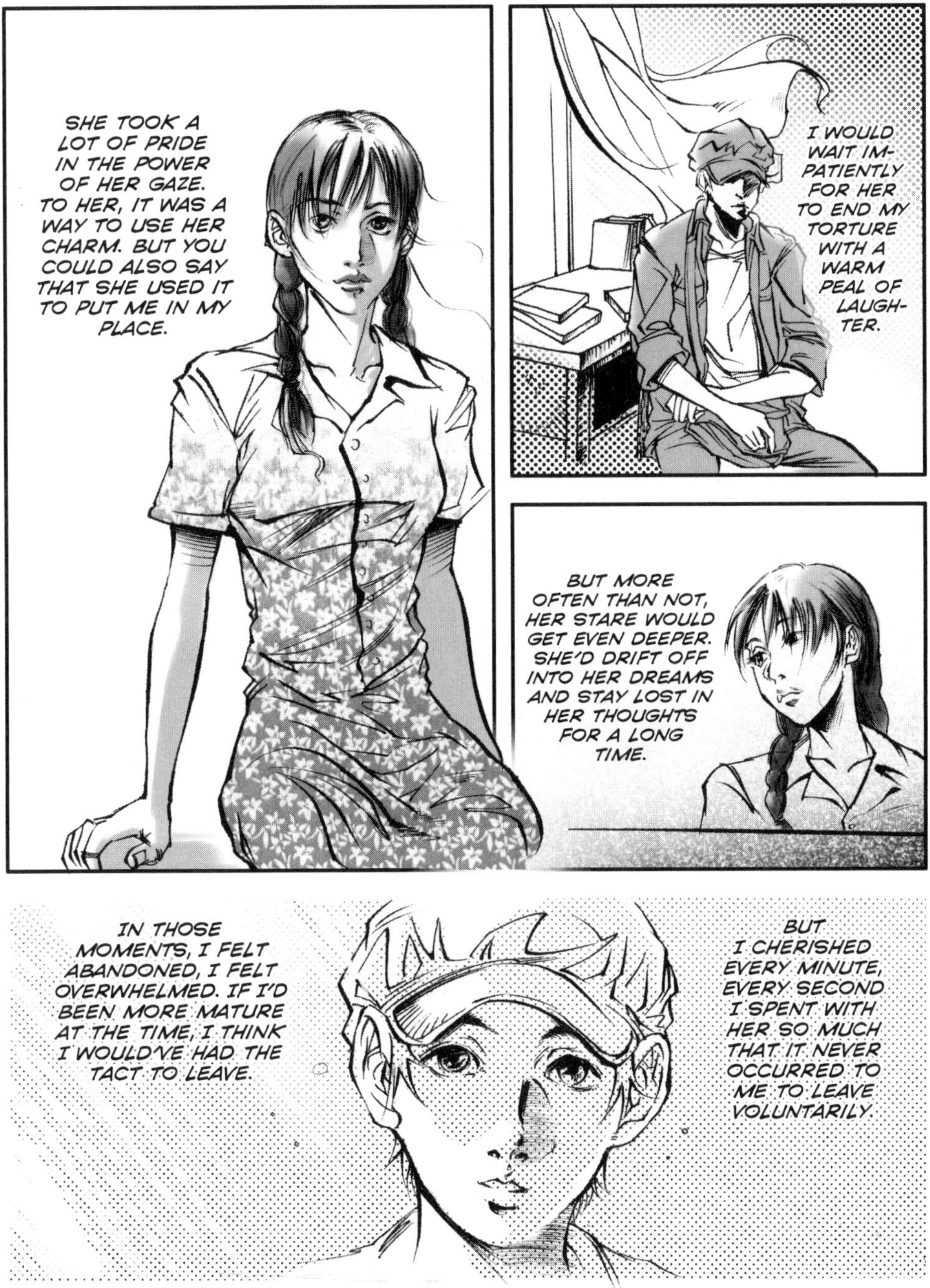
SHE TOOK A LOT OF PRIDE IN THE POWER OF HER GAZE. TO HER, IT WAS A WAY TO USE HER CHARM. BUT YOU COULD ALSO SAY THAT SHE USED IT TO PUT ME IN MY PLACE.
I WOULD WAIT IMPATIENTLY FOR HER TO END MY TORTURE WITH A WARM PEAL OF LAUGHTER.
BUT MORE OFTEN THAN NOT, HER STARE WOULD GET EVEN DEEPER. SHE'D DRIFT OFF INTO HER DREAMS AND STAY LOST IN HER THOUGHTS FOR A LONG TIME.
IN THOSE MOMENTS, I FELT ABANDONED, I FELT OVERWHELMED. IF I'D BEEN MORE MATURE AT THE TIME, I THINK I WOULD'VE HAD THE TACT TO LEAVE.
BUT I CHERISHED EVERY MINUTE, EVERY SECOND I SPENT WITH HER SO MUCH THAT IT NEVER OCCURRED TO ME TO LEAVE VOLUNTARILY.

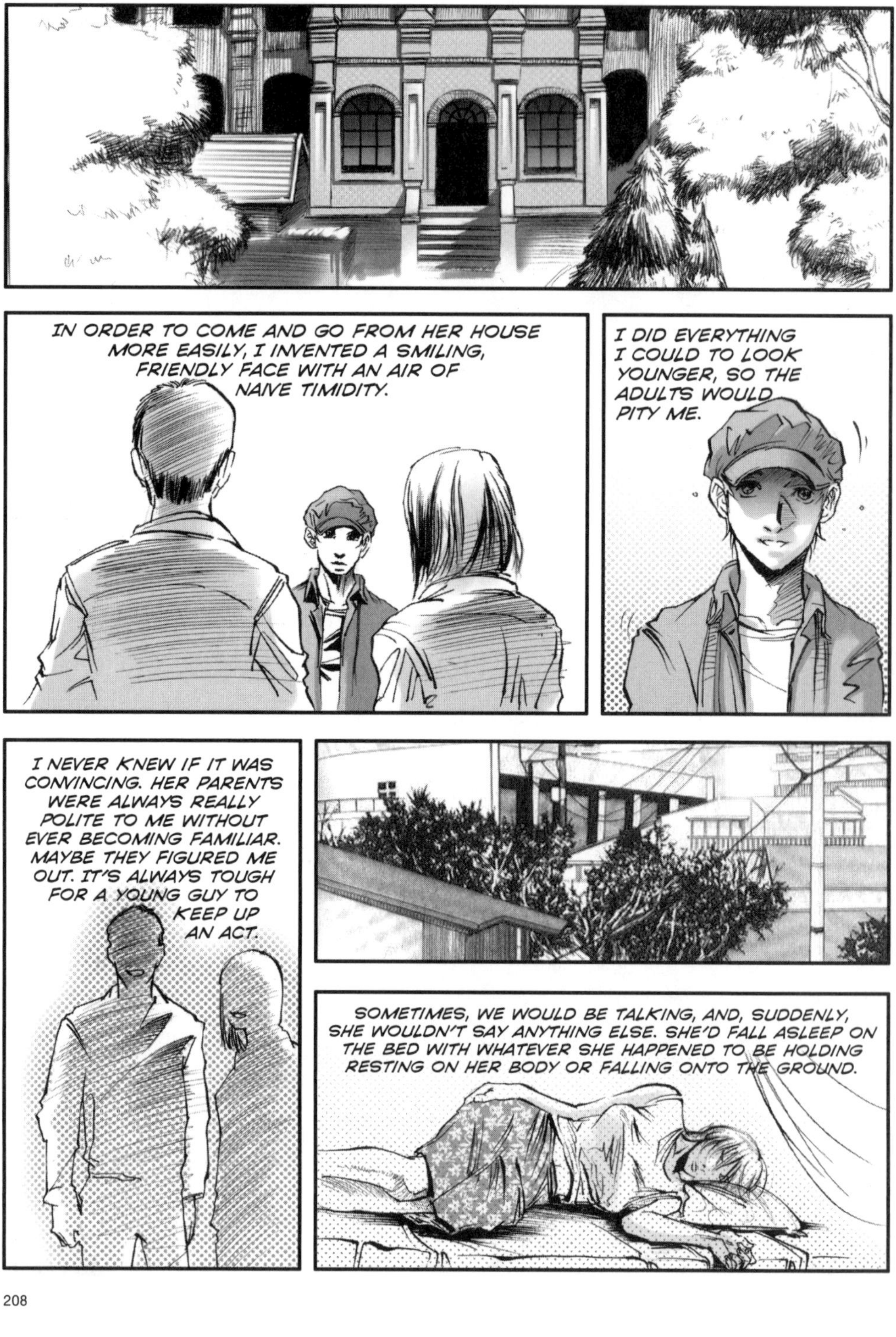
IN ORDER TO COME AND GO FROM HER HOUSE MORE EASILY, I INVENTED A SMILING, FRIENDLY FACE WITH AN AIR OF NAIVE TIMIDITY.
I DID EVERYTHING I COULD TO LOOK YOUNGER, SO THE ADULTS WOULD PITY ME.
I NEVER KNEW IF IT WAS CONVINCING. HER PARENTS WERE ALWAYS REALLY POLITE TO ME WITHOUT EVER BECOMING FAMILIAR. MAYBE THEY FIGURED ME OUT. IT'S ALWAYS TOUGH FOR A YOUNG GUY TO KEEP UP AN ACT.
SOMETIMES, WE WOULD BE TALKING, AND, SUDDENLY, SHE WOULDN'T SAY ANYTHING ELSE. SHE'D FALL ASLEEP ON THE BED WITH WHATEVER SHE HAPPENED TO BE HOLDING RESTING ON HER BODY OR FALLING ONTO THE GROUND.

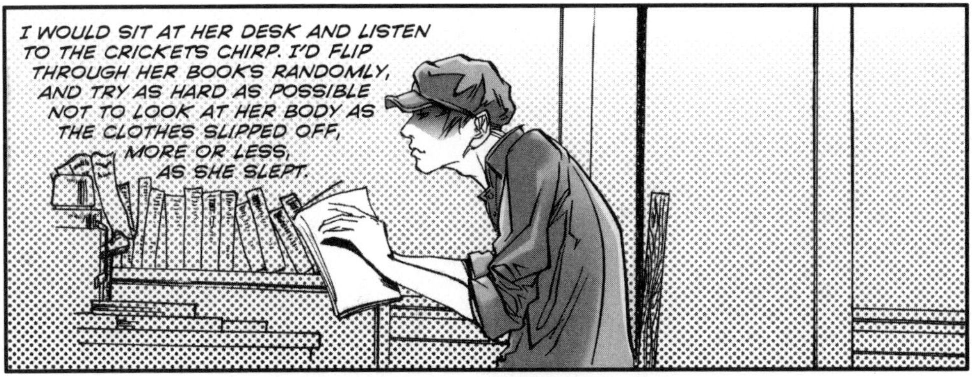
I WOULD SIT AT HER DESK AND LISTEN TO THE CRICKETS CHIRP. I'D FLIP THROUGH HER BOOKS RANDOMLY, AND TRY AS HARD AS POSSIBLE NOT TO LOOK AT HER BODY AS THE CLOTHES SLIPPED OFF, MORE OR LESS, AS SHE SLEPT.

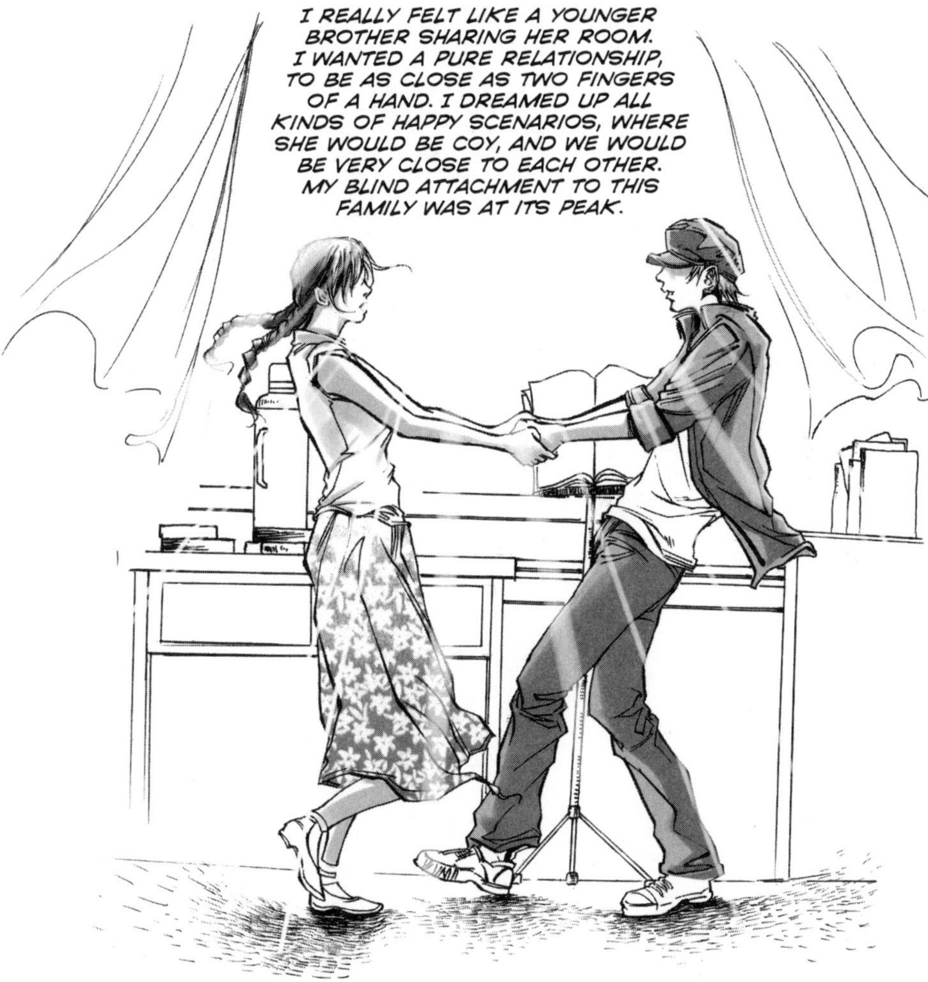
I REALLY FELT LIKE A YOUNGER BROTHER SHARING HER ROOM. I WANTED A PURE RELATIONSHIP, TO BE AS CLOSE AS TWO FINGERS OF A HAND. I DREAMED UP ALL KINDS OF HAPPY SCENARIOS, WHERE SHE WOULD BE COY, AND WE WOULD BE VERY CLOSE TO EACH OTHER. MY BLIND ATTACHMENT TO THIS FAMILY WAS AT ITS PEAK.

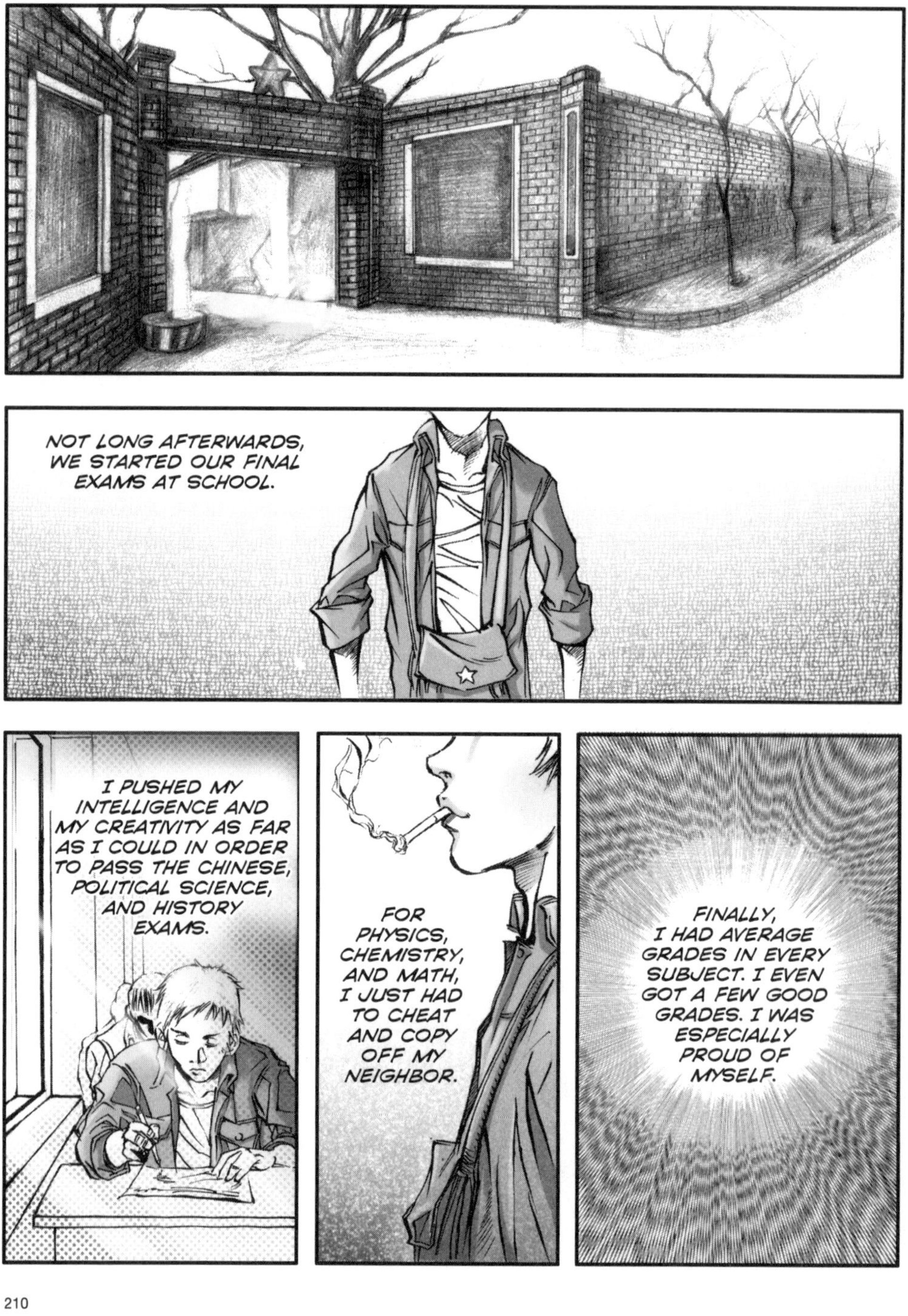
NOT LONG AFTERWARDS, WE STARTED OUR FINAL EXAMS AT SCHOOL.
I PUSHED MY INTELLIGENCE AND MY CREATIVITY AS FAR AS I COULD IN ORDER TO PASS THE CHINESE, POLITICAL SCIENCE, AND HISTORY EXAMS.
FOR PHYSICS, CHEMISTRY, AND MATH, I JUST HAD TO CHEAT AND COPY OFF MY NEIGHBOR.
FINALLY, I HAD AVERAGE GRADES IN EVERY SUBJECT. I EVEN GOT A FEW GOOD GRADES. I WAS ESPECIALLY PROUD OF MYSELF.

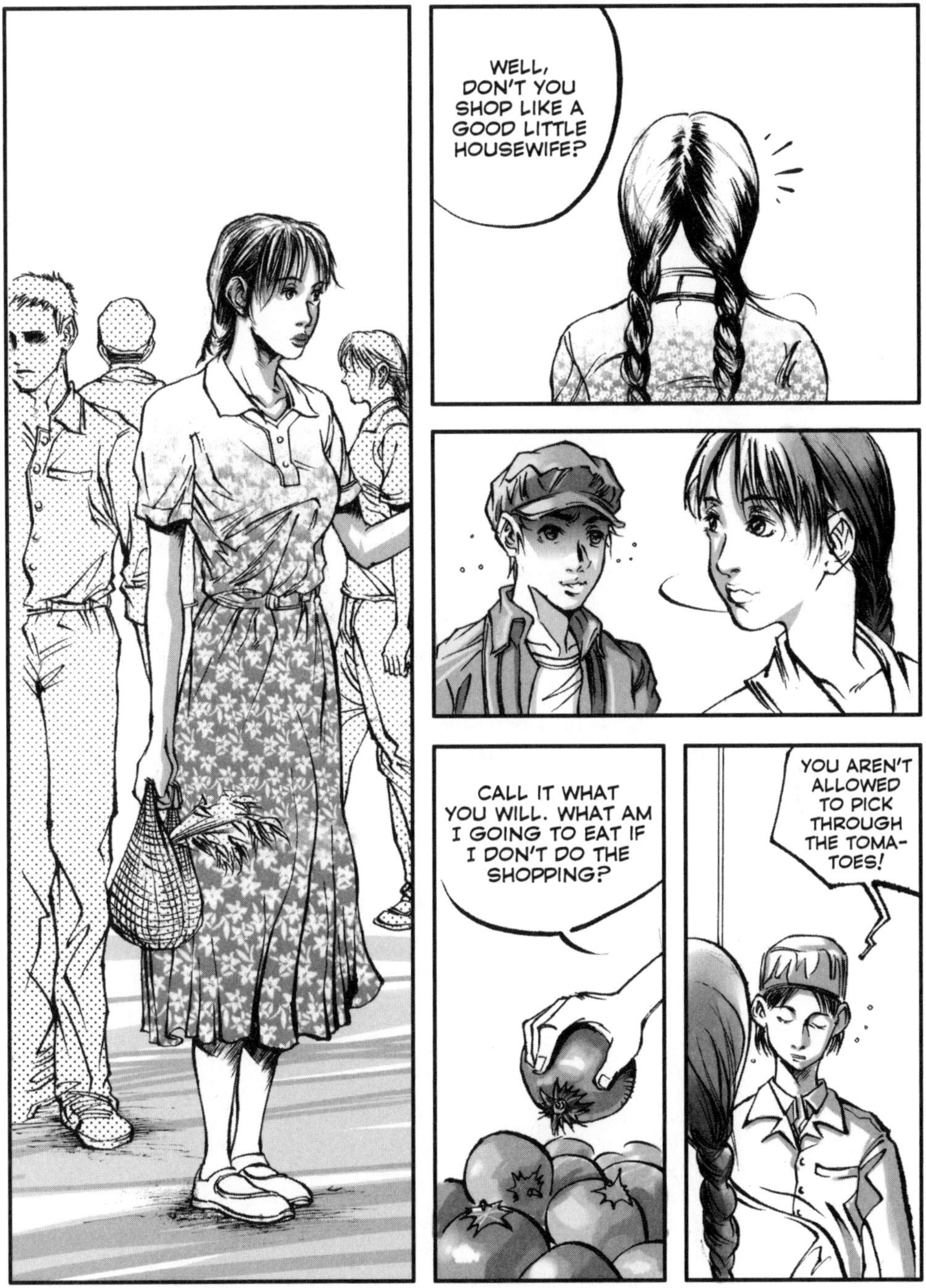
WELL, DON'T YOU SHOP LIKE A GOOD LITTLE HOUSEWIFE?
CALL IT WHAT YOU WILL. WHAT AM I GOING TO EAT IF I DON'T DO THE SHOPPING?
YOU AREN'T ALLOWED TO PICK THROUGH THE TOMA- TOES!

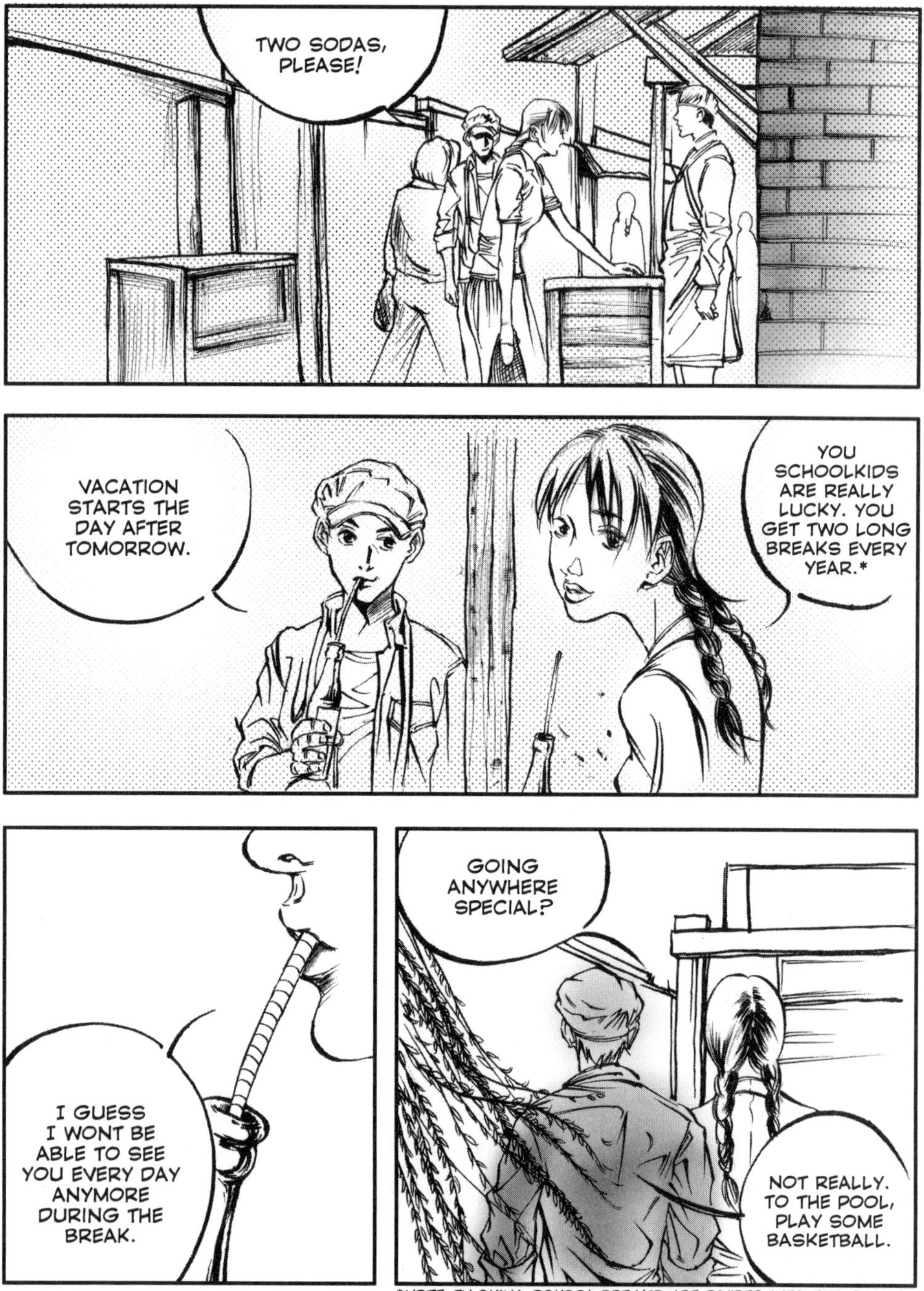
TWO SODAS, PLEASE!
VACATION STARTS THE DAY AFTER TOMORROW.
YOU SCHOOLKIDS ARE REALLY LUCKY. YOU GET TWO LONG BREAKS EVERY YEAR.*
I GUESS I WONT BE ABLE TO SEE YOU EVERY DAY ANYMORE DURING THE BREAK.
GOING ANYWHERE SPECIAL?
NOT REALLY. TO THE POOL, PLAY SOME BASKETBALL.

**NOTE: IN CHINA, SCHOOL BREAKS ARE DIVIDED INTO TWO PERIODS: WINTER VACATION, WHICH STARTS AT THE CHINESE NEW YEAR, AND SUMMER VACATION (JULY/AUGUST).*

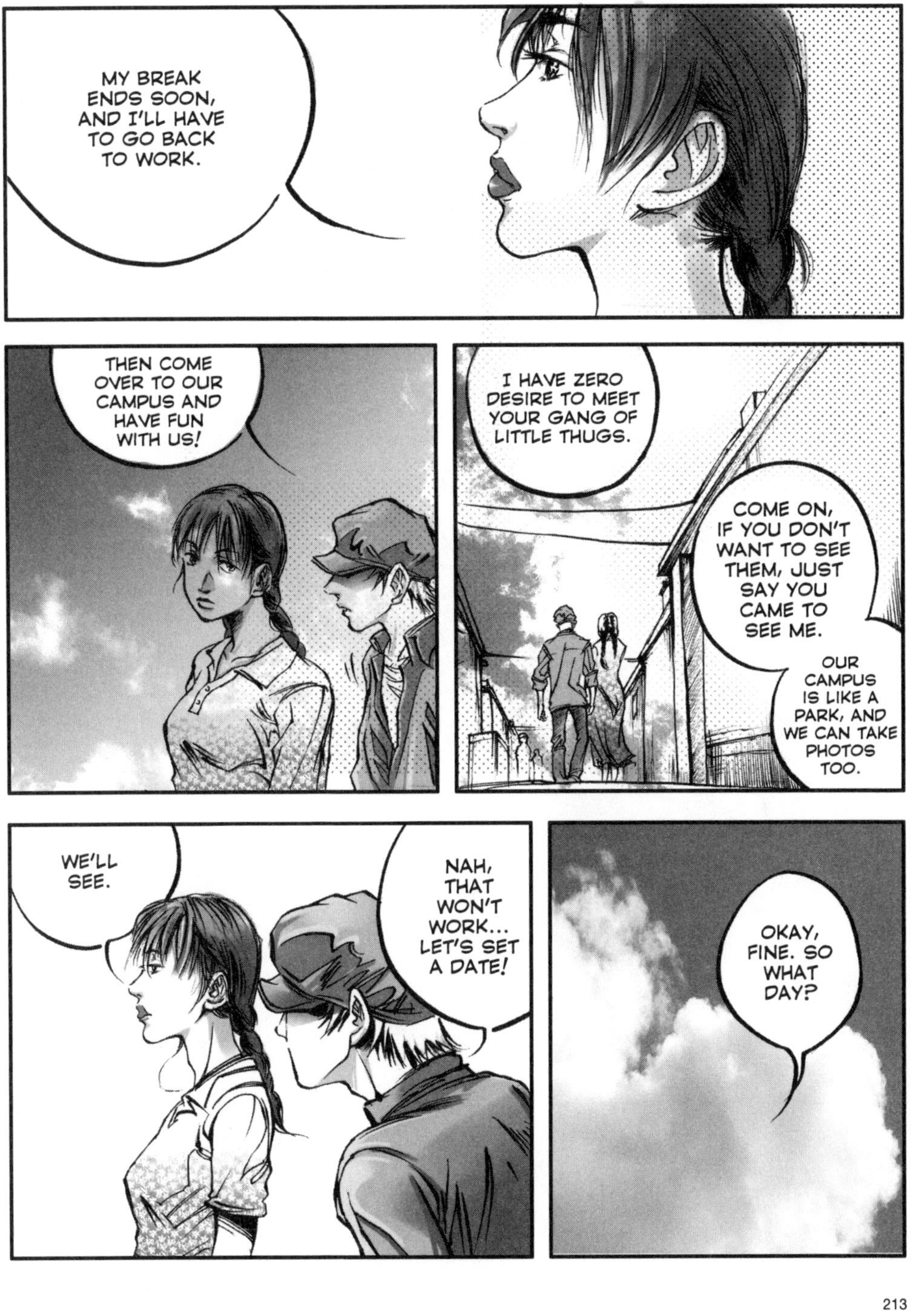
MY BREAK ENDS SOON, AND I'LL HAVE TO GO BACK TO WORK.
THEN COME OVER TO OUR CAMPUS AND HAVE FUN WITH US!
I HAVE ZERO DESIRE TO MEET YOUR GANG OF LITTLE THUGS.
COME ON, IF YOU DON'T WANT TO SEE THEM, JUST SAY YOU CAME TO SEE ME.
OUR CAMPUS IS LIKE A PARK, AND WE CAN TAKE PHOTOS TOO.
WE'LL SEE.
NAH, THAT WON'T WORK... LET'S SET A DATE!
OKAY, FINE. SO WHAT DAY?

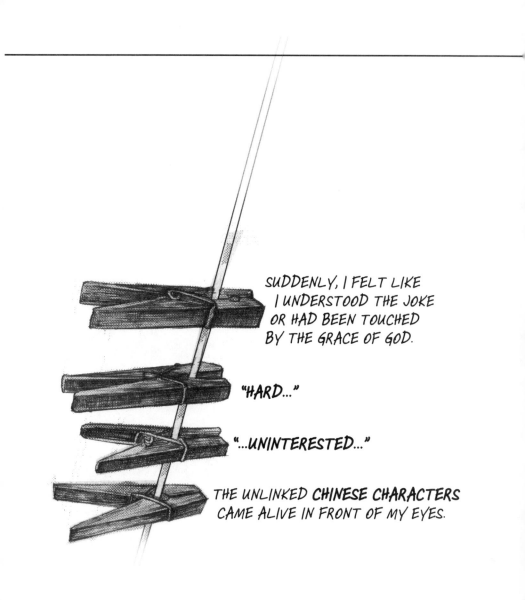

SUDDENLY, I FELT LIKE
I UNDERSTOOD THE JOKE
OR HAD BEEN TOUCHED
BY THE GRACE OF GOD.

"HARD..."

"...UNINTERESTED..."

THE UNLINKED **CHINESE CHARACTERS**
CAME ALIVE IN FRONT OF MY EYES.

mi lan and me...

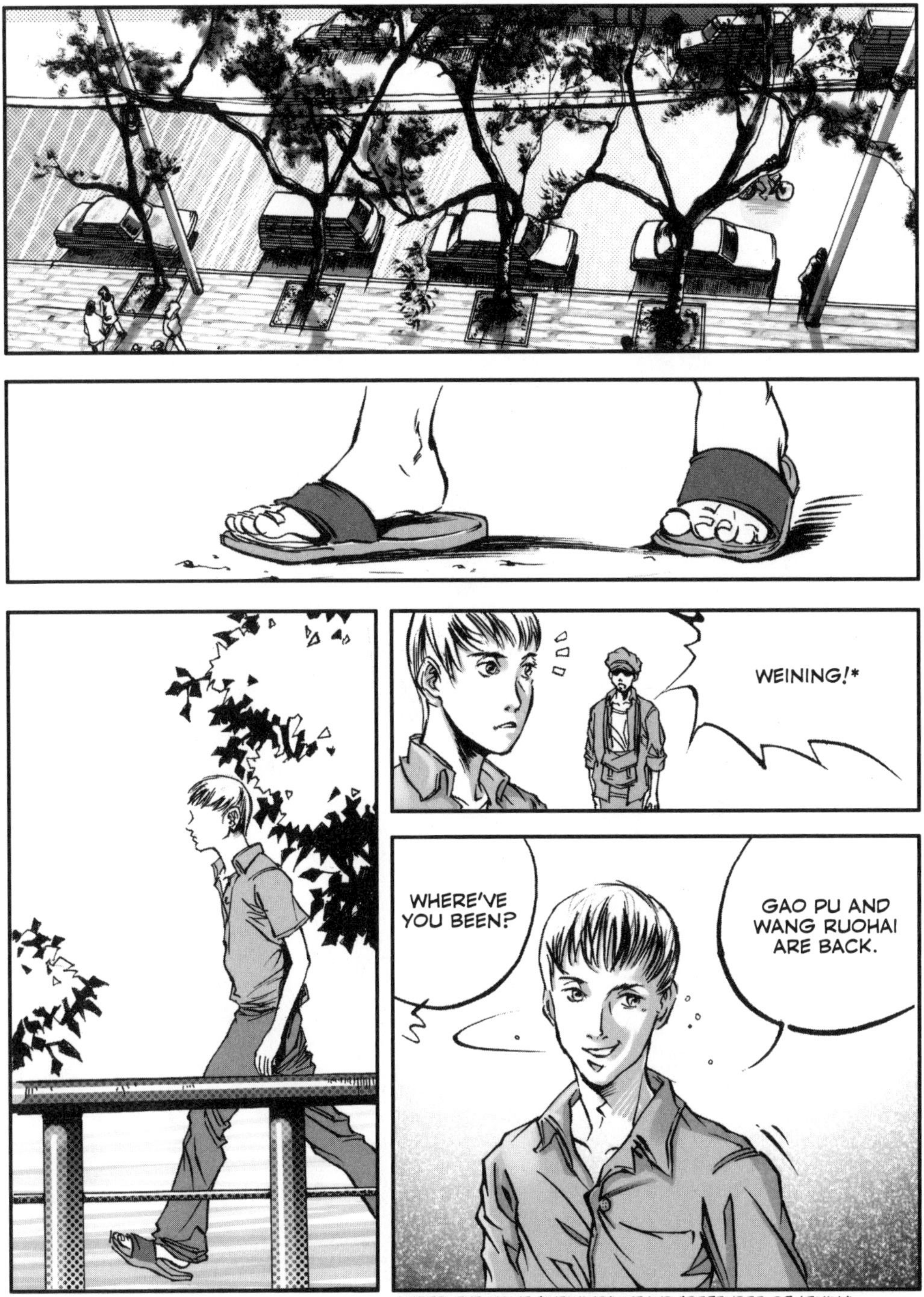
WEINING!*
WHERE'VE YOU BEEN?
GAO PU AND WANG RUOHAI ARE BACK.

*NOTE: THE NAME "WEINING" MEANS "DEFENDER OF LENIN." IT WAS A VERY COMMON FIRST NAME DURING THE CULTURAL REVOLUTION.

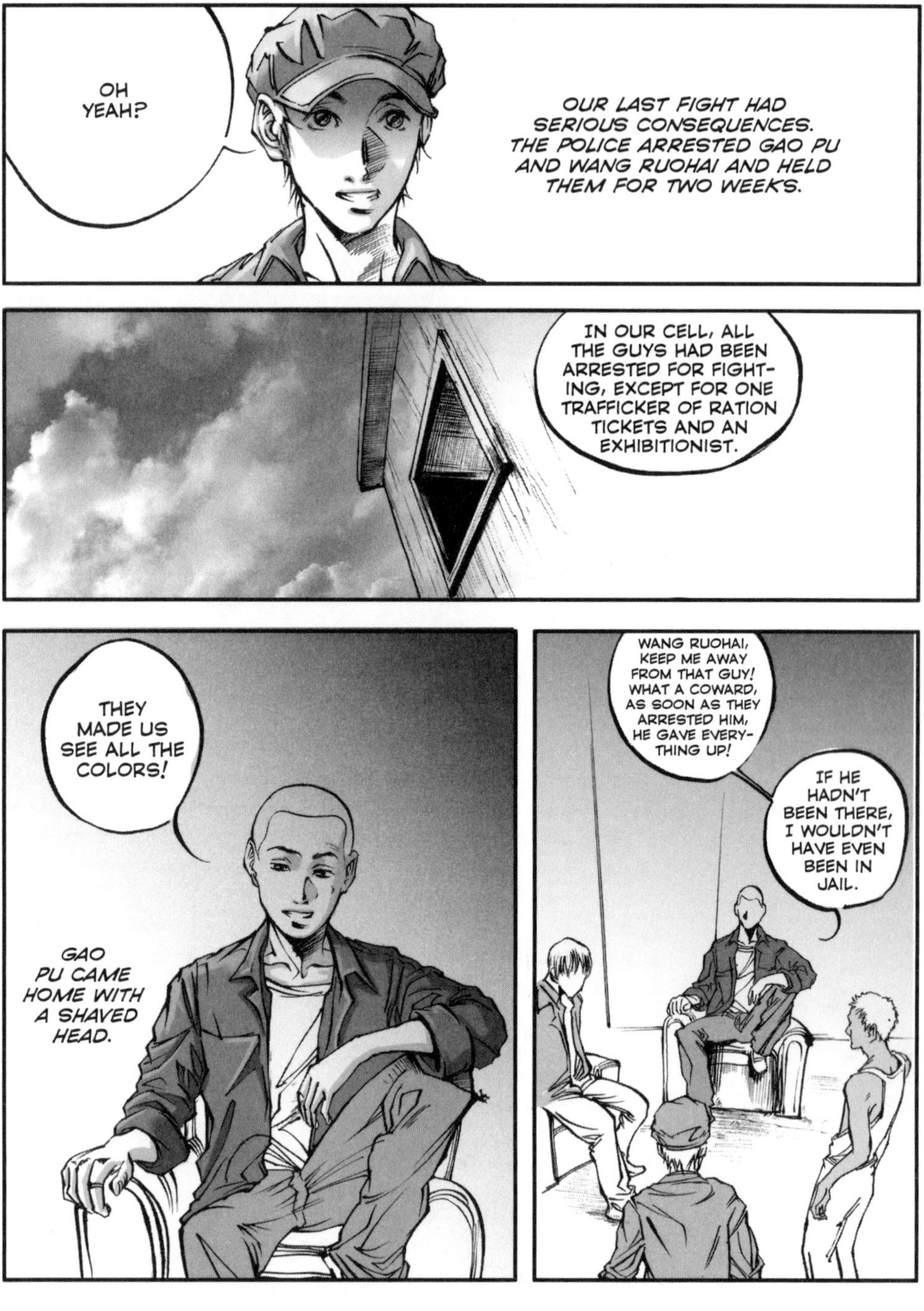
OH YEAH?
OUR LAST FIGHT HAD SERIOUS CONSEQUENCES. THE POLICE ARRESTED GAO PU AND WANG RUOHAI AND HELD THEM FOR TWO WEEKS.
IN OUR CELL, ALL THE GUYS HAD BEEN ARRESTED FOR FIGHTING, EXCEPT FOR ONE TRAFFICKER OF RATION TICKETS AND AN EXHIBITIONIST.
THEY MADE US SEE ALL THE COLORS!
GAO PU CAME HOME WITH A SHAVED HEAD.
WANG RUOHAI, KEEP ME AWAY FROM THAT GUY! WHAT A COWARD, AS SOON AS THEY ARRESTED HIM, HE GAVE EVERYTHING UP!
IF HE HADN'T BEEN THERE, I WOULDN'T HAVE EVEN BEEN IN JAIL.

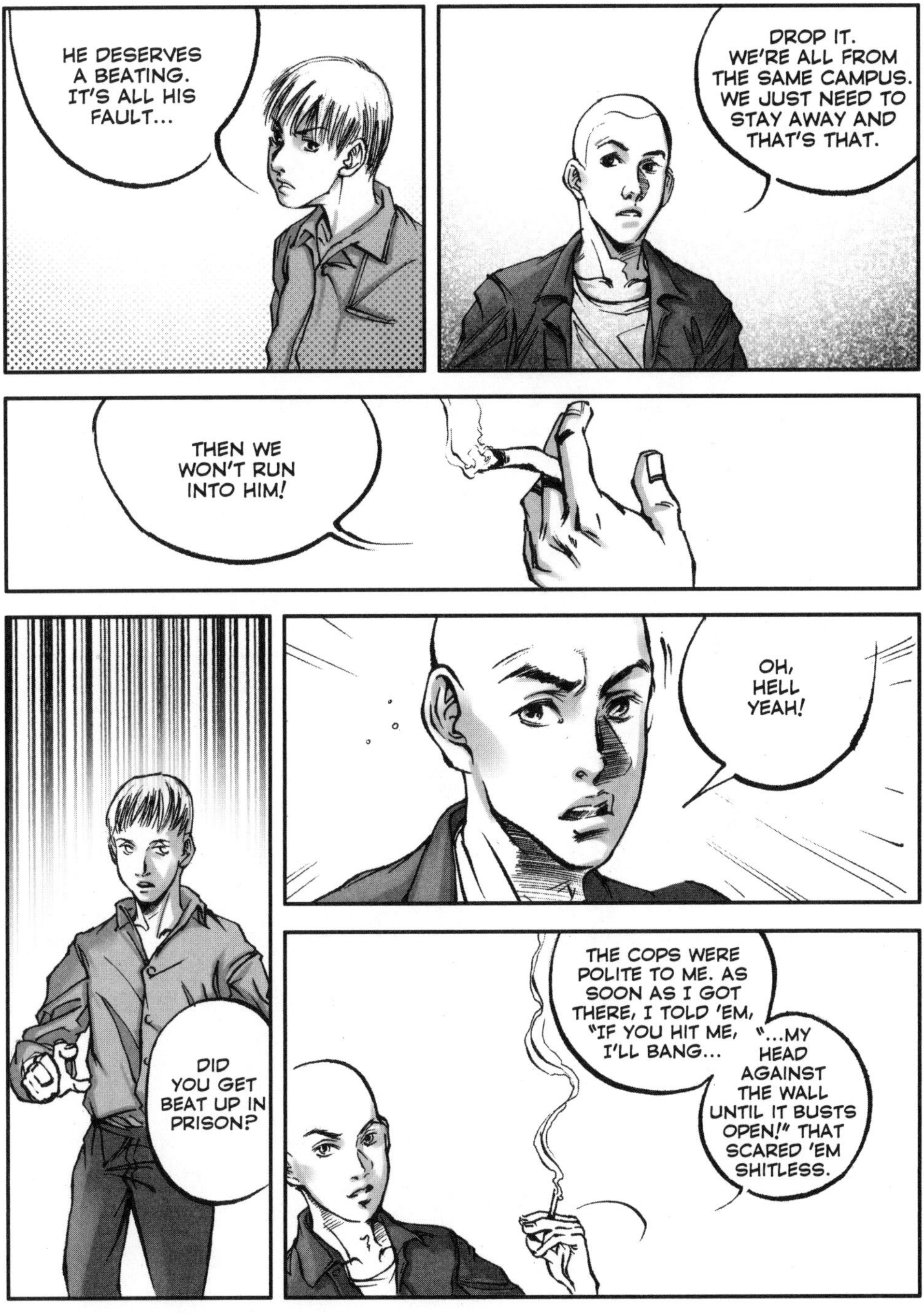
HE DESERVES A BEATING. IT'S ALL HIS FAULT...
DROP IT. WE'RE ALL FROM THE SAME CAMPUS. WE JUST NEED TO STAY AWAY AND THAT'S THAT.
THEN WE WON'T RUN INTO HIM!
DID YOU GET BEAT UP IN PRISON?
OH, HELL YEAH!
THE COPS WERE POLITE TO ME. AS SOON AS I GOT THERE, I TOLD 'EM, "IF YOU HIT ME, I'LL BANG...
"...MY HEAD AGAINST THE WALL UNTIL IT BUSTS OPEN!" THAT SCARED 'EM SHITLESS.

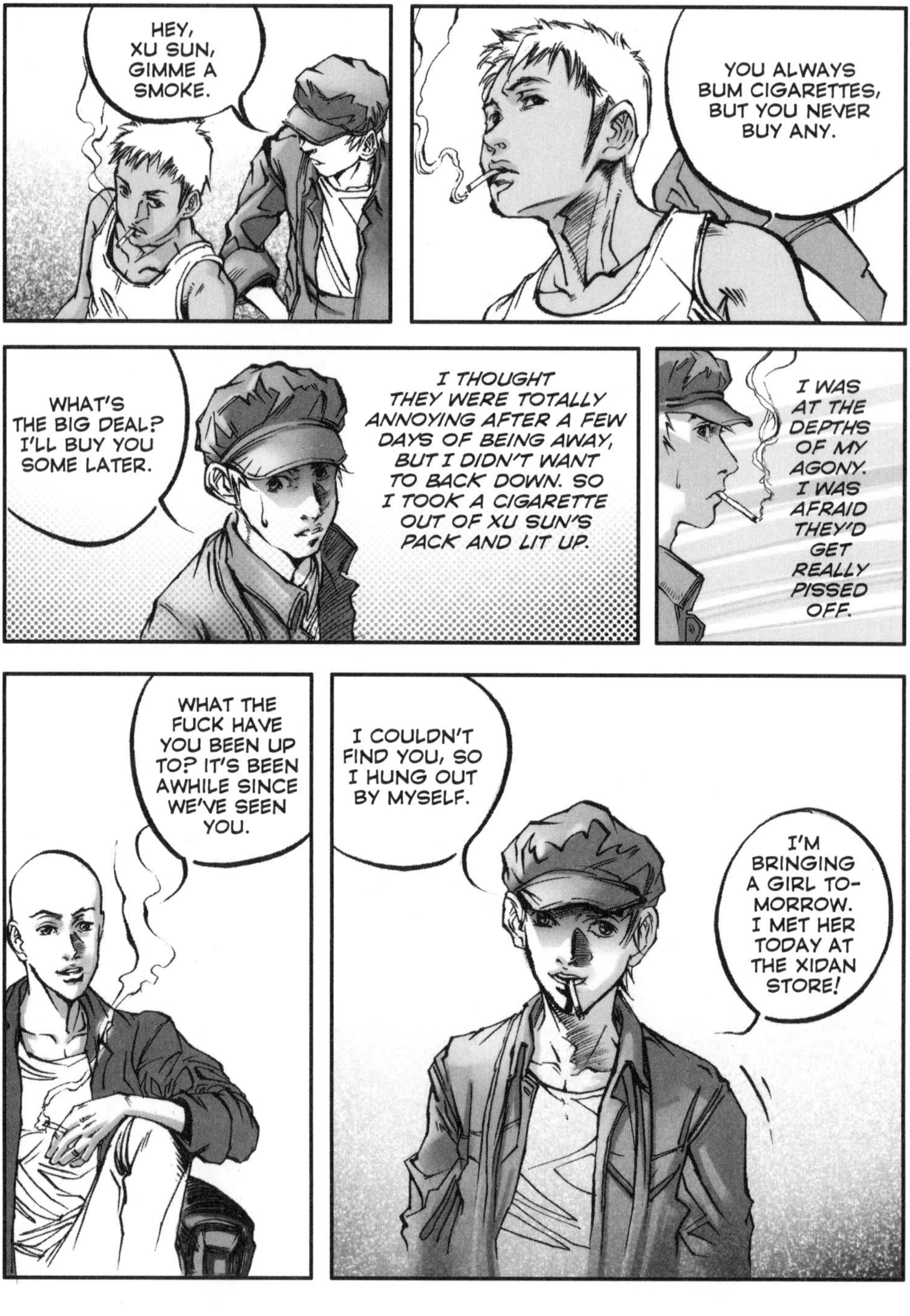
HEY, XU SUN, GIMME A SMOKE.
YOU ALWAYS BUM CIGARETTES, BUT YOU NEVER BUY ANY.
WHAT'S THE BIG DEAL? I'LL BUY YOU SOME LATER.
I THOUGHT THEY WERE TOTALLY ANNOYING AFTER A FEW DAYS OF BEING AWAY, BUT I DIDN'T WANT TO BACK DOWN. SO I TOOK A CIGARETTE OUT OF XU SUN'S PACK AND LIT UP.
I WAS AT THE DEPTHS OF MY AGONY. I WAS AFRAID THEY'D GET REALLY PISSED OFF.
WHAT THE FUCK HAVE YOU BEEN UP TO? IT'S BEEN AWHILE SINCE WE'VE SEEN YOU.
I COULDN'T FIND YOU, SO I HUNG OUT BY MYSELF.
I'M BRINGING A GIRL TO-MORROW. I MET HER TODAY AT THE XIDAN STORE!

WE TOOK HER TO A HILL.

THEY WERE ALL SITTING ON A BENCH SMOKING.

I WAS CONVINCED THEY WERE ALL SLOUCHING ON PURPOSE...

...WHEN THEY SAW US COME UP THE HILL

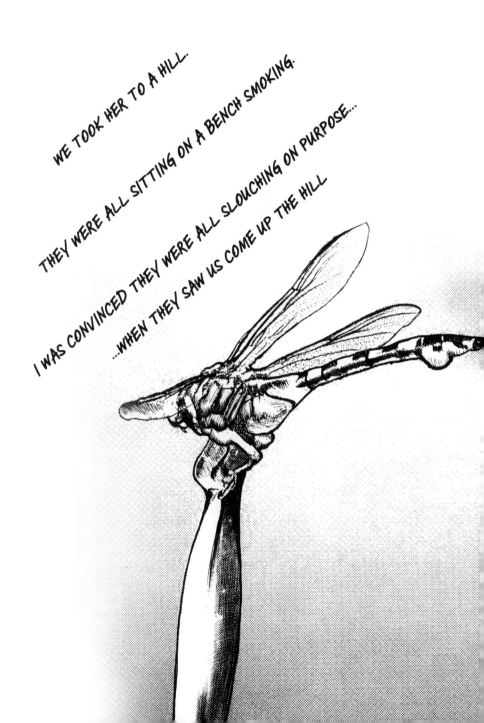

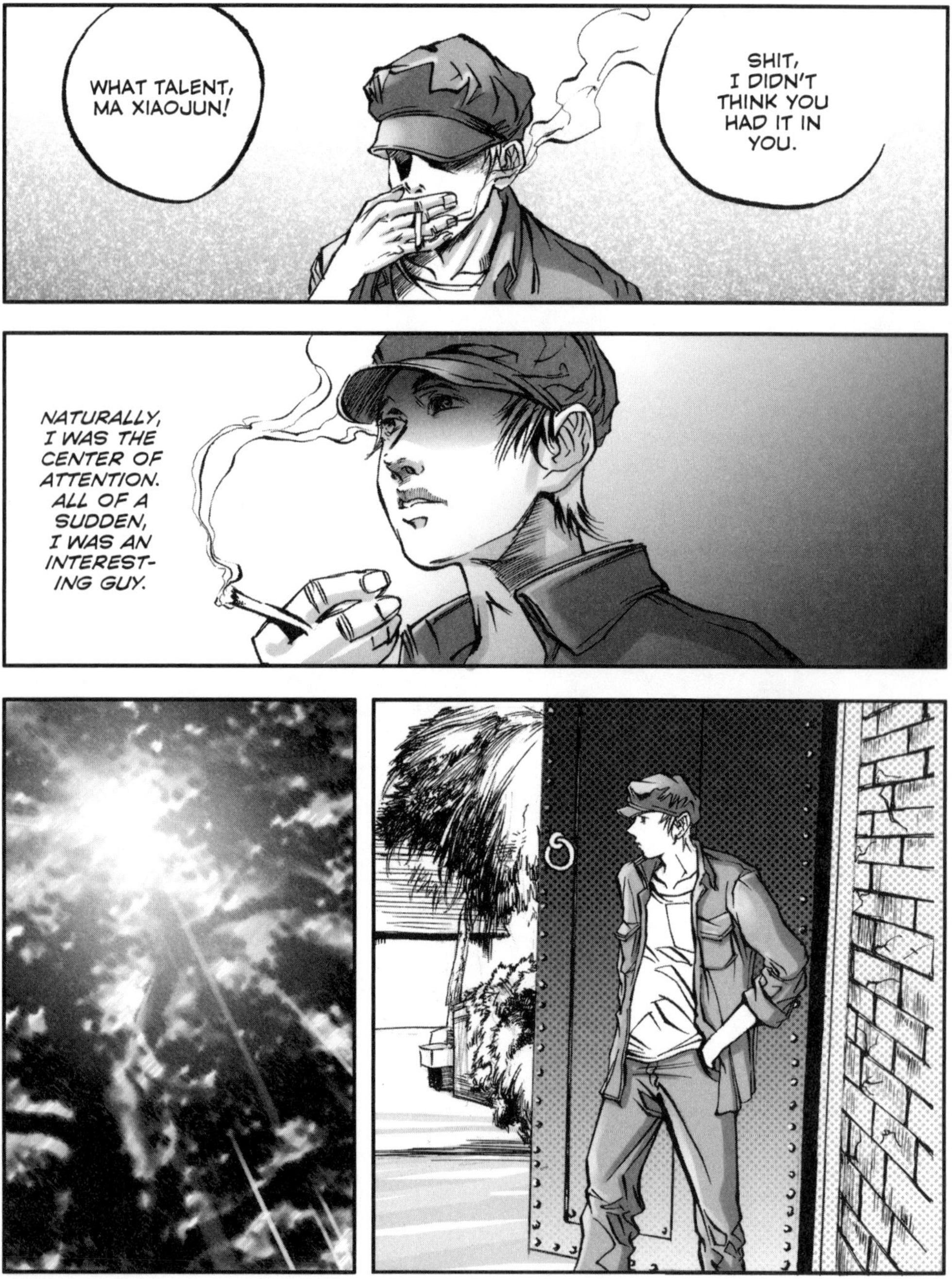
WHAT TALENT, MA XIAOJUN!
SHIT, I DIDN'T THINK YOU HAD IT IN YOU.
NATURALLY, I WAS THE CENTER OF ATTENTION. ALL OF A SUDDEN, I WAS AN INTERESTING GUY.

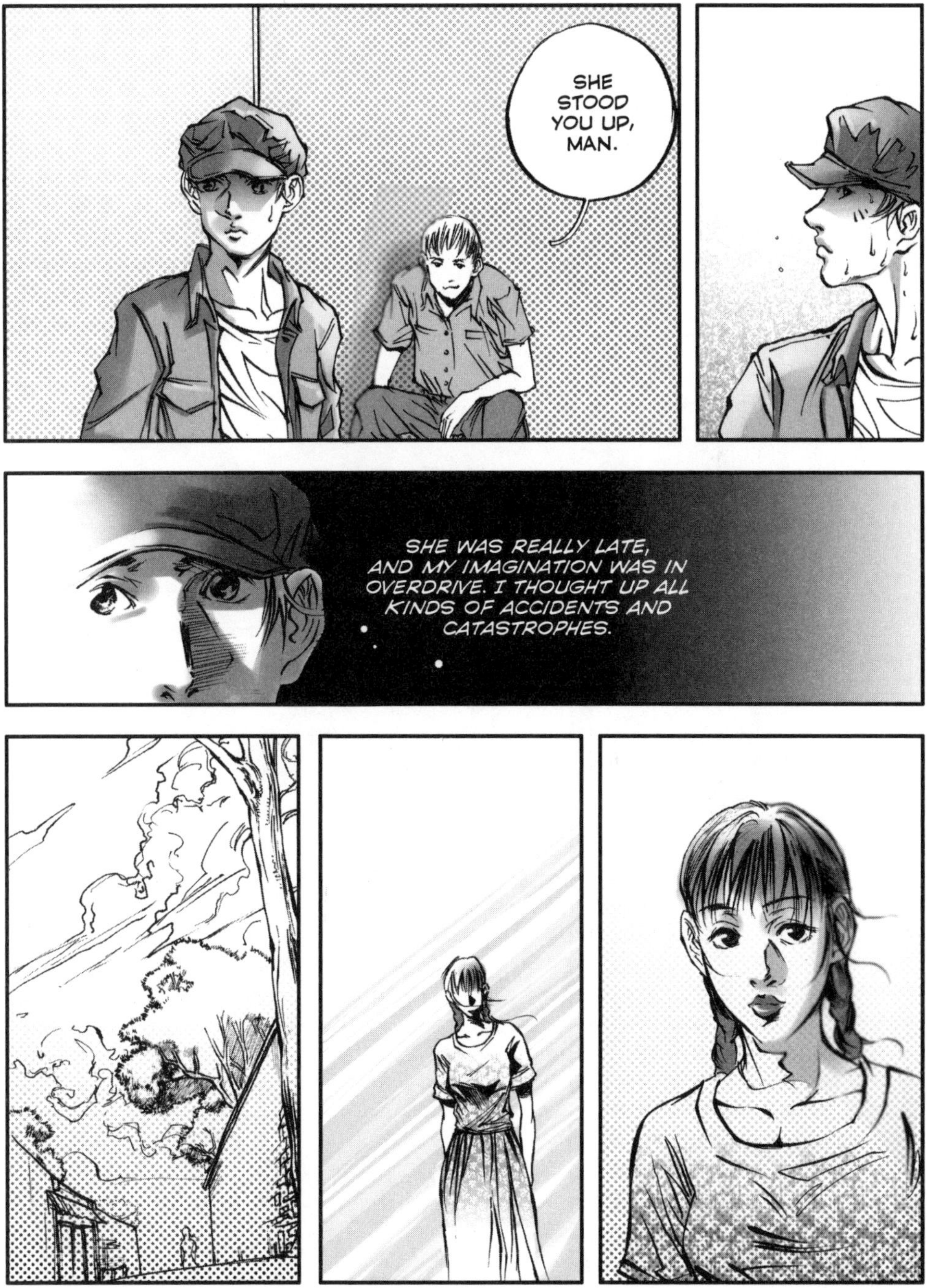
SHE STOOD YOU UP, MAN.
SHE WAS REALLY LATE, AND MY IMAGINATION WAS IN OVERDRIVE. I THOUGHT UP ALL KINDS OF ACCIDENTS AND CATASTROPHES.

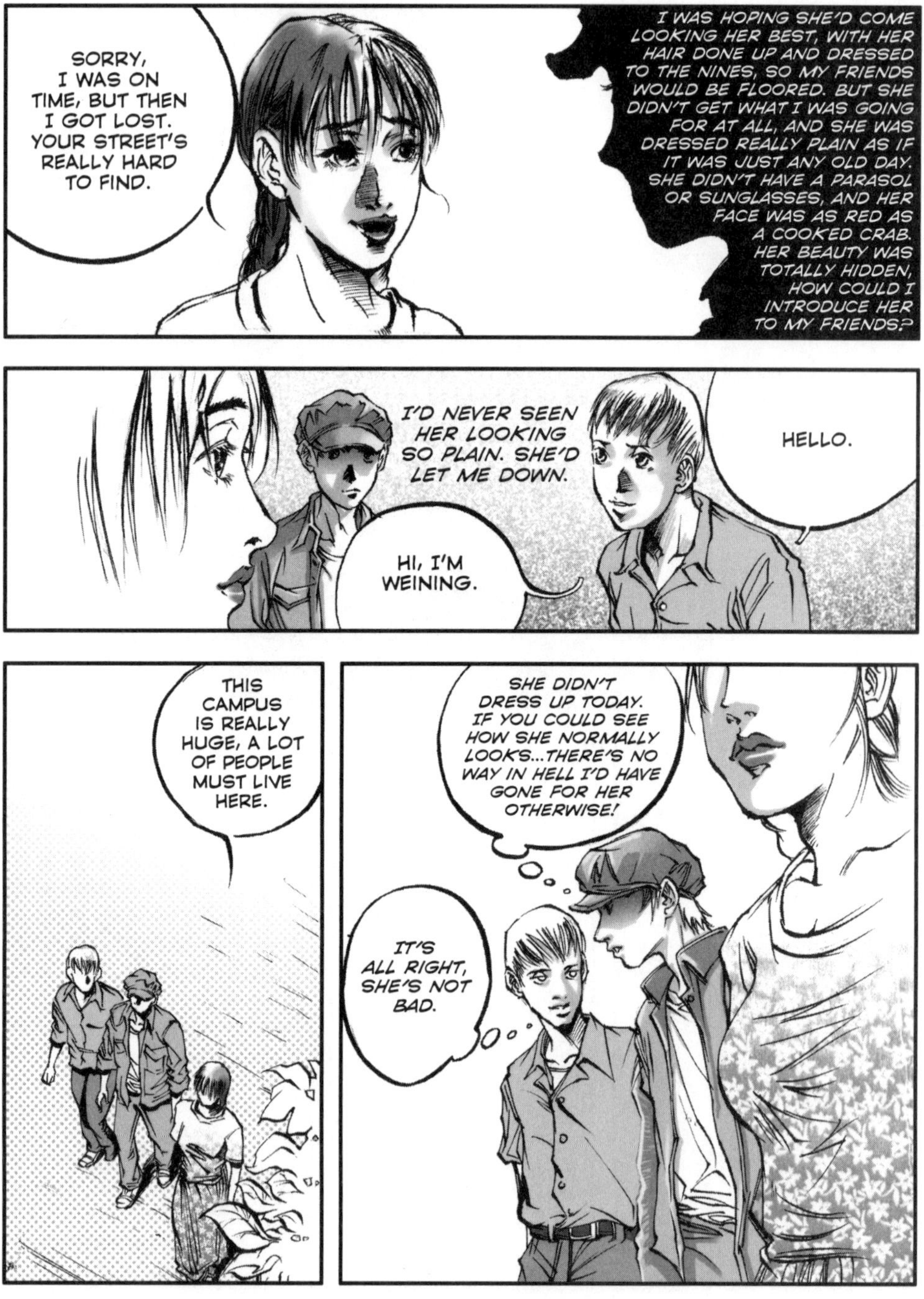
SORRY, I WAS ON TIME, BUT THEN I GOT LOST. YOUR STREET'S REALLY HARD TO FIND.
I WAS HOPING SHE'D COME LOOKING HER BEST, WITH HER HAIR DONE UP AND DRESSED TO THE NINES, SO MY FRIENDS WOULD BE FLOORED. BUT SHE DIDN'T GET WHAT I WAS GOING FOR AT ALL, AND SHE WAS DRESSED REALLY PLAIN AS IF IT WAS JUST ANY OLD DAY. SHE DIDN'T HAVE A PARASOL OR SUNGLASSES, AND HER FACE WAS AS RED AS A COOKED CRAB. HER BEAUTY WAS TOTALLY HIDDEN, HOW COULD I INTRODUCE HER TO MY FRIENDS?
I'D NEVER SEEN HER LOOKING SO PLAIN. SHE'D LET ME DOWN.
HELLO.
HI, I'M WEINING.
THIS CAMPUS IS REALLY HUGE, A LOT OF PEOPLE MUST LIVE HERE.
SHE DIDN'T DRESS UP TODAY. IF YOU COULD SEE HOW SHE NORMALLY LOOKS...THERE'S NO WAY IN HELL I'D HAVE GONE FOR HER OTHERWISE!
IT'S ALL RIGHT, SHE'S NOT BAD.

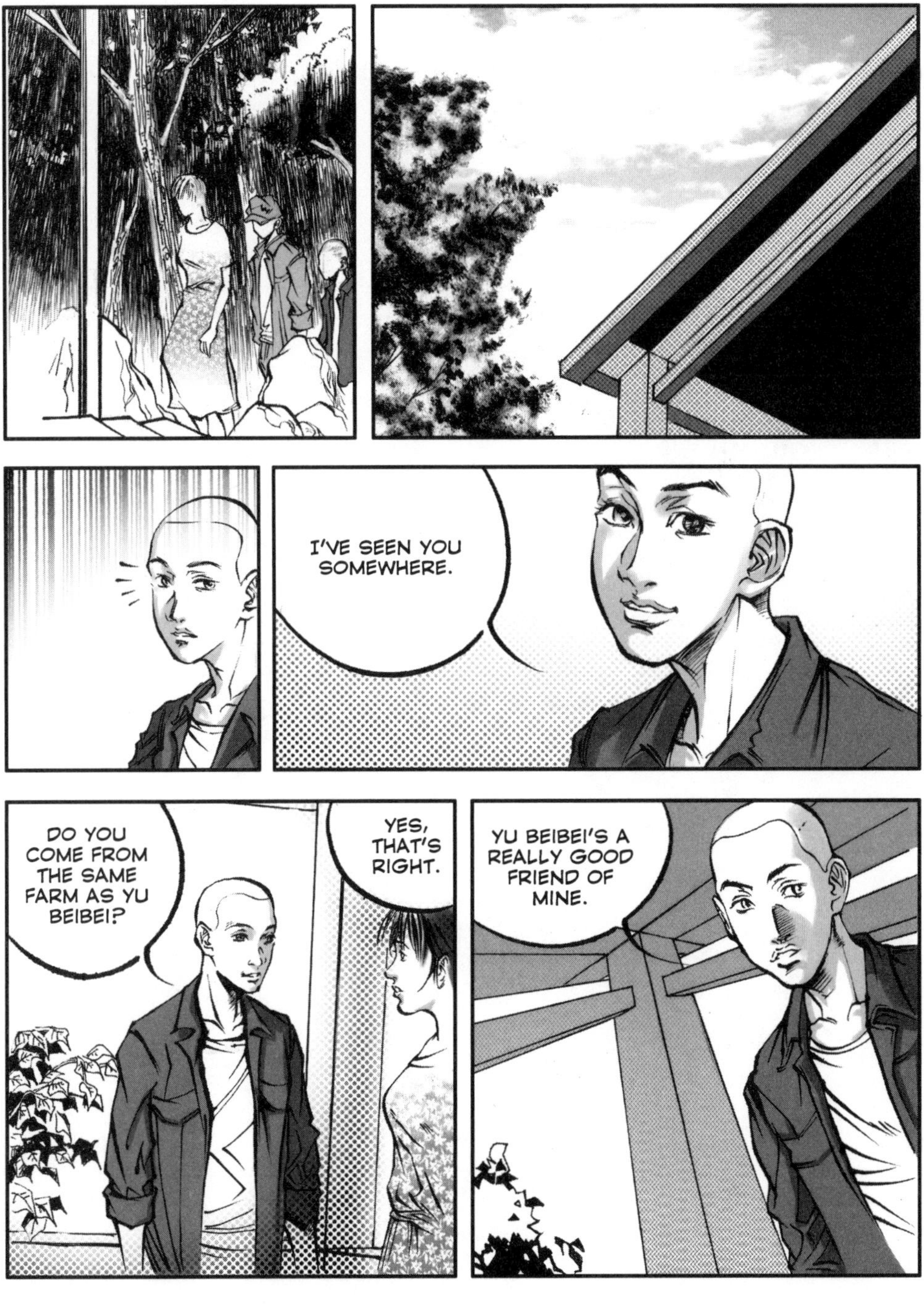
I'VE SEEN YOU SOMEWHERE.
DO YOU COME FROM THE SAME FARM AS YU BEIBEI?
YES, THAT'S RIGHT.
YU BEIBEI'S A REALLY GOOD FRIEND OF MINE.

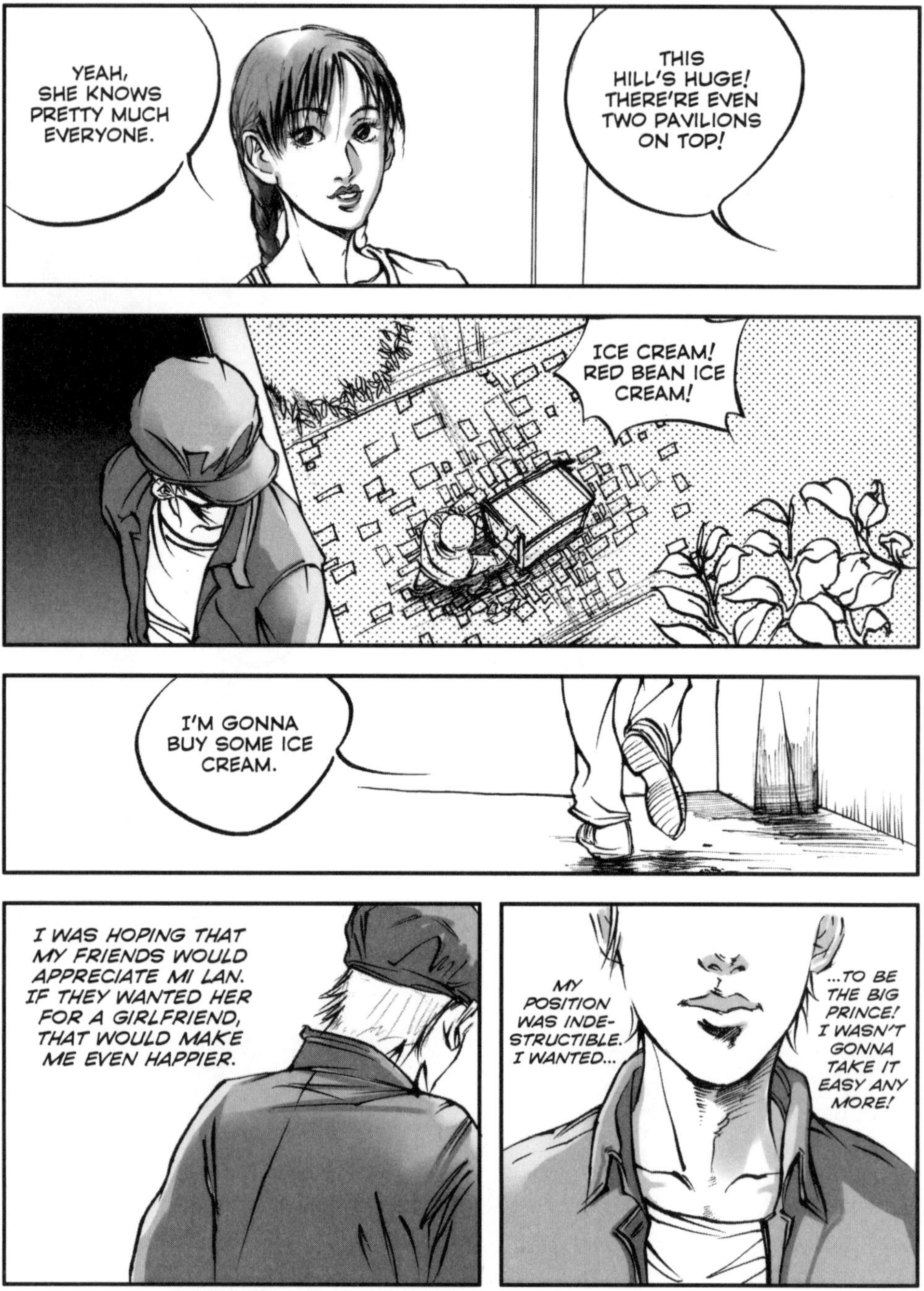
YEAH, SHE KNOWS PRETTY MUCH EVERYONE.
THIS HILL'S HUGE! THERE'RE EVEN TWO PAVILIONS ON TOP!
ICE CREAM! RED BEAN ICE CREAM!
I'M GONNA BUY SOME ICE CREAM.
I WAS HOPING THAT MY FRIENDS WOULD APPRECIATE MI LAN. IF THEY WANTED HER FOR A GIRLFRIEND, THAT WOULD MAKE ME EVEN HAPPIER.
MY POSITION WAS INDE-STRUCTIBLE. I WANTED...
...TO BE THE BIG PRINCE! I WASN'T GONNA TAKE IT EASY ANY MORE!

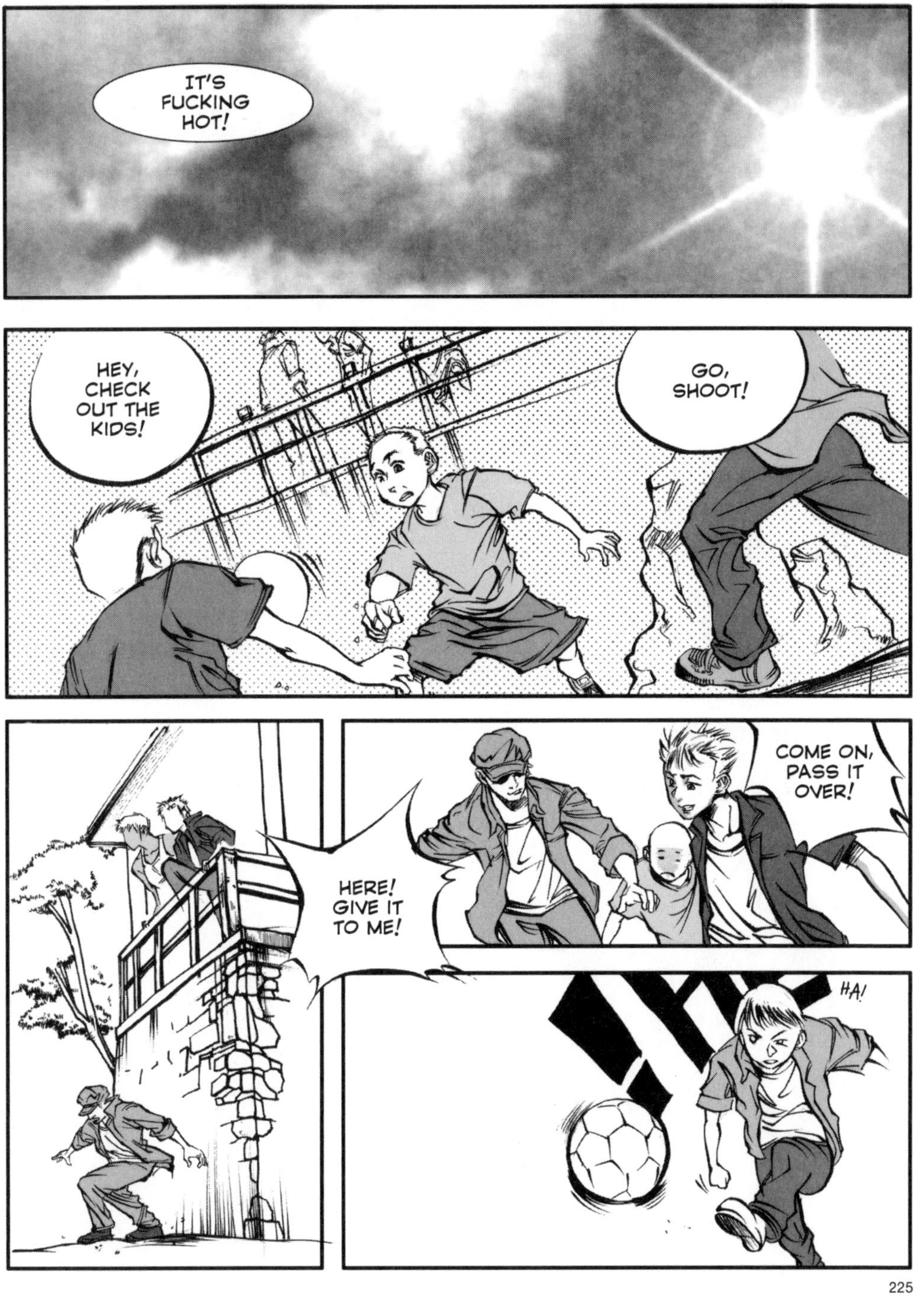
IT'S FUCKING HOT!
HEY, CHECK OUT THE KIDS!
GO, SHOOT!
HERE! GIVE IT TO ME!
COME ON, PASS IT OVER!
HA!

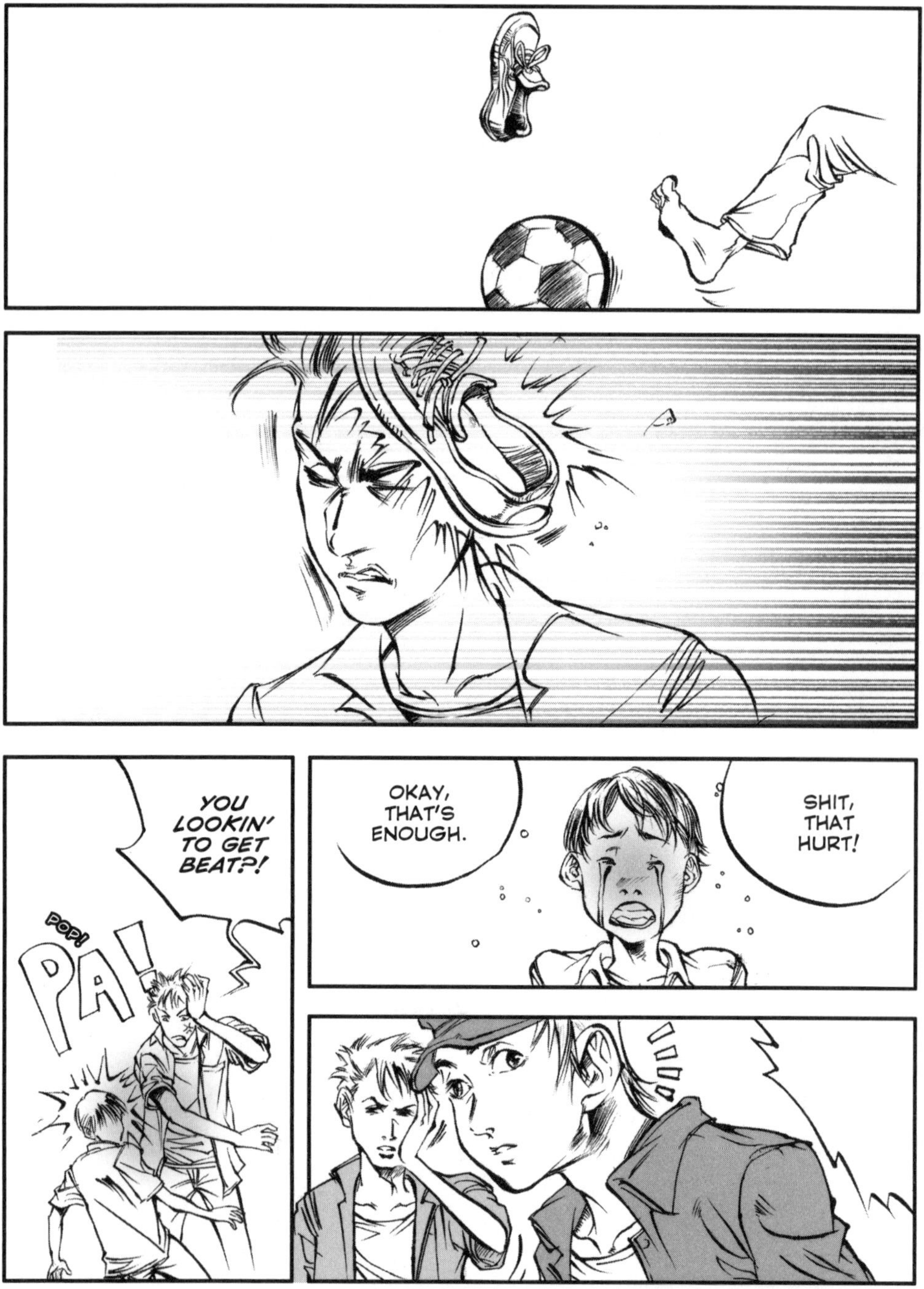
YOU LOOKIN' TO GET BEAT?!
POP!
PA!
OKAY, THAT'S ENOUGH.
SHIT, THAT HURT!

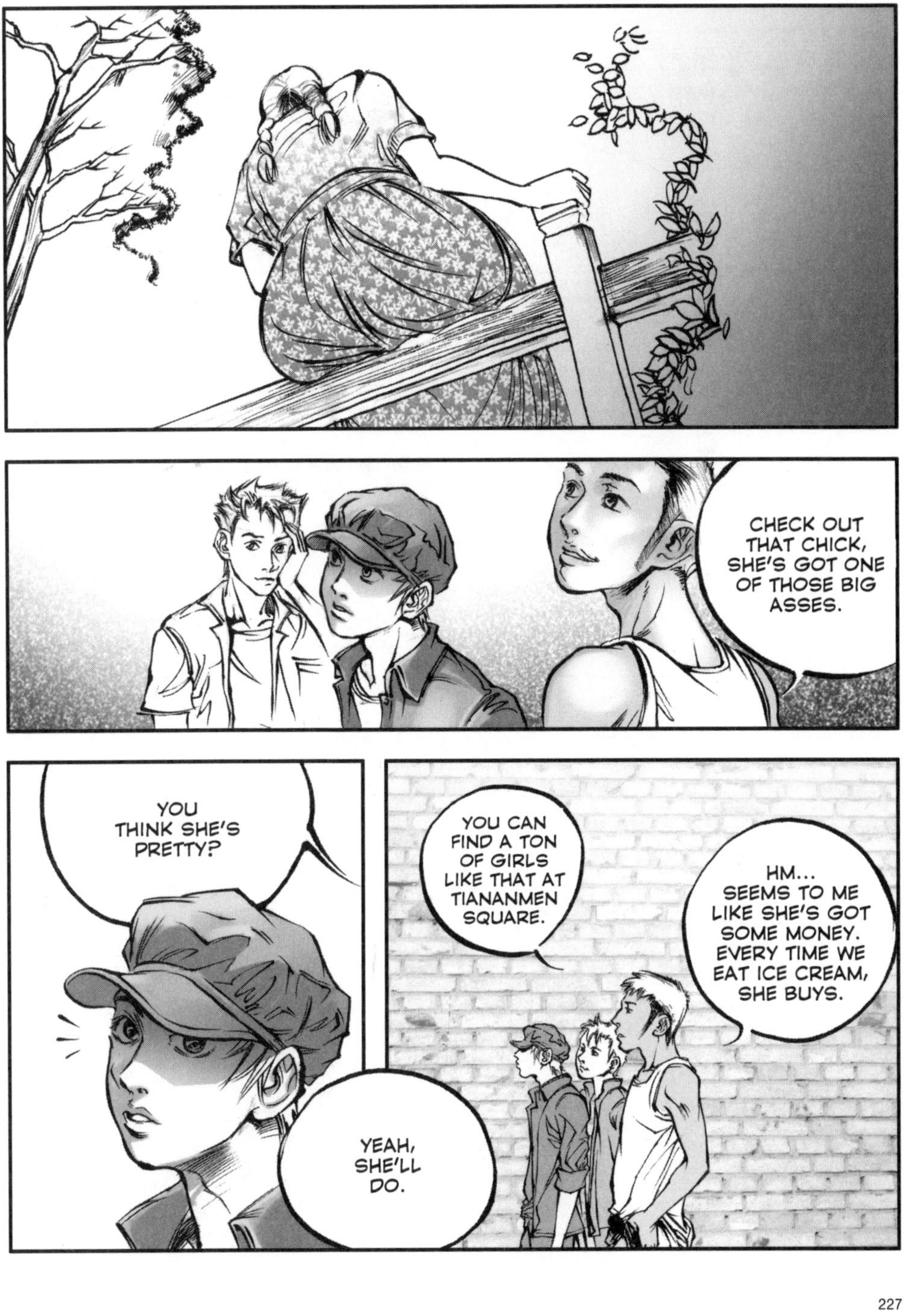
CHECK OUT THAT CHICK, SHE'S GOT ONE OF THOSE BIG ASSES.
YOU THINK SHE'S PRETTY?
YEAH, SHE'LL DO.
YOU CAN FIND A TON OF GIRLS LIKE THAT AT TIANANMEN SQUARE.
HM... SEEMS TO ME LIKE SHE'S GOT SOME MONEY. EVERY TIME WE EAT ICE CREAM, SHE BUYS.

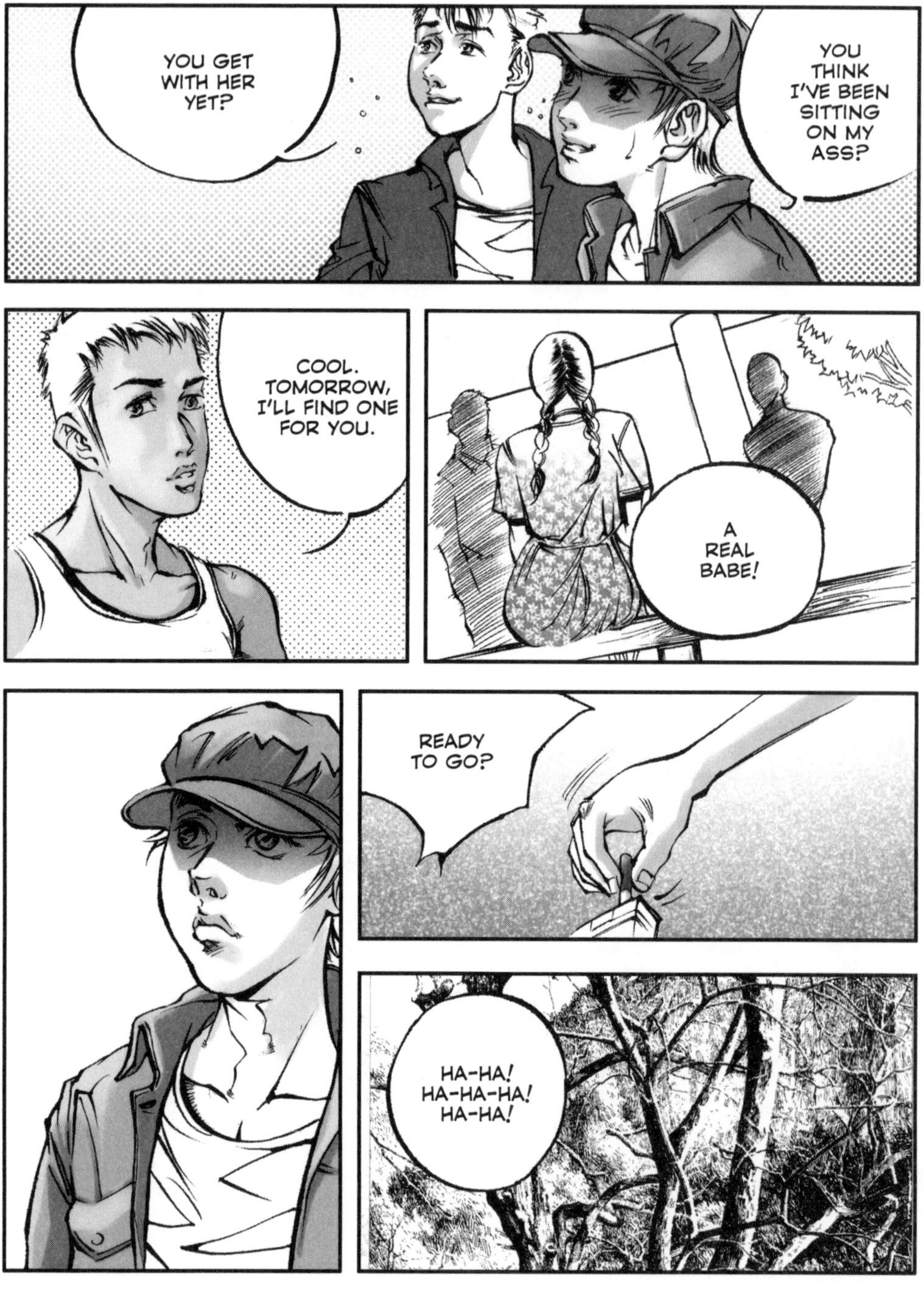
YOU GET WITH HER YET?
YOU THINK I'VE BEEN SITTING ON MY ASS?
COOL. TOMORROW, I'LL FIND ONE FOR YOU.
A REAL BABE!
READY TO GO?
HA-HA! HA-HA-HA! HA-HA!

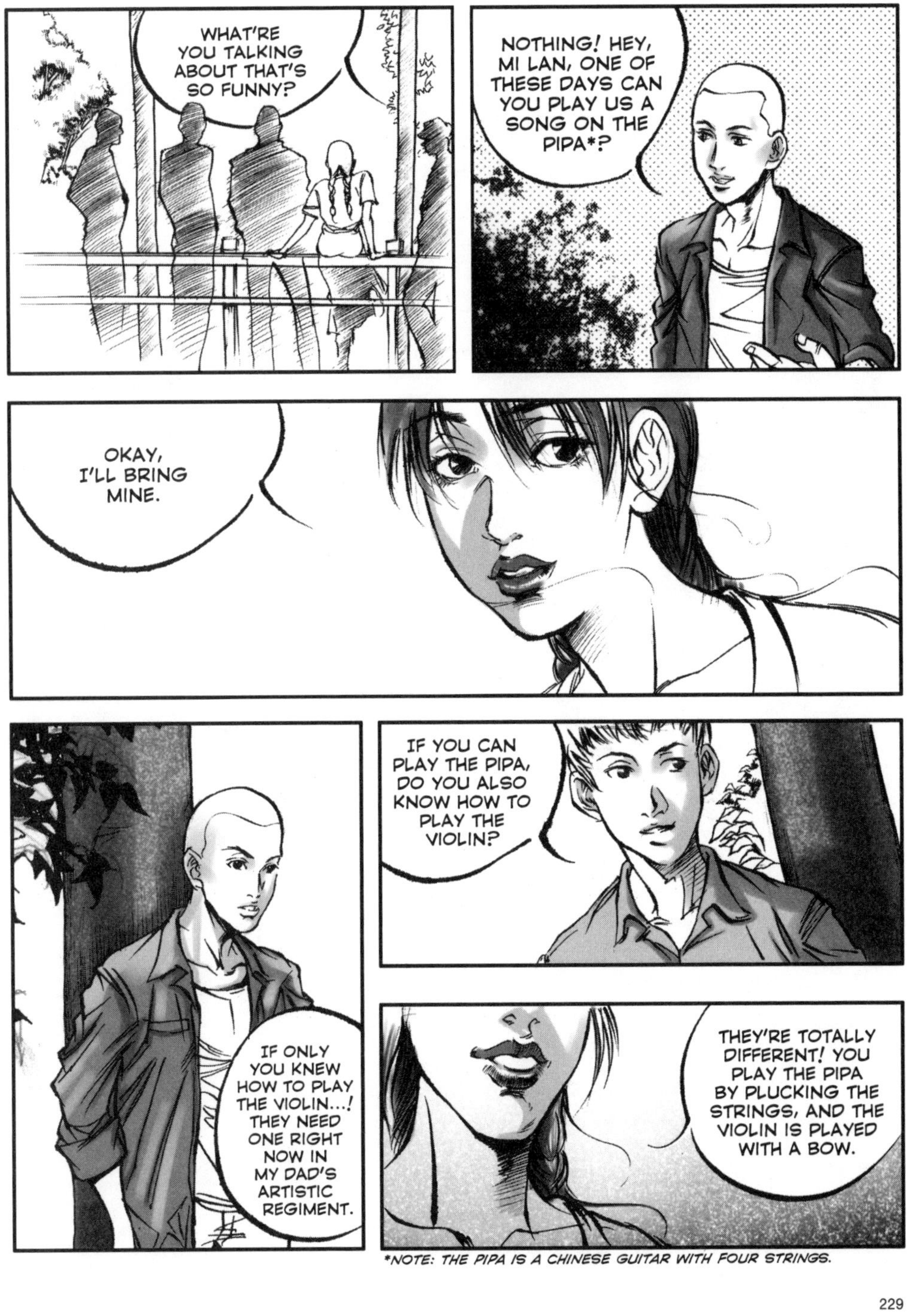
WHAT'RE YOU TALKING ABOUT THAT'S SO FUNNY?
NOTHING! HEY, MI LAN, ONE OF THESE DAYS CAN YOU PLAY US A SONG ON THE PIPA*?
OKAY, I'LL BRING MINE.
IF ONLY YOU KNEW HOW TO PLAY THE VIOLIN...! THEY NEED ONE RIGHT NOW IN MY DAD'S ARTISTIC REGIMENT.
IF YOU CAN PLAY THE PIPA, DO YOU ALSO KNOW HOW TO PLAY THE VIOLIN?
THEY'RE TOTALLY DIFFERENT! YOU PLAY THE PIPA BY PLUCKING THE STRINGS, AND THE VIOLIN IS PLAYED WITH A BOW.

NOTE: THE PIPA IS A CHINESE GUITAR WITH FOUR STRINGS.

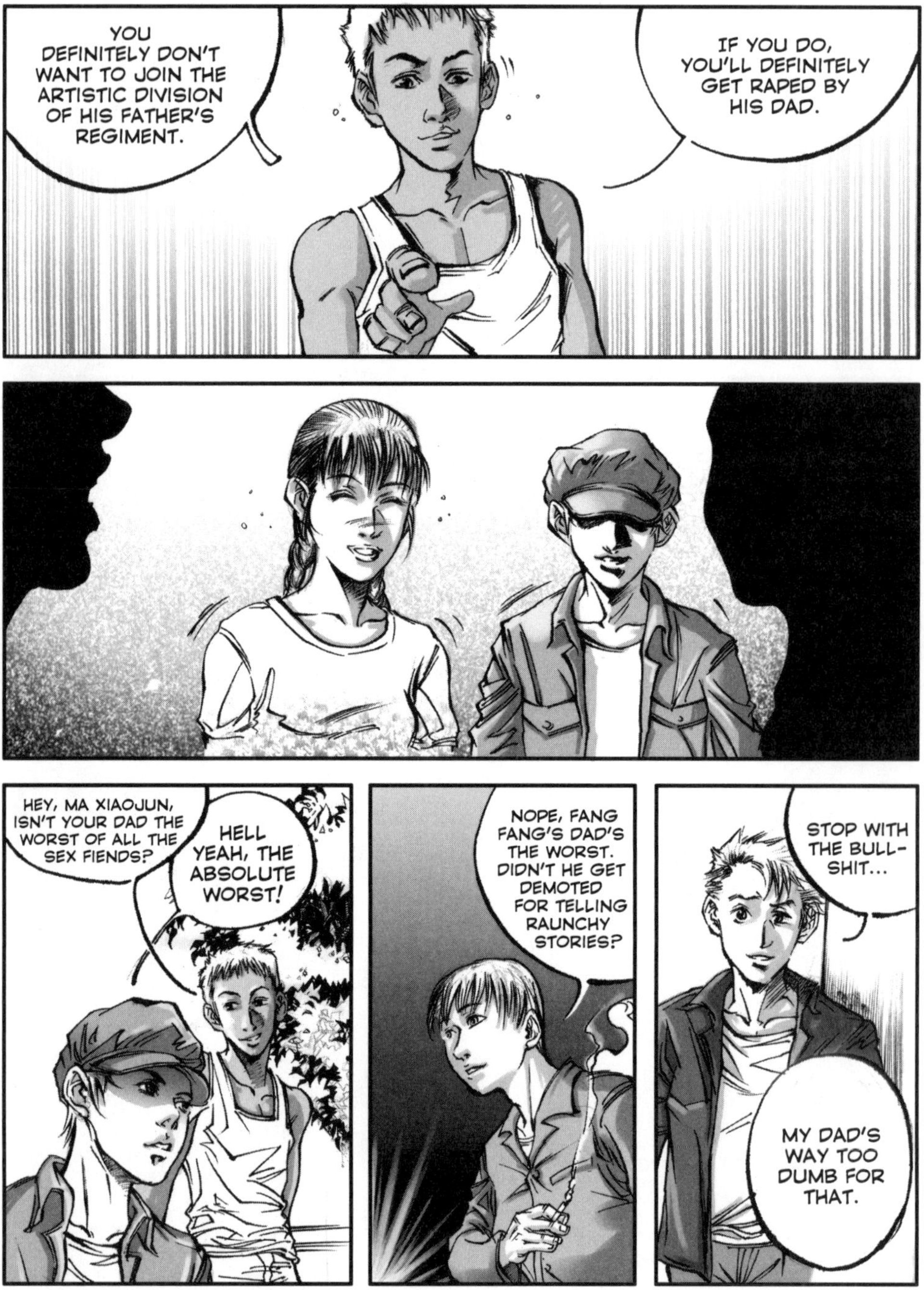
YOU DEFINITELY DON'T WANT TO JOIN THE ARTISTIC DIVISION OF HIS FATHER'S REGIMENT.
IF YOU DO, YOU'LL DEFINITELY GET RAPED BY HIS DAD.
HEY, MA XIAOJUN, ISN'T YOUR DAD THE WORST OF ALL THE SEX FIENDS?
HELL YEAH, THE ABSOLUTE WORST!
NOPE, FANG FANG'S DAD'S THE WORST. DIDN'T HE GET DEMOTED FOR TELLING RAUNCHY STORIES?
STOP WITH THE BULL-SHIT...
MY DAD'S WAY TOO DUMB FOR THAT.

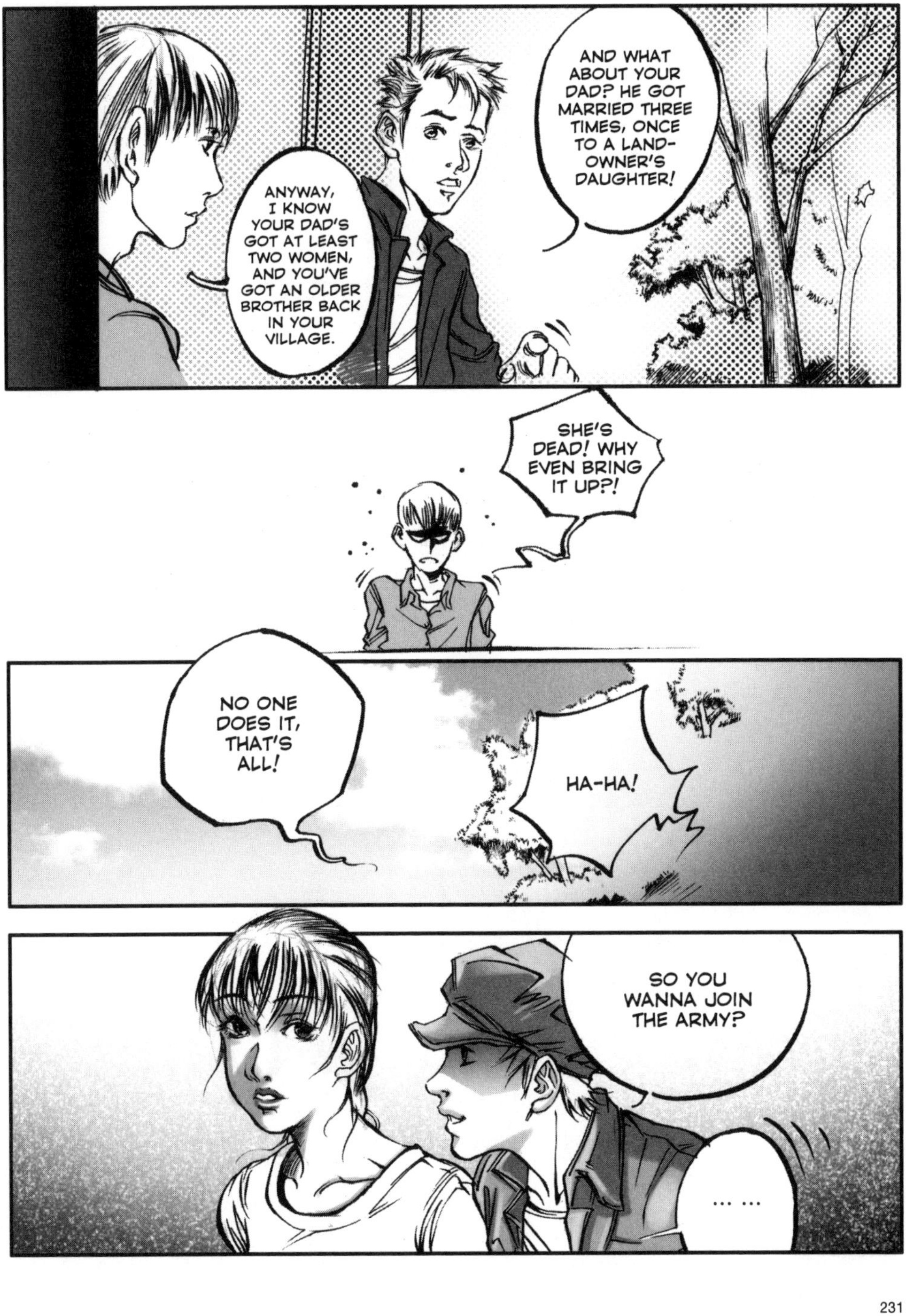
ANYWAY, I KNOW YOUR DAD'S GOT AT LEAST TWO WOMEN, AND YOU'VE GOT AN OLDER BROTHER BACK IN YOUR VILLAGE.
AND WHAT ABOUT YOUR DAD? HE GOT MARRIED THREE TIMES, ONCE TO A LAND-OWNER'S DAUGHTER!
SHE'S DEAD! WHY EVEN BRING IT UP?!
NO ONE DOES IT, THAT'S ALL!
HA-HA!
SO YOU WANNA JOIN THE ARMY?
... ...

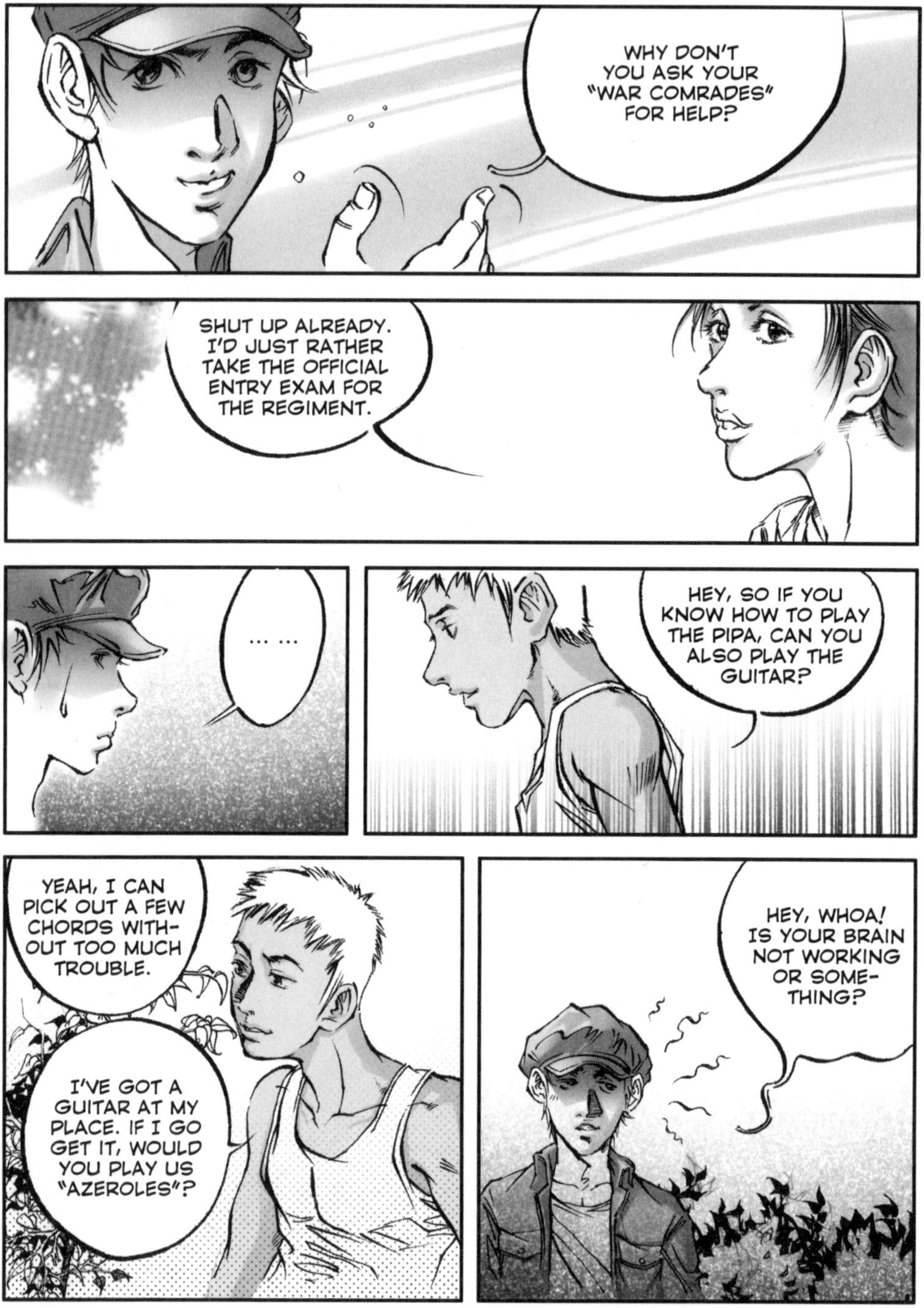
WHY DON'T YOU ASK YOUR "WAR COMRADES" FOR HELP?
SHUT UP ALREADY. I'D JUST RATHER TAKE THE OFFICIAL ENTRY EXAM FOR THE REGIMENT.
... ...
HEY, SO IF YOU KNOW HOW TO PLAY THE PIPA, CAN YOU ALSO PLAY THE GUITAR?
YEAH, I CAN PICK OUT A FEW CHORDS WITHOUT TOO MUCH TROUBLE.
I'VE GOT A GUITAR AT MY PLACE. IF I GO GET IT, WOULD YOU PLAY US "AZEROLES"?
HEY, WHOA! IS YOUR BRAIN NOT WORKING OR SOMETHING?

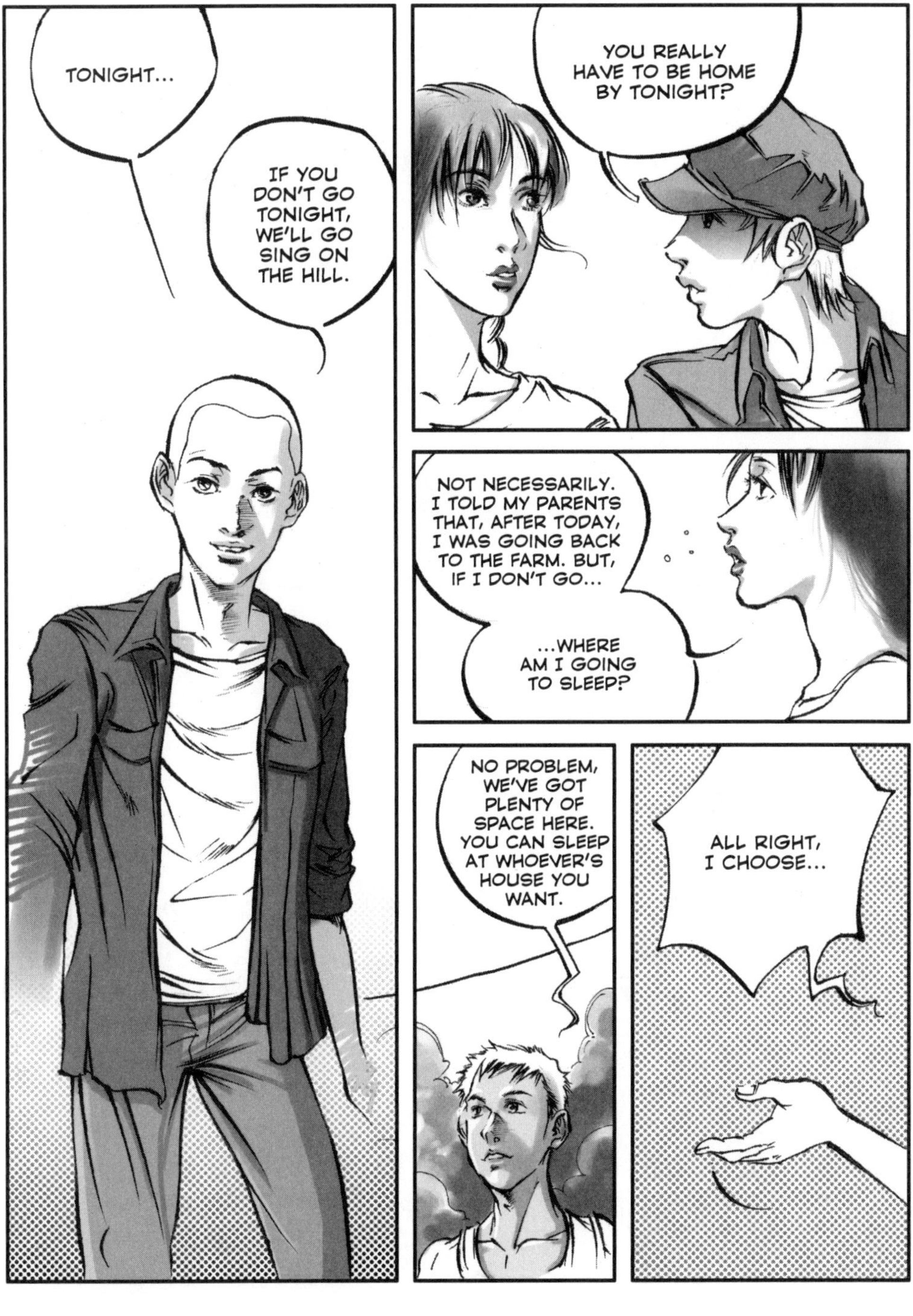
TONIGHT...
IF YOU DON'T GO TONIGHT, WE'LL GO SING ON THE HILL.
YOU REALLY HAVE TO BE HOME BY TONIGHT?
NOT NECESSARILY. I TOLD MY PARENTS THAT, AFTER TODAY, I WAS GOING BACK TO THE FARM. BUT, IF I DON'T GO...
...WHERE AM I GOING TO SLEEP?
NO PROBLEM, WE'VE GOT PLENTY OF SPACE HERE. YOU CAN SLEEP AT WHOEVER'S HOUSE YOU WANT.
ALL RIGHT, I CHOOSE...

EVERYONE WAS STARING AT ME.

WHEN I GOT HOME,
I LOOKED IN THE MIRROR AND
SAW THE BLOODY SCRATCHES
FROM HER NAILS ON MY
NECK AND CHEEKS.

TO THE TOUCH, THEY BURNED WITH SADNESS.

WHILE I TREATED MYSELF WITH MERCUROCHROME,
I TOLD MYSELF THAT SHE COULD HATE ME IF SHE WANTED,
BUT SHE WOULD REMEMBER ME FOR THE REST OF HER LIFE.

to be continued...and completed in volume 2

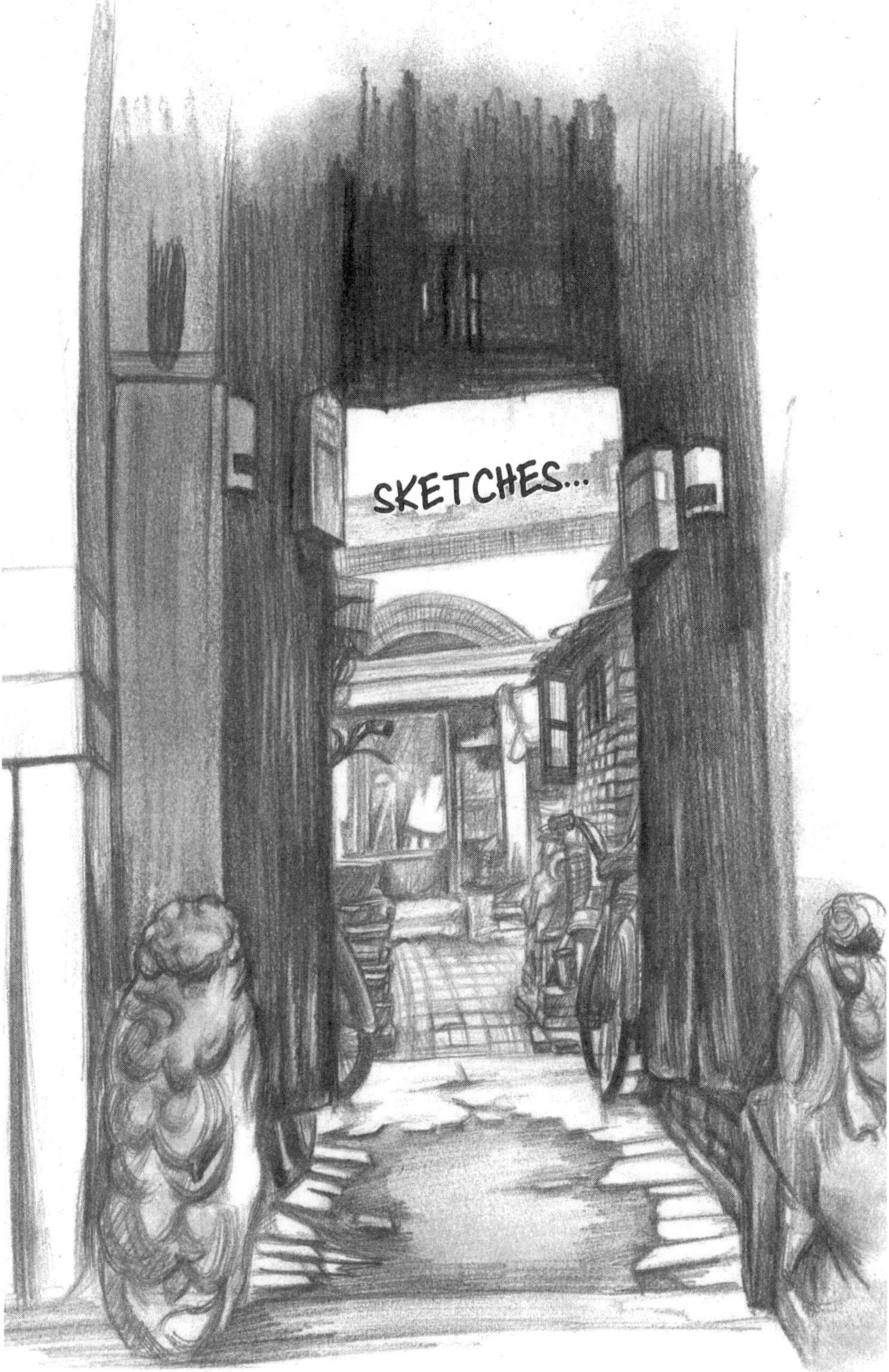
SKETCHES...

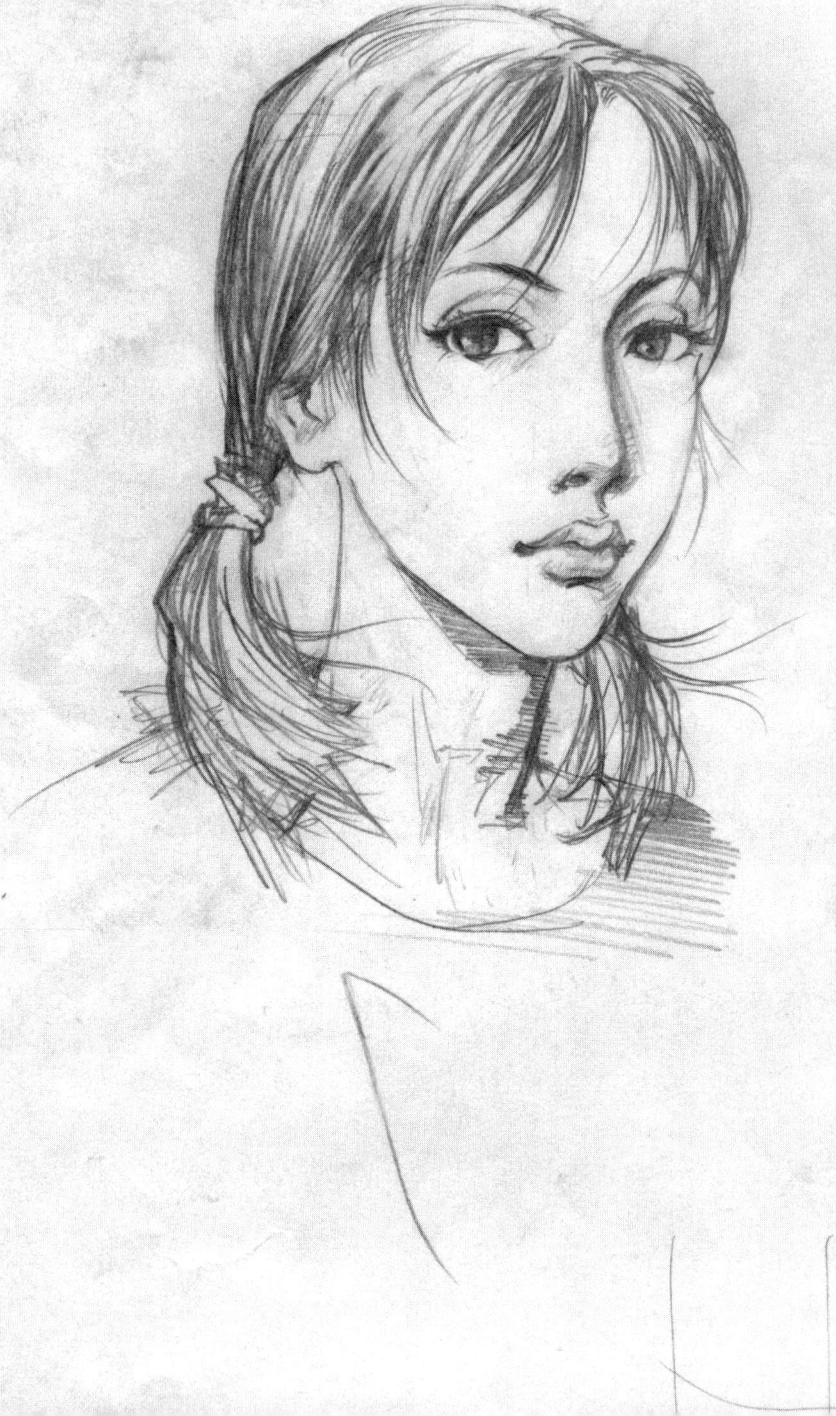

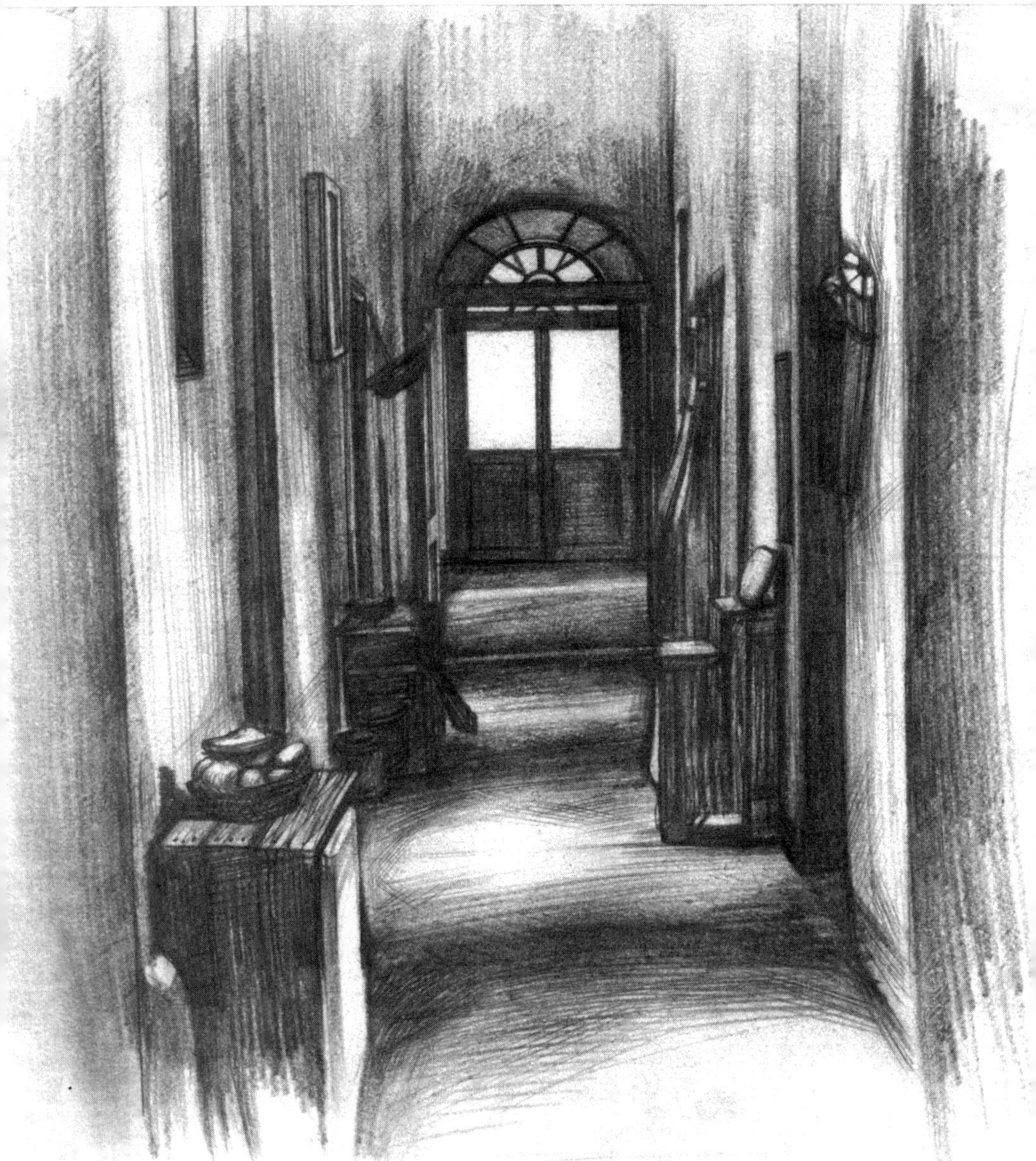

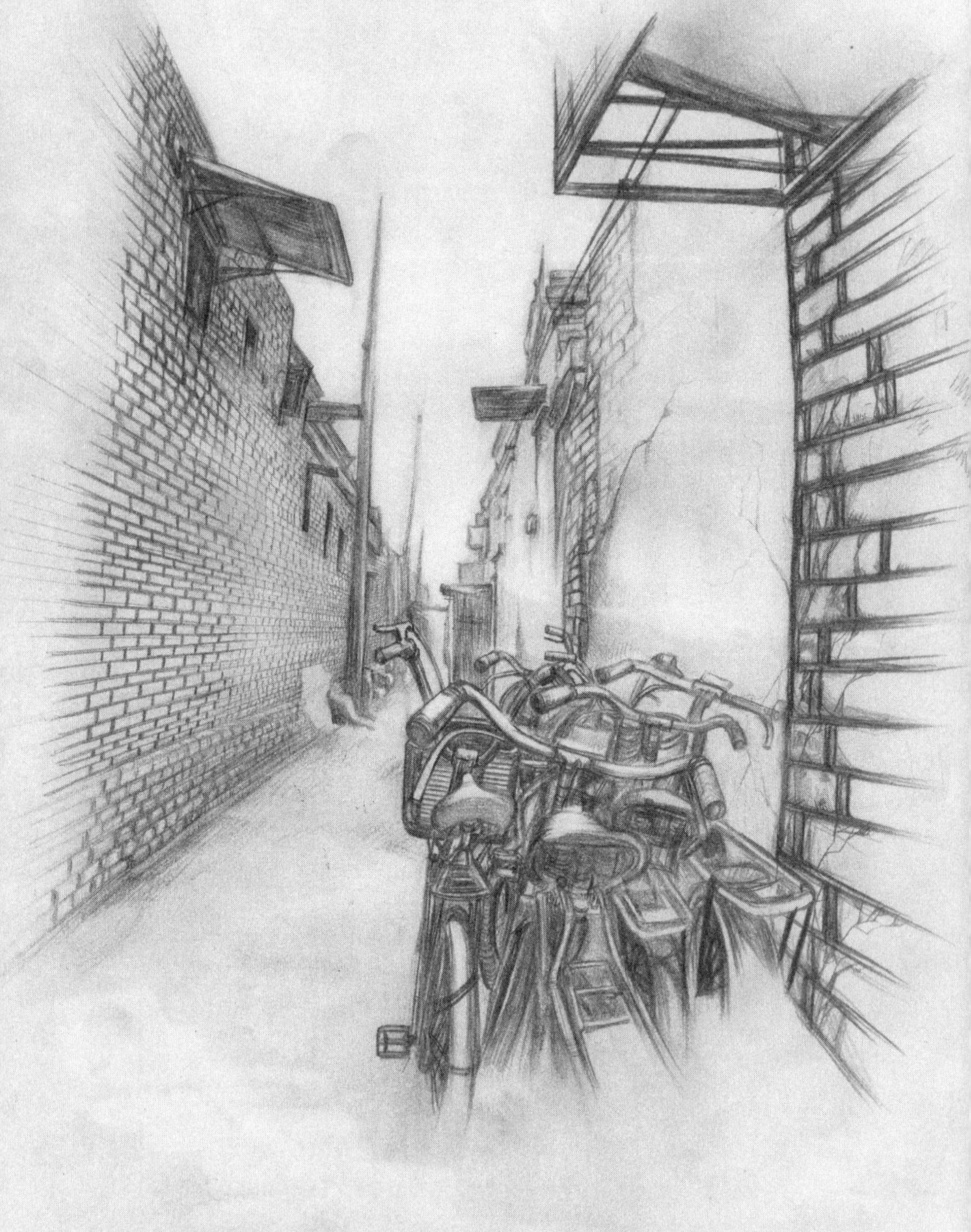

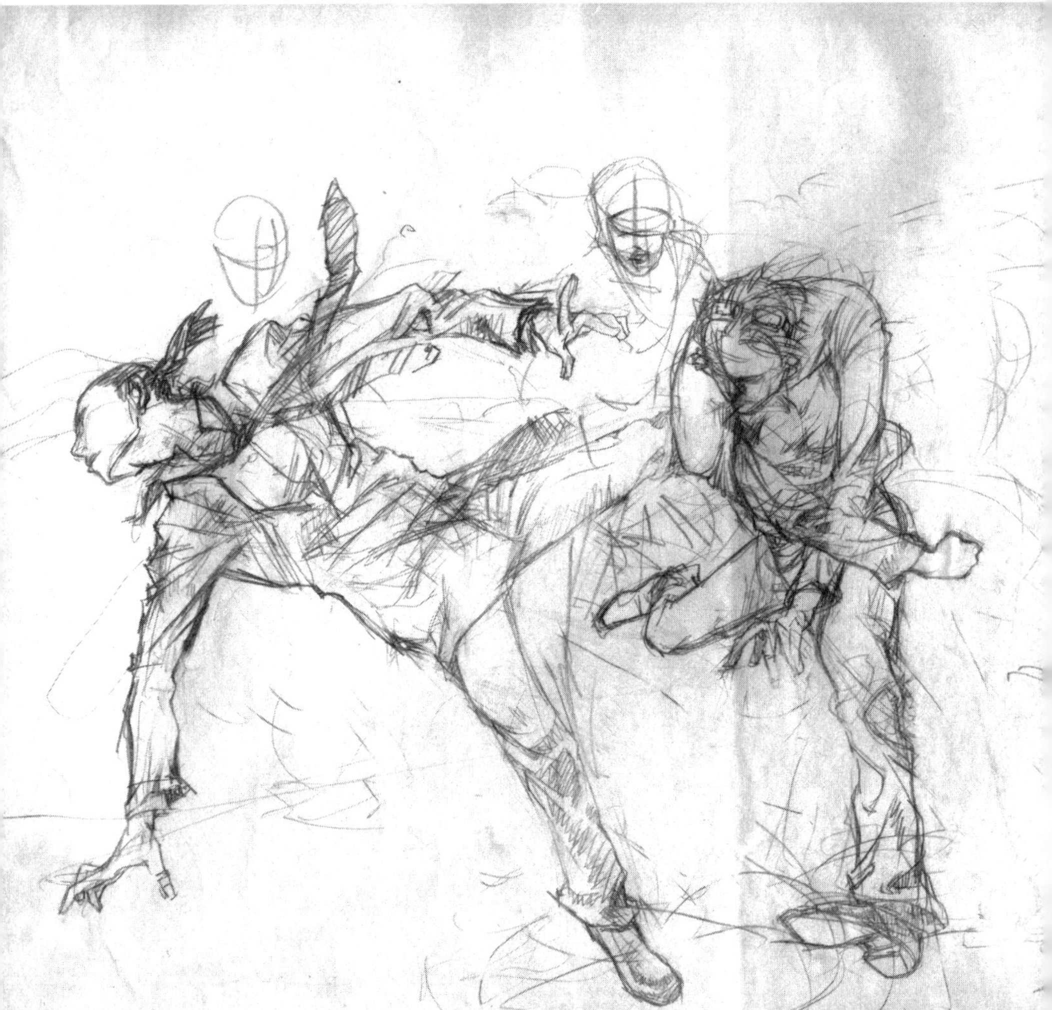

WILD ANIMALS ①

SONG YANG

Translation: J. Gustave McBride

Lettering: Tania Biswas

WILD ANIMALS Vol. 1 © XIAO PAN – SONG YANG – 2006. All rights reserved. First published by Modern Press - China.

English translation © 2008 by Hachette Book Group USA, Inc.

Yen Press
Hachette Book Group USA
237 Park Avenue, New York, NY 10017

Visit our Web sites at www.HachetteBookGroupUSA.com and www.YenPress.com.

Yen Press is an imprint of Hachette Book Group USA, Inc. The Yen Press name and logo are trademarks of Hachette Book Group USA, Inc.

First Yen Press Edition: September 2008

ISBN-10: 0-7595-2938-8
ISBN-13: 978-0-7595-2938-0

10 9 8 7 6 5 4 3 2 1

BVG

Printed in the United States of America